THE CHALLENGE OF CHANGE FOR JUDICIAL SYSTEMS

International Institute of

Administrative Sciences Monographs

Volume 14

Edited by Marco Fabri and Philip M. Langbroek

Vol. 13. R. Gregory and P. Giddings (Eds.), Righting Wrongs
Vol. 12. Y. Fortin and H. Van Hassel (Eds.), Contracting in the New Public Management
Vol. 11. S. Nelen and A. Hondeghem (Eds.), Equality Oriented Personnel Policy in the Public Sector
Vol. 10. L. Rouban (Ed.), Citizens and the New Governance
Vol. 9. A. Kouzmin and A. Hayne (Eds.), Essays in Economic Globalization, Transnational Policies and Vulnerability
Vol. 8. J. Corkery, T. Ould Daddah, C. O'Nuallain and T. Land (Eds.), Management of Public Service Reform
Vol. 7. A. Hondeghem and EGPA (Eds.), Ethics and Accountability in a Context of Governance and New Public Management
Vol. 6. J.G. Jabbra and O.P. Dwivedi and IASIA (Eds.), Governmental Response to Environmental Challenges in Global Perspective
Vol. 5. IIAS and the United Nations (Eds.), Public Administration and Development
Vol. 4. IIAS (Ed.), New Challenges for Public Administration in the Twenty-First Century
Vol. 3. IIAS Working Group on Social Security Systems (Eds.), Transformations in Social Security Systems
Vol. 2. M. Garrity and L.A. Picard (Eds.), Policy Reform for Sustainable Development in the Caribbean
Vol. 1. A. Halachmi and G. Bouckaert (Eds.), Public Productivity through Quality and Strategic Management

ISSN: 1382-4414

The Challenge of Change for Judicial Systems

Developing a Public Administration Perspective

Edited by

Marco Fabri

Senior Researcher at the Research Institute on Judicial Systems of the National Research Council, Bologna, Italy

and

Philip M. Langbroek

Teacher and Researcher at the Institute of Constitutional and Administrative Law, Utrecht University, The Netherlands

IOS Press
Ohmsha

Amsterdam • Berlin • Oxford • Tokyo • Washington, DC

ISBN 1 58603 062 0 (IOS Press)
ISBN 4 274 90392 3 C3034 (Ohmsha)
Library of Congress Catalog Card Number: 00-106319

Publisher
IOS Press
Nieuwe Hemweg 6B
1013 BG Amsterdam
The Netherlands
fax: +31 20 620 3419
e-mail: order@iospress.nl

Co-Publisher
International Institute of Administrative Sciences - IIAS
Rue Defacqz, 1
B-1000 Brussels
Belgium
fax: +32 2 537 9702
e-mail: iias@iiasiisa.be

Distributor in the UK and Ireland
IOS Press/Lavis Marketing
73 Lime Walk
Headington
Oxford OX3 7AD
England
fax: +44 1865 75 0079

Distributor in the USA and Canada
IOS Press, Inc.
5795-G Burke Centre Parkway
Burke, VA 22015
USA
fax: +1 703 323 3668
e-mail: iosbooks@iospress.com

Distributor in Germany
IOS Press
Spandauer Strasse 2
D-10178 Berlin
Germany
fax: +49 30 242 3113

Distributor in Japan
Ohmsha, Ltd.
3-1 Kanda Nishiki-cho
Chiyoda-ku, Tokyo 101
Japan
fax: +81 3 3233 2426

CRC prepared by G.J. Wiarda Institute, Utrecht University, Boothstraat 6, 3512 BW Utrecht, The Netherlands.

PRINTED IN THE NETHERLANDS

Preface

From its very inception the discipline of public administration has exclusively had a very one-sided interest in the effectiveness and efficiency of executive power. The functioning of the legislative power and of the Judiciary are only taken into account in the handbooks of public administration as far as the Executive is influenced by them. This is all the more remarkable, for in all countries the Legislature, as well as the Judiciary, are confronted with many problems linked to ineffectiveness and inefficiency which concern a lack of managerial attention, and which have a negative impact on their legitimacy. The courts and the judicial apparatuses are overburdened with unresolved cases and a backlog of work. Failures and mistakes by all parties concerned are an inevitable consequence of this situation. Not only is criminal law affected by this situation, but also private and public law cases: insufficient justice is rendered as a result. Citizens lose their confidence in the good functioning of the different branches of the Judiciary. Court cases are protracted beyond reasonable time-limits. In such circumstances justice is only affordable by men of means. The drive of the public prosecutor and the courts for efficiency, however, stands in a tense relationship with the due process of law. In this climate of a legitimacy crisis and with the judges and public attorneys having an image problem, policy makers are attempting to influence or even dominate the judicial branch of government.

All European countries have major problems in this respect. A lack of good management and the non-application of sound organisational principles have a negative affect on the functioning of their judicial systems. Without a more efficient managerial approach, rendering justice is hardly possible. Law and public administration, public administration disciplines, depend on each other for the effective realisation of their principles. On the other hand, they may also be at cross-purposes.

At a fundamental level, the principles of justice and (new) public management conflict with one another. At an institutional level, the relationships between ministerial policy makers and judges, and between judges and public attorneys are becoming increasingly strained. At the organisational level, the management of court procedures, the prosecution, rosters, human resource management, and the application of Information and Communication Technology (ICT) are failing. At an operational level such problems as dilemmas in setting priorities, balancing justice and efficiency in a day to day context, the application of performance indicators, the furtherance of a growing transparancy – with the help of ICT – are all encountered.

The study before you is based on the notion that the discipline of public administration can provide an extremely valuable contribution for the attainment of justice by a translation of sound principles of management applied within the Judiciary and the courtrooms. If the above diagnosis is well-founded, then the co-operation between the legal and public administration disciplines will lead to a very valuable enrichment of both theory and practice.

A certain reluctance from legal colleagues to accept public administrative support in the organisation and functioning of the Judiciary is quite understandable. The co-operation of lawyers and public administration specialists requires from the latter a sensitivity for the specifically legal dimensions of the work of the courts. On the other hand, judges and magistrates realise the difficult phase through which the courts in most countries are passing. Many of them are becoming aware that the situation at the court level cannot be improved by legal measures alone. Improvement of legal procedures has to be accompanied by improvements in the work flow, by changes in the organisational culture and by an enhancement of client orientation. In this respect, administrative law and administrative science represent two sides of the same coin.

The content of this study has mainly been influenced by the results of the 1999 Annual Conference of the European Group of Public Administration (EGPA), whose general theme was 'Delivering and Managing Justice in the 21st Century' ('*Rendre et Gérer la Justice au 21 Siècle*'). The EGPA was hosted by the European Public Law Centre in Athens and by its Director, Professor Spiridon Flogaïtis. The Conference itself was held at Cape Sounion, about 60 km south of Athens.

Miss Olga Zygoura, Legal Assistant at the Greek Council of State, wrote the main outlines for the discussion in the Working Groups during the Annual Conference. The EGPA is very grateful to Professor Flogaïtis and to Miss Zygoura for having provided an excellent opportunity for bringing theorists and practitioners together on this subject of great practical and theoretical importance.

At the Conference in Cape Sounion, a Permanent Study Group on "Management and Delivery of Justice" was set up, which will convene during the Annual Conferences of the European Group of Public Administration. This study officially launches the new Permanent Study Group. I hope that a lasting cooperation between lawyers and public administration specialists will be fruitful in providing the necessary improvements within the judicial sphere.

Mention also has to be made of the subsidies by the Dutch Ministry of Justice, the Research Institute on Judicial Systems, Italian National Research Council, Bologna, Italy and the Faculty of Law of Utrecht University, the Netherlands, which with their support wish to emphasise the importance of the subject - not only in a national context but also in a European one - by making the publication of this study possible.

Ignace Snellen
President of EGPA

Contents

Part III
Changing Positions of Courts in Society

Part IV
Governance and Change of Courts and Public Prosecutors' Offices

Part V
Courts, Public Prosecuters Offices' and ICT

The Challenge of Change for Judicial Systems
M. Fabri and Ph.M. Langbroek (Eds.)
IOS Press, 2000

Developing a Public Administration Perspective on Judicial Systems in Europe

Philip M. Langbroek and Marco Fabri

1 Introduction

During the last few decades the field of public administration in most European countries has largely neglected the management of the courts, prosecutors' offices and in general what we could call 'judicial institutions'[1] (North, 1994; Powell and Di Maggio, 1991). During the 1990s, governments, courts, and public prosecutors' offices were confronted with some major societal developments, leading to increased attention for courts and judges by many European governments. For this reason, together with the European Public Law Centre in Athens, The European Group of Public Administration (EGPA) in 1999 organised an international conference on the subject of management and delivery of justice. The aim of that conference was to develop a perspective on judicial institutions that public administration had ignored for too long. The conference was quite successful, because it brought together policy makers, judges and scholars in the field of the organisation of justice who would otherwise not have met so easily. As a consequence of this success, the EGPA founded a permanent study group on 'management and delivery of justice'. It is the aim of this collection of articles to provide this study group with a preliminary basis on which to work. With this collection – which contains several contributions to the conference and some original contributions – we want to show that judicial institutions must be a field of interest for public administration studies.

This introductory chapter starts with a general description of the necessities and motives for the development of a public administration perspective on judicial institutions. After that, we will provide a brief description of the conference keynote speeches in section three. Next, we briefly introduce the different contributions that have been organised in five sections. Section 4 describes and summarises the steps in recent policy developments concerning judicial institutions in some European countries. The fifth section is dedicated to the changing positions of judicial institutions within state and society. Section 6 focusses on what we call 'Governance and change of courts and public prosecutors' office'. In this section we have contributions that deal with quality management, judicial administration issues, performance measurements, and specific case studies on the recruitment and selection of judges as well as on the juvenile

1 We would like to reiterate that the word 'judiciary' can sometimes be misleading, because in some countries (e.g. Belgium, France, Italy) it can also include the public prosecuters.

courts. The seventh section assembles contributions on Information and Communications Technology in the courts and prosecutors' offices. We think that the subject is of great importance, because ICT developments tend to generate changes in organisations autonomously, and we do not think courts and prosecutors' offices are immune to this tendency.

We conclude this introduction in section 8 with some suggestions for future research with the hope that public administration scholars will finally contribute to the development of knowledge on judicial institutions.

2 Why a public administration perspective?

Traditionally, in European countries the judicial institutions are entirely left to the judicial professions.[2] Judicial organisations are ruled by law, judges and public prosecutors are the professionals. This means that in the decision-making process the juridical perspective prevails over the organisational one. However, during the 1990s pressures for change grew to a sufficient extent for governments to take some action – often, but not always inspired by the American example (Röhl, 1993).[3] These pressures had different characteristics. For example, the European integration and the economic and cultural globalisation develop alongside the rise of international law firms. Judicial organisations, courts and judges, prosecutors' offices and prosecutors are confronted with an increase in cases with an international – and thus more complex – dimension. Some aspects that deserve to be mentioned separately are the increasing importance of EC law, in the form of guidelines and regulations, and of the case law of the EC Court. (Vervaele, Betlem, de Lange, Veldman, 1999). Another factor is the case law of the European Court of Human Rights, especially on article 6 of the European Convention on Human Rights, concerning 'the right to a fair and public hearing within a reasonable time by an independent and impartial tribunal established by law'. The court's standard seems to be that even the appearance of partiality should be avoided[4] (Van Dijk and Van Hoof, 1998, 390-479). Lawyers increasingly specialise in a narrow domain of the law, e.g. medical liability, environmental law, contracts, or intellectual property rights. Next to this, medical and biotechnology give rise to questions concerning ethics, criminal law as well as intellectual property rights. These questions are brought to the courts.

This may be a lesser problem in criminal law, but within the domain of civil law this causes increasing problems for the courts, since judges generally do not specialise as much as many practising lawyers do. Apart from this there is a tendency that the salaries of specialised lawyers are much higher than the salaries of judges, so (suppo-

---

2 An exception is the work of Shimon Shetreet (1976).
3 See the contributions by Fabri and Van der Doelen in this collection.
4 E.g. ECHR October 23, 1985, *Benthem* v. *The Netherlands*, Series A. 97; ECHR September 1995, *Procola* v. *Luxembourg*, Series A. 326.

sing that money also makes our judges tick) it is not self-evident that the best lawyers sit on the bench. For lawyers in Europe, big money cannot be earned at the bar. Often lawyers do not deal with judicial proceedings at all any more. This is an indication that the fusion of (international) enterprises and contract law seems to be a financially more rewarding business.

During the last decade, there has been an increase in all kinds of cases, civil, family, penal, and administrative, in most European countries. Without additional measures these increases created backlogs and procedures taking more than two years and sometimes even more than five years. Part of this situation is that drugs and drugs-related cases still make up a considerable proportion of the work of the criminal justice system. Another aspect is that courts are confronted with asylum seekers pleading their cases, and find themselves confronted with immigrants who – even if they have been living in Europe for several years – do not speak the language of the country they are living in. Together with increasing legal restrictions on the immigration of asylum seekers, this builds up to quite a challenge for judicial control and for the courts.

Moreover, an alternative to court proceedings is emerging throughout Western Europe. Alternative dispute resolution aims at the settlement of a conflict without the judgement of the courts.

Most judicial organisations have not had and do not have the capacity to deal with massive numbers of cases, let alone the other demands placed upon the shoulders of the judiciary, like managing relations with the justice departments, with the political domain and with the public.

The effect of these and other tendencies is that the legitimacy of the courts and public prosecutors' offices is at risk. There is no way of denying or ignoring these ongoing developments and holding on rigidly to traditional and juridical professional values. The question is how governments, courts and judges, prosecutors' offices and prosecutors have and will react to these developments. The political environment is not necessarily friendly towards the judicial institutions. Driven by their wishes to be re-elected and by political programmes that promise an increased effectiveness and efficiency of government and of governmental services, politicians play the tune of accountability – one dimensionally interpreted as 'value for taxpayers money'. Managers from justice departments in Great Britain, the Netherlands and Italy, at a very different level, try to introduce aspects of the so-called *new public management* (Fortin and Van Hassel, 2000) into judicial organisations. So judicial professionals are confronted with efforts to introduce organisational values into their institutions. In this climate, politicians tend to invest in judicial organisations only if courts and public prosecutors' offices are able and willing to demonstrate the effectiveness of these investments.

It appears that there is an unavoidable answer to these circumstances: judicial institutions need an organisational perspective. Ultimately, it is inevitable to rethink the institutional setting, the functioning, and the resources of courts, prosecutors' offices, and related organisations in order to make them responsive to the dynamics of modern society, and even to redesign judicial proceedings. We consider it one of the tasks of public administration to contribute to these efforts - which have already been started by different national governments within the European Union under the pressures of societal developments.

3 Keynote speeches: management & efficiency *versus* judicial values

The keynote speeches at the Cape Sounion Conference reflect the societal and judicial developments mentioned above. They reveal the tensions between the traditional juridical values upheld by the juridical professions, on the one hand, and the efficiency and effectiveness of the works of courts and judges demanded by politicians and implemented by managers with an organisational perspective, on the other.

Zygoura starts her exposé with an ironical report on Ubu Roi, by Alfred Jarry. The question 'why are judges opposed to reforms?' is answered by referring to judicial independence and impartiality. In the story of Ubu, he abolishes the judicial justice system. For Zygoura this is a basis for questioning the idea of an organisational development of judicial systems. She warns of a justice system too closely related to the executive branch of government. Therefore she questions the relation between judicial independence and striving for judicial efficiency, the relation between judicial activism and the constitutional position of the judiciary, the relation between efforts to reduce the number of cases by rising the registration fees on the one hand and the right of access to justice on the other, the relations between the organisational development of judicial institutions and the institutional guarantees of judicial systems. What may be considered as the real product of a judicial system?, she asks. Furthermore, Zygoura describes the judicial system of Greece from a constitutional perspective, from a perspective of the agents of justice, and from the perspective of judicial procedures. Mrs. Zygoura indicates that Greek court organisations have a problem finding enough personnel for supportive services in the lower echelons. Procedures take too much time, because of too many formalities and complexities.[5]

Loveday briefly describes the policies of the Conservative Governments in Britain during the eighties and the nineties. Recognising the problems of the courts, like reducing delays and the introduction of the so-called 'fast track', he points to the policies for evaluating the performance of the courts. This is done by measuring the throughput of courts and crime clearance rates by policing agencies. Loveday doubts if the effectiveness and efficiency of courts and policing agencies may be adequately measured and stimulated by this kind of performance measurement. He indicates the

5 Unfortunately, Mrs. Zygoura did not consider the text of her keynote speech: 'Rendre et gérer la justice au XXIe siècle' to be fit for publication in this collection.

ineffectiveness of these policies from the points of view of public trust. And he relates the policies of performance measurements to bad working relations within the offices of the judicial system in Great Britain and Wales. He warns of an unprincipled managerialism in the field of justice.

Christophe Tchakaloff gives an outline of the traditional legitimacy of the continental justice systems as a matter of constitutional principle. This concerns judicial independence, the judicial institutions, access to justice, and respect for international and supranational legal norms. But she also indicates that the legitimacy of the justice systems is contested in practice, caused by slow proceedings, the fact that judicial language is often incomprehensible to citizens not versed in the law. This is combined with the growth in the numbers of cases in all judicial domains. Strategies for change are directed at a new orientation of the justice system towards society. This aim offers all kinds of possibilities, the most promising being the efforts to reduce crime in the metropolitan areas by bringing justice to the neighbourhoods, the introduction of more simple and faster procedures, and the introduction of management techniques into the judicial organisations. Of course, while doing so, the judicialisation of social relations such as in the USA should be prevented. From the process of developing judicial cooperation within the European Union as agreed upon in the Amsterdam Treaty, ChristopheTchakaloff expects positive influences on the development of international exchange between judges, courts and judicial organisations.

These keynote speeches underline the inevitability of managing courts and judges. It is necessary to reinforce the legitimate position of the courts and judges in society and within the state. The organisational development of courts and judges, however, should not be at the expense of constitutional values of judicial independence (Schmitt, 1928; Kägi, 1937; Vile, 1967; Shapiro, 1981) and judicial impartiality. Organisational development is not a value in itself but should be directed at the support and maintenance of the societal functions of the courts. To that end, a new balance between judicial accountability and judicial independence should be developed. A juridical approach of accountability of the courts focusses especially on damages.[6] We hold that accountability for the courts should be seen in a broader, societal perpective.

4 Policy developments concerning the justice systems

The governments of Great Britain, France, Italy and the Netherlands have organised various efforts to change the ways courts and judges perform their jobs. The aims of all these efforts are directed towards improving the societal benefits from justice.

So, in Great Britain the Woolf Report proposed to improve access of justice, to reduce the complexity of procedural rules and to modernise terminology. According to *Blake*, the most important element of Woolf's proposals was to give the courts the

6 For example, Olowofoyeku (1993).

competences necessary to take responsibility for proceedings. This is the system that has been introduced. Nowadays the debate focuses on the issue of whether an efficient case management system requires the active participation of the judges or whether court administrators can be entrusted with much of the work. Implemented changes restrict possibilities for contesting parties to use procedural law for their own purposes. Therefore, efficiency and reliability cause the British justice system to step unavoidably away from the strictly adversarial character of proceedings in civil law systems.

Jean writes that in France, since 1987, management support for the court administrations has been developed, especially at the appellate courts. Nowadays this management support functions by means of ICT systems. This is seen as a necessity, since an increasing number of French citizens apply to the courts in civil proceedings. During the past three years a legislative programme has started. This programme aims at changing civil and penal proceedings, increasing their speed and stimulating negotiations between parties instead of judicial decision-making. It is also directed at the development of evaluation systems to monitor the productivity of the courts. These quantitative measurements cannot yet deal with factors like the procedural strategies of the lawyers of insurance companies. Especially the field of penal law needs coordination efforts between municipal authorities and public prosecutors' offices to deal with the volume of crime and to increase the effectiveness of justice in order to improve societal conditions in difficult neighbourhoods. Part of this partnership is the instalment of legal establishments and justice within these neighbourhoods. Some of the debate in France concerns the positions of judges in society. According to Jean, the tendency is to stimulate that lawyers direct their efforts at negotiations and not at adversarial proceedings, and that the functions of judges is restricted to those cases where negotiations have failed. Furthermore, a start has been made with the separation of public prosecutors' offices and the courts, since public prosecutors' offices will have to follow national prosecution policies. Within the domain of the courts and within the domain of the public prosecutors' offices new balances will have to be developed between managerial and judicial functions, and between professional values and organisational accountability.

The Italian Government seems to give the improvement of the efficiency and the effectiveness of the courts a serious priority, enacting several law reforms in the last decade. From the several actions undertaken by Parliament and the Ministry of Justice described by *Marini*, we mention two mainly procedural reforms: the civil reform of 1995 and the criminal one of 1989. The ultimate goal of both reforms is to reduce the excessive length of the proceedings and their negative consequences such as backlogs, pre-trial detention, and the length of time between the date of the crime and the eventual trial. These reforms made the work of public prosecutors and judges more complex, and as a result of that, the length of the proceedings is still a very serious and unresolved problem. At the structural organisational level Parliament merged the first instance courts to try to reach some economy of scale, and in addition it enlarged the jurisdiction of the single judge, instead of a panel of three, in an attempt to increase productivity. Ten years ago the Justices of the Peace were introduced to deal with the minor civil cases. In the year 2000 minor criminal cases will be attributed to them as well. Furthermore, important investments have been made concerning the adoption of information and communication technologies. It is not clear if these major reforms and innovations have been analysed and evaluated, and this would be a typical task for public administration scholars.

In the Netherlands several changes have taken place during the last decade. The administrative justice system was completely reorganised with the introduction of the Administrative Law Act, investments in new courtbuildings were made on an extensive scale and ICT has been introduced in the courts. Furthermore minor offences have been removed from the criminal domain and placed within the domain of administrative justice. Most cases at first instance are dealt with by one judge. During the last few years experiments are being carried out so as to shorten civil proceedings. Alternative dispute resolution has drawn the attention of the legal professions.

From the organisational perspective four major developments have taken place, as *Brommet and Cleiren* describe. First of all the Public prosecutors' offices have been disconnected from the court organisations. Public prosecutors' offices now function under the leadership of a committee of prosecutors general at the national level. The Minister of Justice has political accountability for the public prosecutors' offices, and may give them guidelines. Second, the organisation of courts and judges has also drawn some attention from the policy-makers. The courts' supporting services are part of the justice department. Management of the courts is a joint task of judges and the management of the courts' supporting services, and is carried out at the courts' district level. Furthermore, increased attention has been paid to court performance measurement. Third, a project for the organisational development of the courts was initiated by some judges and the Ministry of Justice in 1996. It mainly focussed on the judges and their wishes for their courts and for the national judicial organisation. This resulted in the development of a separate judicial organisation for the courts and the courts' supporting services. However, this development is still going on. As Mrs. *Eradus* indicates, judges are willing to accept their separate responsibility for a new Dutch judicial organisation. A new Act on the Judicial Organisation will be sent to Parliament in the autumn of 2000. The proposed Act institutes a Council for the Judicature in order to enhance and facilitate a further organisational development of the courts, but also to function as a buffer between politics and the courts. The Council, for example, will divide the government funding amongst the courts. The general idea is that in this way a good balance can be structured between judicial independence, judicial accountability, and efficiency. Thus the societal legitimacy of the courts can be achieved. When the reorganisation of the Dutch judicial system is completed, the judicial organisation will be able to take care of its own interests and will be able to live up to political and societal demands for its accountability.

Considering these governmental efforts a few tendencies can be discerned. Judges are under pressure to take responsibility for the judicial and organisational performance of their courts. For many judges the acceptance of managerial responsibilities for their court organisations is not self-evident. Case management requires that the responsibility for proceedings is taken over from contesting parties by the court. Governments are willing to invest in the organisational development of their justice systems. The idea that it is better to keep conflicts away from formal court proceedings, be it penal or civil, has taken hold in all the countries described. In some countries, like Italy and Great Britain, measures for the improvement of the judicial system seem to be taken primarily by the government. The role of judges in the processes of reform is not clear and further analysis is needed. For example, in Italy all the managerial positions at the Ministry of Justice are held by judges or prosecutors. The Dutch Government has combined a top-down with a bottom-up approach. This means that not only judges in management positions are involved in the change. Court performance measurement is an issue in all countries, either to assess the investments necessary to make courts perform according to newly set standards, or to be able to hold courts accountable. The issue of the relation between judicial independence, measurement of court performance and accountability for the courts deserves prolonged attention by lawyers and scholars in public administration.

5 The changing positions of courts in state and society

As is clear from the descriptions of governmental policies, judicial independence and judicial accountability are still sensitive issues, because the institutional complexes of courts, judges and ministries of justice/Lord Chancellor's departments are forced into some organisational development. This means that relations between those executive parts of the government that are under political scrutiny of parliament on the one hand, and the judicial branches on the other should be studied again both from the perspective of accountability and from the perspective of judicial independence.

According to the contribution by *Drewry* the British Lord Chancellors' Department (LCD) evolved into a bureaucratic office with roughly the same relationships with other parts of government and the public as other British departments have. This means that elements of the *new public management* can be recognised in the relations between the LCD, the courts and the public: agencies, charters and public service agreements are accepted tools there. In this respect the administration of justice looks very much like an ordinary public service organisation. Judicial independence plays a major role, but judges play a role in developing those new tools and in improving the work of the courts, and they are quite often engaged in public debate on matters concerning the judicial organisation.

In the Netherlands the development of *new public management* has taken its own course. An awareness that the judicial system should earn it is legitimacy not only by sound juridical judgements but also by providing adequate services as well, has developed during the last few years within the courts, as *Langbroek* describes. The separation of powers had its divide between the administrative service organisations of the courts and the courts themselves. The effectuation of so-called *integral management* within the courts and the administrative service organisations made public servants and judges equally responsible for the organisational functioning of the courts. The struggle against backlogs and delays in penal, civil and administrative proceedings demands a pro-active attitude from managing judges and from managing public servants within the court organisations. To that end even the courts have to develop policies regarding their contacts with the media, the way procedural law is implemented, and how equal or comparable cases should be decided upon. This has a lot to do with the objective to earn and maintain public trust in the courts.

Tsobanoglou describes the development of the Greek judicial system from an historical- sociological perspective. From that point of view, the Greek judicial system demonstrates all the signs of the normal administrative services of the Greek state. Tsobanoglou signals the lack of interrelations and the lack of interaction between the system of law and regulations, on the one hand, and Greek society on the other. Law can hardly be made effective, because it is not adapted to the ways the real Greek society functions. In general, he signals a very formalistic approach to law by administrative bodies and by the courts, a lack of providing grounds to back up judicial decisions, and huge delays and backlogs in judicial proceedings, practically making the courts inaccessible for ordinary citizens, the 30,000 Greek lawyers notwithstanding. Furthermore, the culture of Greek judges is one of maintaining their social separation. The President of the Greek Supreme Court signals these failures and recently made some proposals for reform - also because Greece is a EU member. However, if the Greek elites do not recognise that the effectiveness and service quality of their judicial system is a prerequisite for further economic integration and development, these reform proposals may be in vain.

Dakolias and Thachuk's contribution bring to our attention the fundamental dilemma between judicial independence and judicial accountability. The dilemma is posed in relation to the problem of eradicating corruption from the judiciary, as one of the most important issues, particularly in some countries, in the planning stages of judicial reform. The article puts in a correct perspective the consequences of corruption not only for the administration of justice but for society in general and provides an opportune warning on the always tipped balance between independence and accountability.

We conclude for Great Britain and the Netherlands that the courts are no longer only part of the public domain as they always were because of their activities as juridical decision-makers. Nowadays they are also part of the political domain in their relationship with the public. Only as far as the relations of the courts with the executive branches of government and with parliament are concerned, does the constitutional demand of judicial independence prescribe that judges and politicians hold back if it comes to criticising each other (Kirby, 1998). Courts and judges, as regards the contents of their judgements, are accountable to the law and to the public in general, and not to the traditional political domain. Therefore, the buffer function of a Council for the Judicature or of a Lord Chancellors Office are different solutions to maintain the necessary separation of powers. Next to that, awareness of the possibility of corruption within the judicial system requires from all branches of government, including the courts, from the media and from the public that the accountability of courts and judges be effectuated.

In the light of the Greek experience, a prerequisite to an organisational development of courts and of a judicial system seems to be that the judicial system and the body of law and regulations are adapted to societal developments. This prerequisite has not yet been met in Greece. It is questionable whether only formal changes in Greek law and institutions will suffice in order to achieve that momentum.

6 Governance and change to the courts and public prosecutors' offices

In this section six contributions provide an example of some issues that have been under scrutiny in some countries in Europe concerning governance and changes to the courts and prosecutors' offices. What we would like to stress is the variety of interests and approaches to the study of the judicial systems which have, however, a common denominator in the effort to look for change for a better administration of justice.

Van der Doelen's contribution deals with the efforts that are taking place in the Netherlands to promote a better quality of justice. In September 1998 the Netherlands started a major project of Reinforcement of the Judicial Organisation (PVRO) as a response to increasing pressure from the press, the public and the political body to increase the quality of the administration of justice. In particular, emphasis is put on courts' performance developed through the coherent and shared vision of some organisational aspects such as: leadership, strategy, personnel management, and resource policy. Some of these efforts were stimulated by the Trial Courts Performance Standards developed in the United States, that single out quite a few items to measure the quality of courts such us: accessibility, duration and timeliness, equality, fairness and integrity, independence and accountability, and public trust.

What is interesting to note is that in the United States as well as in Canada and Australia the debate about the performance of the courts and prosecutors' offices has advanced hand in hand with the one developed for other public administrations. Amazingly, European courts seem much more afraid of performance measurements than their American counterparts, even if lately some attempts are taking place in France, in the Netherlands, and in particular in Great Britain and Wales.

Loveday's paper highlights the problems of measuring performance through the application of the *new public management* to criminal justice agencies in Great Britain and Wales. In his contribution Loveday shows how difficult it is to apply performance measurements to the public sector and to the judiciary in particular. The difficulties in identifying the outputs and outcomes of both the judiciary and the prosecutors' offices, create almost insurmountable problems in the evaluation process. The sometimes exasperated *mania* to measure performance by means of quantitative criteria could lead to an inaccurate conclusion, and subsequently to an incorrect implementation of new government policy. This does not mean that we do not have to pursue some kind of performance measurements for the judicial sector at all, but it means that we should carefully identify valid and reliable indicators for each system, without borrowing 'turn key' solutions, in particular from the United Stated, that are sometimes not readily applicable in the European context. One of the problems is certainly the lack of studies on judicial administration carried out by European scholars.

This is what *Fabri* claims in his contribution. Starting from a brief genesis of the discipline of judicial administration in the United States along with the figure of the court manager, he ends up with the need for studies on European judicial systems from a public administration perspective. For too long the study of the administration of justice has been the monopoly of legal scholars with an embarrassing lack of empirical analysis that embraces concepts of organisational theory, public and judicial administration, and management.

In particular, in continental Europe the dominance of the legal formalistic approach to the management of courts and prosecutors' offices has led to several organisational dysfunctions along with a dominant position of judges and prosecutors in judicial policy making. This situation makes any innovation process very difficult and tends to keep the judicial system away from the reforms that are interesting other fields of public administration. The independence of the judiciary is still a strong shield to preserve the *status quo* and to keep the administration of justice away from the benefits that can come from a multidisciplinary approach to its study and analysis. The challenge for change in the European judicial systems should also be endorsed by public administration scholars who should introduce new competence and knowledge in this field, as happened several years ago in the United States.

Among the problems that affect courts and prosecutors' offices, two have been underlined by the contributions by Duvillier and Buitendam. *Duvillier* argues that the public prosecutor in Belgium is what Mintzberg (1979) calls a professional bureaucracy. Actually many courts and prosecutors' offices in continental Europe have the features of a professional bureaucracy and this is certainly one of the main obstacles to promoting innovation processes. Once the kind of organisational configuration that has characterised several judicial institutions has been recognised, the question is how the organisational defences can be overcome to stimulate a process of change. For example, what kind of change levers should be activated, what kind of strategy, what kind of skills should be developed?

A partial answer comes from *Buitendam*'s contribution which gives an outline of the current recruitment, selection and training policy for judges in the Netherlands. This is a central issue for anyone who wants to promote change within the judiciary. She argues that if one wishes to make changes to an organisation, the organisational actors must change too. The problem, however, is in which direction the change should go. For example, in order to promote a better management of courts, would it be better to develop management competences among the judges or among the administrative personnel? Or would it be more effective to 'borrow' these competencies from outside the organisation?

Mestitz's contribution focuses on the Italian juvenile justice system and its differences and analogies with other European juvenile justice systems. It is interesting to note how in this paper the concept of the judiciary as a system is determinant to analyse the features and the problems of the juvenile subsystem. The complexity in this case is very great due to the interactions of many institutions that have to pursue different and sometimes divergent goals. Emphasis is put on the lack of independence and competence of lay judges as well as on the dominant role of prosecutors and judges.

Thanks also to these contributions, we can perceive that throughout Europe there is a refreshing air of change that involves courts, prosecutors' offices and related institutions such as Ministries of Justice, Departments of Prison, Probation, etc. It is a matter of fact that public administration scholars have traditionally preferred to direct their studies towards the Executive and the Legislative branches, leaving the judicial institutions on an exclusive field for legal professionals. Only recently have many Western countries experienced the increasing role of the judiciary in their democratic life, with various events that have certainly highlighted the important and growing role of the judiciary in our societies (Tate and Vallinder, 1995). The pressure for change in the public sector has finally also involved the judicial institutions that for many years have been a world apart from the other fields of public administration.

In addition, the progress in the European Union has been pushing towards an integration of the different judicial systems. This produces increasing interest concerning the institutional setting, the procedure, the functioning and the performance of the different judicial systems. Many governments in Europe have found out how their judicial systems are in quite a crisis, they do not respond as quickly as they should to societal demands, and they seem to be hostages of a legal cage that has slowed down - if not totally avoided - innovation processes.

7 Courts, public prosecutors' offices and information communication technology (ICT)

In this section of the book we have collected four contributions that are quite different from each other, showing that the field of public administration is very wide and is often cultivated with different tools. Much depends on the scholarly backgrounds that affect research methods, techniques, concepts used to interpret phenomena, and in this section we have four different good examples.

The article presented by *Van de Donk* shows how the judicial system, maybe a good last in the public sector, has been recently touched by information and communication technology and how this exposition is going to affect its functioning as well as the actors' behaviours. In particular, the paper briefly describes three information technology tools adopted in some Dutch courts and prosecutors' offices. These tools, at least initially, have focused on decisional support systems for sentencing but, and this should be particularly notable for public administration scholars, information technology is largely considered to be one of the most important change factors for judicial systems as, indeed, it has already been in other public administration sectors. In the Netherlands a strong movement towards judicial reform is taking place and information technology is seen as a *conditio sine qua non* for the success of the reform processes.

The adoption of information technology raises many questions about judicial independence and accountability due to the fact that, among other aspects, technology makes the judicial system more visible. It increases the quantity and quality of available information and, in doing so, it can contribute to decreasing the information asymmetry which is one of the causes of the organisational power structure. It certainly promotes the introduction of new processes and new routines, but only where the opportunity for change is recognised and internalised by the actors. These latter will see the change when they will believe in it.

The study of ICT and the judicial system should not be different from the studies that deal with the introduction of information technology in organisations. Particularly from the angle of a public administration scholar or practitioner, the focus should not be on technicalities but on the interactions between technology and the organisation as a whole.

This is well pointed out by *Contini*'s article, based on an interesting field research, which tells us that to try to understand technology's potential to change - but we could also relate this to innovation in general - we should focus on the interactions between the innovation object and the receiving organisation. It is through the in-depth study and analysis of these interactions that we can really enrich our knowledge about innovation processes and lead the actors towards a beneficial change for the organisation. On many occasions wonderful highly sophisticated tools have been rejected or, even worse, metabolised by the practices and behaviours of the organisational actors. Contini's argument is that a perspective of change has to deal with the formative context of the organisation, with its micro-ecology of actions - the sedimentation of knowledge and routines that characterise the organisation - more than merely the technology itself. Technology is an artefact which is always reinvented by the users. Through the comprehension of this reinvention process, it is possible to develop our knowledge about innovation processes and then to stimulate organisational change. Only in this way will the implementation of information technology not be just a *celebration of a rite* but will really affect the functioning of the organisation.

Contini's paper has correctly drawn our attention to the fact that we should avoid a goal displacement when information technology is introduced in an organisation (Orlikowski and Robey, 1991). Information technology should bring a perceived benefit to the functioning of courts such as visibility, accountability, quality of decisions, speed and cost of the proceedings, meaning that the mere implementation of computers, sophisticated case flow management systems, video technology, intranet, and decision support systems will not necessary create any change as regards organisational behaviour. Technology is a great opportunity for change, it is a kind of 'Trojan horse', but it is not a self-executing program, a 'plug and play' tool, it needs to be carefully sustained to give the expected results as well as outcomes that cannot originally be foreseen (Barely, 1986; Rice and Rogers, 1980; Weick, 1990; Zuboff, 1988).

Nowadays judicial systems have a great opportunity to implement changes to improve their functioning, their workflow, their decision making by the use of technology (Harrington 1991). Good examples are described in both Staechelé's and Poupa's contributions. *Staechelé*'s paper shows how the implementation of decisional support systems as well as the various Internet applications in France, are certainly important to stimulate a process of change in the judiciary that cannot be postponed any longer. The list of interesting initiatives taken in France as regards technology and the courts should now be followed by field research to develop our knowledge on the concrete functioning of what has been implemented, along with its benefits for the judicial system.

Poupa's contribution, with the description of the progressive implementation of electronic publication of legal information in Switzerland, shows how technology can generate new opportunities between the private sector and a public organisation. Once again the attention should not be on the technology itself but on the interaction process between the technology and the judicial system and the change effects of this interaction in actors' behaviours.

All the four papers, at a different level of analysis, show how technology is probably the most important factor of change for judicial systems. There is no doubt that technology will increasingly affect the administration of justice, and many questions will be looking for answers by public administration scholars.

What we would like to emphasise, once more, is that knowledge and action are strictly related (Argyris and Schön, 1978; Senge, 1990). The more knowledge we produce about these interaction processes, the greater are the possibilities of change – even in a field such as the judicial one, which is traditionally considered very slow in changing. The introduction of information technology in the judicial systems, is a great opportunity to produce studies and analysis to keep constantly alive a knowledge learning process which is a fundamental engine to promote organisational change.

8 Concluding remarks: a public administration research perspective for judicial systems

Throughout Europe, governments try to adjust their judicial systems to our (post-)modern times. Greece seems to be an exception in this respect, because the Greek Government has not yet recognised the problems of judicial administration. In most countries this is primarily a matter of redesigning judicial procedures and of reorganising the courts and the public prosecutors' offices. In Greece more of a complete change of its legal culture seems to be a prerequisite.

In general, convincing judicial professionals of the usefulness of an attitude directed more towards the judicial organisation and towards society than their professional values, is at issue here. Organising these changes is not something unique. It only seems natural that organisations, profit and non-profit, orient themselves towards their societal (political, social, technological, market, media, public) surroundings. Consultants make a living out of helping these organisations to develop strategies in order to determine their future.

This means different choices can be made as to what changes in a judicial organisation are the most essential and who will be responsible for implementing these changes. These choices are related to the traditions of the separation of powers and the special position of courts, judges and public prosecutors within the organisation of the state. Judges are not competent to change the rules and nature of judicial proceedings as far as the legislature is competent to do so (Schmitt, 1928; Kägi, 1937). The position of the courts regarding the executive and the legislature is less clear concerning the organisation of justice, however. Much is dependent on how the concept of a court is defined constitutionally. For example, does the concept of a court only consist of judges or does the concept imply the administrative service organisations as well? And how does the independence of the judiciary relate to the competences of, for example, a justice department regarding the organisation of courts and public prosecutors' offices?

The field of justice is a field of traditional professions. Generally speaking, the traditional professions in the field of law do not give much of attention to the organisation and its societal surroundings which they work in (Kronman, 1993). They handle sets of values internalised during professional education and training. In the field of law these values concern the rule of law (the idea of a *rechtsstaat* in continental countries). So lawyers, judges, barristers, solicitors and public prosecutors are focussed on the content of the law, of legislation, and of jurisprudence. In general, their professional perspective does not give them the outlook necessary to cope with major societal developments and with the organisational demands as a consequence thereof. So governments and justice departments have taken the initiative to start a process of change - in Great Britain, in France, in Italy and in the Netherlands. Not to mention the changes in Belgium where the Dutroux affair has urged the Government to change the judicial system.

When governments start to implement inevitable changes in their judicial organisations, members of the judiciary seem to find themselves in a peculiar position. They seem to have the choice between either welcoming these changes, anticipating them and adapting themselves to them, or to step aside and leave the changes to others. The last-mentioned choice will leave the management of change to others. In professional organisations this seems to be a normal pattern. Within judicial organisations possibly a distinction can be made between different responsibilities: organisational management, judicial management and the traditional judicial tasks of presiding over hearings and deciding cases, the judicial 'core business'. It is a matter of choice how these different responsibilities are organised, related and accounted for. But this choice is related to another one, namely the choice for a certain amount of responsiveness regarding the court's organisational and societal surroundings. Societal and organisational responsive courts require an altogether different kind of management than courts that adhere exclusively to fulfilling traditional judicial functions, leaving the 'responses' to other institutions. This choice concerning what kind of organisations courts should be, is directly related to the answer to the question how far political accountability for the courts may reach. The rule of law and the idea of *rechtsstaat* state that the political accountability for the courts necessarily is a restricted one. Therefore, the choice for the development of courts as organisations that are capable to live up to demands of public accountability by themselves seems inevitable.

So far, governments have tried to modernise their judicial systems by developing instruments and competences so as to give courts and judges greater control over and responsibility for court proceedings. Speed of procedure is the main issue of case management. Comparing Anglo-American and continental adaptations of judicial proceedings, we see a debate going on in Great Britain and Australia about reducing the adversarial system and giving courts and judges a greater grip on and responsibilities for judicial proceedings.[7] On the continent, for example in the Netherlands, however, voices are heard indicating that ADR is more attractive because it gives parties a greater grip on the proceedings and the outcome thereof. Italy seems to be wrestling with the disadvantages of adversarial penal procedures introduced ten years ago, without changing the still inquisitorial organisational setting and culture (Fabri, 1994; Pizzi and Marafioti, 1992). This case shows us the necessity to reiterate to the legal professionals that the law is just one of the levers of change and quite often not the most important one.

---

7 The Woolf Report advises that the courts should be given the responsibility for guiding a case on to the appropriate procedural track. These tracks are: small claims, fast-track and multi-track, and to make the court responsible for dealing with a case in conformity with the chosen track.
See www.open.gov.uk./lcd/interim, chapter 6. The major change consists of the courts being responsible for the timetable, not the contesting parties.

Looking at the current adaptations in judicial proceedings, looking at governmental efforts to develop a responsive judiciary and looking at the major societal developments of our time, which are the most urgent questions for research?

We think the public administration perspective on judicial institutions should combine *static* and *dynamic* themes.[8]

Static themes concern the institutional relations within a judicial system and the institutional relations between a judicial system and its societal and political surroundings. For example, the institutional position of courts both within their own state and within the European Union and with particular attention to the jurisdiction of the European Court of Human Rights could be the subject of research. Thanks also to the contributions presented here, the dilemma between judicial independence and accountability and their relations with the political systems still seem an important research issue, since it is still a sensitive one in many European countries (Di Federico, 1996). Special attention should be devoted to the relations between the courts and the public. Researches could develop themes referred to as the public trust, the media and the support and legitimacy of the courts.

Dynamic themes concern the ways courts and judicial institutions adjust themselves, but also affect the changing societal circumstances. For example, on the one side, researches who will deal with the process of societal globalization and the changing position of courts and prosecutors' offices would be of great interest as well as research concerning the changing role of the legal professions. On the other side, court judgments but also international prosecutorial initiatives are going to deeply affect the globalization process.

A mixture of dynamic and static elements can be found in the perspective of court management, which is a very important research field to develop, particularly in Europe. A great deal of research is needed into the management of court services concerning proceedings, workflow and judgments. Above all, there is a strong demand for techniques and methods to measure and evaluate judicial institution performance. The definitions of concepts of efficiency, effectiveness, and quality management have to be improved in order to be useful for the judicial systems. Research into the training of judges, prosecutors, court managers, and judicial personnel is always a priority, since without it no change can take place (Armytage, 1996). In addition, we can see technology as a meta-theme that cuts through all the static and dynamic elements identified. It is a matter of fact that technology can be considered the strongest tool for change and it is already affecting the way in which justice is done (Anderson, 1993).

---

8 These themes are the summarized outcome of a questionaire amongst researchers, policy-makers and judges visiting the workshops on management and delivery of judges during the EGPA Conference in 1999.

So, the domain of management and delivery of justice is quite broad. We feel that the public administration perspective should not be restricted to a sociological one concerning courts and judicial organizations. Culture is also a point to attend to, as are the legal settings in which courts have to function. Traditional constitutionalist perspectives on the organization of courts and judges no longer suffice to generate solutions for their problems nowadays. This having been said, we view the function of a public administration perspective on judicial organizations as generating different kinds of comments and knowledge on what courts and judges do. A traditional function of scholars in law is the review of judicial decisions. With their comments they contribute to the development of the law. In a similar way the tasks of scholars in public administration could be seen as describing and analysing the organisational functioning of judicial institutions, meaning that the focus is on subjects like policy analysis, justice outcomes and services, evaluation programmes, citizen satisfaction, and quality of justice. The judicial functions within the European states are far too important to leave to the legal professions alone. Thus, the dynamics of the checks and balances concerning courts and judges can be reinvented once more to keep our rule of law and our '*rechtsstaat*' alive.

References

Anderson, R., Borgersen, E., Brest, P., Fenwick, W. J. Sher, 'The Impact of Information Technology on Judicial Administration: a Research Agenda for the Future', in: *Southern California Law Review*, vol.66, (1993), pp. 1761-1812.

Argyris C. and D. Schön, *Organizational Learning: A Theory of Action Perspective*. Reading, MA., Addison-Wesley, (1978).

Armytage, Livingston, *Educating Judges: Towards a New Model of Continuing Judicial Learning*, The Hague/Boston/London: Kluwer Law International, (1996).

Barely, Stephen, *Technology as an Occasion for Structuring: Evidence from Observations of CT Scanners and the Social Order of Radiology Department*, in:*Administrative Science Quarterly*, n.31, (1986), pp.78-108.

Blankenburg, E., F. Bruinsma, *Dutch legal culture*, Deventer/Boston, (1994).

Dakolias, M.J. Said, *Judicial Reform, A Process of Change Through Pilot Courts*, The World Bank, Washington, (1999).

Dijk, P. van, G.J.H. van Hoof, in collaboration with A.W. Heringa, J.G.C. Schokkenbroek, B.P. Vermeulen, M.L.W.M. Viering, L.F. Zwaak, *Theory and Practice of the European Convention on Human Rights*, The Hague/Boston/London: Kluwer Law international, (1998).

Fabri, M., 'Theory versus practice of Italian criminal justice reform', in: *Judicature*, vol.77, n. 4, (1994).

Fortin, Yvonne, Hugo van Hassel, *Contracting in the new public management, From Economics to Law and Citizenship,* Amsterdam, Oxford, (2000).

Di Federico, G., 'Prosecutorial Independence and the Democratic Requirement of Accountability', in: *Italy: Analysis of a deviant case in a comparative perspective*, Working Papers Irsig-Cnr, Bologna, Lo Scarabeo, (1996).
Harrington, J., *Organizational Structure and Information Technology*, London: Prentice Hall, (1991).
Kägi, O.W., *Zur Entstehung, wandlung und Problematik des Gewaltenteilungsprinzipes*, Universität Zürich, Zürich, (1937).
Kirby, M., *Attacks on judges a universal phenomenon*, Paper presented at the winter leadership meeting of the American Bar Association, Section of litigation, at Maui, Hawaii, January 5, (1995)
download from: http://www.hcourt.gov.au/speeches/kirbyj/maui.htm.
Koers, A.W., *Driemaal is scheepsrecht. De modernisering van de rechterlijke organisatie*. Den Haag: SDU, (1999).
Kronman, A.T., *The lost lawyer, Failing Ideals of the Legal Profession*, Cambridge, London, (1993).
Langbroek, P.M., 'De publieke verantwoordelijkheid voor rechtspraak', in:*Tijdschrift voor de rechterlijke macht*, (1994), pp. 405-413.
Langbroek, P.M., 'Naar een rechtsplegingskunde', *Tijdschrift voor de rechterlijke macht*, (1995), pp. 323-328.
Mintzberg, Henry, *The Structure of Organizations*, Englewood Cliffs, NJ., Prentice Hall, (1979).
North, C. Douglass, *Istituzioni, cambiamento istituzionale, evoluzione dell'economia*, Bologna, Il Mulino, (1994); tit. orig., *Insitutions, Institutional Change and Economic Performance*, Cambridge University Press, (1990).
Olowofoyeku, Abimbola, *Suing Judges, A study of Judicial Immunity*, Oxford, (19-93).
Orlikowski, Wanda and Daniel Robey, 'Information Technology and the Structuring of Organizations', in: *The Institute of Management Sciences*, (1991), pp.143-169.
Osborne, D., Gaebler, T., *Reinventing government: How the entrepreneurial spirit is transforming the public sector*, Reading: Addison Wesley, (1992).
Pizzi, William and Luca Marafioti, 'The new Italian Code of Criminal Procedure: The Difficulties of Bulding an Adversarial Trial System on a Civil Law Foundation', in: *The Yale Journal of International Law*, vol.17, n.1, (1992), p. 3.
Powell, W. and P. Di Maggio, *Institutionalism in Organizational Analysis*, Chicago: The University of Chicago, (1991).
Rice, R.R. and E.M. Rogers, 'Reinvention in the Innovation Process', in: *Knowledge*, vol. I, 4, (1980), pp. 499-514.
Röhl K.F., *Gerichtsverwaltung und Court Management in den USA*, Köln, (1993).
Schmitt, C., *Verfassungslehre*, Berlin, (1928).
Senge, Peter, *The Fifth Discipline. The art and practice of the learning organization*, New York: Doubleday Currency, (1990).
Shapiro, M., *Courts, A comparative and political analysis*, Chicago, (1981).
Shetreet, Shimon, *Judges on trial, a study to the appointment and accountability of the English judiciary*, Amsterdam, New York, Oxford, (1976).

Tate, Neil & Torbjön Vallinder, (eds.), *The Global Expansion of Judicial Power*, New York: New York University Press, (1995).
Vervaele J.A.E, co-ed.: G. Betlem, R. de Lange, A.G. Veldman, *Compliance and enforcement of European Community law*, The Hague, (1999).
Vile, J.C., *Constitutionalism and the separation of powers*, Oxford, (1967).
Weick, Karl, 'Technology as Equivoque: Sensemaking in New Technologies', in: Goodman, P., L. Sproull and Associates, (eds.), *Technology and Organizations*, San Francisco, Jossey Bass, (1990), pp.1-43.
Zuboff, Shosana, *In the Age of the Smart Machine*, New York, Basic Books, (1988).

Part I

Keynote Speeches: Management & Efficiency *versus* Judicial Values

The Challenge of Change for Judicial Systems
M. Fabri and Ph.M. Langbroek (Eds.)
IOS Press, 2000

Address to the EGPA Conference, Cape Sounion, Greece

Barry Loveday[1]

I am very pleased to be able to address you today at the start of this year's conference which has as its theme 'Delivering Justice in the 21st century'. In my opinion it is entirely appropriate that this subject should be a matter of consideration and debate at a conference such as this rather than being confined as it has perhaps traditionally been in the past to lawyers, constitutionalists and practitioners. This is because, as we have learned in the UK, the tide of reform within the public sector has certainly embraced the criminal justice system which like other services has been required to demonstrate greater economy, efficiency and effectiveness.

In this address, I intend to discuss some of the developments which have taken place or which are taking place in England and Wales in the delivery of criminal justice. Although the demand for 'value for money' was initiated in the 1980s by the Conservative Government led by Margaret Thatcher it is particularly noticeable that 'New Labour' has decided to continue the pressure to improve performance within all public services. That, as many will be aware, certainly includes agencies within the criminal justice system which for the very first time is now the subject of a Strategic Plan to improve the overall efficiency of the 'system' in the delivery of justice.

Now I would like to stress that there are clear reasons for supporting a number of the aims identified within that Plan. Reducing delay and fast tracking serious cases along with the more general objective of promoting confidence in the criminal justice system are laudable aims and are unlikely to generate much dissention. It may be the case, however, that how the range of objectives set by government are to be achieved will be a matter of dispute. Thus (and I must not pre-empt my own paper on this!) a commitment to the continued application of performance measurement and performance management by New Labour to the public sector is fully reflected in its Strategic Plan for criminal justice. Within this document all 'agencies' are subject to performance targets and performance monitoring. In addition, the Government makes clear that within the new 'Business Plan' the primary aim of the Government will to be encourage greater co-ordination between differing agencies and ultimately to begin to 'manage the system as a whole'. While this objective does, of course, reflect continuing Government interest in improved efficiency, it may also pose problems. Not the least of those is whether criminal justice is in any sense amenable to performance measurement. Can we really make a judgement about the work of the courts on the

1 University of Portsmouth, Great Britain.

basis of throughput? Can we make any real judgement about the effectiveness of policing on the basis of the arrest rate achieved or the crime clearance rate? I very much doubt it! Yet the general thrust of 'reform' remains (as with the earlier Conservative Government) closely linked to numbers, throughput and target attainment. This is a matter of concern, particularly in England and Wales where only a year ago the Glidewell Review of the Crown Prosecution Service was to provide in some considerable detail the 'downside' of performance management. Here within the CPS and in order to achieve targets set by the centre, discontinuance and downgrading of offences became a regular feature of CPS case management. Nor in the pursuit of efficiency gains did matters end there. One further discovery of the Glidewell Review of case management related to 'case termination' where it was learned that when the outcome of a prosecution was thought to be, in any way, uncertain then discontinuance was likely. So it was that in cases involving an offence of violence against the person nearly a third (29%) could, year on year 'be expected to be terminated'. With however more certain offences, motoring offences for example, the percentage termination rate fell to just 1%! Nor did the CPS prove to be that good at prosecuting errant police officers accused of committing the most serious offences, as the Butler Inquiry has recently informed us. That is, however, a separate issue that cannot be considered here.

Not surprisingly given the frequency of non-prosecution in cases of serious personal crime, public confidence in the criminal justice system, as was to be vividly described by David Rose in successive newspaper articles, fell dramatically. Ironically, there appeared to be some interesting correlations between public confidence and CPS performance levels. As public confidence fell most steeply in the mid-1990s the CPS was, according to its own Annual reports, reaching most of its targets. Indeed to judge by the content of those Reports there appeared to be no conceivable reason why anyone would wish to question what it did and how it fulfilled its function. Yet within months its Director and Chief Executive was to accept and implement organisational change that radically altered the structure of the CPS while also effectively reversing the whole management approach which had until then characterised its operation. As the Glidewell Report was to identify, the 'performance culture' and associated management style had generated considerable animosities within the organisation. As Glidewell was to relate in relation to the management of the CPS :

> 'It seems that many staff fear that if they are critical of management this will at best prevent them from progressing in their careers and at worst may endanger their jobs. We have warned ourselves against taking these assertions at face value ... It is, however, clear that a form of management which breeds this amount of unhappiness and mistrust amongst its employees cannot be sound. At the very least it shows a failure of management at some levels to succeed in communicating to their staff what it is they are doing or seeking to do and why' (Glidewell Chap. 1, para. 25).

Just what organisational culture was created by the 'performance culture' was to be identified in an eternal survey conducted by the Glidewell Inquiry. Personnel were to be asked to comment on the attributes of the person who might be expected 'to get on' in the CPS. Respondents were to state that :

> 'Towing the line, secretiveness and even intimidation were held in higher regard than being a good manager of people, communicating well, having a high level of professional skill or being open and frank and supportive to colleagues' (Glidewell Chap. 5 para 22).

Under a new Director the CPS is now in the process of rebuilding and re-establishing its credibility. It is expected that in the future a less centralised, cost driven and 'performance approach culture' will be attained which remains an integral part of the 'New' Public Management and provides a continuing lesson for other criminal justice agencies and those within the wider public sector.

The Anglo-American perspective on criminal justice

Along with the application of NPM to criminal justice has come, as one distinguished academic has described it, the increasing Americanisation of criminal justice policy in the UK. (Rutherford, 1996). From the application of 'zero tolerance policing' through to a growing commitment to the private provision of services in the criminal justice field, particularly the expansion of private prison capacity, criminal policy has rather faithfully reflected similar developments in the United States. Much of this particularly during the early 1990s reflected the influence of James Q. Wilson on a Conservative Government that was keen to pursue a 'war on crime' based on mandatory sentencing, increased prison capacity and retributive justice. In political terms being seen to be 'tough on crime' was politically attractive and traditionally this policy area was monopolised by the Conservative Party. It is probably fair to say that one of the most interesting features of New Labours' election in 1997 was this party's success in replacing the Conservatives as that which could be most trusted on crime, law and order. But being 'tough on crime and tough on the causes of crime 'while becoming the most successful soundbite in recent Labour Party history, has also come at some cost. The strategy of 'triangulation' developed by Clinton's Democrats in America (and more traditionally known as 'stealing the opposition party's clothes') and pursued by New Labour has meant that the criminal policy in the UK has, as has been argued most recently by Andrew Rutherford in England, been pushed to the right as in the run up to the 1997 election each party espoused more punitive policies to deal with the perceived crime problem.

One result of this has been the difficulty in distinguishing between the policies of New Labour and that of its predecessor in the criminal justice field. As is being increasingly recognised domestically the flagship legislation of New Labour, the Crime and Disorder Act of 1998 encompasses a range of punitive measures which, inter alia, will now criminalise the behaviour of children under 10 years of age. There are indeed many facets of the Act with which the former Conservative Government would have been entirely comfortable. But my purpose here is not to analyse that legislation but to identify two features surrounding it which are of some interest. First, following a long and quite undistinguished 'British tradition' of apeing all things American, virtually no interest was taken in criminal policy as developed in Europe, even though there remains much to learn from policy development in this area from fellow Europeans. Instead the development of criminal policy continues to reflect what presumably is seen as best practice in the United States. This is, to say the least, difficult to understand! With a prison population which per thousand population remains one of the highest in the world and a murder rate which is unparalleled in Europe one might legitimately ask who might learn from whom?

Secondly, the legislative programme embarked upon by New Labour appears to take a highly mechanistic view of the role of the criminal justice system, being as much 'result-orientated' as its predecessors. New Labour appears to be as managerialist in its approach to improving efficiency as the Conservatives were in the past.

Achieving results has been clearly identified in the Government's Strategic Plan mentioned earlier. There is, however, a real danger that in seeking 'results' particularly when these may be identified for election purposes, the Government will intervene to 'encourage' the achievement of objectives it has set both individual agencies and the criminal justice system as a whole. For a number of reasons, of which you will be aware, it may be difficult for criminal justice agencies to achieve objectives when there are so many environmental and other factors at play over which they have no influence. For a government committed to improving performance this may lead to greater central intervention and the further erosion of professional discretion at an operational level.

Finally, the managerialist approach to criminal justice which has been pursued by successive governments may come at some additional cost. For, as has been argued by Rutherford and others the commitment to managerialism may easily replace interest in a commitment to principled policy. For as has been argued by one commentator concerning the impact of managerialist ideology on criminal justice in Britain :

> 'The virtue of managerialism is that it is divorced from any substantive normative or political values. Indeed it transforms the absence of principled policy, for example along the lines of justice and fairness, from a vice into a virtue'. (Jones, 1993).

To this might be added the danger that the cult of managerialism may only serve to reinforce what Rutherford has described as 'pragmatic expediency'. This danger becomes ever greater when efficiency gains are effectively cost-cutting exercises which have little concern with either quality of service delivery or 'outcomes' rather than 'outputs'.

In conclusion, I would like to say that the theme of this year's conference might enable us to explore the problems surrounding the 'delivery of justice' and perhaps begin to come to some conclusions as to how it may be better delivered. Even if we are unable to come to any firm conclusions it is likely that the exploration of this issue may generate new insights into the delivery of justice within European Member States which may prove to be instructive and from which we can all expect to learn. I am therefore sure that we can all look forward to a productive and rewarding conference here at Cape Sounion.

References

Rutherford, A., *Transforming Criminal Policy Spheres of Influence in the United States, the Netherlands and England and Wales during the 1980s*, Waterside Press, (1996).

Jones, C., *Auditing criminal justice*, BJC, (1993).

The Review of the Crown Prosecution Service, Presented to Parliament by the The Attorney General Sir Iain Glidewell, by Command of Her Majesty, June 1998. Download from: http://www.official-documents.co.uk/document/cm39/3972/contents.htm

The Challenge of Change for Judicial Systems
M. Fabri and Ph.M. Langbroek (Eds.)
IOS Press, 2000

Gérer et rendre la justice au XXIème siècle: La justice continentale

Marie-France Christophe Tchakaloff[1]

1 Introduction

Dans notre système démocratique, la justice est un pouvoir, une autorité publique, un principe éthique, une administration qui touche à la vie quotidienne de chaque citoyen. C'est dire que la justice peut présenter tous les ingrédients d'une grande utopie mobilisatrice pour le XXIème siècle.

En ce sens d'ailleurs, un double constat confirme le besoin européen de justice. D'une part, tous les Etats européens se recentrent autour de l'objectif de justice. Certes, celui-ci n'est pas nouveau. Il a plus particulièrement été prôné dans les périodes tumultueuses de l'histoire. Mais aujourd'hui, il doit permettre de satisfaire et propager 'l'Etat de droit', Etat constitutionnel qui se façonne dans la démocratie et le respect des droits de l'homme et des libertés fondamentales. D'autre part, l'administration de la justice est au cœur de réflexions et des réformes de tous les Etats européens du fait de ses décalages sociaux et de sa difficile gestion. Le 'monument' que représente 'l'ensemble Justice' a été modifié, transformé, mais derrière le replâtrage, le plan de la construction d'origine souvent très ancienne reste perceptible.

Le thème de nos travaux est ardu. Déjà Richelieu dans son testament politique estimait 'plus aisé de reconnaître les défauts de la justice que d'en prescrire les remèdes'. Aussi me bornerai-je dans ce rapport introductif à lancer quelques pistes concernant la justice continentale, d'abord à partir d'interrogations sur la légitimité de la justice continentale, et ensuite sur l'efficacité de cette justice.

2 Sur quelle légitimité repose la justice des etats à tradition continentale?

Si la légitimité de fondement de la justice continentale est incontestable, sa légitimité fonctionnelle est pratique et contestée.

1 Professeur de Droit public, Directeur de la recherche et des publications à l'Institut international d'administration publique, Paris (France).

2.1 Une incontestable légitimité de fondement:

La justice est enracinée et garantie dans chaque constitution écrite, notamment sur quatre points essentiels. En premier lieu, la justice est garantie dans son indépendance. Cette indépendance est consacrée dans chaque Etat conformément à ses règles constitutionnelles de séparation des pouvoirs. Il faut insister sur le fait que l'indépendance de la justice est une règle de droit, et pas seulement un principe éthique, qui prémunit les juges contre les incohérences éventuelles de la justice.

En deuxième lieu, la justice est garantie dans son organisation institutionnelle. De nombreux pays fonctionnent sur la base de deux ordres de juridictions répartis entre l'ordre judiciaire et l'ordre administratif: la Grèce, la Finlande, l'Italie à partir de 1889-1890, les Pays-Bas et le Portugal. En France la dualité est un legs de la révolution de 1789, le Conseil constitutionnel a reconnu à ce principe valeur constitutionnelle.[2] Et la justice administrative française tend parfois à se considérer autonome du fait de sa spécificité et oublier que l'organisation de la justice ne vise pas seulement l'ordre judiciaire.

En troisième lieu, l'accès direct des citoyens est garanti en Grèce, aux Pays-Bas, au Portugal, en Espagne où ce droit d'accès a été élargi par la constitution de 1978, en Finlande grâce à une disposition adoptée en 1995 sur le 'droit à une justice audition'.

Enfin, en respectant l'échelle des normes constitutionnelles le juge doit assurer le respect de la norme internationale. Cette primauté du traité sur la loi a deux effets. D'une part, elle s'impose à tous les juges, quel que soit leur domaine, civil, pénal ou administratif, et à toutes les juridictions même spécialisées, et quelle que soit leur place, instance d'appel et de cassation. Et la primauté fait de ces juges des juges de la loi nationale.

D'autre part, cette primauté rappelle que les pays européens sont façonnés par une autre administration de la justice que la leur: justice transnationale, du Conseil de l'Europe et de l'Union européenne. (La même obligation de primauté s'impose au Royaume-Uni mais sur le fondement d'un acte spécifique: l''European Community Act').

Ces quatre caractéristiques engendrent quatre obligations pour l'administration de la justice. Elle doit mettre en œuvre les moyens nécessaires pour accomplir les missions; elle doit ouvrir l'accès des plaideurs. Elle doit organiser le déroulement de l'instance conformément aux règles de procédure. Elle doit faciliter les voies de recours sans lesquelles il n'y aurait pas d''Etat de droit'.

Comment le respect de ces obligations dans les différents Etats continentaux est-il perçu? La question est fondamentale puisqu'elle conditionne la crédibilité de l'administration de la justice et les domaines à privilégier pour la moderniser.

---

2 Décisions du 22 juillet 1980 et du 23 janvier 1987.

2.2 La légitimité de la justice contestée en pratique:

Certes les relations des juges avec les médias, les 'affaires' qui empoisonnent l'indépendance de la justice dans l'Etat par immixtion du politique suscitent l'intérêt mais aussi la critique de l'opinion publique. Mais des critiques de fond sur le fonctionnement et la gestion de la justice, sont proférées dans les Etats. Elles émanent des citoyens justiciables, des serviteurs même de la justice et même de la classe politique qui invoque le 'gouvernement des juges' lorsqu'elle est mise en cause.

La justice paraît lourde, dans son organisation et dans sa gestion: parce qu'elle est lente en raison du jeu des délais, parce qu'elle est pesante compte tenu des degrés de juridiction, parce qu'elle est désuète, routinière et qu'elle semble souvent incompréhensible notamment du fait de son vocabulaire et de sa terminologie.

Plus la justice facilite l'accès des citoyens, plus elle s'asphyxie et explose. Le procès civil s'est multiplié partout, il a triplé en France entre 1975 et 1995. Au pénal, des affaires complexes ralentissent l'instruction (terrorisme, délinquance organisée, affaires financières) et produisent un double effet: d'un côté le juge conscient du retentissement de son application du droit sur des centaines de milliers de personnes, comme dans le cas de conventions collectives en droit du travail, évite de se précipiter, d'un autre côté des contre-pouvoirs s'organisent.

Le système judiciaire ne s'est que très partiellement adapté. Les effectifs de magistrats et de fonctionnaires de justice sont insuffisants malgré leur progression. Les tentatives d'assouplir la gestion des effectifs ont été limitées. Les stocks d'affaires gonflent. Pourtant les méthodes de travail se sont améliorées particulièrement grâce à l'informatique. Et, pour améliorer 'le temps magistrat' le recours aux procédures rapides s'accroît. Mais il n'y a plus beaucoup de gain de productivité à attendre des moyens matériels actuels.

Ce scepticisme généralisé, ces retards dans les affaires, cette incapacité de plus en plus patente à bien gérer la justice, conduisent à reconsidérer son fonctionnement.

3 Comment assurer l'efficacité de la justice continentale?

Cette interrogation oblige à répertorier les moyens d'une véritable stratégie de changement, avant de présenter quelques pistes de perspectives pour l'avenir (je ne prétends présenter une étude exhaustive).

3.1 Les moyens internes d'une stratégie de changement:

– A titre préliminaire une remarque s'impose. Dans les Etats européens à tradition continentale la justice est une administration publique particulière; non pas parce qu'elle rentre en relation avec la morale par les normes de comportement qu'elle impose et qu'elle sanctionne; non pas parce qu'elle croise la politique (l'amnistie peut être régulatrice de la vie sociale et politique, la prescription est une forme de sécurité juridique); non pas parce qu'elle interfère avec la psychologie. Mais parce que la justice est un service public, sans aucune vocation entrepreneuriale: elle ne se préoccupe ni de la concurrence, ni du marché. Et, à ma connaissance, dans lesdits Etats européens continentaux, il me semble qu'il n'existe pas de privatisation poussée de la justice.

Ces caractéristiques fortes engendrent d'ailleurs en partie la faiblesse de la gestion de l'administration judiciaire...Les réformes se poursuivent dans tous les Etats européens depuis 20 ans.

Après le rapport de la commission de réflexion sur la justice dite 'commission Truche' du nom du premier président de la Cour de cassation, le premier ministre a ouvert le chantier de la réforme de la justice dès sa déclaration de politique générale en juin 1997. Des textes législatifs et des mesures d'accompagnement échelonnées dans le temps ont été adoptées ou sont en préparation. La priorité est accordée à la justice quotidienne avec la loi relative à l'accès au droit et à la résolution amiable des conflits du 18 décembre 1998 qui distingue l'accès au droit de l'accès à la justice, et avec une nouvelle procédure de compensation judiciaire pour des peines de moins de trois ans. D'autres textes réforment le fonctionnement de l'organisation judiciaire: tel le projet de loi constitutionnelle prévoyant l'avis conforme du Conseil de la magistrature élargi pour nommer les magistrats du parquet, qui va dans le sens d'une plus grande protection de ces magistrats face à l'exécutif, ou bien la loi sur l'efficacité de la procédure pénale du 23 juin 1999.[3]

– Dans une perspective globale, il semble que les missions du juge doivent être recentrées face au nouveau contexte social. Concrètement, ce recentrage suppose notamment:

- d'orienter la justice vers son environnement, notamment la ville pour l'adapter aux impératifs urbains ou pour créer des pôles spécifiques de contrôle et de répression de la délinquance économique et financière (bientôt à Paris, Marseille, Bastia et Lyon);
- de mettre en place des procédures simplifiées pour amoindrir les délais, d'introduire des formes simplifiées de justice en développant la médiation, la conciliation, par exemple avec un médiateur communal sur le modèle norvégien;
- d'insérer dans certains cas le juge dans la société en créant sous l'influence du droit anglo-saxon un juge citoyen partageant son temps entre une activité professionnelle rémunérée et un rôle d'assesseur dans un tribunal. L'atout de ces mesures de rénover progressivement l'institution ne doit pas occulter deux risques possibles. D'une part, l'atomisation de l'institution judiciaire par la justice de proximité. Or il ne faut pas oublier que cette forme de justice plutôt qu'une alternative à la justice traditionnelle est un travail en amont sur la délinquance. D'autre part, l'extension du judiciaire dans la vie sociale 'ou judiciarisation' sur le modèle américain. Cette tendance est déjà largement inscrite dans nos systèmes européens.

3 Cf. Jean-Paul Jean 'Les réformes de la justice, Regards sur l'actualité', La Documentation française, février 1999, pp. 17-36.

– La gestion prévisionnelle des effectifs devrait être adaptée. Cet aspect recouvre en partie le précédent en y adjoignant la formation et le déroulement des carrières, très différents d'un Etat à l'autre. En tous cas, la justice continentale est une justice de carrière. L'élection des juges ne peut que rester marginale. Sans doute conviendrait-il, au moins en France, de multiplier les fonctionnaires de justice en leur confiant une partie substantielle de la gestion de l'administration de la justice. Ces fonctionnaires déchargeraient les juges d'une tâche de gestion qui alourdit leur fonction. Et ils auraient l'avantage d'être parfaitement adaptés à la gestion ce qui permettrait, peu-être, de la rationaliser et de la moderniser.

3.2 La prospective européenne à intégrer:

Dans l'espace européen commun, l'ignorance entre eux des systèmes judiciaires engendre des blocages très importants. Une coopération ou entraide judiciaire organisée amoindrirait les inerties nationales. Il est clair que la justice, plus que la monnaie ou la politique étrangère, est au cœur de la souveraineté des Etats nations, comme le rappelle la ministre Elisabeth Guigou - Cahiers du radicalisme, juin 1999 p. 83 –. Il ne s'agit pas de retirer aux Etats ce qui dans la justice émane de leur culture et de leur tradition, (la famille, la filiation ou le divorce, ou même certaines procédures). Mais chaque administration nationale y gagnerai si la coopération s'opérait à partit de délimitations claires. Délimitations des modes opératoires de coordination, par exemple pour donner compétence à un seul tribunal pour citer des jugements contradictoires... ce qui serait un bienfait dans le cas des contentieux franco-allemands relatifs à la garde d'enfants des couples bi-nationaux. Délimitation des secteurs d'harmonisation aux domaines que chaque organisation nationale seule à des difficultés à maîtriser, tels que la criminalité, la corruption ou le blanchiment d'argent.

Cette perspective suppose une nouvelle impulsion, et celle-ci paraît tout à fait possible depuis l'entrée en vigueur du traité d'Amsterdam qui renforce la coopération judiciaire prévue par le traité sur l'Union européenne.

Part II

Policy Development in the Justice Systems

Modernising Civil Justice in Engeland and Wales

Charles Blake[1]

1 The beginning of reform

The process of change to the structure and management of civil litigation began before the election of a Labour Government in May 1999 but developed apace after that date. The initial reason for change was the interim report by Lord Woolf published in 1995[2] and the final version published in 1996.[3] Lord Woolf was asked by the previous Conservative Government in 1994 to review the process of the civil courts in England and Wales with a view to:

- improving access to justice
- reducing the complexity of the procedural rules and modernising terminology
- removing unnecessary distinctions of practice and procedure.

The first of these admirable aims was essentially a political question. It required consideration of the funding of civil litigation which would involve an inquiry into the operation of legal aid, the possibility of introducing contingency fees, the remaining restrictive practices within the professions of barrister and solicitor and fees charged to litigants for the issue of proceedings. In fact Lord Woolf was neither asked to, nor did he intend, to go very far down the road of considering how far the state should be willing to subsidise litigation and for whom. That was not the subject of a review until Labour came to power in 1997 and decided to carry out a comprehensive review of the system of legal aid. That is not further considered in this chapter. The author has examined the outcomes of that review from the perspective of social policy in a forthcoming article.[4] Other questions were more important to Lord Woolf. These might include the detailed rules of procedure (the High and County Courts had different procedural rules), the distinction between the hierarchy of courts having civil jurisdiction (essentially a question of whether there was any need to preserve the separate High and County Courts with their different levels of Judge with different rates of pay), whether a more active form of case management should be introduced

---

1 Charles Blake is a sollicitor.
2 Interim report by Lord Woolf to the Lord Chancellor on the Civil Justice System, HMSO, London, June 1995 (hereafter 'Interim Report').
3 Final report by Lord Woolf to the Lord Chancellor on the Civil Justice System, HMSO, London, July 1996 (hereafter 'Final Report').
4 Forthcoming in *Social Policy Review*, summer 2000.

and what part might be played by alternative dispute resolution such as mediation, conciliation or arbitration.

Lord Woolf was astute enough to realise and to spell out that a truly radical reform package might indeed have to merge the County and High Courts. Part of the initial steps necessary for this change had been put in place before his inquiry began. Most financial limitations on the jurisdiction of the County Court had been removed. So why did he not first recommend the abolition of the distinction and the complete merger of both types of court? The further changes to the system of litigation in terms of common procedural rules would then be simpler to implement. To discover the answer to this often asked question it is necessary to read between the lines of his interim report. He says, very firmly that: 'High Court Judges, and only High Court Judges, should deal with the most demanding cases in the system'.[5] But he gives no reasons. Moreover, he fails to notice that many of the cases dealt with by High Court judges turn solely on questions of fact. This is true whether the judge is presiding over a jury trial for an indictable offence or a High Court trial for, say, negligence by a professional person. The amount of money and, therefore, compensation, involved in the civil cases may well be substantial but there is no magic in figures or numbers.

Lord Woolf goes on to say that 'for constitutional reasons it is essential that the separate status of the High Court Judge is maintained and not undermined in any way.'[6] This too is an assertion. He may have meant that the public law jurisdiction to review administrative acts was reserved the High Court. But even this is an exaggeration. A public law point can always be raised in defence to, for example, a claim by a public body brought to recover money in the lower courts.

At the time when he wrote there were difficulties about rights of audience. Barristers automatically obtained rights of audience in all courts immediately on being called to the Bar. By contrast, solicitors only obtained such rights in the County and Magistrates courts, that is, the lower civil and criminal courts. To obtain such rights in the higher courts in 1996 it was generally necessary for a solicitor to pass an elaborate series of tests and courses.[7] Not surprisingly, not many bothered. Most solicitor higher court advocates were former barristers who had transferred from one profession to the other and brought their qualification with them.

The uncomfortable truth about merger of the County and higher courts was that the High Court judges would, almost unanimously, have opposed the proposal. On that basis the remainder of any reforms suggested by Lord Woolf might have fallen and that was a risk he was not prepared to take. The opposition from High Court judges would have been based on nothing more than self-importance. High Court judges receive knighthoods and a higher salary than their County Court colleagues. It was and remains possible to be promoted from the County to the High Court but it is

5 Page 74, Interim Report.

6 Page 74, Interim Report.

7 The system has since been considerably relaxed as a result of the passage of the Access to Justice Act 1999. It is now easier for solicitors to become qualified as High Court advocates.

uncommon. If a chief officer of police has to start a career as a constable it is hard to see why some judges are drawn almost exclusively from the Bar, and why all judges do not have to begin their judicial careers in the lower courts and compete on merit for promotion. But such is not the English way of ordering the judiciary. Understandably, Lord Woolf did not want to jeopardise his entire venture by recommending changes that had no prospect of being accepted. He had other plans for the judiciary to which we should now turn.

2 Case management

The interim report of Lord Woolf had this recommendation as its main theme.[8] He said in many places in the report that the adversarial tradition of civil procedure in England and Wales had to be substantially modified so as to remedy its defects. These were said to be excessive cost, excessive delay, inadequate information provided by each party about the case, improper usage of the limited resources of the judiciary and the court system and inappropriate use of expert evidence. The principal solution to all of these problems was to give the courts the power, indeed the duty, to control the progress of each case. This was designed to encourage settlements, or, where a case could not be settled, that it came for hearing within a reasonable time. The length of the hearing should itself be limited to what was necessary to establish the essential issues between the parties. To succeed, case management would have to achieve two main aims. First, a strict timetable for the conduct of the case must be set. Secondly, the case must be supervised as it proceeds in accordance with the timetable, indeed in order to ensure that it does so.

To a large extent this is the system that has been introduced.[9] The courts are now responsible for the conduct of, and progress in, all cases except those that lead to default judgments because the defendant does not respond to the proceedings or those where the claimant obtains an early summary judgment. This change was not without its critics. The Bar and the leaders of the solicitors' profession were sceptical about the effectiveness and alleged reductions in cost likely to arise from case management. They pointed out that, under the existing system, the great majority of cases were settled between the parties before a hearing so there was no need for special steps to be taken to induce that which happened in any event. This objection of heavy handedness was pressed very hard on Lord Woolf between the publication of his interim and final reports. But it did not succeed. It is too early to assess the merits claimed for the new system against the fears of its detractors because empirical research on the effect of the reforms only began in 1999 and is not yet complete. However, it is worth setting out briefly both the nature of the objections to the Woolf reforms and the response made by Lord Woolf and others to those criticisms. In particular the question

8 See pp. 26–48, Interim Report.

9 The details are very complicated but a brief look at the Civil Procedure Rules, 1999 (HMSO, London) will demonstrate the new powers and duties of the courts in managing cases.

will be discussed whether an efficient case management system requires the active participation of the judges or whether court administrators can be entrusted with much of the work.

3 What may be wrong with case management?[10]

3.1 Funding

The Woolf reforms came about at a time when both major parties in England had decided that high taxation and high spending were policies that lost elections and, therefore, ideological reasons apart, had to be abandoned. More had to be done, by fewer public servants, for less money. The consequences are that it is not clear, even in 2000, whether the resources necessary to implement the reforms will be made available. It is interesting to note that the Court Service (the Government agency responsible for the administration of the civil and criminal court system) has recently discovered that the number of civil cases commenced after the Woolf reforms were implemented in April 1999 has fallen by 23%.[11] The reasons are unclear. It is possible that practitioners are very wary of new procedures and have held back on new cases preferring to reach an out of court settlement or, at least, to postpone the issue of proceedings until the last possible moment taking account of limitation of actions defences. It is also equally likely that the reforms are working too well. One of their important features is that each party must disclose important information held about an incident that may become litigious before an action is begun. This less combative and more cooperative approach required by the reforms may have led to many actions being settled or abandoned before papers are filed in court. Whatever the answer the Court Service, acting on the requirements of the Treasury, has raised its fees to cover the anticipated deficit. There is a fundamental objection to requiring the parties to fund the entire cost of the court system. As a matter of principle this approach ignores the public importance and effect on the development of the law of having disputes dealt with by and before the courts. But, if the mathematics have been done correctly, resources will not be a problem in implementing Woolf.

3.2 Technology and other case management tools

Quite simply, the technology necessary to track cases efficiently was not available in April 1999 and will not be installed in the courts for some time yet, possibly not until 2001. Further, much training of court officials and judges was and remains necessary to make the reforms work according to plan. The professions moved with alacrity to

10 This section draws on the lengthy discussion about case management and the Woolf reforms in Zuckerman and Cranston (eds.), *Reform of Civil Procedure: Essays on 'Access to Justice'*, Clarendon Press, Oxford 1995.

11 Consultation paper on proposed increases to court fees (Court Service, London, January 2000), available on Court Service web site www.courtservice.gov.uk

inform and educate their members about the nature and effect of the changes. But, as with resources, there must always be some concern that the tools needed to do the job will not be accessible when and where they are needed. The lack of current research prevents any judgment being made on this point.

3.3 The Mutuality of reform

Apart from resources and technology the courts must be able to adhere to their part of the bargain. If practitioners are to be disciplined into being more cooperative and less confrontational and more conscious of the need to adhere to timetables laid down by the court, the courts themselves must be able to accommodate hearings on the day fixed. Should this exceptionally not be possible, they must be ready to compensate the parties and their lawyers for wasted time. At first the Court Service resisted the imposition of this obligation. But, after pressure from the professions and consumer groups, and perhaps the fear of adverse findings by the courts themselves on the basis of some kind of express or implied contract to make court time available, this attitude has changed. The Court Service will now offer compensation for wasted hearings where the parties are not themselves at fault. So this problem seems to have been managed out of existence.

3.4 Certainty and local flexibility

One of the features of court administration before Woolf was the existence of numerous local, unauthorised but well understood, administrative practices adapting the strict letter of procedural rules to local circumstances. It may seem strange that such practices can survive in a small, compact and densely populated country. Some practitioners were rather proud of local customs and practices which went contrary to the law. It is not yet clear whether all of these local variations have died out but it seems from some random inquiries made by the author, that they probably have. So the objection based on the need for local flexibility does not seem to have much force today.

3.5 The cost of case management

The immediate effect of the courts having greater powers to direct the course of conduct in cases is that the point at which costs are incurred has shifted back to the beginning of legal actions and even before they are commenced. The shorthand phrase that has come to embody the Woolf reforms is 'front loading'. That is, much of the work has to be done before proceedings are filed in order to comply with the requirements of the rules about the contents of the documents that must be filed and the likely timetable that will be laid down if a case is defended. It is no longer sensible for a lawyer to advise a client who is doubtful about bringing proceedings: 'we can issue proceedings and see what the defendant or the insurers do next'. This is a recipe for disaster as control of the action will pass to the court and the necessary preliminary work to keep up to date with the timetable will not have been done. To some extent this is merely a question of timing. Costs must be incurred earlier in the proceedings than they would have been before the reforms were introduced. But the reforms have not been complete in one respect. Lord Woolf wanted the majority of cases not only to be managed tightly by the courts but also for what he called 'fast track' litigation to be subject to fixed costs payable to the lawyers. Such cases would be those where the amount involved was more than in the 'small claims' track (originally to be £3,000 but now increased to £5,000) where informal procedures are followed. The trial would be limited to one day at the most and if possible to three hours. Fixed costs would have worked in two ways. First, the costs as between lawyer and client would have been limited to fixed sums. Secondly, the rule that the loser must normally pay the winner's costs would not be abrogated. But those costs as between the winning and losing party would also have been fixed. The Government decided not to introduce this regime at the beginning of the reforms as there was some uncertainty about the capacity of lawyers to adjust to these reforms speedily enough. The costs of advocacy for the fast track trial are fixed but the costs of preparation are not. They are assessed either in a summary manner at the trial or later by a more detailed process. So, Woolf would have raised initial expenditure but limited the costs of preparation for the trial. Until fixed costs are introduced in the fast track the true effect of the reforms cannot be measured in financial terms to the parties and their lawyers. The Government shows no sign of wanting to move to fixed costs which is regrettable.

3.6 The process of court management and control

One feature of the reforms was a series of sanctions against parties and their lawyers who were in default of complying with timetables for the conduct of the case. It was not clear how far such a regime would lead to endless pre-trial wrangling about who was in default, why and how and whether sanctions should be imposed or not. The rules contain an overall principle that discretionary decisions have to be taken by the courts so as to further the interests of justice but that expedition in the conduct of cases should also become the norm. As stated above, it is difficult to be certain in the absence of research but Lord Woolf's main purpose here was to change the culture of litigation from aggressive partisanship to a mode of cooperation between the parties and their lawyers and between lawyers and the courts. This seems to have had some effect and there appears to be more respect for court orders and a greater degree of cooperation than one might have expected. Some early decisions of appellate courts concerning the operation of sanctions show that a balance is being struck between the imperative of progress and the need to do justice between the parties when there is a good reason for default in compliance with the timetable. One way of achieving this is to make extensive use of intermediate costs orders. If one party is unable to comply with an order for, say, disclosure of a document by a certain day, then an extension may be granted but at the expense of the defaulter. Such costs will be assessed and made payable immediately rather than, as previously, left until the end of the case when, all too often, they were forgotten in the overall reckoning following a trial or leading to a settlement. So far, this aspect of the reforms seems to be working satisfactorily.

3.7 Judges as managers

Here lies a problem that gores to the heart of the Woolf reforms. Is case management compatible with a judicial function? If the judge becomes involved very closely in a case during its preliminary stages, will that judge get to see too many of the internal papers showing the strength and weakness of the case which, arguably, should be adjudicated upon later on evidence placed before the court at the trial? This assumes that judges should only ever do what they have always done. It is most important that decisions about the conduct of cases should be taken by judges and not merely by court administrators. There is room for the use of administrators in marshalling cases and putting them in a suitable state to be placed before judges. Judges must be wary of making irrevocable decisions even on procedural matters before sufficient information is placed before them. But it is the very experience of the judge as a former practitioner (the absence of a career judiciary in England may have this advantage) that should enable a correct judgment to be made on procedural matters yet one which will not compromise the impartiality of the trial process. Moreover, there is no reason to think that the imperative of avoiding delay and moving cases forward will lead to the judges becoming so concerned with the quantitative elements of their performance indicators that they forget about the quality of decision making. The two can be combined. In areas of administrative decision making in England difficulties have arisen. Agencies lay down requirements for their staff to process so many cases in a certain space of time that the question of whether the decision is correct or not is easily forgotten. This has been observed in social security decision making where administrative tribunals have had to cope with an influx of appeals from decisions that may have been taken too hastily. This must be avoided with reforms of the courts.

A related question is the tension between the administration of the courts within budgets fixed by the Government and the necessary independence of the judiciary to make decisions, including those about procedural matters, that do justice between the parties, even if the resources of the court to deal with cases are limited. This was a difficulty foreseen by Lord Woolf and his solution was twofold. First, a senior appellate judge has been assigned as head of civil justice to supervise the reforms. This is not merely a titular role. The post-holder makes it his business to get around the country and see what is happening locally. Secondly, he is assisted by the creation of a Civil Justice Council with wide representation by consumer interests, lawyers, judges and court administrators. The work of this body is widely publicised on the internet[12] and its reports and recommendations are widely read. As with the reforms themselves time is needed to assess its efficacy but it seems to be well aware of the expectations placed upon it.

12 www.cjq.gov.uk

4 Political aspects of reform

As stated above the Government has not merely moved forward with the Woolf reforms. It passed the Modernisation of Justice Act in 1999 with separate but related aims. First, the structure of legal aid has been reworked so as to remove this form of funding from many civil cases. The cost of legal aid was said to be out of control. A suitable alternative has been found which is a form of contingency fee known as a 'conditional fee'. It is not based on a pure percentage of the money recovered by the winning party which is how contingency fees operate in the United States. Instead, the lawyer is permitted to charge an uplift on what would otherwise be payable by the successful party to the successful lawyer. This uplift becomes recoverable from the losing party. If the claimant loses, no fee is payable at all to that party's lawyer. Legal aid is preserved for family and criminal cases. Its abolition will be noticed initially in routine personal injury cases where it is thought to have outlived its usefulness and to be capable of being replaced by conditional fees. There are special arrangements for insurance policies to be taken out by claimants against the risk of losing (negligible in most personal injury cases) the case and having to pay the defendant's legal costs.

Secondly, the Act will increase the number of solicitors who can carry out advocacy in the higher courts. The existing limitations had become unacceptable. Thirdly, the Act creates a Community Legal Service which will bring law and legal advice closer to people by putting in place arrangements all over the country for contracted suppliers to give legal advice to the population at large. The suppliers of such advice might be voluntary sector advice agencies as well as lawyers. The exact workings of the scheme remain somewhat mysterious in the spring of 2000 when it is supposed to begin its work.

5 Administrative tribunals

The Woolf reforms have not touched the work of these bodies which continues to be supervised by the Council on Tribunals. The need for a comprehensive review is urgent. Each tribunal follows its own procedure, sometimes with Woolf – like elements of control by the tribunal and sometimes not. There is a bewildering system of appeals usually to second tier bodies, interrelated to internal reviews and supervision by the courts by way of judicial review. Unfortunately, there is little sign that the Government sees this as a priority. Far more people have dealings with tribunals than with the courts and this is likely to continue.

6 Conclusion

Lying behind the reforms is a political question about the nature of law and dispute resolution in England and Wales. Is it essentially a private matter in which the state creates a framework for the parties to either settle their dispute or battle it out before a judge qualified and authorised to give a binding decision? Or is a dispute between two private people a sign of social breakdown, at least on a small scale, that justifies an active intervention by the state with the possibility of mediation or conciliation also being made available to the parties? There is no one answer to this question depending as it does on the function one attributes to the state, the role played by law in the life of citizens and the system of resolving disputes in place at any one time. The Woolf reforms go some way from the traditional English view that the parties must initially solve their disputes with minimal assistance by the state. An assessment of their success depends on the outcome of pending research.

The Challenge of Change for Judicial Systems
M. Fabri and Ph.M. Langbroek (Eds.)
IOS Press, 2000

Justice. Quels modes d'administration et d'évaluation pour un service public complexe qui doit rendre des décisions en toute indépendance?

Jean-Paul Jean[1]

Culturellement, la justice est une institution très spécifique. Avant de voir comment les principes du management peuvent s'appliquer sur son champ, il faut comprendre les principes essentiels qui guident son action. Cela nécessite une rapide perspective historique (1), une analyse de son mode de fonctionnement (2) et un repérage de tendances lourdes dans lesquelles s'inscrivent ses évolutions actuelles (3).

1 La modernisation de la justice s'inscrit dans une longue histoire

L'organisation de la justice française est profondément marquée par les structures mises en place sous Napoléon, au début du 19ème siècle, après les grands débats de la Révolution. Pendant près de deux siècles, la justice fut soumise tout à la fois à l'emprise des notables locaux et à la puissance de l'Etat. La révision constitutionnelle du Général De Gaulle en 1958 fit entrer la justice dans la sphère de la modernisation de l'Etat par la revalorisation du statut et de la rémunération des juges, par l'amélioration de leur recrutement (création de l'Ecole nationale de la magistrature), par une réforme de l'organisation judiciaire supprimant de multiples micro-juridictions pour établir le tribunal de grande instance comme juridiction de droit commun, ainsi que par la fonctionnarisation des greffes.

Cette rationalisation marquait aussi une reprise en main du pouvoir central sur la magistrature. '*Dans ce nouvel édifice républicain, la justice change simplement de maître*',[2] l'élément le plus significatif étant de faire passer le Conseil supérieur de la magistrature (CSM) de l'emprise des parlementaires à la tutelle du président de la République. Le chef de l'Etat, '*garant de l'indépendance de l'autorité judiciaire*', selon l'article 64 de la nouvelle constitution, '*est assisté par le Conseil supérieur de la magistrature*' dont il nomme les membres, et a la mainmise sur toute la magistrature.

---

1 Substitut général près la cour d'appel de Paris, Directeur de la Mission de recherche droit et justice.
2 L'expression est de Denis Salas, (Salas 1998).

La nécessaire modernisation de l'institution avait pour corollaire l'intégration de la justice dans l'Etat central, en même temps que l'exécutif montait en puissance face au Parlement et aux notables locaux. Mais ce besoin d'administration de la justice sur le mode d'un service public devait se greffer sur une institution archaïque et culturellement très spécifique.

1.1 L'administration de la justice s'est construite lentement

En 1959, c'est par une expression restée dans les mémoires, *'sortir du néolithique'* que le premier président de la Cour d'appel de Paris Maurice Aydalot, lors d'une rentrée solennelle, incitait ses collègues à changer leurs méthodes de travail. En 1968, la création du très actif Syndicat de la magistrature (SM) fût perçue par nombre de juges comme un instrument de modernisation de l'institution judiciaire, par-delà la seule vision corporatiste défendue jusque-là. Les débats publics sur la justice que porta le SM s'amplifièrent par les exigences nouvelles portées par les promotions successives de l'Ecole nationale de la magistrature.

Jeunesse, désacralisation, débat public sur les grandes questions de société des années soixante-dix, soutien des intellectuels, tout se conjugua pour que la scène judiciaire devienne un véritable enjeu. La dénonciation publique de la misère des tribunaux, la revendication sur les moyens de la justice et le statut des magistrats, la négociation avec le politique venaient se combiner avec l'ouverture de l'institution sur la société.

1.2 Comprendre les phénomènes générationnels pour comprendre la modernisation de l'institution

C'est ainsi que les demandes de réforme et de modernisation, sont pour beaucoup nées de l'intérieur même de l'institution. En quelques années, tous phénomènes conjugués, l'institution judiciaire a formé une génération de nouveaux juges dans un débat permanent. Ce sont ces générations, formées dans les années soixante-dix, qui, du simple fait démographique, ont occupé progressivement la plupart des postes de la hiérarchie, en particulier la direction des tribunaux et les postes stratégiques de l'administration centrale.[3]

Ce phénomène générationnel, commun à tous les pays qui recrutent par le biais d'une école d'application, est essentiel pour qui veut comprendre l'évolution des mentalités et des systèmes de valeur dans l'institution judiciaire et expliquer les facteurs de changement. Ainsi, au 1er février 1998, 43% des magistrats[4] avaient entre

---

3 Le ministère français de la justice a la particularité d'avoir pour cadres, principalement, non des administrateurs, mais des magistrats temporairement détachés dans des fonctions d'administration, ce qui contribue à une culture professionnelle très spécifique.

4 Le terme 'magistrat' concerne en France les membres du parquet et les juges, puisque le statut de la magistrature fait de ces deux métiers un corps unique, où l'on peut passer d'une fonction à l'autre, contrairement à la culture anglo-saxonne, voire à d'autres pays latins (Espagne, Portugal) où ces fonctions sont totalement dissociées.

45 et 55 ans, 4.416 magistrats sur 6.496 soit 68%, avaient été recrutés depuis 1981 dont 3.410 par l'ENM (77 %) et 1.006 par une autre voie (concours exceptionnels ou intégration directe, concernant des personnes bénéficiant déjà d'une expérience professionnelle). Les femmes, qui n'ont pu accéder à la magistrature qu'à partir de 1946, représentent aujourd'hui la moitié des magistrats.

2 Une organisation administrative et budgétaire de construction récente

L'ouverture de la justice au débat public et ce renouvellement générationnel ont beaucoup contribué à la discrète modernisation d'un service de la justice géré pendant de très longues années de façon totalement archaïque. La création d'une direction d'administration générale ayant en charge pour l'ensemble du ministère de la Justice les questions de budget et d'équipement ne date que de 1964. Il a fallu attendre 1967 pour que la fonctionnarisation des greffes soit mise progressivement en œuvre, et les années soixante-dix pour prendre en compte les évolutions démographiques dans l'implantation des tribunaux. Furent ainsi crées en région parisienne les tribunaux de grande instance de Créteil, Nanterre et Bobigny et une cour d'appel à Versailles. Après l'augmentation des recrutements des juges et des greffiers, les années 1974-1984 correspondirent au développement des équipements judiciaires.

Mais les tribunaux étaient gérés à l'économie par les collectivités locales et le transfert des charges budgétaires des juridictions à l'Etat ne fût effectif qu'en 1987. La gestion des juridictions à partir de son administration centrale est donc récente. La mise en place de services administratifs déconcentrés dans les cours d'appel, dotés des moyens de la délégation budgétaire, de suivi et d'évaluation de l'activité des juridictions, est seulement maintenant en train d'aboutir, appuyée par une très forte implantation d'informatique et d'outils de gestion.

2.1 Une administration qui concerne les juridictions, mais aussi les questions pénitentiaires et la prise en charge des mineurs

La justice française a aussi la particularité d'intégrer dans son champ de compétence et son budget, non seulement les juridictions, mais aussi l'administration pénitentiaire et les services de la protection judiciaire de la jeunesse (qui prennent en charge les mineurs protégés et les mineurs délinquants), alors que n'existe pas un niveau de gestion déconcentrée commun.

Le budget de la justice, s'il représente environ 27 milliards de francs, intègre ces trois composantes. Or, chaque secteur (prisons, mineurs, juridictions) a été à son tour une priorité budgétaire, avec quelques dominantes: les années 1960-1970 furent celles du programme des structures d'accueil des mineurs, les années 1986-1989 ont été consacrées à la réalisation du programme de 13.000 nouvelles places de prison et à la rénovation des équipements pénitentiaires.

C'est depuis le début des années quatre-vingt-dix qu'a succédé un effort significatif sur la construction et la rénovation et l'équipement, en particulier informatique, des juridictions, et sur la revalorisation salariale des magistrats. Cet effort, accompagné d'un discours sur la modernisation et la gestion, a progressivement transformé l'institution. Parler de 'productivité judiciaire' n'est plus un tabou aujourd'hui pour une institution qui a absorbé une très forte augmentation de son contentieux civil et nombre de réformes législatives, montrant par là même de réelles ressources d'adaptation.

2.2 La place de la justice dans la société s'est profondément modifiée

Par la masse des affaires qu'elle traite, la justice a aussi pris une place réelle dans la vie des Français. Le contentieux des affaires civiles qui lui sont soumises a triplé en vingt ans. La justice hérite de toutes les questions que la famille, l'école, le quartier, les institutions ne savent plus traiter. La prison accueille une population marquée de plus en plus par les ruptures familiales, l'illettrisme, la pauvreté, la toxicomanie, les troubles psychiatriques. La pénalisation de la vie sociale,[5] amplifiée par la médiatisation des affaires et la pression des victimes, la mettent en permanence sous les feux de l'actualité. La 'judiciarisation' des débats publics signifie que le juge doit trancher de tout au nom du droit.[6] Cette demande sociale de justice, cette exigence de contre-pouvoir indépendant, ne sont que des transferts de la légitimité accordée précédemment à l'Etat et aux dirigeants. Le couple justice–média légitimé par l'opinion publique est en train de construire un '*tiers-pouvoir*' selon l'expression de Denis Salas.[7]

Et pourtant, paradoxalement, alors qu'ils la saisissent de plus en plus, les Français doutent de leur justice. Toutes les enquêtes d'opinion convergent. Plus de deux-tiers ne lui font pas confiance et ont une mauvaise image d'elle. Plus de 75% lui reprochent de mal fonctionner et d'abord d'être lente et coûteuse. Plus de 80 % la jugent 'vieillote' et 'soumise au pouvoir politique'.[8] Leur première demande concerne l'accès à la justice pour les moins riches et l'accélération des délais de traitement des affaires.

2.3 D'importantes réformes en cours nécessitent une stratégie d'évaluation

Depuis trois ans, s'est mis en place un important programme de réformes législatives, touchant au statut des magistrats, à la procédure pénale et à la procédure civile, accompagné à fois d'une forte augmentation des moyens, mais aussi d'une exigence plus grande vis-à-vis des résultats d'activité des juridictions.

On peut relever quelques tendances lourdes de ces changements.[9] Les réformes visent à accélérer et diversifier les réponses de la justice et à poser les jalons d'une 'économie de la justice' pour favoriser la justice négociée. La justice pénale, en recourant à des personnes extérieures et des associations, doit répondre 'en temps réel' et se fonder, pour la petite délinquance, plus sur des modes de réparation que

---

5 Garapon et Salas (1996).

6 Jean (octobre 1997).

7 Salas (1998).

8 Guigou (février 1998). Cf. aussi l'enquête effectuée en 1997 à la demande de la Mission de recherche droit et justice, disponible sur son site web http://www.msh-paris.fr/gipjustice

9 Pour une analyse complète cf. Jean (février 1999).

des modes de sanction. Mais, dans le cadre judiciaire, les droits de la défense doivent être renforcés, la détention provisoire, limitée, et la situation des prisons, améliorée. La justice civile doit permettre le recours plus facile au conseil, à la transaction, plutôt qu'au mode contentieux, et doit améliorer ses délais de réponse.

Pour ce faire, la justice a été dotée d'importants moyens supplémentaires (en augmentation de 14% ces trois dernières années en tant que priorité gouvernementale) et a été le premier poste de l'Etat bénéficiaire de créations d'emplois (par exemple 422 créations de postes de magistrats sur la même période, ou encore 1000 éducateurs pour mineurs, pour un effectif actuel de 3000). En matière immobilière, la justice devient le premier investisseur de l'Etat (1,5 milliard d'autorisation de programme pour l'année 2000) et la construction d'un nouveau palais de justice à Paris constitue un des principaux 'grands travaux' des prochaines années.

Malgré l'augmentation significative de ces moyens budgétaires, la pression sur la justice demeure très forte et l'administration centrale développe ses moyens d'analyse et d'évaluation des résultats pour justifier de la bonne utilisation de l'argent public. En effet, par exemple, alors que le contentieux civil d'affaires nouvelles diminue depuis deux ans, les délais de jugement ont tendance à repartir à la hausse. L'élaboration d'indicateurs de résultats devient un enjeu essentiel pour les décideurs, et s'effectue en associant au maximum des responsables des juridictions. Il convient en effet d'éviter une vision purement quantitative qui ne permettrait pas d'expliquer des phénomènes complexes intégrant par exemple les stratégies des professions juridiques et judiciaires pour lesquelles la justice représente aussi un marché, en particulier les avocats et les compagnies d'assurance.

3 Les évolutions de la justice française s'inscrivent dans des tendances lourdes

Ces réformes s'intègrent dans des tendances lourdes de la justice française et conduisent à aborder quelques débats de fond qui conditionnent les évolutions futures.
Si l'on considère comme évidente la question du poids grandissant des normes européennes et de la montée de la coopération judiciaire dans l'espace de l'Union Européenne, quelques débats peuvent être mis en évidence, concernant le métier même de magistrat (1), la part grandissante des politiques publiques dans les stratégies judiciaires (2), la question de la territorialisation de l'intervention judiciaire (3), la distinction qui ne peut être que grandissante des fonctions de magistrat du parquet et de celles de magistrat du siège (4), et enfin, la professionnalisation de l'administration des juridictions et le développement de la culture de l'évaluation (5).

3.1 Le magistrat généraliste ou spécialiste?

L'évolution des méthodes de travail conduit à mieux distinguer la fonction généraliste pour laquelle le magistrat est formé, de la nécessaire spécialisation dans certains contentieux.

Ainsi, dans le domaine de la lutte contre la grande délinquance financière et la criminalité organisée, la complexité des affaires et l'internationalisation des échanges ont à la fois nécessité et permis l'amélioration de la coopération judiciaire européenne et la mise en place de magistrats de liaison auprès de pays étrangers. Viennent d'être créés des 'pôles financiers' à Paris, Bastia, Lyon et Aix, permettant aux procureurs et aux juges d'instruction de se voir adjoindre des collaborateurs venant du ministère des Finances dans le cadre d'un travail en équipe.[10] Ces sites spécialisés, qui devraient concerner à terme de six à huit juridictions, disposent aussi d'un 'plateau technique' informatique (logiciels de gestion de dossiers complexes, scannerisation...) et préfigurent ce que devront devenir certains services de la justice pour sortir d'une gestion artisanale et se hisser au niveau de spécialisation nécessité par l'enjeu.

Dans toutes les grandes juridictions, cette distinction entre différentes 'spécialités' (délinquance financière, mineurs, délinquance de rue, exécutions des peines, questions commerciales....) existe pour les parquets. Pour les magistrats du siège, les fonctions de juge spécialisés sont institutionnelles (juge des enfants, juge de l'application des peines, juge d'instance), ou purement fonctionnelles (juge de la famille). Dans les petites juridictions, la fonction généraliste constitue par contre le modèle référent. On s'aperçoit à travers la question de la mobilité et de l'avancement des magistrats, qu'il existe une forte dichotomie entre les juges anciens, très motivés par ces fonctions spécialisées ou généralistes, et ceux qui les occupent d'abord pour des raisons de rapprochement géographique ou d'avancement. Or, il n'existe pas de gestion prévisionnelle des carrières des magistrats et la structure du corps fait que toute une génération est bloquée dans son avancement par la précédente qui a bénéficié d'une conjoncture démographique exceptionnelle, ce qui engendre frustrations et immobilisme. Il manque en conséquence une réflexion sur le métier de juge, distinguant la carrière professionnelle du contenu même de la profession, dissociant le grade et l'emploi.

3.2 La participation des juridictions aux politiques publiques

L'institution judiciaire doit faire face, en matière civile comme en matière pénale, à ce que l'on dénomme des 'contentieux de masse'. Derrière les représentations de la justice que s'en fait le grand public, se vit une réalité toute autre, avec des milliers de professionnels d'une institution confrontée souvent aux contentieux répétitifs (pension alimentaire ou loyer impayé, conduite en état d'ivresse, vol....) mais qui concernent à chaque fois une situation personnelle, un individu à juger. C'est ainsi que sont rendues chaque année plus de dix millions de décisions pénales et plus de deux millions de

10 Sur la conception de cette action européenne, cf. Jean (mai 1997).

décisions civiles que toute une armée d'intervenants doit préparer et mettre en œuvre: greffiers, avocats, huissiers, éducateurs, policiers, surveillants de prison, agents du trésor public, associations....

3.2.1 Une forte pression sur le champ pénal

Si l'on ne s'en tient qu'aux affaires pénales excluant les contraventions en matière de circulation routière, les parquets reçoivent chaque année près de cinq millions de procès-verbaux, dont deux tiers concernent des affaires non élucidées.[11] Pour les affaires traitées selon un mode non administrativé, les parquets ont été contraints de diversifier leurs modes d'intervention, pour éviter le renvoi devant la juridiction, en développant la médiation, la réparation, avec l'appui des professionnels ou d'associations. Une attention toute particulière a été portée à la prise en compte et la reconnaissance des victimes, là encore avec un fort relais associatif.

Ces évolutions de modes de réponse se sont effectués en relation privilégiée avec les élus locaux qui, se faisant le relais de leurs administrés, interpellent très souvent la justice, en particulier les parquets, pour que soient assurées des réponses efficaces à la délinquance quotidienne, pour que soit maintenu l'équilibre des quartiers menacés par des bandes, organisées ou non, se livrant aux trafics et à la violence. Pour institutionnaliser ces rapports entre les parquets et les municipalités, sont signés des 'contrats locaux de sécurité' à l'initiative des préfets. Des 'maisons de la justice et du droit' sont créées dans une soixantaine de ville, en partenariat entre la justice et les municipalités. Dans ces lieux, situés, dans les quartiers 'difficiles', sont mises en œuvre les actions de médiation, de réparation, l'accompagnement des associations. Toutes ces actions s'inscrivent dans le cadre conceptuel de la 'politique de la ville', politique publique interministérielle destinée en particulier pour la justice et la police à mieux prévenir et répondre à la délinquance urbaine.

Toujours sur le plan pénal, l'orientation politique majeure de ces dernière années a été le 'traitement en temps réel', mode de comparution rapide et simplifié devant les juridictions de l'auteur d'une infraction. Ce mode massif de traitement des affaires de délinquance quotidienne, qui correspond à une forte demande sociale, exerce une forte pression sur les juridictions, mais est de plus en plus critiqué par les juges qui y voient une sous-justice 'à la chaîne'.

Ce qui est certain, c'est que ces nouveaux modes de réponse à la délinquance font subir une pression forte sur la justice et nécessitent une organisation et des négociations qui modifient profondément le fonctionnement autrefois 'distancié' de l'institution.

3.2.2 Une redéfinition de la place du juge

Plus généralement, la **place du juge**, et le périmètre du champ judiciaire sont en constant mouvement. Les citoyens souhaitent un accès plus facile au juge et le législa-

---

11 On estime par exemple que l'auteur d'un cambriolage est identifié une fois sur dix.

teur multiplie les textes,[12] tout en dénonçant l'encombrement de l'institution qu'ils contribuent à noyer sous le flot continu des contentieux. Est-ce le juge qui doit être au plus près de la vie quotidienne, ou sont-ce plutôt les garanties du droit (accès au dossier, débat, aide juridique qualifiée, voie de recours) qui doivent se développer dans la vie sociale?

La loi sur l'accès au droit et les modes alternatifs de règlement des conflits du 18 décembre 1998 ouvre une piste essentielle en matière civile. Ce n'est pas de plus de juge, mais plus d'une justice garante, d'une justice recours dont nos concitoyens doivent bénéficier. Ainsi, par exemple, des dizaines de milliers de saisines pour la modification du montant d'une pension alimentaire, de plus en plus fréquentes du fait de la précarité des situations matérielles des individus, pourraient être évitées grâce à l'élaboration puis la diffusion de barèmes indicatifs. Dans nombre de contentieux dits 'de masse', les procédures de médiation, de conciliation, de tentative de transaction pourraient même devenir obligatoires, une éventuelle saisine du juge en cas d'échec restant toujours possible. Cette évolution est conditionnée par l'évolution du métier d'avocat et sa réorientation sur la fonction de conseil plutôt que sur l'action contentieuse, en particulier quand le justiciable bénéficie de l'aide judiciaire.[13]

3.3 Une politique judiciaire qui s'inscrit sur un territoire

Une meilleure adaptation des réponses de la justice aux populations concernées pose la question de la bonne répartition des ses moyens sur tout le territoire. Une mission de **réforme de la carte judiciaire** a été créée fin 1997 par Madame Guigou, ministre de la justice, pour revoir l'implantation des lieux de justice face aux évolutions économiques et démographiques. La méthode retenue rompt avec les tentatives précédentes par la mise en place d'une approche essentiellement fondée sur une analyse des besoins et de la situation locale de chacune des 1158 juridictions de métropole. Son expérimentation a commencé en 1999 sur les 227 tribunaux de commerce, en particulier sur le ressort des cinq cours d'appels qui, du fait de l'héritage historique, comptent à elles seules la moitié des juridictions à niveau très faible d'activité. Cette première démarche a aboutir à une première suppression de 36 petits tribunaux de commerce.

Cette approche nécessite une nouvelle culture, plus proche de celle de la Délégation à l'aménagement du territoire (DATAR), du concept d'unité historique et socio-économique de 'pays', de la prise en compte de la notion 'd'agglomération' (plusieurs communes voisines), la réflexion sur les 'villes nouvelles' (grands ensembles urbains construits depuis les années soixante). La vision et le fonctionnement administratif classique autour de la structure administrative du département, créée par la révolution,

---

12 Par exemple, plus de 13.000 textes comportent des dispositons pénales.

13 Pour une vision européenne de ces questions cf. 'Pour une nouvelle justice civile. La crise d'efficacité de la justice civile en Europe', Actes du colloque de Paris 1999 de l'association MEDEL (magistrats européen pour la démocratie et les libertés) éd. Annonces de la Seine. Synthèse disponible sur le site de MEDEL http://www.cidadevirtual.pt/asjp/medel.html

sont dépassés. Mais cette nouvelle approche se heurte à la rigidité des règles de procédures et compétences territoriales, au civil comme au pénal.

Les nouvelles formes de communication, en particulier Internet, modifient aussi totalement la donne. La notion de justice de proximité a totalement évolué. Elle ne peut plus s'évaluer en termes seulement géographique. Il faut distinguer, comme en matière de santé, quel est pour le citoyen le premier niveau d'information pertinent, puis quels sont les services plus spécialisés auxquels il peut accéder. Est ainsi nécessaire un premier niveau généraliste (impayés, contentieux locatifs, questions familiales, petite délinquance par exemple) avec des juges polyvalents, et un niveau plus spécialisé (contrats, droit international, délinquance financière....) avec des juges rompus à ces contentieux.

3.4 La distinction renforcée entre parquet et juridictions, entre procureurs et juges: les deux magistratures

L'évolution des rapports entre, d'une part, les magistrats du siège (qui composent la juridiction) et, d'autre part, les magistrats du parquet, est patente et nécessaire. L'effet conjugué du rapprochement des garanties statutaires des magistrats du parquet de ceux du siège et de l'extension du champ des prérogatives du parquet au détriment du siège dans le domaine pénal, ainsi que les pesanteurs de la dyarchie[14] dans la gestion des cours d'appel et des tribunaux, ont provoqué des prises de position radicales des premiers présidents. Ces derniers ont pris en 1998, au sein de leur conférence générale, une délibération unanime pour demander une séparation plus nette des deux fonctions, au moment même où le Parlement allait délibérer sur la réforme du Conseil supérieur de la magistrature (CSM) qui confirmait au contraire l'unité du corps des magistrats.

Face à cette montée en puissance du parquet qui anime des politiques publiques et est l'interlocuteur judiciaire des partenaires extérieurs, les premiers présidents ont choisi la voie d'une 'distinction' plus marquée dans les fonctions judiciaires qui irait jusqu'à affirmer, comme dans la plupart des autres pays européens, que seuls les juges du siège composent la juridiction, le parquet n'étant qu'une partie au procès. Cette évolution, qui n'est pas dans la tradition juridique française, s'inscrit parfaitement dans une conception d'extériorité de la justice par rapport à l'Etat qui sera un des débats essentiels de ces prochaines années. Elle est aussi en rupture avec les pratiques réelles et la volonté des juges des enfants, des juges d'instance et des juges de l'application des peines qui jouent un rôle essentiel par exemple dans la négociation avec les partenaires extérieurs comme les conseils généraux pour disposer de structures adaptées pour les mineurs placés, avec les sociétés d'HLM[15] pour limiter les expulsions ou encore avec les services sociaux pour trouver des solutions d'hébergement aux sortants de prison.

14 Le premier président et le procureur général gèrent conjointement chacune des 33 cours d'appel, le président et le procureur chacun des 181 tribunaux de grande instance.

15 Habitation à loyer modéré, responsables du logement social.

3.5 La professionnalisation et la déconcentration de la gestion des juridictions

3.5.1 La notion de service public de la justice

Trop longtemps, la justice s'est considérée comme une institution à part. Si le débat a évolué rapidement ces dernières années, les termes doivent en être précisés, car il serait dangereux de ne considérer la justice que comme une administration ordinaire.

L'administration de la justice est un service public qui doit être soucieux de la qualité de ses prestations.[16] L'application du concept de service public à l'institution judiciaire, qui n'est pas une administration comme les autres, est aujourd'hui un fait acquis. Si elle est en train de devenir une vraie administration moderne, il lui manque une culture de la gestion des ressources humaines, pour ses 62.000 fonctionnaires et 6.500 magistrats de l'ordre judiciaire. L'enjeu est aussi de développer une **démarche qualité**, centrée en particulier sur l'accueil des publics exclus qui composent l'essentiel des justiciables. L'expérimentation en cours de 'guichets unique de greffe',[17] la mise en place de services d'accueil et d'orientation, le développement de la place des associations travaillant avec la justice vont en ce sens. Le respect de délais raisonnables de jugement, de réponse effective à chaque justiciable, de compréhension et d'effectivité des décisions doivent être des soucis constants.

3.5.2 La nécessité de développer l'évaluation

Mais, par delà de réels effort de mise en œuvre d'outils statistiques performants liés à l'informatique de gestion, il manque encore dans la justice française une vraie **culture de l'évaluation**. Par exemple, dans le domaine pénal, très peu d'études mesurent l'impact réel du traitement en temps réel (TTR) qui accélère les comparutions des auteurs de délinquance de voie publique. Que produit ce dispositif en termes de résultats: assiste-t-on à une dégradation de la qualité des procédures liée, d'une part, à ce mode d'organisation et, d'autre part, à la déqualification et au moindre contrôle des agents et officiers de police judiciaire, les victimes ont-elles une meilleure réponse, les auteurs récidivent-ils moins...?

Sont actuellement élaborés des indicateurs de résultat par juridiction, intégrant des ratios entre le nombre d'affaires jugées, par contentieux, et le nombre de postes de magistrats, par exemple, les chiffres de population.... Ces indicateurs de 'productivité' ont été diffusés à toutes les juridictions pour la première fois lorsqu'ils ont servi de base en 1998 à la localisation des créations de postes de magistrats du siège et du parquet. Ces indices ont été pondérés pour prendre en compte certains éléments spécifiques (nombre de mineurs pour les postes de juges des enfants, types d'établissements pénitentiaires pour les postes de juge de l'application des peines....). Les réactions ont été fort nombreuses, car les écarts entre juridictions, par exemple au niveau du nombre de jugements civils rendus par magistrat, pouvaient être très importants.

---

16 Cf. Guigo (1998).

17 Regroupement de tous les services de premier niveau à l'entrée d'un même site judiciaire.

Mais, globalement, une fois le premier choc passé, les juridictions ont accepté un système plus objectivé que par le passé, en faisant valoir leurs spécificités propres. A partir d'une démarche quantitative, peut donc s'engager un débat plus qualitatif sur l'affectation des moyens dans les juridictions.

Ces exigences d'analyse de performance des juridictions deviennent de plus en plus importantes avec le renforcement des moyens budgétaires et les créations de postes dans la justice. Les parlementaires s'étonnent en effet à juste titre de ce que, malgré des augmentations significatives d'effectifs, et une diminution des affaires civiles depuis trois ans, les délais moyens de jugement et les stocks continuent d'augmenter dans la plupart des juridictions.

Les magistrats s'intègrent progressivement dans cette culture de l'évaluation, mais demandent légitimement à être associés à son élaboration et à sa mise en œuvre. Ils craignent aussi que la pression permanente de la productivité soit incompatible avec la fonction même de juger une affaire individuelle qui peut demander beaucoup de recherches et de débats. Le renforcement des garanties du procès équitable en application de la convention européenne des droits de l'homme conduit aussi à un alourdissement et donc à un allongement des délais de procédure. Le productivisme de ces dernières années n'a aussi été permis que par l'instauration quasi généralisée du juge unique en première instance, et par le recours à l'informatisation et aux procédures simplifiées. Or, les gains de productivité dûs à ces deux derniers éléments ont sans doute aujourd'hui atteint leur limite et la revendication du retour à la délibération collégiale est d'autant plus légitime qu'elle émane de jeunes collègues qui doivent se former au contact des plus anciens.

4 Conclusion. Justice, une exigence renouvelée

4.1 Parquet et politique de l'Etat

Le rapport entre le pouvoir exécutif et le parquet est en France un débat très politique, compte tenu de la tradition forte des prérogatives de l'Etat face à l'exigence incontestée d'une justice indépendante. Par delà toutes les différentes réformes, l'engagement (respecté) du garde des sceaux de ne plus intervenir auprès des parquets dans les affaires individuelles marque une rupture significative, en cohérence avec la possibilité de donner des instructions générales définissant une politique publique.

Les projets de réforme (statut de la magistrature et rapports entre le ministère de la justice et les parquets) prévoient une plus grande autonomie pour les procureurs. Paradoxalement, plus le parquet s'autonomise, plus il bénéficie d'un statut protecteur qui le rapproche du juge du siège alors que les statuts de ces deux magistratures devraient se différencier.

Il faut donc bien distinguer, d'une part, l'autonomie des magistrats du parquet dans les décisions individuelles, d'autre part, les directives de politique publique qu'ils doivent mettre en œuvre, car, selon les termes de la Constitution, '*le gouvernement détermine et conduit la politique de la nation*'. En particulier, la politique de sécurité, si elle doit être adaptée au contexte local, ne peut dépendre des seules humeurs ou des opinions d'un procureur, dont la politique pénale doit être en cohérence avec les orientations nationales et faire l'objet d'une évaluation.

4.2 Des magistrats qui vont être de plus en plus exposés

La contrepartie de l'extension des pouvoirs, et donc de la montée en puissance des procureurs, est, vis-à-vis d'eux, l'attente d'une plus grande transparence (on demande désormais au parquet de motiver les classements sans suite, par exemple), et une obligation de rendre compte (à travers des rapports réguliers à la hiérarchie et au ministère, ou encore la justification publique de choix de poursuites).

C'est la même chose pour le juge du siège. Plus son rôle social et politique est important par exemple, les décisions récentes en matière de politiques publiques de santé (sang contaminé, amiante, vaccinations) ou en matière politico-financière, et plus à son tour il est exposé. Une partie de la magistrature, historiquement, se complaisait parfaitement dans la tranquillité de l'anonymat et le confort de l'impuissance.

En conséquence, le **niveau d'exigence** vis à vis des magistrats monte légitimement. Le débat est souvent posé sur le terrain de la responsabilité personnelle du magistrat, alors qu'il devrait plus l'être sur celui de l'évaluation et du rendu-compte, selon le concept anglo-saxon d''accountability'.

Ainsi, le débat sur l'insuffisance professionnelle des juges (essentiellement les retards injustifiés) commence légitimement (mais encore de façon embryonnaire) à être traité sur la plan disciplinaire par le Conseil supérieur de la magistrature, en plus des manquements déontologiques. La question de la responsabilité est par contre mal posée dans le débat public, car elle ne doit pas toucher la liberté juridictionnelle qui constitue l'essence même de la fonction et qui ne peut être contestée que par les voies de recours devant une juridiction supérieure.

Le débat est d'autant plus compliqué en France que les chefs de juridictions (conjointement, premier président et procureur général pour les cours d'appel, président et procureur pour les tribunaux de grande instance) sont aussi les responsables de l'administration et de la gestion, dans un cadre hiérarchique. Il existe donc une grande concentration des pouvoirs, voire souvent une confusion entre les pouvoirs juridictionnels et les pouvoirs d'administration, qui doivent entraîner chacun un régime différent de responsabilité.

Il est donc essentiel que les fonctions d'évaluation et de contrôle d'activité distinguent nettement, d'une part, l'administration et le fonctionnement du service public de la justice, à partir de concepts et de méthodes déjà utilisés dans d'autres administrations, d'autre part, de l'activité individuelle du magistrat dans sa fonction juridictionnelle dans laquelle son indépendance ne peut être remise en cause.

La mise en œuvre concomitante de principes gestionnaires et du respect de principes constitutionnels nous invite donc à une subtile alchimie.

Références

Garapon, Antione et Denis Salas, 'La République pénalisée', dans: *Hachett coll. Questions de société*, (1996).
Guigou, Elisabeth, 'Justice, restaurer la confiance', dans: *L'état de l'opinion*, Sofres éd Seuil, (février 1998).
Guigou, Elisabeth, 'La justice au service du citoyen', dans: *Le service public de la justice*, éditions Odil Jacob, (1998).
Jean, Jean-Paul, 'La justice sans le pouvoir', dans: *Le Monde Diplomatique*, (mai 1997).
Jean, Jean-Paul, 'La judiciarisation des questions de société', dans: *Revue Après-demain*, (octobre 1997).
Jean, Jean-Paul, 'Les réformes de la justice', dans: *La documentation française, Régards sur l'actualité*, (février 1999).
Salas, Denis, *Le tiers pouvoir. Vers une autre justice*, Hachette littérature, (1998).

The Challenge of Change for Judicial Systems
M. Fabri and Ph.M. Langbroek (Eds.)
IOS Press, 2000

The System of Justice in Italy: Signs of Evolution

Luigi Marini[1]

1 Introduction

During the last four years the beginning of a drastic evolution of the system of justice has taken place in Italy: this has affected its laws and structures and the civil and criminal proceedings. The description in a few pages of the meaning and extent of what many have defined as a true 'revolution' is no easy matter, also because it was connected with the profound changes that concerned the political system at the beginning of the last decade.

At least a short outline of the basic aspects is necessary to try to understand that evolution, since the Italian system of justice has some peculiarities within the framework of a continental, European legal system. First, I will give some general information about the organisation of the courts, the Italian judiciary, and some aspects of its social function in Italy. Second, I will describe the main features of the change brought about in the Italian judicial system during the past ten years.

2 General features of the Italian judicial system

2.1 Constitutional backgrounds

The Italian system of justice cannot be understood, and its essential characteristics noted, unless the values – set out by the Constitution in Articles 104, 105, and 110 – are understood. The constitutional law, which immediately after the Second World War completely put an end to the experience of Fascism and affirmed the substantial equality of citizens before the law, opted for the functional and organizational independence of the Judiciary from the Executive. A specific organ, the *Consiglio superiore della magistratura* (*C.S.M.*),[2] is responsible for the management of careers in the Judiciary: from training to transfers, from disciplinary matters to organizational choices of judicial activities within the offices. The Minister of Justice has an auxiliary function, namely he has to supply the offices with personnel, equipment, pre-

1 Luigi Marini is a member of the Italian Judiciary.
2 The Higher Council of the Magistracy (CSM) is composed of 33 members, among them the Head of State, 10 members appointed by Parliament and the remaining coming from the Judiciary, and represents the link between the legislative and the judicial power.

mises and funds. The Minister can initiate disciplinary proceedings against one or more judges, but only the *C.S.M.* is entitled to issue the relevant decision.

In this system, the Public Prosecutors are not only members of the Judiciary, but have, substantially, the same guarantees awarded to the judges; among them, their non-removal as well as their freedom of decision and of action in respect of every citizen, included the members of the Executive, must be underlined. To this end, it must be recalled that, according to the Italian Constitution, the Public Prosecutor is not entitled to choose whether or not to instigate an inquiry, or to bring an indictment: he has to submit the case to the Judge of preliminary invesigation, who is the only authority entitled to decide to discontinue a criminal case. If we add to this the fact that the law enforcement officers must inform the Public Prosecutor of every reported crime brought to their attention, we can understand that the number of criminal cases heard and tried every year by Public Prosecutors and Judges is very high.

2.2 Career judges and honorary judges

The Italian justice system still reflects the guidelines of the Napoleonic Codes: its structure and rules are not a product of the local 'community' and judges are neither elected nor appointed by the political power of the day. Appointment is based on the results gained in an entrance examination, and the judge is a civil servant, although with a special status. Members of the Bar and the Judiciary follow separate and not interchangeable careers, and have a different cultural approach: a judge represents the State, whereas a lawyer represents a person who has to request a specific provision from the State, or, alternatively, has to defend himself. This difference has unfortunately taken on negative features and the two categories nowadays almost contradict one another.

Career judges are traditionally entrusted with justice, and 'honorary' lay judges have had, at least until recently, a secondary and supporting role. In Italy honorary judges, who are not professional judges[3] nowadays have different competences: some of them co-operate with the judges sitting in the Courts and in the Offices of the Public Prosecutors; others work as experts in specialized courts;[4] some of them are elected to the Courts of Assizes[5] for short terms; others, finally, fulfil the functions of Justices of the Peace and are only competent in civil matters.[6]

The institution of Justices of the Peace where was set up in 1995, and from that time onwards honorary judges have acquired a more important role in Italy. In 1999

3 The judges who perform their functions but have not sat any public examination are considered honorary judges; their function is temporary and they can be duly rewarded. The payment for some of them, such as the Honorary Associated Judges and the Justices of the Peace, is proportional to the quantity of work done.

4 For example in the Juvenile Courts.

5 Sections of the courts trying particularly serious offences (e.g. murder) and composed of 6 lay judges and 2 career judges.

6 Justices of the Peace will also try minor offences and impose non-custodial sentences from the spring of 2001.

the Justices of the Peace dealt with 851,907 civil cases, whereas career judges heard a total of 2,603,154 civil cases at first instance. Furthermore, in 1998 a limited number of honorary judges[7] were entrusted with around 600,000 civil cases instigated before May 1995 and which were still pending in the courts.

2.3 *Diffusion of courts and offices*

Judicial institutions are scattered all over the Italian territory. The Offices of the Justice of the Peace number 848, while the Courts of First Instance amount to 166 and there are 220 detached Divisions of these Courts. The Offices/Courts of First Instance total 1,322 (with 166 Offices of the Public Prosecutor: one in every Court); the Courts of Appeal total 29, with the same number of Offices of the Public Prosecutor.

Such a large number of Offices/Courts of First Instance implies that the workload of many of them is small,[8] and brings comparatively high costs as well as management problems. For this reason the Government is attempting to reduce the number of offices in order to improve the overall efficiency. However, Italy is a young democracy, in the past the country was occupied by foreign powers for centuries and was affected by endless domestic conflicts: for many communities the presence of a judicial office is still a political and a symbolic sign of great importance. For this reason the governmental policies are being strongly resisted within Parliament and certain communities.

It must be stressed that before 1998 the Offices/Courts of First Instance were even more numerous. Traditionally, apart from the Courts of First Instance there existed another judicial organ, the *Pretura* (Single judge court of limited jurisdiction), generally with jurisdiction in civil cases and minor offences.[9] By an Act of 1997 the 165 *Preture* were merged with the other courts (*Tribunali*), which became the only judicial Offices of First Instance composed of career judges. We shall consider that issue shortly.

2.4 *The demand for judicial interventions in Italy*

The Italian justice system may seem very contradictory. On the one hand, the efficiency of the system is considered to be very low, because of the excessive length of civil and criminal proceedings. On the other hand, the same justice system also appears particularly efficient: the results achieved against the instigators of Mafia crimes and the investigations and trials effected by the 'Clean Hands Pool' provided, at least from an external point of view, a demonstration of the great investigative abilities and remarkable professionalism of the judges.

---

7 The Act concerned provided for the establishment of 1,000 honorary judges, while initially about 320 judges were in service; during 1999 their number rose to 791 following a new selection.

8 In more than 400 Offices of the Justice of the Peace only 2 judges sit, while in 37 of the 166 Courts no more than 10 judges sit and another 43 have between 11 and 15 judges.

9 Likewise there were 165 Single judge Courts of limited jurisdiction, with their relevant Offices of the Public Prosecutor, in addition to the 164 Courts of that time.

We should therefore assume that the Italian demand for judicial interventions is particularly complex. The number of cases submitted every year to the system of justice is very high, and some aspects of social life are extremely delicate and require strict control. During recent years, the yearly average of new civil cases has amounted to about 3,780,250;819,265 of which are brought before a Justice of the Peace,[10] while the Offices of the Public Prosecutor receive about 4,482,025 reports of crimes every year, and about 1,281,424 of them lead to a formal indictment.[11] Important observers have stressed the 'anomaly' of the Italian demand for judicial interventions, underlining that because of a lack of filtering instruments and of the distrust of citizens in the Public Administration, claims and conflicts that should be dealt with elsewhere, are brought before the judges. Furthermore, the afore mentioned principle according to which the Public Prosecutor cannot drop a case autonomously, increases the actions required of the judge. In addition to the very high number[12] of cases, we should consider the level of propagation and the danger posed by organized crime, with the subsequent necessity of highly qualified explanations from the system. The quantity of criminal proceedings against dozens of serious criminals every year is not diminishing, and such activities absorb the energies of a remarkable number of career judges.

3 Procedural and organisational provisions for the Italian judicial system

The justice system currently has 9,109 career judges (the judges working in the Judicial Offices number about 4,400), 4,700 Justices of the Peace (about 2,700 already in place),[13] in addition to about 2,600 honorary judges who assist the judges and the career Public Prosecutors, and 1,000 of them hearing the civil cases filed before May 1995. About 37,000 administrative officials, included those working in the Ministry of Justice and its Divisions, assist the judges.

It must be underlined that judges and administrative officials are assigned to a large number of offices, of a small scale, and that the choice of allowing citizens have a judicial office in their community implies relevant additional costs, also in terms of effectiveness.

10 The number of cases before a Justice of the Peace is rapidly increasing, from 179,688 in 1996 to 354,607 in 1999.

11 The fact that more than 25% of the reports of crimes received by the Offices of the Public Prosecutor result in a formal indictment, requiring the determination of a judge, places the Italian justice system very far from the levels of the common law systems, and represents as an unbearable burden for the judges. The causes of this phenomenon are very complex and cannot be described in this survey.

12 For the Offices/Courts of First Instance we can recall that in the period 1997-1998 the yearly average of *new cases* assigned to every Public Prosecutor was about 1,000 (with peaks up to about 1,900); ordinary civil cases were about 350 for every judge (except the simplest cases); criminal cases tried by every judge amounted to about 380.

13 The number of 4,700 Justices of Peace was established by the Act of 1991, which also provided that they had criminal jurisdiction. Full implementation will only be attained (Act no. 468 of 1999) in 2001.

For those reasons, the share of the budget that the State assigns yearly to the services of justice is currently under discussion, as it seems excessively low: at the beginning of the 1990s it amounted to about 0.9% of the total budget, it increased a little in subsequent years and in 2000 it reached 1.4%. In particular, many think that the number of judges and administrative officials is insufficient to meet the demand for judicial interventions and that the premises and technologies utilized are inadequate. Most Italian judges however, always have asserted that the existing of judges would be sufficient if the State would invest more resources in organisational and material provisions and if the 'anomalous' parts of the demand for judicial would be eliminated.

3.1 The rules governing the trial and its 'guarantees'

The Italian legal system provides very profound differences between penal and civil proceedings, but both of them involve a considerable expenditure of energy and activity on the part of the justice services.

Traditionally civil proceedings are strictly ruled, by law. In each case the law prescribes the issue which has to be decided upon by the judge, the evidence to be heard and the length of the proceedings; therefore, the judge's power to modify the subject of the proceedings, to decide whether or not to hear certain evidence or to accelerate the procedure is very limited. This has resulted in a great number of cases lasting too long and has also created undesirable practices by judges and lawyers who give very little attention to the necessity for simplicity and expeditiousness. Furthermore, the Italian legal system always gives parties the opportunity to appeal against the Tribunal decisions before the Court of Appeal and before the Court of Cassation. As a consequence, the judges of the Tribunals and of the Courts of Appeal[14] must devote a great deal of time to drafting the grounds of appeal, as the 'superior' judge determines the appeal, for the most part, merely by examining the contents of these grounds.

After the assessment that the length of civil proceedings was continually increasing, in 1995 a reform was introduced which has modified some of the rules of procedure in order to make the proceedings simpler and more expeditious. The reform has gradually resulted in a significant improvement in the quality and also in the average length of civil proceedings.[15]

Maybe, the problems concerning criminal proceedings are more complex. Like the Spanish and French legal system, the Italian system originates from an 'inquisitorial'

---

14 During the years 1997-98, civil decisions delivered by Tribunals have amounted to, on average, about 917,000 per year, and the appeals before the Courts of Appeal have numbered, on average, about 33,243, equivalent to more or less 3.6%.

15 About 5 years after the reform on May 1995, it is now possible to make a preliminary evaluation of the length of the proceedings before Tribunals: 5.4 years were needed on average to obtain a decision before the reform, it is now around 2,5 years. This evaluation is bound to change in time, however. It has to be reiterated that only about 50% of the civil proceedings end with a Tribunal decision and that they end much sooner.

penal procedure, in which the investigating judge (*giudice istruttore*) was the one to interrogate the defendant, to evaluate and collect the evidence, to decide on guilt. In 1989, with a radical reform, a new trial model, similar to the common law model, was introduced and it has removed the investigating judge (*giudice istruttore*) from the stage of judicial investigation by transferring it to the Public Prosecutor (Pubblico Ministero). It is nevertheless a hybrid model which, for example, introduced plea bargaining and the simplified trial, but retained strong elements of the Italian juridical tradition. The Public Prosecutor cannot refuse to proceed against the indicted person not even when he becomes a prosecution witness; the Public Prosecutor can gather elements during the investigation which, in some cases, have the value of evidence at the hearing; there are no juries; grounds for the decisions must be provided by the judge; every decision[16] can be appealed against, before the Court of Appeal and eventually, before the Court of Cassation. Only at the end of all the appeal procedures the sentence can be executed.[17]

The new criminal procedure system, which has opportunely abandoned its *'inquisitorial'* character, has brought along profound contradictions. An *'adversary'* system may be successful only if a very small number of trials take place in Court, if the sentence becomes immediately enforceable and can be appealed against in few cases, if the judge is not compelled to state the grounds for the sentence or can state them succinctly. In Italy, on the contrary, the sentenced person has a right (apart from the cases we are going to mention) not to suffer the punishment until all the appeals have been heard; a very large number of trials are on average very long, so that in many cases the punishment is finally imposed many years after the beginning of the trial. This situation makes preventive detention very important: in serious cases and if the defendants are recidivists, the Public Prosecutor can ask the judge to issue a warrant of arrest, even before the indictment has been formulated; consequently, the indicted person may remain in prison many months before and during the trial.[18] Anyway, as preventive detention has deadlines fixed by law, it often occurs that a person is released after he/she has been sentenced if the sentence has been appealed against and is not final; subsequently, when all the appeals against the judgement have been heard, the person will return to prison to resume serving the whole sentence.

As we can see, the Italian criminal procedure provides for the coexistence of *'civil law'* and *'common law'* institutions and that leads to results which are often contradictory. In the last few years, especially starting from the event referred to as

16 With the exception of those decisions where the defendant is sentenced only to a non-custodial penalty for misdemeanours.

17 The Constitution – which views the fascist model as a negative model – for the protection of citizens against every abuse, states that the citizen has to be considered innocent until the conviction becomes final and furthermore states that every penal judgement can be appealed before the Court of Cassation.

18 However, the warrant for pre-trial detention issued by the Judge for preliminary investigations or by the Court can always and repeatedly be challenged before a specialised division of the Court commonly called 'The Court of Freedom' (Tribunale della Libertà).

'Mani pulite' ('*Clean hands*')[19] a large part of the political world and of the Bar has denounced the excessive power of the Public Prosecutors with regard to the way they gather the evidence and has criticized the utilization of preventive detention. These problems have led to some amendments being made to the criminal procedure. At first, the Constitutional Court introduced some instances when judges are no longer competent;[20] afterwards, in 1999, Parliament amended Article 111 of the Constitution by introducing the principle of the so-called 'giusto processo' ('*fair trial*');[21] in 1999 some amendments were also introduced into the Code of Criminal Procedure. These amendments make the trial more complex and increase the duties of the Public Prosecutor during the inquiries.

All these reforms have led to an increase in formal activities and have made the job of the 'magistrati' ('*judges and public prosecutors*')[22] more demanding. This factor, together with the very high number of trials, has progressively led the judicial authorities into difficulties; consequently, the time necessary to bring trials to a conclusion has grown longer.

3.2 The organisation of the courts and the work of the judiciary[23]

In the last few years a great deal of attention has been paid to the effectiveness of the Courts not only by the *C.S.M.* and the Ministry of Justice but also by the ministries and authorities in charge of audit controls. There are structural and operational problems in the judicial system which have been accounted for in different ways. Responsibility for the poor service has been laid on the judiciary, on an excessive number of courts, on a lack of resources or on the inefficient use of these courts. Probably, all these explanations have some truth in them:

19 Under the label 'Clean Hands' a number of investigations and trials for corruption and related offences were instigated. They started in 1992 in Milan and caused a great sensation because they involved important Italian politicians and businessmen.

20 Some examples: if a Judge, upon the request of the Public Prosecutor, has delivered a decision concerning a person under investigation, he cannot hear the case of that same person/defendant at a later date. A judge who has judged a case cannot hear a different but related case or a case involving different defendants related to those he has already heard.

21 In other words the new Article 111 changed the Italian legal tradition. It provides that statements made by a person during investigations have no probative value unless the person confirms them before the trial Judge. To fully understand the import of this provision it must be considered that, in Italy, the defendant, even if during the investigations he/she had agreed to be questioned, has the right to lie, the right to silence and the right to answer only to some questions during the trial: there is no offence of 'contempt of Court'.

22 An example: during the investigations, the lawyers and the persons under investigation are entitled to a considerable number of formal notices and notices concerning the filing of trial pleadings and papers. Another example: a first instance trial, in the case when the defendant is under arrest, may involve from 3 to 8 members of Judiciary, and such a number may rise to 11-16 if the defendant appeals against conviction to the Court of Appeal or to the Court of Cassation, which occurs quite frequently.

23 Translator's note: the original word *Magistrati* applies to Judges and Public Prosecutors. They are all part of the Judiciary, albeit with a different status. 'The Judiciary' or 'members of the Judiciary' have been chosen so as to preserve the original extensive meaning.

a The high number of courts scattered around the territory has already been mentioned. No doubt such a system is wasteful in energy, many courts are necessarily endowed with limited resources and personnel and are not highly productive.
b As to the distribution of resources, it must be stressed that in the past, when judicial statistics were not available, resources were assigned to courts according to inconsistent and ill-chosen criteria and it has proved quite difficult to restore a correct and efficient practice.
c However, recent assessments have shown that there is a real need for an increase of human resources and equipment.
d It is more difficult to deal in a few lines with the claim that a good share of responsibility for the so-called 'Justice crisis' rests with the Judiciary. Such a charge not only stems from a generic dissatisfaction which the public may have towards 'professionals' since they are obviously liable to make mistakes and consequently – sooner or later – to disappoint 'their clients' (as happens – for instance – to hospital doctors). It is also based on the specific responsibilities vested in the members of the Judiciary by Italian law as to the management of the judicial service.

As already said, pursuant to Articles 104 and 110 of the Constitution, the Judiciary is granted a high degree of independence not only as far as judicial duties are concerned but also as to the direction and organisation of the courts. The 'Chief' in a Court is, in fact, a member of the Judiciary while the head of the clerical staff co-operates with him in the organisation of the service. It is important to note that a member of the Judiciary (who is under the supervision of the *C.S.M.* and not of the Ministry of Justice) is also the head of the Court office which manages the internal workload, including the number of judges and clerks to be assigned to the specialised sections. Finally, a member of the judiciary decides on the use of courtrooms, and on funds for the purchase of computers, telephones and other equipment.

The above points highlight how the Italian legislation attaches greater importance to safeguarding the independence of the Judiciary than to the efficiency of the 'production system' also with regard to the management of the courts. It would be unfair, however, to deny that, on the whole, the members of the Italian Judiciary have underestimated the need to make the courts' activities efficient and cost-effective.[24] In the last few years, however, a marked evolution has occurred and both the *C.S.M.* and the Ministry of Justice[25] are working to improve the judicial system efficiency.

---

24 This issue is extremely sensitive and should not be commented upon lightly. Past experiences under fascism have undoubtedly influenced the Judiciary who tend to reject controls on the merits of their activity and other kinds of 'interference' on the part of the Executive. From such suspiciousness arose the claim that the activity of the Judiciary cannot be 'quantified' and also the conviction held by many members of the Judiciary that protecting people's rights demands high quality work which ought not to be conditioned by budget or production standards.

25 The Government elected in 1996 was strongly committed to the reform of public administration and – as shown further – brought about extensive changes also in the judicial service.

4 Policies for reform

The process of reforming the judicial system started in 1989 when the new Code of Criminal Procedure came into force, and was greatly accelerated starting from 1996 when Mr Prodi became Prime Minister.

In the period 1989 - 1996 two important measures were adopted: the institution of the Justice of the Peace by a law of 1991, which became operational in 1995 in the civil field only, and the reform of the Code of Civil Procedure which - also starting in 1995 - simplified trials.

In 1996 the new Minister of Justice launched a comprehensive initiative for the reformation of justice, which included a 'package' of co-ordinated bills to be submitted to Parliament. For the first time proposals were made on the basis of a systematic design aimed at tackling the quantity and quality of the demand for judicial intervention (decriminalisation of a number of offences), the structure of the courts (the merging of the two first-instance courts *Tribunale* and *Pretura;* sub-division of the courts in the 5 largest metropolitan areas), strengthening the courts in southern Italy, and enlarging the jurisdiction of the Justice of the Peace (attribution of criminal jurisdiction). All these bills were passed by Parliament in the years 1997-1999. They dealt with complex matters which can only be briefly sketched out here.

4.1 'Giudice unico' di primo grado (Court of First Instance)

This is possibly the most important reform and the most complex. It concerned the structure of the courts and civil and criminal trials. Up to 1999, first-cases could be tried by two completely independent courts: the *Tribunale,* where the most serious cases were dealt with by three judges sitting together, and the *Pretura* (from the Latin *'praetor')* where a single judge heard the less serious cases.

Such a situation entailed an increase in the number of courts as well as the existence of many smaller courts, and it also led - in many cases - to a duplication of trials when the relevant acts fell partly under the *Tribunale* jurisdiction, partly under the *Pretura* jurisdiction. The reform aimed to change this. The *Pretura* and *Tribunale* were merged in all the 164 then existing benches. Obviously such a process, concerning courts that were once totally independent, took a tremendous organisational effort: structures and work patterns had to be changed as well as the assignments, activities and habits of the members of the judiciary and of the clerical staff.

Apart from such structural reform, the law provided for changes in criminal and civil trials aimed at significantly decreasing the number of trials where three judges instead of one were required.

Thanks to the decrease of the amount of cases requiring three judges and also thanks to the larger size of the courts, this reform is expected to increase the courts' productivity and efficiency.

4.2 Depenalizzazione (decriminalisation)

Thanks to the entry into force in January 2000 of a 1999 law, the courts' caseload was reduced. A considerable number of petty crimes were decriminalised, judges were no longer required to deal with them and could also speedily conclude the trials related to the decriminalised offences already under way. This measure was adopted in order to cope with the 'abnormally' high number of cases. It was estimated that in this way the investigations and trials should decrease by 10-12%.[26]

4.3 The jurisdiction of the 'Giudice di Pace' (Justice of the Peace)

The courts' caseload will be further reduced following the attribution of criminal jurisdiction to the Justice of the Peace. The use of the Justices of the Peace has proved successful; the length of civil trials is considerably shorter. Naturally, the Justices of the Peace hear the simplest cases, in fact few of their decisions are appealed against. However, the number of cases submitted to the Justices of the Peace is sharply increasing and this is causing some difficulties.

Given such success, before August 2000 – as established by a Law of December 1999 – the Government will set the rules for simplified criminal trials before the Justice of the Peace, who will hear offences concerning less serious breaches of the law (abuse, defamation, slight injury...) and will inflict penalties other than detention.

4.4 Increasing the personnel in southern courts

Starting mostly from the end of the 1980s, an increasing number of judicial and clerical staff have been assigned to the courts in southern Italy. Since 1992, when the mafia carried out two massacres in which Judge Falcone and Judge Borsellino were killed, public opinion started to demand a tougher reaction against the mafia and a strong reaffirmation of the rule of law in southern Italy.

However, although judicial and clerical personnel in southern courts were increased, there were little requests for assignments in that area and the members of the Judiciary who served in the south were generally juniors who – after 2 or 3 years – succeeded in being transferred elsewhere. In order to keep Judiciary members longer in the so-called 'difficult' courts (yearly identified as such by the *C.S.M.*) a 1997 law provided for some economic and career benefits for those members of the judiciary who served in 'difficult courts' for at least 4 or 5 years. Up to date this measure has proved useful.

---

26 Such a percentage is not sufficient, according to judges, to solve the problems related to an excessive workload, also due to the fact that the decriminalised offences were simple cases which did not require much work on the part of the judges, prosecutors and staff.

4.5 Organisational reforms

Such a brief account of the legislative reforms cannot provide a comprehensive overview of the complexity of the operation carried out, which required co-ordinating the discussions on several bills and was further complicated by a difficult political climate and by a strong confrontation in Parliament between the majority and the opposition on some justice issues.

The amendments of some Laws and of the Codes of Procedure were only an aspect of the Government action in the justice field. Great emphasis was also placed on the reform of the central administration and the organisation of the courts.

The first step in this direction was a general reform of the public administration. The 1996 Cabinet and their successors, who took charge in December 1999, focussed on ministry structure rationalisation, service decentralisation, the reform of public mangers' functions, changes in the national budget and in the budgets of governmental bodies and the introduction of methods for management control. The political choice to reduce state expenditure and rationalise investments bound and stimulated all parties to innovation. The Minister of Justice, too, acted towards this goal to the extent allowed by the independence of the courts. It should be mentioned that since 1996 some 50 young statisticians, about 100 business graduates and 26 young organisational analyst have been recruited and the use of information technology has been greatly promoted. It was a large investment in technical professional competence, which until recently was quite scarce in the Judicial system. Such competence is being applied mainly to management and organisation.

The second step was a structural change in the organisation of the courts. The establishment of a statistics department enabled the Ministry of Justice to make the first assessment of macro data concerning courts: information about personnel, workflows, the length of trials and the output percentage of each section.

Consequently, the first comparative assessment of the needs of each court was carried out and a partial readjustment of resource and personnel distribution was commenced. In the past reliable evaluation systems were not available[27] and the distribution of resources and personnel followed criteria which were not entirely rational.[28]

At the Ministry of Justice, in addition to the review of resources, an analysis of the organisation of courts is being carried out by internal analysts and external consultants; a great deal has still to be done to devise new organisational patterns and technical solutions to improve the judicial system efficiency.

Once more it must be stressed that in general requests for judicial intervention are marked by great complexity, which bears on the Italian judicial system. Social and economic conditions greatly differ in different parts of Italy and the work of the

27 The only statistical data available were those gathered by the National Statistics Institute (*Istat*) which naturally were not tailored to the organisational and management needs of the Ministry of Justice.

28 An example: there are offices of the Public Prosecutor where there is a staff of 8 or 9 members per Prosecutor and other offices of the same kind where they have no more than 4.

Judiciary differs accordingly, not only as to the object and the complexity of trials,[29] but also with regard to the professional approaches and working methods of lawyers, the co-operation of the local people, the efficiency of the public administration, etc. This situation makes organisational analysis and attempts at management innovation especially difficult. In spite of this, the increasing priority given to the efficiency of justice really seems to have become a well-established trend in Italian politics.

5 Conclusions

The Italian political system is going through a transitional phase which has caused great strain on the judicial system. Although only some political parties have explicitly proposed to amend the statuary provisions concerning the structure of the Judiciary,[30] the majority of politicians seem to be convinced that in recent years many members of the Judiciary have over-used their discretion. As a result, and with the support of the majority of the Bar, Parliament has approved some important amendments to criminal procedural rules aimed at reducing 'the pre-eminence' of the Public Prosecution during hearings and the extent of judicial discretion.

A comprehensive evaluation of what has happened and is still happening is beyond the scope of this article, but it is important to point out that the Judiciary has to face a 'revolution' as to its functions and prerogatives and it is requested to restore the efficiency of the judicial service in a state of general uncertainty and also of internal dissent.

Moreover, the Bar is also going through a difficult phase: the number of lawyers in Italy is very high,[31] professional standards vary greatly and there are deep internal disagreements. At present, the relations between the Judiciary and the Bar are particularly tense and this certainly does not help the positive evolution of the judicial system.

In spite of this, during the last four years the trend towards transformation has gained ground. The Government and Parliament have introduced innovations based on a systematic reform project and concerning both legal and organisational issues.[32] The Judiciary and the administrative staff, on their part, have started to appreciate the

29 In southern Italy, for example, courts have to deal with a considerable number of criminal cases and lawsuits related to social security benefits. In northern Italy, instead, civil trials concerning industry and business are more frequent. Moreover, courts in the south and courts in some metropolitan areas in the north have to deal with organised crime offences which absorb a great deal of energy.

30 In May 2000 a number of referendums will take place in Italy. One of them aims to introduce a strict distinction between Judges and Public Prosecutors as far as their careers are concerned. Such a distinction may result in the weakening of Public Prosecutors' independence. Another referendum aims to change the way *C.S.M.* members are elected.

31 At the beginning of 1999 there were some 90,000 lawyers and every year their number increases by about 10-11,000.

32 In addition, on 22 March 2000, the Government submitted a bill aiming to appoint 1000 new members of the Judiciary. Such a number is thought to be necessary to clear the judicial backlog.

import of the change and the *C.S.M.* and the Ministry of Justice have been at pains to improve and update professional standards.

In conclusion, the conditions for a more modern and efficient judicial system have been created and the resulting system will be able not only to fight harder against organised crime but also to meet all the rightful expectations of the public.

References

AA.VV., *Il Sistema giudiziario italiano*, Roma: Ed. Consiglio superiore della magistratura (1999) (volume con testo in Italiano, Francese, Inglese, Spagnolo, Tedesco).

AA.VV., 'Il Giudice unico', numero monografico n. 2-3, (1998), di *Documenti Giustizia,* Rivista edita dal Ministero della Giustizia.

AA.VV., *Economia e criminalità,*, Roma: Ed. Camera dei Deputati, (1993).

AA.VV., 'Dei delitti e delle pene', in: *MicroMega*, n. 1, (2000), Milano (Gruppo L'Espresso).

AA.VV., *La Giustizia del Quotidiano*, Torino: Ed.Gruppo Abele, (1999).

AA.VV., 'Il sistema giustizia alla prova delle riforme', in: *Questione Giustizia*, n. 4/97, Milano: Ed.Franco Angeli.

AA.VV., *Governo dei giudici*, Milano: Ed.Feltrinelli, (1996).

Ciro Riviezzo (a cura di), 'Giudice unico di primo grado', in: *Gazzetta Giuridica*, Milano: Ed.Giuffrè, (1998).

Colombo, G., *Il vizio della memoria*, Milano: Ed.Feltrinelli, (1996).

Ferrajoli, L., *La cultura giuridica nell'Italia del Novecento*, Roma-Bari: Ed. Laterza, (1999).

Lazzaro, *Il Giudice unico*, Milano: Ed. Giuffré, (1999).

Marini-Vaudano, 'Giustizia, istruzioni per l'uso', supplemento al n. 20 di*Avvenimenti* (con informazioni in 7 lingue per i cittadini stranieri).

Marino, *Il Giudice unico*, Napoli: Ed. Simone, (1998).

The Challenge of Change for Judicial Systems
M. Fabri and Ph.M. Langbroek (Eds.)
IOS Press, 2000

Managing and Delivering Justice in the Netherlands in the 21st Century

Towards an Empowerment of the Judiciary

Christina P.M. Cleiren and Edo C. Brommet[1]

1 History

1.1 Phase 1 (1988 –1994): Decentralisation of management and the introduction of planning and control

The changes presently taking place in the management of the Dutch Judiciary must be placed in the perspective of a development that was set in motion during the latter half of the 1980s.

The increased caseload and the first round of Dutch Government cutbacks triggered a drastic reorganisation of the Dutch judicial organisation. At that time, the judicial organisation comprising the Judiciary and the Public Prosecutions Department, and its management (personnel, offices, and finances) fell entirely under the Secretary of State for Justice.

The perception that the judicial organisation and many other implementing organisations will function better if management authority and responsibilities are placed at as low a level as possible led in 1990 to the appointment of a governing director in each district: the Director of Legal Support (DLS). This director was made head of the department of all official support personnel, and was given control of all budgets and responsibility for the other management positions. Up until then these tasks and responsibilities had been largely implemented in a classic centralist manner at the Ministry.

The Presidents of the judicial tribunals and heads of the public prosecutor's offices remained heads of the 'legal' personnel bearing responsibility for policy, i.e. the efficient running of the administration of justice and law enforcement. Other than that, there was barely any policy at all within the Judiciary. Cases were brought and handled without there being any explicit steering process.

The introduction of the DLS structure did not result in integral management in the sense that policy and management were controlled from one central point. The

---

1 At the time they wrote this contribution, both authors worked at the Dutch Ministry of Justice, the Hague, the Netherlands. Today Cleiren is a Professor in Criminal law at Leiden University.

directors and their magisterial opposite numbers had to coördinate management and policy by covenant. In other words: it was a dual model.

Once the DLSs had made their entrance the Ministry of Justice substantiated the steering and accountability relationship with the districts by way of a planning and control cycle.

Although this cycle could only be maintained with the DLSs in formal terms, it quickly became clear that Presidents and Chief Public Prosecutors could by definition exert considerable influence on the management of their authorities. There was no point, for example, in making management agreements with a DLS about the number of criminal cases to be settled if the President had the final say on drawing up the court timetable.

At the same time the Ministry and the management of the PPD, at that time the meeting of Procurators-General, discovered planning and control as an instrument that could be used to steer law enforcement up to a certain level better than the circulars that were previously used. As from 1992 the national priorities of the PPD, such as fraud, traffic and the environment, formed a fixed part of the management agreements that were made annually with the Chief Public Prosecutors.

In actual practice, the steering and accountability relationship between the Ministry and the districts was extended to the Presidents and the Chief Public Prosecutors. Although they did not bear a formal responsibility for management, there was an increasing commitment to the management agreements among them. Most of the Presidents became willing to answer to the Ministry for the development of their judicial tribunal's operating performance. Appendix 2 offers an overview of the management tools used in the planning and control cycle.

1.2 Phase 2 (1994 – 1998): The reorganisation of the Public Prosecutions Department

In 1993, the public, the press, and Parliament expressed fierce criticism on the running of the Department, and this directly resulted in a reorganisation. The criticism concerned a number of releases of suspects, believed to be caused by procedural errors of the PPD. The Secretary of State for Justice set up the so-called Donner Committee, and in 1994 the Committee made the following recommendations:

- to convert the PPD into one organisation instead of the function which until then was attached to the individual courts.
- to place the policy and control under one roof both nationally and at local level instead of the existing dual model (national: meeting of Procurators General and Ministry, local: Chief Public Prosecutor and Directors of legal support).

The Committee had suffered some criticism from the Chief Public Prosecutors about the DLS structure. This may or may not have to do with people being too quick to take out their own powerlessness, fully in or part, on the – often troublesome – management apparatus. The advice of the Donner Committee was in any event logical from an integral management viewpoint.

At the beginning of 1995 a 'Committee of Procurators General' was formed on an informal basis as a national management committee of the PPD. At the same time the reorganisation of the PPD started. The planning and control cycle was being directed more and more at the Committee in its capacity as the PPD management, and much less towards the individual Chief Public Prosecutors. The Committee was accountable for the implementation of the 1997 and 1998 annual plans that received the approval of the Minister of Justice.

As from 1 January 1998 the new relationships has been settled in formal terms. The fact that the PPD's policy mandate is conferred on the Committee directly by the Minister, while the management mandate - as is the case with other justice sections - runs via the Director-General, made the new structure relatively complex:

- Policy frameworks for the PPD are laid down by the Minister of Justice; partly long-term, but in any event also annually and linked to the national budget cycle; the Committee has a policy implementation mandate.
- Management frameworks for the PPD are set by the Director-General; the Committee has a management mandate.
- At each stage of the planning and control cycle policy and management are explicitly linked to each other.
- The new Judiciary (Organisation) Act contains a number of procedural regulations for specific directives that the Minister of Justice can give to the PPD.
- The heads of the Public Prosecutor's Offices are integral managers of their offices and are as such accountable to the Committee.

1.3 Phase 3 (1994 – 1998): The debate on the management of the judiciary

Developments in the Judiciary had a different dynamic. Between 1994 and 1998, discussions took place concerning the administration and management of the administration of justice, which discussions had been prompted by several internal and external factors.

- The Hoekstra Committee was set up by the Cabinet, mainly to study the intended reorganisation of the PPD. Its report was published in 1995, and formed the main external basis for this discussion. The report proposed a type of integral management for the Judiciary, where the management of means would be assigned to management committees to be formed for every court.
- Furthermore, many Presidents had increasing doubts on the viability of the dual system. The judicial tribunals have been modernised at a fast pace over the last ten years. The link between the content and quality of the administration of justice, on the one hand, and management, on the other, has become increasingly stronger. Many members of the judiciary recognised the fact that an organisation that is already so complex can no longer be kept on course by two captains.
- Last but not least, a small, but active number of Judiciary members were aware that to a certain extent the administration of justice would have to adapt to the changing demands of society in the late 1990s. If they did not, the Judiciary

would lose its effectiveness, and eventually its legitimacy. All these factors contributed to the start of 'Project ZM (Judiciary) 2000', which also concluded that the management of the judiciary would have to be strengthened.

In view of these developments, the desirability of also introducing integral management to the judiciary and charging either the Presidents or management committees with its implementation was also subscribed to by the Presidents and the Procurators General at the Supreme Court. They did however assert that introducing integral management, and especially the duty of accountability to the Minister of Justice, would bring about considerable risks concerning the institutional independence of the Judiciary. This is why they proposed the founding of a national Council for the Administration of Justice which would, for instance, consult directly with the Lower House for the setting of the budget.

At the end of 1996, the Lower House adopted a motion where the Secretary of State for Justice was asked to set up a Committee, which would make recommendations concerning the future organisation and equipment of the Judiciary. This so-called Leemhuis Committee comprised mainly external experts, but also a number of Judiciary members. In its work, the Committee was able to use the results from discussions and reports from previous years.

The Leemhuis Committee reported in January 1998, and made the following recommendations:

- To form a Council for the Administration of Justice, which constitutes a guarantee for the institutional independence of the Judiciary;
- To join the courts and district courts in terms of management, as this increases the manageability of the administration of justice at local and national level;
- To introduce integral management in each of the courts;
- To develop a modern personnel and quality policy, and pay specific attention to improving working processes;
- To earmark 250 million Euros during the coming Parliament for improving capacity, necessary investments in information technology, and other innovative developments.

2 The process in 1998

After the Dutch parliamentary elections in 1998, the report of the Leemhuis Committee played a role during the formation of the new Cabinet. The coalition agreement of August 1998 for the second Cabinet of Prime Minister Wim Kok, included the most important recommendations from the Leemhuis Committee. Due to limited financial room, the budget increase was set at 15 million Euros for 1999, rising to 65 million Euros in 2002.

In order not to lose time, officials from the Ministry of Justice organised a conference during the formation of the coalition. The conference was attended by representatives from the Judiciary and by a number of outsiders – the implementation of the recommendations from the Leemhuis Committee was the main point on the agenda. The majority of delegates concluded that it was about time that the Judiciary itself took responsibility for this reorganisation.

In June, the first plan of action for a 'Reinforcement of the Judicial Organisation Project' was drawn up. It emphasised the management of courts, the implementation of a professional personnel policy, the improvement of working practices, encouragement to focus on the community, and future developments relevant to the administration of justice.

At the start of July 1998, the Presidents of the courts gave their support to this plan of action, and indicated their willingness to commission the project.

At the end of August, they appointed a 'Core Team' from their members, and a Project Manager who would be responsible for the further preparation of the Reinforcement of the Judicial Organisation Project.

In August, the new Justice Minister Job Cohen took office, and was given responsibility for the reorganisation of the Judiciary. On 2 September 1998, he discussed the Leemhuis Committee report with the Select Committee for Justice. He stated that he broadly subscribed to the Leemhuis recommendations, but that he wanted to incorporate them in an overall plan for the future of the administration of justice. The Justice minister gave a commitment that an 'outline' of the administration of justice in the 21st century would be submitted to the Lower House no later than December 1998. The plan quickly assumed the working title 'White Paper'.

During the next few months, the Ministry of Justice worked hard on this paper. The intensive round of consultations on a draft version of the White Paper, held in November by the Justice Minister and the departmental management, was particularly important. The 'professional body' for the Judiciary, the Dutch Association for the Administration of Justice, held a special place in these consultations, and eventually agreed to the policy proposals contained in the White Paper.

During the same period, the Judiciary continued the planning of the Reinforcement of the Judicial Organisation Project. During the planning, there was full co-ordination with the Ministry of Justice, and the main points of the JIP were incorporated in the White Paper.

As promised by the Justice Minister, the final version of the White Paper was sent to the Lower House before Christmas 1998, after it had received approval from the cabinet.

3 Administration of Justice in the 21st century

The policy document 'Administration of Justice in the 21st century', contains five central **aims:**

- To offer 'tailor-made administration of justice' to citizens, which includes room for out-of-court settlements, and alternative dispute resolution (ADR).

- To reduce the processing times, which requires specific investments in capacity and a redesign of business processes.
- To increase the accessibility of the courts, which means an increased use of modern means of communication.
- To strengthen equality before the law and unity of law, which requires the introduction of more information, registration, and expert systems.
- To stimulate the external focus of the administration of justice, which requires regular studies of how those subjected to the administration of justice rate the service.

These aims can only be achieved if the organisation of the administration of justice is strengthened. The ambitions require an organisation responsible for its own management and strong and powerful management aimed at achieving results at national and local level. The introduction of integral management in the courts and simultaneously setting up a Council for the Administration of Justice are the most important pillars of strengthening the judicial organisation.

The Council for the Administration of Justice will be the body that takes on responsibility for the Judiciary, as set out in the Reinforcement of the Judicial Organisation Project.

The details and the implementation of the reorganisation are organised along three tracks:

- First, there is the aforementioned **Reinforcement of the Judicial Organisation Project**. This comprises those elements of the reorganisation for which the Judiciary itself is responsible. The setting up of local committees, development of a personnel policy for legal personnel, and the redesign of business processes are not the type of subjects that can be detailed by civil servants behind desks.
- The future relationships between the Secretary of State for Justice, the Council for the Administration of Justice, and the management committees of courts will have to be laid down properly in an amendment of the **Judicial Organisation Act**. This should respect both ministerial responsibility for expenditure on the administration of justice, and judicial independence. Whichever way the tasks of the Council for the Administration of Justice are organised, legislation will have to answer a number of difficult questions.
- Finally, there are a number of activities within the framework of administration of justice in the 21st century that will be carried out under the direct responsibility of **departmental management.** They include preparations for setting up the Council for the Administration of Justice, the introduction of a new budget system, but also the administrative joining of courts and district courts. All of these projects will be carried out in close co-operation with the Judiciary. In some cases, these projects are led by project leaders from the Judiciary, albeit under the responsibility of civil servants.

The legislation and formal preparations are due to be completed on 1 January 2002.

4 Current state of affairs

Exactly one year before this EGPA annual conference, the Justice Minister and the Lower House signalled the kick-off for the reorganisation. They were agreed that the Judiciary itself had brought the ball into play! During the past year, a number of important steps have been taken.

To start at the **political level**: In April 1999, the Lower House agreed all proposals contained in the White Paper, except for the administrative joining of courts and district courts. Initially, the majority of the Lower House feared that such administrative joining would lessen the specific qualities of the administration of justice in district courts, such as speed and accessibility. The Lower House was strengthened in this opinion by a lobby of district court judges. During a second meeting in June 1999, the Justice Minister managed to convince the Lower House that this fear was unfounded.

The important issue for the **Reinforcement of the Judicial Organisation Project** is that in March the Justice Minister laid down a set of criteria for the Programme Plan, which formulate the requirements the Programme should meet. In fact, the set of criteria draws a clear line between the political responsibilities of the Justice Minister and judicial independence.

In April, the draft programme plan and the set of criteria were approved by the Justice Minister, and sent to the Lower House. There were also extensive discussions on a covenant between the Justice Minister and the Meeting of Presidents, which would formalise the agreements on the implementation of the Programme. On 6 September 1999, all Presidents and the Justice Minister signed this covenant, which constitutes a formal accountability relationship between the 'Core team' and the Ministry of Justice.

The drafts of the **White Papers** that enable the formation of the Council for the Administration of Justice and the formation of management committees for courts are ready. They have been sent to the delegates of a major legislative conference that is to take place in mid-September. At the conference, more than 100 members of the Judiciary and other involved persons will exchange ideas on these White Papers.

In August 1999, a number of important **departmental projects** were started, including the preparations for setting up the Council for the Administration of Justice, the formation of local management committees for courts, and a new design for the budgeting system that will be applicable between the Justice Minister, the Council for the Administration of Justice, and the local management committees.

5 Some conclusions

1. With the decentralisation of management and the introduction of a planning and control system, as described in Chapter 1, the foundations for the current reorganisation have been laid. The Dutch Judiciary was relatively quickly convinced of the need for these activities, but although the management of the judicial

organisation improved, the management limitations within a dual system have also been brought to light.

2. The Judiciary also appeared sensitive to external pressure for reorganisation of the DPP, and to the partly internal signals that the Administration of Justice, too, would have to adapt to a changing society. The judicial powers were not pushed on the back foot, but faced these developments in a realistic manner.

3. The preparatory process for the reorganisation meant the formation of what were often joint committees - enirely in keeping with the Dutch compromise culture. At crucial times (Hoekstra Committee and Leemhuis Committee), an external chairman and external committee members was necessary to establish a breakthrough in relations.

4. During the implementation of the reorganisation, the management of the process will be divided between the Ministry of Justice and the Judiciary. This unique approach requires both sides to show openness and trust, a strong awareness of their own responsibilities, and respect for the responsibilities of the other partner - this is a precarious aspect of the operation.

5. The reorganisation of the administration of justice in the Netherlands will lead to a clarification of the relationship between the Trias Politica. The strengthening of the Judiciary's responsibilities for management in particular will improve the independence, quality, and efficiency of the administration of justice.

Appendix 1

An overview of the management instruments of the judicial organisation in the Netherlands

In this appendix there will be outlined the set-up and operation of the management instruments within the judicial organisation in slightly more concrete terms. The planning and control cycle referred to in the paper plays an important role here.

It is still the case in the Judiciary that most justice is done to the principles on which the management of judicial organisation were founded at the beginning of the 1990s: *managing in outline, managing at a distance and managing according to output*. Central to this is the processing capacity of the judicial tribunals. The cases must after all be settled within a reasonable period of time and in a manner determined by the judiciary itself.

There is generally more detailed management at the Public Prosecutions Department. The national policy priorities of the PPD in the planning and control cycle have up to now been detailed in a fairly specified manner, for instance. The public prosecutor's offices therefore not only had to hear 20% more environmental cases, but also had to apply an environmental chart, set up a local consultation structure and promote expertise. The reorganisation of the PPD did of course also lead to a recalibration of this management concept. Nowadays there is sooner a global planning in advance and a more detailed accountability afterwards.

In practice, the planning and control cycle works as follows:

- In June the substantive and budgetary frameworks for the judicial tribunals and Public Prosecutor's Offices are laid down in the 'planning and division letter'.

This letter lays down the target levels for the development of the processing capacity of the Judiciary, the policy priorities of the Public Prosecutor's Offices are formalised and the provisional budgets for these authorities are determined. This allocation is made with the aid of an objective division system. This allocation system is intended to prevent the decentralised organisation from expending all its energy in trying to acquire resources, but to utilise the available resources as efficiently and effectively as possible.

- During the summer months the judicial tribunals and the Public Prosecutor's Offices draw up their annual plans, based of course on the set parameters.

It is important in this respect that the Public Prosecutions Department and the judiciary mutually co-ordinate the number of criminal cases to be heard. In the new management structure co-ordination between the judicial tribunals, Public Prosecutor's Offices and collective management department will grow in importance.

- In the autumn consultations are held between the Ministry and the Committee of Procurators General concerning, on the one hand, and the judicial tribunals and public prosecutors offices on the other, the annual plans and the proposals for management and budget agreements being based on them.

During these consultations the proposals are checked against the set parameters. Proposals for adjustment are submitted where necessary and possible. In some cases further consultations are held concerning co-ordination within the criminal law system.

- In mid-December the management and budget agreements are confirmed by the Ministry and the Committee of Procurators General. This means that the judicial tribunals and the Public Prosecutor's Offices have their budgets as from 1 January of the year in question and that the way in which they are to be used is also laid down.

The management agreements for the judicial tribunals are largely quantitative and are laid down in the 'planning and control overviews' (appendix). These provide on a single A4 page an insight into the development of what was done in the years t-1 and t, and in the proposals and agreements for the year t+1. The 'weighted production' is determined using a workload measuring system in which the various 'key products' are given a 'weighting factor'. The 'input' and 'output' comprise the absolute numbers of cases brought and settled.

- The realisation of the management agreements is of course monitored before and after the year of implementation. For this purpose correspondence is conducted about the management reports issued by the judicial tribunals and Public Prosecutor's Offices and local consultations are held with the Presidents, other legal authorities and the directors.

In the 'monitoring discussions' the local management gives account to a certain level for the development of the processing capacity of its tribunals. Explanations are sought for deviations from the prognosis, and it is established whether factors that can or cannot be influenced are at issue.

The data from this planning and control cycle lend themselves ideally to consolidation into efficiency figures at judicial budget level. The fact that Justice came second in a comparative investigation of the General Court of Auditors into the application of efficiency figures can be attributed to a significant extent to the planning and control cycle of the judicial organisation.

Giving the processing capacity and the implementation of policy priorities a central position certainly does not imply that no attention is being paid to the quality of management and administration in the management and accountability relationship.

Financial administration (the General Court of Auditors was less favourable on this point!) has in recent years been improved on a project basis, for instance. The results of this project will be embodied in frameworks. Compliance with these frameworks will be monitored through audits, possibly using the self-evaluation approach of the Netherlands Quality Institute. An approach of this nature will also be developed for other areas of administration, such as automation and security.

Appendix II

Diagram 1

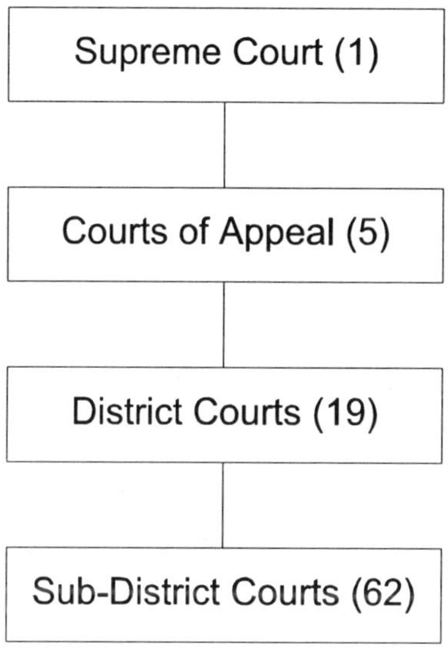

Organisation of the Courts

Diagram 2

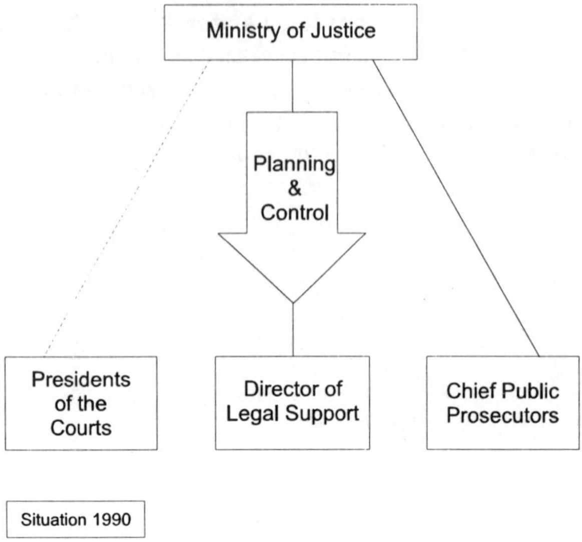

Diagram 3

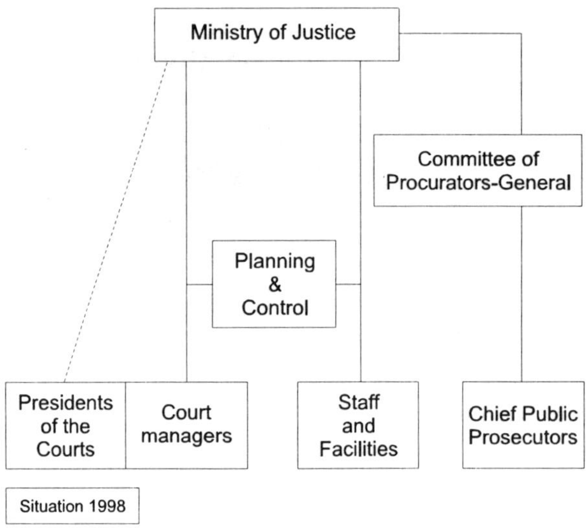

The Power of Innovation

Carla Eradus[1]

Delivering and managing Justice in the 21st century is quite an ambitious theme for a conference. This workshop is concerned with 'the internal organisation of the justice system and the courts and its influence on the effectiveness of the justice system'. In line with this ambition a wide range of subjects was presented in the invitation which we all received. Although they are all important and interesting, I shall only touch upon a few of these subjects in this presentation. I shall do this as a judge from the Netherlands, where I am involved in a programme entitled the Reinforcement of the Judicial Organisation Project, which was started last spring. This programme is part of a larger renewal programme, concerning the working of the judicial system, started when the present Government took office in 1998. Although the judiciary has its own responsibility for the Reinforcement of the Judicial Organisation Project, close relations with the Ministry of Justice are at all times maintained.

Before I explain what we are doing in this programme, the question of why we are in fact doing it must of course be answered. What is the power of innovation in the field of the judiciary? Why change? Although this question sounds a bit naive, it appears difficult to answer; while the answer in itself is important in order to choose the path for innovation.

In most countries represented at this conference the judiciary still holds a respected and comfortable position. Its independence is well guarded. And this at a time when all over the world the executive is in a deep identity crisis and politicians are redefining or trying to redefine the term 'representation'. There seems to be – at least at first sight – no good reason to offer the judiciary as a new toy for administrative science nor to eager consultants. On the other hand, holding a strong position is never a reason to sit back and relax!

Independence has been a welcome excuse to frustrate innovations for years. The result? Sound decisions but low efficiency. Especially the long processing times indicate that something is amiss. But there is more. There is a general feeling that change is necessary to protect independence and ultimately to protect the balance of power as defined by the Trias Politica.

In my view independence consists of two elements: freedom of operation and authority. While everybody thinks that independence only means freedom of operation, it is the growing lack of authority that is really undermining the judges' position and, as a consequence, their role in society.

---

1 President of the Court of Appeal of Leeuwarden, the Netherlands.

In modern life a sound decision is not enough. Maybe it still is for us and some lawyers, but the parties involved want the decision quickly even if this means it is not perfect, they want to understand the decision themselves, they want it to be in line with decisions by other judges and they want it online!

Computer technology is changing the world, it is changing communication and it is changing the distribution of information. The game is changing and if we want to participate we must learn to anticipate. The ivory tower is no jonger a refuge. If we want to play our role in society we need authority. Authority is not a gift that lasts forever, more and more it has to be earned in day to day life, over and over again.
If we look closer at the developments in society, I even expect that at the same time the game is changing the demand for good referees will grow. This is of course not the place nor the time to discuss the developments in society at the beginning of the third millennium. For this moment a raw sketch will suffice.

In short, the changes in society can be described by terms such as: internationalisation, virtualisation (ICT), fragmentation, network society and speed. The bottom line is the following: more and more large structures will be replaced by small units which constantly take part in different configurations, in which borders are not important at all. Developments are the result of several processes and they are not initiated nor controlled by the Government. Although the Government has a role to play as a new kind of process manager, it is expected that trial and error and confrontations will shape our world. In this new world a judge with authority can play an important role to guard the interests of the individual and to stop escalation.

This reflective introduction is not meant to shock you nor my counterpart at the Ministry of Justice. All I want to say is that the judiciary is too valuable to sit back and do nothing and just wait to see what happens. Change must always respect the basic outline of our democratic societies and serve long-term goals. Short-term efficiency operations may seem attractive but can do more harm than good if they destroy an institution that has a history going back centuries! At the same time it must not be denied that efficiency is an element of operating standards for professional organisations.

In the second part of this presentation I will highlight the Dutch Reinforcement of the Judicial Organisation Project which has been inspired by the ideas mentioned in the introduction and combines structural change with more efficiency.

Almost all the courts in the Netherlands participate in this programme which is meant to strengthen their organisation and to prepare them for the future. We largely work on the following:

- Management within the courts;
- The underlying processes;
- Human resource management; and
- The stimulation of external orientation.

The final aspect may be best explained with the following question: what do my partners and clients expect from me?

The levels on which we work are first of all the courts themselves of course. At the same time we work on the interaction between the courts, the second level. At the level of the courts, key issues are the co-operation between the judges and their staff and the management of the court which has to be effective and respect the independence of the individual judge. At the second level, the key issue is to find a method of co-operation between the courts without introducing new forms of hierarchy. 'The judiciary' implies some forms of organisation, but as we speak the ties between the courts are very weak, at least in the Netherlands.

As far as possible, all the work in the programme is carried out by persons from within the judiciary. In this way the available knowledge is utilized. This path has also been chosen because it is expected that in this way the solutions have the support of the people who have to work with them. To do the job properly we train them and there is a possibility of employing internal or external consultants.

The work is organised in twelve national development teams and twenty-six local implementation teams. Twenty-six because this is the number of the local organisations involved in the programme.

Of the twelve national development teams, one team is concerned with the introduction of modern management. In the new situation the management team of a court will be responsible for all matters concerning the operation of the court, especially the use of resources and the generated output. Basically a model is developed which is parallel to a new law on the management of the court.

In order to be able to anticipate future developments, research has to be carried out. That is why another team works on the introduction of a national Centre for Research and Strategy. Most courts are too small to keep pace with the developments in technology, especially information and computer technology (ICT). That is why a test lab will be created to develop and test new instruments for all courts. It is expected that in this way the introduction of new technology can be realised more smoothly and for less money!

In the day to day running of the courts the structuring and restructuring of processes is very important. Not only because of efficiency reasons, but also because of the demands from outside the courts. Speed, transparency, consistency, etc. All these objectives have consequences for the processes involved. Work-flow management is not yet widely used in the Netherlands. There is a team that will collect material and knowledge on work-flow management and develop tools for implementation.

In the Netherlands most laws are quite basic as far as processing rules are concerned. Most processing rules have developed in practice. But practice that differs from court to court. Even in a small country like the Netherlands this gives rise to much confusion. At the same time there is an efficiency incentive for unification. Several teams are working on the unification of processing rules:

- The unification of processing rules in the field of civil law.
- The unification of processing rules in the field of family law.
- The unification of processing rules in the field of administrative law.

For criminal law the main focus is on consistency. Different penalties by different judges in cases that are almost similar give rise to public protest and professional criticism. That is why another team is working on guidelines, a forum for consultation and a databank in the field of criminal law.

Every modern organisation needs good human resource management, especially a professional organisation like the judiciary. To maintain high standards it is important to attract the right people and to keep them trained and motivated. In the near future it will also be difficult to attract enough qualified people because of the growing demand by public and private professional organisations. This team introduces human resource management based on function profiles and output. Output is more than production in terms of numbers, there is also the element of quality. Until now the only instrument for quality have been the Courts of Appeal! Soon a new team will start with the introduction of Quality Management within the judiciary. They will develop a set of tools like indicators and models for questionnaires.

The last two teams I want to mention focus on stimulating extenal orientation. One team promotes the use of the internet and e-mail for electronic communication. The other team is working on a format for dealing with complaints in a way that is satisfactory for the individual who filed the complaint. It also provides an incentive for correction or change if necessary.

Although we are working on several themes at the same time, success is not guaranteed. Innovation is first of all a local affair. Good implementation is essential for real innovation and success. This is the reason why we are creating twenty-six local teams. They know the local situation and priorities.

A complex programme such as that in the Netherlands implies innovation on a operational level but also cultural change, changes in attitude. People have to work together to be successful. Working together implies dependency and trust. To be successful, people also need to know the environment they are working in within and outside the court. Last but not least, it is important to know the public environment, society as a whole. What moves the public, what is the impact of a decision, etc. This cultural element needs special attention for an innovation programme to be successful.

For someone like me who is responsible for the programme itself it is important to motivate people from all levels within the organisation. The best way to do this is to allow them to take part. They have to be involved. Enormous energy can be created once people believe in change and have a personal influence. The same energy can be used to block change once the same people feel lost or misunderstood. People who want to take part are not always equipped to do the (new) job. It is very important to support them, for instance by training or coaching. Innovation has the power to stir inspiration and motivation which enables people to generate energy for real change.

Part III

Changing Positions of Courts in Society

Public Management Reform – A Challenge to Judicial Independence?

Gavin R. Drewry[1]

1 Introduction

This article[2] examines some important constitutional by-products of the 'New Public Management' (NPM) reforms in the United Kingdom, initiated by the Thatcher Government in the 1980s and continued by that government's successors – Conservative, then Labour – in the 1990s, as they have impacted on the administration of justice. It is argued in particular that NPM (happening alongside the growth of judicial review and the impact of European law) has raised some interesting issues to do with traditional and fiercely defended principles of judicial independence.

2 Some problems of comparison

The notorious peculiarities of the 'unwritten' British Constitution and the fact that, in the absence of a 'universal paradigm' of NPM,[3] the UK's version is no more 'typical' than that of any other country that has been reforming its public services, mean that generalisations from the British experience must be treated with caution. In particular, the role of the UK judiciary in constraining government through the exercise of constitutional and administrative law has, at least until recently, been much more limited than in many other countries. And, for the most part, it is only when judges get drawn into the political arena that their claims to 'independence' are regarded as important.

Notwithstanding the impact of globalisation in encouraging a convergence of legal norms, it must be recognised that 'judicial independence' itself is a concept associated very much with Western democracy, the rule of law, and traditions of constitutionalism. And even among Western countries there are important variations in the attributes of judicial independence and the mechanisms used to secure it.

---

1 Professor of Public Administration and director of the Centre for Political Studies at Royal Holloway, University of London, Unitied Kingdom.

2 Parts of this paper draw upon some of this writer's previously published work. See in particular, Drewry, (1992, 187-212) and (1998, chapter 3). See also notes 4 and 15, infra.

3 See Hood (1998, chapter 9).

Elsewhere, it is a characteristic of many authoritarian countries that the judicial process can be called upon – routinely or when thought necessary – to serve the ideological and economic ends of the State.[4]

This chapter makes some reference to a long-standing debate in Britain about whether there is a need to create a 'Ministry of Justice', much of which has been blighted by confusion about what form such a ministry might take. Many countries have ministries of justice; but the model that operates in (say) France, where the judges are recruited into a specialist corps of the civil service, is not easily transposed into the UK context, where judges are recruited from the ranks of mid-career practising barristers. In this and other aspects of this discussion we need to be careful that we are all talking about the same things.

3 The administration of justice – A 'special' public service?

At first sight, the administration of justice possesses many of the characteristics of other public services – health, public transport, education, etc. After all it is 'administered' by salaried public servants and paid for out of national and local government budgets. Justice is an important public good, and adMinistering justice is a crucial, arguably definitive, function of the State. This being so one would expect many of the ordinary ground rules of public administration – to do for instance with regulation of public appointments and tenure of office and with public accountability – broadly to apply.

But in many systems – and the UK provides an important illustrative example – the administration of justice has to a significant extent been treated as a special case and, in particular, been cushioned from some of the rigours of public accountability that operate elsewhere in the public sector. The key to its special status lies in the sensitivities surrounding judicial independence.

4 The imperatives of judicial independence[5]

It must be noted at the outset that the notion of judicial independence is interlinked with other concepts, in particular those of impartiality and neutrality, and we must be careful not to confuse them.[6] For the purposes of this discussion judicial independence is assumed to mean the absence of improper external pressures on the judiciary, and with the capacity of judges – often supported by constitutional safeguards – to resist such pressures without fear of penalty.

4 For a useful discussion of the varied attributes of judicial systems – distinguishing in particular between 'neo-Weberian' and 'dependency-based' models – see Schmidhauser (1987).

5 See Drewry (1991, chapter 3).

6 See Bell (1983, chapter 1).

In so far as the concept is historically linked to the constitutional doctrine of separation of powers the 'improper pressures' referred to are principally those that may emanate from the Executive and Legislative branches of government. However, with Montesqueiu's 18th century advocacy of separation of powers having been overtaken by the more complex realities of modern government, a wider definition may be appropriate. To quote Simon Shetreet:

> 'Independence of the judiciary has normally been thought of as freedom from interference by the Executive or Legislature in the exercise of the judicial function.(...) In modern times, with the steady growth of the corporate giants, it is of utmost importance that the independence of the judiciary from business or corporate interests should also be secured. In short, independence of the judiciary implies not only that a judge should be free from governmental and political pressure and political entanglements but also that he should be removed from financial or business entanglements likely to affect, or rather to seem to affect him, in the exercise of his judicial functions.'[7]

It is apparent, however, that this attempt to extend the definition takes us into a grey area in which 'independence' overlaps with 'impartiality': the former being the protection of judges from improper pressure from government (or business, or anyone else), the latter being the freedom of judges from predispositions – conscious or subconscious – in favour of one section of the community at the expense of another.

When the left-wing UK public lawyer, John Griffith, writes about the 'politics of the judiciary' his complaint is not about judges yielding to improper pressures but about what he believes to be their long-standing subconscious bias in favour of particular categories of litigant (including, in some contexts, judicial bias towards the Executive).[8] And in the recent *Pinochet* extradition cases in the House of Lords,[9] even Lord Hoffman's fiercest critics did not allege that he was in any way pressurised by Amnesty International (a party to the proceedings) to reach a decision of which they approved; the charge against him was that his non-disclosure of his position as the unpaid chairman of a charity linked to Amnesty created an unacceptable appearance of bias. And it was this 'entanglement' (to use Shetreet's word) that led to the unprecedented decision to rehear the case before a differently constituted court.

Although independence and impartiality are different, they are linked. In a pioneering pre-war treatise on administrative law, W.A. Robson started from the premiss that impartiality is a fundamental prerequisite of justice. He then proceeded to argue that such impartiality requires an independent judiciary, noting that, in Britain (as in many other countries), independence has come to be associated with security of tenure:

---

7 Shetreet (1976, 17-19).

8 Griffith (1997, 1993).

9 R. *v*. Bow Street Metropolitan Stipendiary Magistrate, ex p. Pinochet Ugarte (No. 1) [1998] 3 WLR 1456; ditto (No. 2) [1999] 2 WLR 272; ditto (No. 3) [1999] 2 WLR 827. See Malleson (January 2000, 119-127).

> 'Whether or not the decisions of a judge bring satisfaction or anger to the Prime Minister and his colleagues, or to the Lord Chancellor, he cannot be dismissed at will. His tenure is for life, or until retirement, subject only to good behaviour. His salary is fixed and paid out of the Consolidated Fund in order that it may not be subject to that running fire of criticism in Parliament to which all the ordinary items of budgetary expenditure are liable. His conduct cannot even be discussed in Parliament save on a substantive motion for an address for removal from office: an extreme step to be taken only in the event of propriety of the gravest kind. The judiciary is, in effect, part of the public service of the Crown. But a judge is not 'employed' in the sense that a civil servant is employed. He fills a public office, which is by no means the same thing; and part of his independence consists in the fact that no one can give him orders as to the manner in which he is to perform his work.'[10]

The importance of tenure for judicial independence is psychological: unlike the administrator, the judge:

> '(...) can displease an indefinite number of persons an indefinite number of times without any personal consequences ensuing to himself, providing only that he remains sane and does not commit one of those enormities which constitute misconduct. (...) The independence of the judge is (...) of essential importance in so far as it enables the judge to adopt a particular attitude of mind towards the questions which come before him for decision. He can, in short, determine the case before him without fear that adverse results or material reward will accrue to him according to whether the decision does or does not meet with the approval of other persons.'[11]

Writing more recently, Rodney Brazier has suggested four prerequisites for judicial independence:

(i) judicial appointments and promotions should not be subject to uncontrolled Ministerial patronage.
(ii) judges should be free from improper attempts by Ministers, MPs or peers to influence the results of cases still under adjudication.
(iii) that judicial salaries should not be reduced.
(iv) that judges should not be removed from office unfairly or without reason.[12]

He went on to argue that existing UK arrangements broadly satisfy the last three conditions – but he contended that there are serious problems with the first of them.

---

10 Robson (1951, 43-44). The first edition appeared in 1928.
11 Ibid., pp. 46 and 48.
12 Brazier (1989, 69-94, at 74).

The issue of judicial appointments has recently resurfaced, and we will return to it later.

5 The 'traditional' Lord Chancellor and his Department – the buffer and the hinge[13]

The historical custodian of judicial independence in the UK is the Lord Chancellor, a Cabinet Minister who guards the frontier between government, the judiciary and Parliament, being himself a member of all three branches. The Lord Chancellor, whose functions include the appointment, promotion and disciplining of the judiciary, has always – certainly in the past three hundred years or so – been a senior barrister or a Law Lord; i.e. he will himself either have been a senior judge, or a practising member of that branch of the legal profession that has had a virtual monopoly in supplying appointees to the higher judiciary. Although he is a Minister, appointed by the Prime Minister, nowadays party political considerations take second place to the appointee's professional standing as a lawyer; and this Minister sits in the House of Lords, where the intensity of inter-party conflict is generally less than in the Commons.

The Lord Chancellor's Office (LCO) (not then either a 'Government Department', or a 'Ministry') established in 1885 was, for many years, a tiny organisation responsible for judicial and ecclesiastical patronage, though in the 1920s it acquired (from the Treasury) a small branch responsible for the administration of the county courts, which try relatively minor civil cases. It has been observed that, in 1912, when Viscount Haldane moved from being Secretary of State for War, in charge of one of the largest government departments, to become Lord Chancellor, 'he doubtless felt that his new department needed some attention, for it was then not far removed from being an interesting little museum.'[14]

Despite its small size, it was from the beginning a self-important Office, conscious both of its own constitutionally unique status at the interface between Executive and Judiciary, and of the need to protect the sensitivities of the judges themselves. In such a context, the phrase 'administration of justice' seems to have meant something 'administered to' the people, rather as medicine (sometimes nasty medicine) is administered by a doctor to a patient. It is of course important to remember that this was an era long before 'citizen's charters' and of concerns about the user-friendliness of public services. But there is plenty of anecdotal evidence to suggest that the judges who 'administered justice' had little notion of litigants in civil proceedings – still less of defendants in criminal proceedings – being deserving of customer care, or even of much basic courtesy.

---

13 There is a considerable literature on the office of the Lord Chancellor: an excellent bibliography can be found in Polden (1988).

14 Jackson (1977, 583).

The bureaucratic infrastructure that supported the judicial process - what might be called the administration of the administration of justice - was small. And much of it consisted of court officers who were answerable to the judges themselves, and were not then regarded as part of the mainstream civil service; some aspects of administration (particularly of county courts) were under the direction of the Lord Chancellor and his Permanent Secretary - who were members of the same closed fraternity of the Inns of Court from which the judiciary was recruited.

Other Ministers and other departments - even large and important ones - were often wary of challenging the LCO because they were nervous about the sensitivities surrounding judicial independence. And the functions of the Lord Chancellor were generally regarded as being exempt from Ministerial responsibility to Parliament - for the same reason. The legal professions generally, and the judges in particular, were left to regulate themselves. The Lord Chancellor, the principal custodian of judicial independence, took great pains to keep politicians - including fellow Ministers - at a safe distance.

However, the picture was complicated by the fact that the Home Office - headed by a 'political' Minister in the House of Commons - was (and remained until a few years ago) responsible for the criminal courts. During the First World War, Haldane flirted with the idea of converting the Home Office into a Ministry of Justice - leaving himself, as Lord Chancellor, to preside, as judge over a new Imperial Court of Appeal:[15] but moves to set up the latter court never made any headway, and the idea of a Ministry of Justice was anathema to the legal and judicial professions, who (a) never had a clear idea of what it meant, other than to associate it suspiciously with the legal systems of continental Europe, and (b) regarded it (whatever 'it' was) as a potential threat to judicial independence.[16] There was hostility to the idea that the Minister in charge of the courts and judicial appointments should sit in the Commons, exposing the judiciary indirectly to the risk of political pressures.

The supposed importance of retaining the Lord Chancellor's position as a constitutional link between the two branches of government, in order to safeguard judicial independence, was stressed by Haldane's successor, Lord Chancellor Birkenhead, in an essay published in 1922:

> 'if they are totally severed there will disappear with them any controlling or suggestive force exterior to the Judges themselves, and it is difficult to believe that there is no necessity for the existence of such a personality, imbued on the one hand with legal ideas and habits of thought, and aware on the other of the problems which engage the attention of the executive government. In the absence of such a person the judiciary and the executive are likely enough to drift asunder to

15 See the Report of the Machinery of Government Committee (Chaired and substantially written by Viscount Haldane), London: HMSO, Cd 9230, (1918), chapter 10.

16 This writer has written elsewhere about the fractured history of the debate about a UK Ministry of Justice: Drewry (1983, 396-414) and (1987, 502-509). The debate about the Imperial Court of Appeal is discussed in Stevens (1993, chapter 2).

the point of a violent separation, followed by a still more violent and disastrous collision.'[17]

Later, Lord Schuster, the Permanent Secretary of the LCO throughout the inter-war years, was to refer in a departmental memorandum, to the need for 'some link or buffer' between executive and judiciary;[18] later still, his successor, Sir Albert Napier, used the metaphor of a constitutional 'hinge' to describe the Lord Chancellor's position.[19] This remains the conventional wisdom of today: thus the senior judge, Sir Nicholas (now Lord) Browne-Wilkinson, referred in a public lecture in 1987 to the unique constitutional position of the Lord Chancellor as providing 'a flexible and efficient means to transmit the needs of the legal system to the executive and to Parliament.'[20] And Lord Chancellor Mackay quoted the above passage from Lord Birkenhead's essay, with evident approval, in a public lecture in 1990.[21]

6 From LCO to LCD

Even by the 1950s, the LCO still had fewer than 100 staff, some 30 of whom served in the County Courts Branch. One important step towards the partial modernisation of the office of Lord Chancellor happened by accident, in 1948, when the timetable of business in the House of Lords was rearranged so that judicial and legislative sittings usually took place at the same time – the latter in the Chamber of the House, the former in a committee room upstairs. This meant that Lord Chancellors had to choose between sitting in the Chamber (as both a Minister and as Speaker of the House) and sitting as a judge. The former took priority – and this effectively stopped Lord Chancellors sitting judicially on a frequent basis.

Since then successive Lord Chancellors, including the present one, Lord Irvine, have tried to keep the tradition alive by sitting occasionally when Parliament is in recess. But their doing so has been increasingly open to criticism, particularly with the growth of judicial review challenges to the Government and the prospective implications both of incorporation of the ECHR and devolution (where the judges may be called upon to resolve vires disputes between Westminster and the Scottish Parliament and the Welsh Assembly). Moreover, in a case relating to Guernsey,[22] the European Court of Human Rights held, in February 2000, that any direct involvement in the passage of legislation or of executive rules was likely to cast doubt on the judicial impartiality of a person who subsequently decided a dispute involving the interpretation or application of the legislation in question, and that there had in this instance

17 Viscount Birkenhead (1922, chapter 4).

18 Public Record Office, London, Records of the Lord Chancellor's Office: LCO2 3630.

19 Public Record Office, London, Records of HM Treasury: T162 877/E48680, 1944.

20 See 'The Independence of the Judiciary in the 1980s', in: *Public Law*, (1988), pp. 44-57, at p. 45.

21 'The Role of the Lord Chancellor in the Administration of Justice', University of Newcastle, (typescript) 24 February 1990.

22 McGonnell *v.* United Kingdom, (Application no. 28488/95, judgment, 8 February 2000).

been a violation of Article 6 of the ECHR. This decision had nothing directly to do with the role of the Lord Chancellor, but it has reinforced the long-standing concerns of many constitutional commentators about the propriety of a senior Minister sitting as an appellate judge. It is quite possible that the Lord Chancellor's judicial function (and perhaps the Law Lords' participation in legislative debates) will eventually disappear in the wake of the continuing process of House of Lords reform – along with a review of the Lords' appellate role.

The first major step towards upgrading the tiny LCO into a fully-fledged Lord Chancellor's Department (the LCD) predate Mrs Thatcher and the NPM era. It began with the Courts Act 1971, which implemented the main recommendations of the Beeching Royal Commission on Assizes and Quarter Sessions.[23] Section 27 of the Act empowered the Lord Chancellor to appoint such staff 'as appear to him necessary (...) for setting up a unified administrative court service, and (...) generally for carrying out the administrative work of those courts.'

This decision to set up a unified cadre of civil servants, answerable to the Lord Chancellor for court administration, highlighted some of the sensitive issues that lie at the boundary between the judicial function of 'administering justice' and the bureaucratic function of (to use a phrase suggested earlier in this chapter) 'administering the administration of justice.' The Beeching Report had insisted that administrators must 'exercise strong managerial control over all matters affecting the smooth running of the courts other than those which have a direct bearing on the discharge of judicial functions'. The Commission thought it 'very necessary, on constitutional grounds, to provide a visible and effective safeguarding of the position of the judges serving the Circuits (i.e. the regional arrangement of Crown Courts) by assigning to each Circuit a senior member of the judiciary who will have a general responsibility for that circuit and a particular responsibility for all matters affecting the judiciary serving there.'[24] This recommendation was implemented by the subsequent appointment of two Presiding High Court Judges to each circuit.

One area where the court administrator has to be particularly careful not to bruise judicial sensitivities is in listing cases for trial so as to ensure a smooth flow of business through the courts and to ensure that efficient use is made of judicial time, available courtroom space, etc. – and that the convenience of judges is matched by due concern for the interests of the litigants and their advocates, witnesses, jurors, etc. As Jackson has observed:

> 'The administrators must programme the work of the courts but they cannot follow the classical models of administration because they do not control the central operation of the institution, that is the trial and disposition of cases. Inparticular there must be nothing to suggest that the administration controls the judiciary.'[25]

23 London: HMSO, Cmnd. 4153, 1969.
24 Ibid., para. 256.
25 R.M. Jackson (1977, 508).

Interestingly, Jackson has also noted that the establishment of the new Court Service was not welcomed by some of the existing court staff who 'regarded themselves as belonging to a special category and resented becoming "mere" civil servants'. This writer's experience in talking to judges and legal administrators confirms that, even to this day, many of the latter are more sensitive on the subject of judicial independence than are many of the judges themselves. As we will see later, there have been recent moves to increase the 'managerial' role of the judges themselves.

7 The Lord Chancellor, accountability and the administration of justice in the early 'New Public Management' era

We have noted already that the election of the Thatcher Government in 1979 marked the beginning of a radical programme of New Public Management reforms throughout the UK public service.[26] This has continued, perhaps even accelerated, under the New Labour administration of Tony Blair.[27] What effect has the NPM had on the administration of justice'

So far as the administration of the courts was concerned, the initial impact was slight. The Beeching reforms had bedded down, and the Lord Chancellor's Department was much bigger than it had been 30 years previously, but the prevailing assumption remained that justice was, and should – on constitutional grounds – remain a special case, particularly when it comes to resource allocation, and to matters of public accountability, scrutiny by Parliament and complaint handling.

One illustration can be seen in a report on the Administration of the Courts, produced in 1986 by a committee set up by the legal reform group JUSTICE to inquire into the machinery for dealing with public complaints about the administration of the courts. It discusses, in particular, the role of the Parliamentary Commissioner for Administration (the Ombudsman), who in 1984 had reached a '*concordat*' with the Lord Chancellor's Department about the location of the boundary line between 'administrative and judicial' – defining the kinds of case that the Ombudsman would be permitted to investigate. However, the concordat subsequently broke down following the LCD obtaining counsel's opinion that court staff supplied by the LCD, but working under the instructions of judges, did not come within the purview of the Parliamentary Commissioner Act 1967. The Lord Chancellor subsequently agreed to amend the law in order to bring his Department within the purview of the Ombudsman.

An interesting feature of the JUSTICE report was its overwhelming preoccupation with judicial independence, to a point where it virtually lost sight of any legitimate claims of public accountability. Some of the language used is extraordinary. At one

26 There is now a very large amount literature on the nature and development of NPM. See, in particular Hughes (1998); Flynn (1997); Peters and Savoie (1998); Oliver and Drewry (1996); Pollitt (1993); Pollitt and Boukaert (2000); Lane (1997); Zifcak (1994); Hood (1991, 3-20); Hood (1998).

27 For an overview see Rhodes (2000, 151-166).

point it considered the possible objections to extending the powers of the PCA to include investigations of judicial behaviour, a change favoured by some members of the Committee. One objection, it said, 'is that, as the Ombudsman reports to the House of Commons, this would encourage MPs *to pry into the affairs of the judiciary'* (emphasis added). But this objection was then promptly rejected on the grounds that the PCA is an independent officer who 'would only investigate a complaint if he were satisfied that it was serious', and, the Report continues, 'if a serious complaint is made, it would seem better that it should be investigated by an independent person of the standing of the Ombudsman than for it to become the subject of ill-informed speculation in Parliament'.[28]

However, some members of the JUSTICE committee did recognise that the increasing tendency for public authorities to be involved in litigation will make it 'increasingly difficult for the public to accept that judges are independent when the head of the judiciary, who is responsible for their behaviour, is also a leading member of the government'. One solution, they suggested, would be to restrict the role of the Lord Chancellor to being head of the judiciary and Speaker of the House of Lords – which 'would be a logical solution if as some have suggested, a Ministry of Justice is set up, with its departmental Minister in the House of Commons'. However, the Report stopped short of making a positive recommendation along these lines.

Judicial independence had also been invoked to justify the Thatcher Government's decision, in 1979, to exclude the Lord Chancellor's Department and the Law Officers' Department from the purview of the newly-established Commons Home Affairs Select Committee. The Leader of the House, Norman St. John Stevas (as he then was) warned of the threat to judicial independence that might arise:

> 'If a select committee were to investigate such matters as the appointment and conduct of the judiciary and its part in legal administration, or matters such as confidential communications between the judiciary and the Lord Chancellor (...)' [29]

Ten years later Stevas admitted that the exclusion of the LCD had been on the insistence of the then Lord Chancellor, Lord Hailsham, to whom he had deferred on 'tactical' grounds so as not to jeopardise the implementation of the package of select committee reforms.[30] The order of reference of the Home Affairs Committee was changed in 1991 to allow it to inquire into 'the policy, administration and expenditure of the Lord Chancellor's Department (including the work of staff provided for the administrative work of courts and tribunals, but excluding the consideration of individual cases and appointments)'.

28 *The Administration of the Courts*, London: JUSTICE, 1986, para. 4.14. Emphasis added.
29 HC Debs. 25 June 1979, cols. 35 et seq.
30 Evidence to Select Committee on Procedure, The Working of the Select Committee System, HC 19-II, 1989-90, para. 742.

Lord Hailsham was an arch traditionalist, a staunch defender of judicial independence, and a fierce opponent of any attempts to expose any aspect of the judicial process to greater public scrutiny. He denounced proposals to establish a Ministry of Justice as being 'constitutionally very dangerous' and a menace to the independence of the judiciary[31] – though in another context he had also acknowledged that the Lord Chancellor was, in effect, a Minister of Justice.[32] As Lord Chancellor, from May 1979 to June 1987, he played a substantial part in cushioning the administration of justice – and particularly the judges themselves – from some of the early impact of the NPM revolution. His interpretation of his role, at the interface between Executive and Judiciary, was very much in line with the 'buffer' and 'hinge' metaphors, cited earlier.

However, the NPM changes – including the downsizing of the civil service and the quest for more rigorous financial monitoring and control did not exempt the LCD. Lord Hailsham himself initiated a wide-ranging review of the civil justice system – which reported soon after he left office.[33] And toward the end of the Hailsham era some of the judges were beginning to detect the auguries of change. In 1987, Sir Nicholas Browne-Wilkinson, then Vice Chancellor of the Supreme Court (later Lord Browne-Wilkinson, the senior Law Lord) delivered a public lecture in which he identified several developments in the last 30 years or so that, in his view, posed a threat to the continuing independence of the administration of justice.[34] The point on which he laid greatest stress had to do with the recent development of financial management and value for money disciplines (themes central to the NPM programme) relating to public expenditure, and their application to the Lord Chancellor's Department:

> 'the requirements of judicial independence make the Lord Chancellor's Department wholly different from any other department of state. It is not for the executive alone to determine what should be the policy objectives of the courts. It is not for the executive alone to determine whether or not particular procedure judicial procedure provides 'value for money'. Justice is not capable of being measured out by an accountant's computer (...) [U]nder our constitution it is for the judge to determine what is just, and what is not just, subject always to legislation passed by Parliament. As a result of such policy being applied to the Lord Chancellor's Department, that department is being required to formulate policy and to make determinations as to 'value for money' according to financial yardsticks and without, for the most part, even consulting the judges.'

31 *The Guardian* (26 May 1986).

32 Evidence to the Home Affairs Committee, *The Prison Service*, 1980-81, HC412, Evidence, QQ. 995-6. With reference to Lord Hailsham's opposition to this Committee being allowed to inquire into the business of the LCD it should be noted that prisons are a Home Office responsibility.

33 *Report of the Review Body on Civil Justice*, London: HMSO, 1988, Cm. 394.

34 'The Independence of the Judiciary in the 1980s', loc. cit. n. 19.

Thus, he went on: 'The Lord Chancellor's own position, representing as he does simultaneously both the independent judiciary and the interests of government, is becoming more and more difficult, since the price to be paid for obtaining funds for the administration of justice is dependent on satisfying the Treasury that any particular course represents, in their terms, value for money'. He went on to argue that, while the fixing of the total budget for the administration of justice must (as with health or education) be a political act, judges must, *in the interests of judicial independence*, be involved in the preparation of the estimates and in the allocation of the budget once it has been voted by Parliament. By the same token, judges should be more involved in the formulation of legal policy. Sir Nicholas suggested that 'there should be a collegiate body of judges charged with responsibility for taking policy decisions on behalf of judges' – funded by the Lord Chancellor's Department, but accountable to the Lord Chancellor for its expenditure of those funds.

Even if we accept the general diagnosis, the pro-, it is hard to see how it would advance the cause of judicial independence. Lord Chancellor Mackay later opined in another public lecture that: 'the intensity of political conflict in the House of Commons (...) makes it desirable, in our system, that the judiciary should not become directly involved in the politically-charged process of obtaining resources'. And, he went on , 'the Lord Chancellor serves to insulate them from that process'.[35] So we can add the metaphor of 'insulation' to those of the 'buffer' and the 'hinge'.

8 The Mackay era

Lord Hailsham retired from the office of Lord Chancellor in June 1987 and, after a brief interregnum with Lord Havers, Lord Mackay of Clashfern took over the post – which he occupied until the defeat of John Major's Government ten years later. Mackay had been a Law Lord (i.e. a senior appellate judge) prior to his appointment and he had no record (as had Hailsham) of being an active party politician. He was, by background a Scottish advocate rather than an English barrister, so he was not, as his predecessor had been, a member of the closed fraternity of the Inns of Court in London. This may help to explain why tensions that had been building up between the Judiciary and Government now came to the surface.

The context in which this happened was the Civil Justice Review, inherited from Hailsham. In January 1989, three Green Papers on legal services and the legal professions were published. One was entitled The Work and Organisation of the Legal Profession,[36] which proposed relaxing the barristers' long-established monopoly in respect of advocacy in the higher courts, and introducing a new system for licensing advocates. A lay-dominated advisory committee would advise the Lord Chancellor,

35 'The Role of the Lord Chancellor in the Administration of Justice', loc. cit. n. 20.
36 London: HMSO, Cm. 570.

> 'on the education, qualifications and training of advocates appropriate for each of the various courts. The Lord Chancellor should be required to consult the judiciary before reaching decisions as a result of advice tendered by the Advisory Committee, although the final decision would be for him (...) Professional bodies whose members wish to offer advisory and advocacy services will be required to submit their proposed codes of conduct for the endorsement of the Advisory Committee whose role it will be to ensure that such codes of conduct embody the approved principles (...) The Government proposes that the Lord Chancellor should prescribe by statutory instrument the principles which must be embodied in these codes (...) The Government is not prepared to leave it to the legal professions to settle the principles which these codes should adopt because they will be of great importance both to the administration of justice and to the public.'

Hereupon, many leading barristers, and senior judges, went on record as saying, often in very colourful language, that this posed a gross threat to judicial independence and the rule of law. In the Lords' debate on the Green Papers,[37] the Lord Chief Justice, Lord Lane, attacked the new advisory committee procedure as a movement towards executive control over the judiciary, adding for good measure that: 'Oppression does not stand on the doorstep with a toothbrush moustache and a swastika armband (...)'. Lord Donaldson, Master of the Rolls, said that, if necessary, he would tell the Government to 'Get your tanks off my lawn'. The former Lord Chancellor, Lord Hailsham, said that he was 'shocked' by the prospective threat posed to judicial independence by the proposal that 'a member of the executive [i.e. the Lord Chancellor], advised by an advisory committee which is staffed secretarially by his own department and composed of a majority of persons unqualified in the law' would take charge of deciding who was qualified to practice in the courts.

To cut a long story short, the Lord Chancellor eventually modified the original proposal by giving senior judges a power of veto in respect of the codes, and the row subsided. The amended proposals were implemented in the Courts and Legal Services Act 1990. But the bemused observer was left wondering if the proposals in their original form really did threaten the constitutional order, or whether this outcry from judges and lawyers was a self-interested knee-jerk response on the part of an articulate professional pressure group which is strongly represented in Parliament. This is not the first time that Lord Chancellors have crossed swords with the judges, nor is it the last (there have, for instance, been continuing controversies in the 1990s about government moves to restrain judicial discretion in aspects of criminal sentencing). But it was a uniquely intense confrontation, and it was psychologically important in exposing the constitutional fiction that, in the tough era of the New Public Management, the judges cannot always count upon 'their' Lord Chancellor to 'insulate' them against the cold winds of financial discipline and rising expectations; to add a footnote to this, however, it is interesting to note that Tony Blair's Lord Chancellor, Lord Irvine – responding to calls (in the context of continuing discussion of House of Lords re-

37 HL Deb., 7 April 1989, cols. 1307-1480.

form), for an end to his dual role as Minister and judge – recently told the Worldwide Common Law Judiciary Conference in Edinburgh that his unique position enabled him to act as a 'buffer' between the government and the judiciary.[38] *Plus ça change.*

9 The Lord Chancellor's Department today

If Lord Haldane were to return to Earth, looking for his 'little museum', he would find that it has long been demolished, and replaced with a massive modern edifice in Victoria Street, London SW1 – in many respects a Ministry of Justice, though not of the sort that he himself advocated in 1918.

In the early 1990s two important developments took place. First, responsibility for the funding and organisation of the magistrates' courts service in England and Wales was transferred from the Home Office to the Lord Chancellor's Department. About 50 Home Office civil servants moved to the LCD. The second, linked to the first, was the appointment of a junior Minister to the Lord Chancellor to answer in the House of Commons for the operation of the courts. The former move represented an important consolidation of 'justice' functions, formerly divided untidily between two ministries. The second represented a further 'normalisation' of parliamentary accountability for the administration of justice, along with the extended remits of the Home Affairs Select Committee and the Ombudsman, already noted.

The growing political salience of judicial decisions – in particular, the growth since the 1970s of judicial review and now the incorporation of the European Convention on Human Rights into UK Law by the Human Rights Act 1998 – has heightened public interest in the backgrounds of the judges and the way in which they are appointed. Perhaps the NPM process itself has contributed to the growth of judicial review: with Ministers, impatient to see results sometimes cutting legal corners; with public bodies sometimes using the courts to challenge decisions; and with 'empowered' citizens looking for new avenues to assert their rights and entitlements.

The Home Affairs Committee made early use of its extended terms of reference to look at the judicial appointments system,[39] and vacancies are now generally advertised. But the Blair Government and Lord Irvine have dragged their feet on earlier half-promises to set up a judicial appointments commission.[40]

Meanwhile, the Blair Government has continued a major overhaul of the machinery of justice begun by its predecessor – building in particular upon proposals on 'access to justice' arising from an inquiry conducted by Lord Woolf, the Master of the Rolls.[41] An important feature of the Woolf reforms is judicial case-management – including timetabling, with penalties for non–compliance. The Government published

38 *The Times* (6 July 1999).

39 *Judicial Appointments Procedures*, 1996-96, HC 52.

40 See Drewry (1998, 1-7). The issue of judicial appointments is discussed at some length in Malleson (1999, chapter 4).

41 Woolf, *Access to Justice – Interim Report*, LCD, (1995); Woolf, *Access to Justice – Final Report*, LCD, (1996). Also Middleton (1997). For a critical commentary see Zander (1998, 382-389).

a White Paper in December 1998.[42] The Access to Justice Act 1999 established a Legal Services Commission to establish and oversee a new Community Legal Service and a Criminal Defence Service, and paved the way for allowing conditional fee agreements to fund litigation. Apart from the substance of these changes (some of which have been highly controversial), it is interesting to note that the judges themselves - led by Lord Woolf - are now playing a key role in designing, initiating, legitimating and managing important changes in the administration of justice.

Today, the Lord Chancellor's Department is a massive departmental empire of about 11,000 civil servants (a little bigger than the Ministry of Agriculture, a little smaller than the Home Office, and about twice the size of the Diplomatic Service). Most of the staff work in two Next Steps executive agencies - the Court Service (8,600 civil servants) and the Public Trust Office (545). Its annual budget is around £2.3 billion - of which around 70 percent is for legal aid. A quick look at the LCD's Organisation Chart[43] and at its Annual Reports[44] confirms that the landmarks of NPM are everywhere. Agencies, Charters - and now Public Service Agreements, that must accompany all departments' bids for three-year funding under the new financial arrangements announced in the summer of 1998.[45] There is a Courts Charter setting out commitments to improved standards of service to court users. And of course developments like the Woolf reforms, mentioned earlier, have a strong flavour of NPM.

In summary, there can be no serious question about the continuing importance attached by both the political and the legal culture to maintaining the independence of the Judiciary from improper Executive and political pressure. However, there has been an increasing tendency to treat the administration of justice as a public service, much like any other - particularly in the context of resource allocation. The Lord Chancellor and his Department have become more and more like any other 'spending' Minister and Ministry. And, without conceding ground on the 'independence' issue, the judges themselves seem to have recognised the legitimacy of enhanced external scrutiny - and they themselves have become intermittent but active participants in major policy debates to do with legal services.

42 *Modernising Justice*, Cm 4155.

43 The most convenient source is the LCD section of the *Civil Service Yearbook*, published annually by the Stationery Office, London.

44 See *Annual Report 2000-2002*, Cm 4206, April 2000. This and other relevant LCD documentation can be downloaded from the web: http://www.open.gov.uk/lcd/lcdhome.htm – click on 'what's new' for the latest items.

45 See *Economic and Fiscal Strategy Report 1998*, Cm. 3978, June 1998; *Modern Public Services for Britain*, Cm. 4011, July 1998; *Public Services for the Future: Modernisation, Reform, Accountability*, Cm. 4181, December 1998.

References

Bell, *Policy Arguments in Judicial Decisions*, Oxford: Clarendon Press, (1983), chapter 1.

Brazier, R., 'Government and the Law: Ministerial Responsibility for Legal Affairs', in: *Public Law*, 1989, pp. 69-94, at p. 74.

Drewry, Gavin and Dawn Oliver, 'Parliamentary Accountability for the Administration of Justice', in: Oliver and Drewry, (eds.), *The Law and Parliament*, London: Butterworths, (1998), chapter 3.

Drewry, G., 'The Debate About a Ministry of Justice – A Joad's-Eye View', in: *Public Law*, 1987, pp. 502-509.

Drewry, Gavin, 'Justice and Public Administration: Some Constitutional Tensions', in: R.W. Rideout and B.A. Hepple, (eds.), *Current Legal Problems 1992*, volume 55, Part II, Oxford: Oxford University Press, (1992), pp. 187-212.

Drewry, G., 'Lord Haldane's Ministry of Justice – Stillborn, or Strangled at Birth', in: *Public Administration*, 61, 1983, pp. 396-414.

Drewry, G.*, Judicial Appointments, Public Law*, (Spring 1998), pp. 1-7.

Drewry, G., 'Judicial Independence in Britain: Challenges Real and Threats Imagined', in: P. Norton (ed.), *New Directions in British Politics*, Aldershot: Edward Elgar, (1991), chapter 3.

Flynn, N., *Public Sector Management*, 3rd edn., (1997).

Griffith, J.A.G., *Judicial Politics Since 1920*, Oxford: Blackwell, (1993).

Griffith, J.A.G., *The Politics of the Judiciary*, 5th edn., London: Fontana (1997).

Hood, C., 'A Public Management for All Seasons', in: *Public Administration*, vol. 69(1), (1991), pp. 3-20.

Hood, C., *The Art of the State*, Oxford University Press, (1998), chapter 9.

Hood, C., *The Art of the State*, (1998).

Hughes, O., *Public Management and Administration*, 2nd edition, (1998).

Lane, J-E., (ed.), *Public Sector Reform: Rationale, Trends and Problems*, (1997).

Malleson, K., *The New Judiciary*, Ashgate Press, (1999), chapter 4.

Malleson, K., 'Judicial Bias and Disqualification after Pinochet (No. 2)', in: *Modern Law Review,* 63 (1), (January 2000), pp. 119-127.

Middleton, P., *Review of Civil Justice and Legal Aid*, LCD, (1997).

Peters, B.G. and D.J. Savoie, (eds.), *Taking Stock: Assessing Public Sector Reforms*, (1998).

Oliver, D. and G. Drewry, *Public Service Reforms: Issues of Accountability and Public Law*, (1996).

Polden, P., *Guide to the Records of the Lord Chancellor's Department*, HMSO, (1988).

Jackson, R.M., *The Machinery of Justice in England*, 7th edn., Cambridge University Press, (1977), p. 583.

Pollitt, C. *Managerialism and The Public Services*, 2nd edition, (1993).

Pollitt, C. and G. Boukaert, *Public Management Reforms: A Comparative Analysis*, (2000).

Rhodes, R.A.W., 'New Labour's Civil Service: Summing-up Joining-up', in: *Political Quarterly*, 71(2), (2000), pp. 151-166.
Robson, W.A., *Justice and Administrative Law*, 3rd edn., London: Stevens, (1951), pp. 43-44.
Schmidhauser, John R., 'Alternative Conceptual Frameworks in Comparative Cross-National Legal and Judicial Research', in: Schmidhauser, (ed.), *Comparative Judicial Systems*, Butterworths, (1987).
Shetreet, S., *Judges on Trial*, Amsterdam: North Holland, (1976), pp. 17-19.
Stevens, R., *The Independence of the Judiciary: The View from the Lord Chancellor's Office*, Oxford: Clarendon Press, (1993), chapter 2.
Viscount Birkenhead, *Points of View*, vol. 1, London: Hodder and Stoughton, (1922), chapter 4.
Zander, M., 'The Government's Plans on Civil Justice', in: *Modern Law Review*, 61(3), 1998, pp. 382-389.
Zifcak, S., *New Managerialism: Administrative Reform in Whitehall and Canberra*, (1994).

Reinventing the Least Dangerous Branch of Government:

Judicial Independence and the Accountability for the Administration of Justice, Courts and Judges in the Netherlands

Philip M. Langbroek[1]

1 Introduction

The Dutch courts and judges are currently involved in a process of transformation. This transformation process relates to national and international developments. Those developments are, among other things, population growth, the internationalization of business and trade, the extension of technical means of communication, the increase in the transparency of jurisprudence, the media taking an increasing interest in the courts and spectacular cases, and the increase in organized crime. Cases brought before the courts not only increase in number, but, on the whole, they are increasing in legal complexity as well. These developments not only cause problems for the Dutch courts, but for the Dutch Government as well. What can be done in order to enable the courts to meet changing societal circumstances?

A complicating factor is that relations between politicians and the courts and judges are somewhat disturbed. Dutch politicians do criticize the courts and the magistracy. Politicians feel that the implementation of legal rules in a case brought before the courts does not, most of the time, solve the problem at hand. They feel that this is especially so when a court nullifies important governmental decisions. For example, courts have overturned decisions to close 'coffee-shops' by a mayor. 'Coffee-shops' are coffee-houses where hashish or marihuana may be sold in small amounts. They are illegal from the point of view of penal law, but are tolerated by the Public Prosecutors Office if they meet certain conditions. However, the customers of tolerated coffee-shops sometimes cause trouble in their neighbourhood, and for the mayor of the city this may be an occasion to close them down. So, it is not the violation of penal law but the disturbance of the peace which may be the occasion for such administrative measures. If brought before them, the courts judge such decisions according to the general principles of proper administration.[2] This may lead to a nullification of the decision, and if so, the mayor will have to revise his decision. In

---

1 Institute of Constitution and Administrative law, Utrecht University, the Netherlands.
2 For a brief outline in English, see: Langbroek (1998).

the meantime, the coffee-shop is back in business. Several mayors have published their annoyance with the rulings of the courts in major articles in national newspapers, stating that judges do not understand the ins and outs of public policy making, thus suggesting the intellectual incapacity and inability of the courts.

This disturbance in the relations between the courts and politicians is accompanied by the fact that public investment is necessary in order to enable the courts to meet changing societal circumstances. In this situation, where politicians themselves decide on the funds for such investment, the politicians are tempted to extend public control over the judiciary, while the principle of separation of powers demands that politicians refrain from doing this.

This article concerns recent developments with regard to the Dutch judicial organization and aims to contribute to the development of standards for the relations between the executive and the judiciary within the boundaries of the continental notion of the rule of law, the '*rechtsstaat*'. To that end, I describe a rudimentary notion of the *rechtsstaat* and the position of judges and courts according to *rechtsstaat* theory. I will focus on the different positions of judges, courts, the legislature, the executive and their responsibilities. While doing so, I will give an overview of developments concerning judges and courts in the Netherlands. I conclude this contribution with some remarks on the consequences of the developing changes in the Dutch judicial organization from the point of view of judicial independence and the public accountability of courts and judges.

2 Judicial independence and the *rechtsstaat*: constitutional conditions

In the Dutch juridical tradition the word '*rechtsstaat*' has a somewhat vague meaning, used in political and juridical debates to indicate the existence of legal limitations of state power, according to one's own views. However, more can be said about *rechtsstaat* than the phrase that government should abide by the law. The idea of the *rechtsstaat* concerns the freedom of the citizens from the state. It contains an organizational theory about the design of the state: the separation of powers. The idea of separation of powers was generated in the century of the English Civil War, and was combined with the position of Parliament in regard to the position of the King. Eventually, this idea was laid down in a Constitution in the Cromwell era.[3] In Germany, the concept of *rechtsstaat* was developed during the 19th century. This concept distinguishes between public and private spheres, the borderline being drawn by civil rights. The public/private distinction is combined with the organizational concept of separation of powers.[4] The idea of *rechtsstaat* is not primarily concerned with democracy, but rather with legal certainty.[5]

---

3 Vile (1967).
4 Schmitt (1928, 126-130).
5 Kant (1966); Kägi (1937); Neumann (1980).

The *rechtsstaat* requires a constitution to distinguish between three different state functions: the legislative, the executive, and the judicial function. The legislative function is to establish laws. Laws are legal norms of a general nature. The executive function is to execute laws in more or less concrete cases. The judicial function is to settle litigation by implementing the law, including litigation by public organs and public bodies. These state functions are to be separated organizationally. The separated functions within the state should balance and check each other. The aim of this construction is to control state power and to maintain civil liberties. Hence, the demand for judicial independence has an instrumental aspect concerning the organization of the state, but it does not mean that the judicial system has no relations with other state powers.

Within the theory of the *rechtsstaat*, judicial independence refers to special relationships between the legislature and the judiciary, and between the executive and the judiciary. In the context of a constitution, the legislature has the power to lay down the institutional rules for a judicial organization, for the appointment of judges and possibly for the payment of judges. Furthermore, the legislature has the power to lay down legal rules of conduct of a general nature, e.g. the acts containing procedural law or contract law. The executive and the judiciary have the task of implementing these general rules in concrete cases. Apart from judging conflicts between citizens,[6] the judiciary has the task to judge conflicts between citizens and executive state organs. Therefore, courts and judges should be independent from executive state organs. In the same way, the independence of courts and judges means that they should have nothing to do with citizens whose cases they decide. So, the demand for judicial independence refers to the absence of influence by executive state organs on judicial activities, and it refers to the impartiality of judges as well. Impartiality has two meanings. First, the absence of any relation between a judge and the parties in a lawsuit; second, the absence of any interest of a judge or a court in any outcome of any court-proceedings. The activity of judging must be done disinterestedly.

In Western Europe, the separation between legislative organs and the executive is a weak one. Most of the general rules are established by executive organs, their competence being founded on provisions of delegation in Acts of Parliament. Parliament and government (the cabinet) together form the legislative organ, while Parliament controls the government in its policy-making and executive functions. Government formally needs the confidence of parliament.[7]

The budgets for the departments of government are set by Acts of Parliament but the proposals for these Acts are usually made by the responsible department (the minister and the supporting staff of the departments in question). In most countries the government fulfils its functions supported by a clear parliamentary majority, mostly consisting of a coalition of different political parties, based on an agreement contain-

6 This concept of 'citizen' comprises private organizations.

7 Other remarks could be made on differences of checks and balances between parliamentary systems in unitary states and parliamentary systems in federal states. I abstain from this, however, because it diverts too much from the subject of this article, which focuses on judicial independence.

ing a political programme. Members of parliament belonging to a coalition party, cannot be too critical of the cabinet their parliamentary section supports. Therefore, the checks and balances between parliament and the executive are in effect relatively weak. In this context, the judiciary functions as an important counterweight against the dominant executive. The independence of the judiciary from the executive is an essential guarantee for the freedom of citizens from the state. But this does not mean that there should not be any relationships between courts and judges and their outside world.

Judges cannot work strictly on their own and cannot be isolated socially as if they were superhuman, black boxes of legal wisdom. They need a building, a room and a desk, if possible with a computer. Judges need legal literature, so a court needs a library and someone to organize it. Judges have to be paid. Someone has to take care of the judges' chambers, the courthouse, etc. In modern courts, hundreds or even thousands of cases are dealt with annually. So coordination of judicial activities is necessary, and the help of supportive services is presumably a prerequisite for judges to do their job properly. Hence, managerial arrangements are inevitable. Still, these arrangements are to be made in such a manner that judges can concentrate on the cases brought before them.

3 Responsibility for the courts and the judiciary: conditions in statute law and organizational arrangements

Judicial independence and judicial impartiality are only *negative* guarantees. If they are fulfilled, still nothing happens. Justice still has to be done. So, what preconditions should be met in order to make the counterweight-function of the judiciary work?

According to the Dutch Constitution (*de Grondwet*), the legislature must implement an act on the judicial organization. Judges are appointed to a court by the Crown (in fact: the Minister of Justice). The salaries of judges are arranged by an Act of Parliament, in this respect their position is unique compared to the position of ordinary civil servants. The Judicial Organization Act does mention the Chief Justice, but it does not mention the supportive services of the courts, apart from the functions of the court registrar (the managing director) and the courts' secretaries. These supportive services are institutionalized by official decisions of the Department of Justice only. They function as field organizations of the justice department. The Minister of Justice has complete political accountability for those civil services. So, in Dutch courts, judges work close together with public services for whom full political responsibility applies.

3.1 Responsibilities of judges in Dutch courts; legal arrangements

Every court has a Chief Justice, and every court has an assembly of judges. The assembly of judges decides once or twice a year on the way cases are distributed amongst the chambers of a court, and which judges will be appointed to which chambers of the court. The assembly of judges is not based on the Judicial Organization Act, but is largely a consequence of judicial independence and the professional autonomy of judges.[8] Furthermore, judges are responsible for the legal proceedings appointed to them, and for the decisions in those cases. From a strictly legal point of view, the tasks of judges are restricted to court sessions and preparing judgements.

The legal arrangements for the organization of justice are insufficient from the point of view of actual practices in the courts. The origin of those arrangements goes back to the 19th century, when the volume of the modern case-load was unheard of. Mass production calls for management, even if each product has to be made separately. So, the justice department has arranged for management within the courts. Special contracts have been arranged between the courts, the justice department and its court-supporting field organizations. According to these contracts courts are ruled by a system called 'integral management', referring to management by ordinary civil servants and judges together. So, without any basis in statute law, the management boards of the courts function, presided over by Chief Justices, with some judges as members and the court registrars as the managing directors. At the moment, the justice department has full financial and organizational responsibility for the courts.

This is the actual paradox of judicial independence in the Netherlands: Parliament and Government are closely interwoven, so judicial independence is a necessity in order to counterbalance the executive. Nevertheless, the judiciary depends on the legislature for its financial funds, for procedural law, and for its formal organization, but for its supportive services it depends on the executive, the department of justice, as well.[9]

Although they are quite practicable, in my opinion these arrangements do not comply with modern demands of judicial independence. The ways in which the courts are financed, for example, might influence the ways in which litigation or even penal cases are dealt with. Of course, the idea of the professional autonomy judges have internalized is some safeguard against arbitrariness, but they are not in full control. Decisions on how different cases are to be dealt with are – as a matter of principle – judicial decisions. When seen as a managerial decision only, the manager should be a judge. This is a problem, because many judges do not see themselves as managers, but as autonomous juridical professionals. In fact, their idea of independence goes back to the situation where justice could be done without more or less complex organizational support. This is not the actual situation in the Dutch courts. Social, political and technical changes demand that judges – in order to gain and maintain organizational independence – take organizational responsibilities away from the political domain of the civil service and to bring them within the domain of the courts. Strictly speaking, this implies a change in the legal meaning of the word 'court'. The word 'court' originally refers to judges and their judicial activities only. In the modern context however, the word 'court' refers to the court supporting services as well. I believe that judges do not have any real choice. Their choice is either to accept the

8 The Minister of Justice has ordered regulations concerning the internal organization of the courts.
9 In Germany the same model for the court supporting services applies. See Rohl (1993, 137).

necessary changes or to be driven to the margins of the state. Citizens will try to find other ways to resolve their conflicts if the courts do not change their ways (e.g. arbitration, mediation).

Of course, it is the responsibility of the legislature to make the institutional arrangements that allow judges to take organizational responsibilities. But changing the Judicial Organization Act does not automatically mean a change in the professional attitudes of judges.

According to Shapiro, the common fear among judges in different cultures is the fear of revenge on the part of the party judged against.[10] This, in part, might explain the reluctance of many judges to accept organizational duties. From the point of view of judges' traditional professional attitudes, a change of culture is necessary.

This poses two major problems for the judiciary in the Netherlands:

- How to change the professional attitudes of judges, and
- If the organizational autonomy of courts and the judicial organization would increase, how can they be held accountable for the things they do or do not do?

3.2 Changing professional attitudes

It is not possible to change professional attitudes if the professionals are reluctant to accept those changes. It is very difficult to use changes in attitudes of professionals in an instrumental way.[11] Within any institution or organization, in order to change attitudes some of the professionals should have an idea of what needs to be changed. Even then, to try to evoke organizational change is to take the risk that – if the attempt fails – a powerless and cynical organization remains. To try several strategies for change and to start all over again on many occasions asks a great deal of any organization. Nevertheless, a few years ago the Dutch judicature made a successful start on the way to changing traditional concepts and attitudes.

A few years ago, some judges took the initiative to start a strategic programme for change, 'On the future of the magistracy'. About 20% of the judges took part in this programme. It resulted in recommendations and good intentions for the ways the judicial organization could be rearranged, for the working relations between judges and the people in their supportive services, for the ways courts organize judicial proceedings, for improving the quality of court services, for attuning judgements in similar cases to each other, for introducing up to date programmes for information technology, all in order to meet modern standards. The main institutional recommendation in this respect was to establish a National Council for the Administration of Juctice,[12] meant to buffer the tensions between the political and the judicial domain. This Council would be the management board for the courts. On the one hand, it

---

10 Shapiro (1981).

11 Vennix (1996).

12 'Administration of Justice' is an inadequate term here. The Dutch term is: '*Raad voor de Rechtspraak*'. '*Rechtspraak*' refers to three different items: the activities of courts and judges (generating judgments); the courts and the judges as a societal entity; and the formal judicial organization as a whole. The said Council is supposed to deal with all three aspects from an organizational perspective.

would be the visible head of the courts, it would speak for them in public and negotiate concerning funds for the courts with the justice department and possibly Parliament. On the other hand, it would also supervise and help the courts to function as professional organizations.[13] Projects to elaborate and implement those plans were prepared. So, the attempt for change in the Dutch judicial organization has so far been quite successful.

In the meantime, the Minister of Justice installed a committee of specialists to give advice on the modern organizational and practical needs of a judicial organization. This committee developed an elaborate model of a judicial organization, including a Council for the Administration of Justice, but with more elaborate strategic competence than the judges themselves had agreed upon.[14] The Government adopted most of those recommendations, and developed - coordinated with the programme for court improvement - a programme for modernizing the courts, up to the year 2003.[15]

The public debate concerning these outcomes has focussed on the ways judicial independence may be preserved when a National Council - even if it is part of the judicature and even if it consists mainly of judges - supervises the courts.[16] Two issues are at stake here:

- How are courts to be held accountable for the ways they spend their funds, while preserving their independence?
- What would be the role of such a Council concerning the development of judicial policies?

3.3 Changing judicial accountability

Many politicians are willing to generate funds for modernizing the courts, but demand some kind of control in return. Therefore, some kind of accountability for the courts is necessary, although the demand for judicial independence is recognized. As far as the management of the courts is concerned, the Minister of Justice will be empowered to give orders of a general nature to the Council of the Administration of Justice. The Council of the Administration of Justice will be empowered to give orders of a general nature to the management boards of the courts. The Council will be empowered to remove incompetent members of the management board of a court. At this moment it is not certain if this competence will be given and regulated in a new Judicial Organization Act. Some authors fear that the Minister of Justice will give such orders if social and political upheaval result from a courts' judgement. I agree. In case of societal or political strain a minister usually wants to show some - at least symbolically meaningful - action. On the other hand, however, I think it is inevitable that a public organization like a court is held accountable for what it does. How can accountability for the courts be combined with judicial independence?

---

13 Koers, Langbroek, Vennix, Austen (1997).

14 Adviescommissie toerusting en organisatie zittende magistratuur, Rechtspraak bij de tijd, The Hague 1998.

15 Rechtspraak in de 21^{e} eeuw, Contourennota modernisering rechterlijke organisatie, The Hague 1998.

16 Bovend'Eert (1996); Brenninkmeijer (1998).

3.4 Political and public accountability

It might help to distinguish between political accountability for the courts and public accountability for the courts. Public accountability for the courts is to inspire confidence in judges and the courts (and thus to support judicial authority) and in a maintained level of quality of the court organization by making publicly known how those organizations fulfil their public tasks. Political accountability for the courts refers to the traditional legal lines of command and control from the political centre. Political authorities may be held responsible by a representative body. Questions asked about political responsibilities have to be answered in public, and if a parliamentary majority feels the answers are insufficient, then the political authorities can be forced to resign from public office. Political responsibility is the formal coping-stone of a system designed to maintain the democratic legitimacy of government and its supporting services. In other words: political accountability implies public accountability. Public accountability of elected, political authorities serves the realization of political accountability.

The same holds true for the political accountability for the courts. As a property of the independence of the judiciary, political accountability for the courts is restricted to the organizational conditions for an efficient and effective administration of justice.

There are three differences between political accountability for the courts and public accountability for the courts as far as far as the courts are concerned:

- Public accountability refers to organizational preconditions for the judicature and to judgements given; political accountability refers to the organizational preconditions only.
- Public accountability for the courts does not amount to accounting for one's acts in front of an elected, representative body.
- Therefore, public accountability for judgements cannot result in political authorities or an elected, representative body, enforcing judicial authorities to resign.

From the point of view of the distinction between public accountability and political accountability it seems justified to hold a Council for the Administration of Justice accountable according to the centralizing tendencies of political accountability. The courts may be held publicly accountable. The question is how the position of a Council for the Administration of Justice can influence the courts in the line of political accountability. This question may not be answered without considering the responsibilities of the legislature for the courts and the responsibilities of the courts for themselves.

It is the task of the legislature to regulate the institutional arrangements for the courts: how they are organized, the way members of the management board are to be appointed, the competence of the management board, the way judges and supporting services fit into the court's organization, etc. It is also the task of the legislature to regulate the different procedures before a court of law.[17]

The courts are responsible for the way their organizations comply with the demands of their social and professional surroundings. They organize the ways in which litigation, administrative appeals and penal cases are to be dealt with within legal boundaries. But they also deliver judgements in the cases brought before them. If a party does not agree, it is possible to appeal to a higher court. So, the courts are responsible for the development of the law. And it is their task to ensure legal certainty while doing so. This is one of the reasons for the demand of the *rechtsstaat* that courts and judges be independent and impartial. Therefore, it may not be the task of a Council for the Administration of Justice to influence the development of the law. It should limit itself to the organizational conditions of the courts. The Council may divide funds amongst the courts according to an Act of Parliament, facilitate activities the courts think necessary, e.g. training courses, quality management, provide an intranet for the courts, manage databases with jurisprudence, take care for public relations, etc. From the point of view of judicial independence, I consider a borderline case to be the concept of controlling the managerial qualities of Chief Justices by giving the Council the competence to remove a Chief Justice from a courts' management board (while remaining a court judge). Since, at the moment, management skills are not a judicial stronghold, some control and support seems necessary. In time, however, judges will learn the skills of management, therefore it would be wise to limit the controlling competence of the Council to a term of, for example, ten years. But even without such specific competence, supervision of the courts concerning the ways in which they deal with their public accountability is acceptable. In this respect the Council may be given the necessary competence to give orders to a court organization.

3.5 Effectuating public accountability for the courts

Changes as discussed above will be useless if courts remain the inwardly-oriented professional organizations they used to be. The public accountability for the courts rests, first of all, with the courts themselves. Effecting public accountability for the courts, by the courts, is necessary to generate legitimacy with regard to the courts and their judgements. This means that courts should do a lot more than only dealing with cases and delivering judgements. They have a societal environment to cope with, and, in my opinion, quality management is a key to that end.

In order to support the authority of jurisprudence, supplemental demands may be made on judges and the courts. These demands concern:

- checks against judicial rulings; the comments on court rulings by professional lawyers and legal science;
- the skills and training of judges;

17 In the USA, this is different. There, the Supreme Court makes the rules for the proceedings. See Röhl (1993, 44-46).

- the powers of courts to guide procedures from intake up to and including delivery of the judgment;
- the time it takes to organize hearings and to pronounce judgement;
- the public nature, especially the accessibility of court proceedings;
- the public nature and accessibility of court rulings;
- public relations (journalists, instruction of the public);
- readiness to accept and to answer complaints;
- contact with the bar;
- internal quality controls.

The most important aspects are:

3.5.1 Checks and balances

Checks on courts exist in two forms: those directed against the consequences of judgements in individual cases and those directed against the consequences of a judgement for society as a whole. The natural check on a judgement for an interested party is to appeal to a higher court.

The competence to correct judgements, undesirable from a political point of view, belongs to the legislature. Tax laws, for instance, are changed regularly, because of rulings by the tax section of the Dutch Supreme Court. The law develops because contesting parties seek judgement in a court of law. Scholars comment on the judgement and it may be, or may be not, that adjustments are made in similar cases. Editors of legal journals have an important function in checking the juridical quality of judgements. Thus, for every societal field a body of juridical knowledge exists, and develops.[18]

What should not be done is to make it possible to sue a court or a judge for damages if a court ruling was to be overruled by a higher court.[19] Some immunity on the part of the courts is desirable, because judges should feel free to make contributions to the development of the law.[20]

Another natural check on court rulings are the public comments by the profession, be it judges, the bar or academic lawyers. This might convince a court to change rulings in similar cases. Those comments contribute to the development of the law.

Furthermore, in the Netherlands the Chief Justices of some courts and the coordinating judges of several court sections (administrative law, penal law, family law) meet several times a year to discuss legal developments and to attune proceedings and judgements as to juridical technical matters. For example, the concept of 'interested party', a prerequisite for any appellant to have his case judged on the merits of its content in an administrative court, may be slightly adjusted in rulings after a meeting of judges has taken place. Of course, they do not have the competence to make decisions their colleagues have to comply with, but it is an aid to a stable development of

18 See Cardozo (1924); Cardozo (1921).
19 Olowofoyeku (1933).
20 See Mincke (1999, 65-75).

the law, and thus for maintaining legal certainty. For most judges, to abide by the outcomes of those meetings is a matter of good-fellowship.

3.5.2 Management skills

Judges are highly trained legal professionals. The law is their business. From the point of view of the organization of a court, more has to be done than to hold hearings and to write and deliver judgements. There are court servants who need guidance, courts need their own public relations, guidelines for the bar have to be developed, new judges should be educated, and so on. In order to fulfil their societal functions judges should be trained in order to be able to do so.

3.5.3 Public relations

Courts are paid for out of public funds. Court hearings and court rulings are public events. It could be wise to instruct reporters in some aspects of the cases they are interested in. This is not to engage in public debate concerning a court ruling, but to help the realization of the public function of the court. Even here, limits have to be set, e.g. when may a camera be allowed in a courtroom? Since judgements are delivered in public, it seems only normal that judgements can be obtained at the courts. Modern techniques make it possible to publish judgements on a courts' internet site. Another thing to be done by every court is to publish annual reports on developments in jurisprudence by the court and within their organization. The idea is that courts seek ways to show the public what, how and why they are doing what they do.

3.5.4 Complaints

Nowadays, Dutch courts do not have an elaborated legal system to handle complaints. A court is a professional, service-providing organization. Mistakes are sometimes made, and an organized way of dealing with complaints may be an organizational aid in order to learn from clients what has gone wrong.

3.5.5 Quality management

The independence and professional autonomy of judges make it difficult for them to accept criticism as to the way they do their job. Nevertheless, it is important that everybody in a court is able to learn how certain ways of doing things may be improved. Next to external checks on the activities of judges and the courts, it is possible to organize internal checks. A colleague could observe a judge in a courtroom, and inform him or her what has been seen. Some judgements may be discussed by a team of colleagues. It would even be possible to organize visits to a court by another court, in order to evaluate court performance.

In a word, the public accountability of the courts may be effectuated by showing the public what, how and why courts and judges do as they do, and by showing what they do to improve their organization, their services and their products. The idea behind this is known as 'quality management'. And quality management can help the courts to increase their organizational independence. At the same time it may help to sustain the public legitimacy of the courts.[21]

All in all, Dutch courts are improving their functioning mainly in the legal aspects. But a lot of work still has to be done on the organizational side.

3.5.6 New risks?

The courts' business is to implement the law in conflicts of interest, and in penal procedures brought before them. These judicial activities must be done independently, impartially and disinterestedly. An increased autonomy for the courts combined with efforts to effectuate the public accountability of the courts will probably enhance the independence and the public legitimacy of the courts. But, as courts start functioning as professional service organizations, what happens to the autonomy of individual judges? Some judges want to make a career within the judicial organization. For them, it might be difficult to conform to the organizational values of their court (efficiency!) and to take an independent stand concerning the explanation of the law at the same time. In modern courts, judicial independence will be a matter of judicial mentality. The relations between judges and their organization will be under some strain. Judges will have to cope with this strain, but they should not be left alone; it will also be the task of the court management to provide judges with real freedom to judge a case according to the law and according to their conscience.

4 Concluding remarks

In this article, I have discussed the inevitable changes for the judiciary in the Netherlands. I have written about those changes from the point of view of the *rechtsstaat* and the demand that judges must be independent and impartial. Changes in the Dutch judicial organization are developing. As a consequence, the debate on the ways guarantees demanded by the *rechtsstaat* and the constitution are made operative, shifts from the legal to the organizational domain. The shift in the subject in this debate goes hand in hand with a shift in participants: from lawyers to the organizational professionals. Hence the subject of this conference for scientists in the field of Public Administration. Nonetheless, it is important to notice that the inevitable changes in the judicial organization presumably enable courts to meet new societal challenges, but they do not solve the problems of judicial independence and impartiality. Judges and courts will have interests of their own to cope with. I do not think it would be wise to try to regulate the disinterestedness of judges and courts imperatively on this point, however. Courts and judges should be left free to solve this problem, but it remains the tasks of the legislature, lawyers, scientists and the media to watch and evaluate the doings of the courts, and to make the results known to the public. Furthermore, the public accountability of the courts obliges them to give these public actors full coope-

21 I developed this idea in: Langbroek (1994, 404-413); Shetreet (1976), was a source of inspiration.

ration in fulfilling these public duties. In a modern *rechtsstaat* the checks and balances in and around the courts are, by all modern means of communication, a public matter.

References

Bovend'Eert, P.P.T., 'De rechterlijke organisatie, een nieuwe buitendienst van het ministerie van justitie', in: *NJB*, no. 18, (1996).

Brenninkmeijer, A.F.M., 'Rechtspraak bij de tijd; bespreking van het rapport van de commissie Leemhuis', in: *NJB,* no. 9, (1998).

Cardozo, B.N., *The nature of the judicial process*, Clinton, (1921).

Cardozo, B.N., *The growth of the law*, New Haven, (1924).

Kägi, O.W., *Zur Entstehung, Wandlung und Problematik des Gewaltenteilungsprinzipes*, Zürich, (1937).

Kant, I., 'Anfangsgründe der Rechtslehre', in: *Die Metafysik der sitten*, orig. 1796, Hamburg, (1966).

Koers, A.W., Ph. Langbroek, J.A.M. Vennix, J.M.M. Austen, *De ZM op weg*, Utrecht, (1997).

Langbroek, P.M., 'De publieke verantwoordelijkheid voor rechtspraak', in: *Tijdschrift voor de rechterlijke macht,* (1994), p. 404-413.

Langbroek, P.M., 'General Principles of Proper Administration in Dutch administrative law', in: B. Hessel, P. Hofmanski, (eds.), *Government Policy and Rule of Law*, Bialystok/Utrecht, (1998).

Mincke, G.W., 'Haftung für richterliches Handeln in Deutschland', in: A.W. Jongbloed, (ed.), *Aansprakelijkheid voor optreden door de rechterlijke macht*, The Hague, (1999), p. 65-75.

Neumann, F.L., *Die Herrschaft des Geseztes*, orig. 1936, Frankfurt am Main, (1980).

Olowofoyeku,. A., *Suing Judges, A Study of Judicial Immunity*, Oxford, (1993).

Osborne, D., T. Goebler, *Reinventing government: How the entrepeneurial spirit is transforming the public sector*, Reading: Addison Wesley, (1992).

Röhl, K.F., *Gerichtsverwaltung und Court Management in den USA*, Cologne, (19-93), p. 44-46, p. 137.

Schmitt, C., *Verfassungslehre*, Berlin, (1928), p. 126-130.

Shapiro, M., *Courts*, Chicago, (1981).

Shetreet, S., *Judges on Trial, A Study on the Appointment and Accountability of the English Judiciary*, New York, (1976).

Vennix, J.A.M., *Group Model Building: Facilitating Team Learning Using Systems Dynamics*, Chichester, (1996).

Vile, J.C., *Constitutionalism and the Separation of Powers*, Oxford, (1967).

The Challenge of Change for Judicial Systems
M. Fabri and Ph.M. Langbroek (Eds.)
IOS Press, 2000

Aspects of the Public Justice System in Greece

George O. Tsobanoglou[1]

1 Introduction

I will attempt to present my research on the nature of the Greek public policy field using a genealogical approach to the formation of the State and civil society, the nature of the rule of law and its status in Greece, the conflict between law and society and how this accounts for the present conditions under which justice is administered. The article outlines some of the main genealogical characteristics of the socio-administrative State regime in Europe in order to place the Greek juridical system in its proper perspective and thus to provide an interpretation of essential aspects of the public justice system in Greece.

An analysis of the present-day juridico-administrative system in Greece is a lonely task for social scientists waiting to be thoroughly investigated in the years to come. In this endeavour only a modest attempt can be made and this from an Anglo-American perspective that focuses upon welfare issues. The very fact that justice administrations provide a service for citizens and that the social body participates in this exercise also renders public administration accountable to itself (the citizenry). It is well known how rights and functions relate to the proper administration of justice. Criminology as early social governance still bears this mark as it defines the relations of the state with society.

In Grcccc itself the turbulent post-WW II social history, still awaiting full and calm accountability, has to this day left many issues that one may readily call as 'post-traumatic stress disorder', to borrow the concept from the field of psychiatry. Civil conflict and wars leave many scars and delay institution building. To a degree, the provision of justice and civil protection are the very first that must be put in place. The case of Greece and recent evidence as presented in this report indicate that in the process of social development the country has been experiencing over the past few decades, the main emphasis has been on building up the physical environment, the core infrastructure, while the other measures which may be reffered to as the soft infrastructure, the quality of services, still has a way to go.

Another issue concerns to the proverbial Greek legal formalism that is far removed from social reality. The changing international environment and the increased accountability increasingly demanded of national governments will be the main reference for the future appreciation of legal and society issues in the country.

---

1 Institute for Social Development, Athens, Greece.

2 Background

2.1 *The consequences of the development of civil law and social action. Conditions for administrative reform: a macro-perspective*

In Greece, the conflict between society (*Gesellschaft*) and the legal order (*Verfassung*) has since the Second World War involved an exceptionally undemocratic legal regime embedded within a quasi-militarised 'administrative power'. In a way it resembled the old Continental 'welfare police' of the eighteenth century (Knemeyer, 1983). This administrative grounding was a result of the post-war authoritarian regime's alienation from the common people. When the other post-war European States were building social citizenship systems, placing emphasis on the development of social support professions that started to gain public ground within the professions of the public sector, Greece was not following this trend. Quite the opposite was happening (Tsobanoglou, 1992). For this reason, the hydrocephalic nature of the military apparatus of the state has created an overgrowth and an imbalance, which clearly left outside it both mechanisms for *civil rights protection and the community outside the sheltered politically correct 'public sector'* (Tsobanoglou, 1992). Since law is historically relatively multi-faceted, there is a curious resemblance between administrative regimes within many post-Second World War peripheral states and the welfare administration of the Cameralist German States and their Police Science (*Polizeiwissenschaft*) during the eighteenth century (Tsobanoglou, 1993). It seems that the State in those cases could not confront law as a separate entity but it has had to subvert it within such extra-juridical categories as the Nation (Ethnos), the phylogenetic aspect of nationhood (Phyle denotes race in Greek), etc. Given the atavist nature of the dominant Greek cultural mode in both Greece itself and abroad, one can see how simple the regression to a pre-modern legal state can be. If one adds the legacy of Byzantium and its legal codes, one can see some of the intricate mechanisms in favour of the apologetics of such a regime.

Laws, in order to be administered in daily practice, require a bona fide understanding that as a type of voluntary action it is in line with the spirit and the moral principles of the community. The state, by the admission of the rule of written law, recognises the right of the members of the social body to interact and associate freely. Its role is to side-step in order to regulate whenever such agreements are not respected. One must note that the presence of civil rule and national determination is incomplete if they exist out of context, as in cases that are introduced from without rather than from within. Such determinations are exemplary in Greece's turbulent history from the time when the Bavarian Monarchy established elements of Cameralism in Greece to the pre and post-WW II British and American interest in Greek public affairs (Baerentzen et al., 1987).

In Greek affairs, the socio-administrative situation has been characterised by the popular incapacity of the state apparatus to admit certain conditions for social action, i.e. popular democratic entry into politics. The establishment from above of certain conditions for legal rule, as inscribed by the constitutional and other civil systems, does not necessarily allow for the establishment of the rule of law in practice. To begin with, administrative law in the country has been inadequately socially developed, protected in its daily function by laws of 'secrecy' which inevitably cloud their 'service' character. Similarly, citizens' participation is obfuscated and unrecognised.

The State under the rule of law (*Rechtsstaat*) has historically established the legal autonomy of the society of citizens from the old welfare state. Social regimes, as post-*Rechtsstaat* regimes attest, normally emanate from a regime of social administration in which it is the Law that has to accommodate Society. The accommodation of the juridical order (*Verfassung*) with regard to *Gesellschaft* brings about a system of regulation based upon participation. The lack of such socio-legal institutional accommodation leaves empty the organisational space, which is filled by personal links and kinship ties. This represents a minimum for political integration which is necessary for legitimacy to be maintained within the civil state (patron-client system). Greece in practice has a very weak link between the juridical and the social orders. *It is for this reason that atypical structures of political patronage fill in the void.*

The real face of such a civil state emerges when we begin to look upon the principal modality of the type of labour outside the administration and within the community. The type of labour of the pre-liberal *Gemeinschaft* (society) is that of informal labour. The politico-legal concerns of the State under the rule of law (*Rechtsstaat*) which were superseded by the Liberal Revolution, the Reformation and the Napoleonic Wars, required a new transformation to deal with the *problem of society as a new field subject to state administration.* The main contradiction between labour and the owners of capital was transformed by new reforms that were aimed at the constitution of labour as an 'economic' subject. Labour became the 'consumer' of the products and to this end 'consumption' and the party system enter the equation as regimes implying systems for the integration of private life and the political sphere, respectively. The functioning of the State under the rule of law, was primarily based upon the capacity of the forces of the market (it could be both a political - corresponding to the needs of a nomenclature - and an economic one) to fashion order and social development. The role of the State pertains to that of a civil, as opposed to a military, practice aiming at the maintenance of law and order under a regime centering around the rehabilitation of the marginal, the minorities, the paupers. *Criminology was a new field, the new body of knowledge (gnosis) signalling the constitution of administrative reform away from Cameralist politics and towards a system of social defence that was aiming at the abolition of deadly ostracism and censorship*. By comparison, Greece to this day has failed to develop criminology as an important early social science that would control the conflicts between rights and functions among the social actors, the new social administration, social protection and the citizen.

Liberalism was governed by natural law according to which the measure of government was indicative of the degree of liberty. However, this was the government of the private households, of the private families that required only a partial intervention by the penal department. The form of the police was per se limited only to areas of common law crime since it was unclear as to its broader definition. The collapse of this 'naturalist' model and the subsequent emergence of a 'historical' model in law and in the form of the discipline of sociology proposed a bifurcated trajectory for the epigones of the *Rechtsstaat*. *A positive solution required the formation of a new 'government', a social government, ready to police not single families but a collective order defined as 'population'*. Therefore, the state was in principle to encompass all of 'society', thus making its own separate laws the subject of a new intelligibility, subject to a new type of administration based upon the active social reproduction of labour.

The main crux of this law has been labour law, thus establishing the specific regulatory capacity of an expanded state-form whose aim was the regulation of politico-administrative conflicts. The state gives shape to the laws of a labouring population and develops its actions by the instrumentality of a science of society. Various shades of corporatism are expressions of this development. The state, in either its liberal or social-democratic forms, has been the grid issuing either the order of *the economy (oeconomia) of the families, or the order of population.* Varieties of states from the feudal past may help us define conditions and typologies of corporatist developments within the regions of Europe that have not developed the system of liberal rule. The state predating agrarian capitalism was not at the time the place of a discursive practice regarding the 'government' of either the 'public' or 'private' spheres, as recent debates appear to refer. In fact, the first sound system of 'governance' was that of the liberal *Rechtsstaat*.

The modern conflict within the developing *Rechtsstaat* in peripheral transitional states, understood as the one between law and society, might have, as is quite often the case, a negative side, entailing a return to the old continental 'welfare police', the *Wohlfahrtstaat*, with the addition of armour (the dictatorships in the South of Europe). It appears that the borders of the 'administration' between its civil and military sectors are rather thin and may be easily crossed when the conjuncture dictates reasons for the preservation or restoration of order. The old welfare police state always remains in a state of conflict by virtue of its 'nature' and structure with the impeding *Rechtsstaat*, that attempts to free labour and to establish the law and labour contract across the realm, in order to develop a process of democratisation (*democratisierung*).

The social state (*Sozialstaat*) allowed the regulation of the 'marginal', the poor and the other disinherited, as a precondition for the security requirements for the 'freeing' of labour, i.e. of its voluntarist aspect. Early liberalism was to be reinforced during the 1930s with the emergence of unique ensembles of state regulatory mechanisms for the control and reproduction of labour conditions. *The regulation of the working conditions for the reproduction of labour by no means undermined the voluntary nature of the offer of labour. Action was always the result of 'free-consent'*.

The post-war Greek State represents a curious amalgam of a peripheral pre-liberal political form whose paternalistic and 'clientelist' politics represent an interesting example of historic backwardness concerning law and society. *Legislation is enacted but its application is practically blocked.* Similarly, all kinds of legislation including that, which involves issues of health and safety, the physical integrity of citizens, remains not in force as it is considered a foreign legal transplant.

3 Approaches to the Greek civil society

The relationships between states and their citizenry are not, as a general measure of understanding, uniform or even homogenous. Political history, the historical continuity and discontinuity of the national democratic forms, the established notions of social protection and the modalities of social 'welfare', with their associated notions of social citizenship, all constitute and subsequently define the methodologies with which we may measure the relationship between the citizen and the administration in a national and subsequently supranational territory. The design of a certain methodology which will allow evidence to be established for the hidden reality, which is in effect a citizenry without an effective socio-economic representation, as is the case in many national situations, is as important as it is necessary. This methodology will have to be produced in each case bringing in elements of a national quality to the general development of modern international social science. In our case elements of a national sociology of the Greek state and society will have to be produced and communicated so as to be able to take account of the position of the citizens and the quality of their national and local administration.

Although it is generally considered that Greek legal culture is rather polyphonic (the number of lawyers in the country is calculated to reach 30,000 by the turn of the century), being influenced by strong Napoleonic institutions and a German administrative tradition, post-war Greece did not develop those post-war European welfare institutions and the associated social administration, local government, unemployment benefits, a general system of labour regulation with associated labour market institutions and a national health and pension system. The legislative workload during the past 20 years is as follows: over 2,178 Laws have been enacted, about 14,248 presidential Decrees and some 17,638 Ministerial Decisions have been produced. From these, about 92 Laws have been related to public administration (Pagakis, 1998). The post-war years in Greece have been marked by extraordinary politico-administrative and socio-legal changes. Great gaps in basic human and political rights developed so that we can really begin to consider the Restoration of Democracy, July 1974, and EEC membership as landmark dates in the process of normalisation and democratisation of present-day Greece (Tsobanoglou, 1993a, 1993b; Alevisatos, 1986). It is therefore habitual practice among Greek politicians to compete as to their capacity to legislate as they view such action as the very epitomy of political practice.

In Greece when the rare issue of a conflict between a citizen and the administration arises, *the decisions of this Body of Controllers appear to be narrowly-defined legal interpretations that* might be out of context regarding the particular case in question as they refer to general legal protocols, that of course do not describe each case in detail. It is up to the professional to define the connection and to deliver an opinion. Most of the time, it depends largely on who the claimant is; the reference to the general directives lacks special effect in the world of practice, which modern administrative law would require. The abstract reference to law, lacking as it does the relevance to the case in question, leaves the citizen outside the protective measures of modern administrative law. The role of the auditor is usually interrogatory rather than mediatory. The body of controllers and auditors remains an instrument of the administration to control the administrative process. It is a characteristic of this process that it is being carried out in a formalised, legalistic way, that is outside citizens' rights and modern administrative practices. They usually carry out controls of a financial auditing nature, giving rise to corruption issues that remind one of the roles of the financial police in other countries.

4 Dealing with conflicts and how the courts manage or do not manage such affairs. The political plateau and the views of the judges

The regime of political patronage which is still the dominant relationship between the citizen and the administration is a regime of a moral nature, that is to say a regime that is based on a moral patronage economy (Arlacchi, 1983). *Under this regime, the very notion of employment is considered as part of the regime of such clientelist relations, which permeates all levels of access to public administration institutions.* In a very basic way, information is an issue for it is highly controlled and it is produced and disseminated by those in clientelist and professional control. The legal profession has traditionally opposed any information sharing with the administration. Their purpose has been to control basic information requirements of the population regarding socio-administrative issues such as social security, employment, and taxation. In the past attempts by the Greek administration to introduce systems of social control to the administration (1735/86 Law) were reduced to a state of inertia.

Social controls in society are realised by 'regulating' the occupational categories, the professional groups, and the general accounting infrastructure that defines basic incomes, taxation categories, and other professional groups. By licensing their activities and the basic control of the work qualifications they regulate social employment categories. In fact, the issue of professional mobility is very important in defining the process of work and political and social empowerment of the citizenry. *The lack of a comprehensive system of nationally registered occupations, with their subsequent skill and professional development requirements,* for example a very clear separation between mental and manual work, a clear process defined in terms of a pay scale, conditions of work, work remuneration and systems of evaluation and control pertinent to knowledge-based work indicate that social mobility is certainly not defined by the work process itself since this process is controlled politically by the clientelist system (Mavrogordatos, 1997).

When basic social and labour rights are practised, few aspects for citizens' with complaints may become regulated in an alternative way. However, in the Greek situation the main accountability issues regarding citizens and the administration are only just beginning to be taken into account. The anaemic regime that governs the national health system supports private interests in hospitals, which although they offer 10% of the total services they acquire over 40% of the public expenditure. This system is not a matter of contracting out, as commonly happens in the rest of Europe and America, but it is a politically-oriented distribution of public resources, by the political administration, to the benefit of certain private political interests. The issue of the pension funds is a similar case in point. Workers, farmers, merchants, the self-employed and employers funds in the Social Security Agency and the other Funds were until faily recently (1985) kept with State Banks with virtually no interest given. Today, the Banks charge practically no less than the general rate, the Funds are obliged to be deposited with the State Banks, and they usually have to be charged the normal usurious lending rates the Greek Banks charge. The pension funds are not able to manage their assets as they are governed by state banking rules and regulations.

While this is the case with the state institutions, the private institutions appear to act outside any formal control channels since the distance between the nominal and the formal under the law is distinct from the affective and the informal in practice. The legal regime is part of the public space, the space of the public citizens. Outside public organisations, informal and atypical forms abide, for there is very little support in social emergency cases for issues such as unemployment, social security and access to alternative means of dispute resolution. The absence of a recognised third sector also weakens the bargaining position of the citizens as the administration habitually turns simple procedural cases into litigation issues. From then on, it is money and time that determines the outcome. (There is no free legal aid as such which is akin to established services in other European legal environments.)

Constitutional Reform is currently an ongoing process in Greece including the relevant decrees that regulate the 'sensitive area of Justice Administration'. The President of the Highest Administrative Court in a speech to the Athens Bar (12/02/-2000, To VEMA, 14/02/2000, p. A15) expressed his eagerness to discuss proposals for reform provided the organisational structure of the Court and the interests of the profession are safeguarded. The setting in place of incentives for the 'quality careers of the administrative judges and the enlargement of the pool of qualified staff for the Council of State (Supreme Administrative Court) constitute the two parameters of the professional interest', according to the Judge with reference to the chronic congestion in the process of the distribution/administration of justice the President of the Supreme Court mentioned that the solution to this situation lies in: 1) the rational organisation of the courts so as not to have judges overworked and underworked, 2) the reform of the education of lawyers and the way in which they practice so as not to use court proceedings to satisfy personal financial needs, 3) the setting up of processes for ensuring transparency in the public administration so as to persuade the citizen of the legality of the administrative decision in question.

In a similar vein, a few days later the President of the Supreme Court (Areios Pagos) made some recommendations that will ease the notorious congestion in the Courts. The court delays in the distribution of justice are phenomenal, reaching levels of actual justice being refused in cases taking over three to five years to come before the court. This damages the funcioning of the courts and negates the very existence of the provision of justice. The economic exchange relations in the community and society, the regulation of conflicts, commercial activity, the protection of human rights all require judicial protection, which, in practice, is denied. The void in judicial protection due to the delays in the administration of justice has currently drawn the attention of the European Court of Human Rights which reprimanded Greece for this situation. This case overload which is not screened at all ends up in the Supreme Court being turned into a Small-Claims Court! A system of case screening has recently only been introduced in Council of State (High Administrative Court) proceedings but not in the Supreme Court. Such a case screening system ought to be introduced at the very beginning of the civil litigation process, thus recognising the importance of Alternative Dispute Resolution (ADR) mechanisms. The long delays in court appearances also dilute the witness system for it then becomes contaminated with bribed witnesses. The President of the Supreme Court suggested the following recommendations for the distribution of justice and the improvement of the Court system in the country to become a reality.

These are:

a. The institution of out-of-court settlements in civil cases must be enforced. It has been be legislated but its application has unfortunately been suspended.
b. The system of witness evidence without direct appearance must be abolished.
c. The Supreme Court must establish a system for filtering cases so that it ceases to occupy itself with unfounded claims of minor importance.
d. Improvements in 'interrogation' and the 'bankruptcy' law process must be implemented.
e. The constitution of the 'justice police' must be realised.
f. Improving the institution of self-governance of justice is also an issue.
g. Economic independence must be provided for the functioning of justice and the decisions of the institutional organs must be honoured. (To Vema, 27/02/2000, A57 Interview with Supreme Court President S. Matthias to I. Mandrou.)

5 In closing

As seen above developments associated with quality service have not yet found their way into the apparatus of the Greek administration. This, despite extensive funding from the EU and the periodic legislation which declares the necessity for citizenship involvement. If law is not implemented and it is costly for the citizen to establish his/her status, then social activism ought to exist. The voluntary sector ought to be allowed to operate and to be voluntarily financed.

The weak organisational development of the economy and polity is best exemplified in the weak professional qualification regime that leaves the relationship of the legal profession and the courts economically in contradiction. In effect, the role of law in the operability of civil society and its economy, i.e. the very constitution of the 'circulation' sphere, the contracts, the transactions, omits certain key issues.

The practice of law and the administration of justice, its distribution and its equity are a 'problem' currently recognised in the country. What is not clearly understood by the elite is that further institutional participation in the EU decision-making structures requires a complete recognition that modern 'governance' structures are grounded on organisational contexts that a) realise that the role of law in the 'economic' sphere is based on the circulation and distribution of goods and services, b) a qualification regime needs to be established and 'professions' need to be recognised which are subject to legal and professional standards, and c) disputes need to be 'regulated', preferably at the place of their formation and solved in the workplace if possible.

When attempting to deal with the administration of justice in Greece one is facing great challenges. Part of the problem is the lack of sufficient research, the weak status of sociology of law in the country, including sociology itself, and the lack of researchers in the relevant Ministries of Justice, the Court System, the Ministry of 'Public Order' (the Police), and the weak status of Criminology as a specific scientific field. The field of justice research is not as yet constituted in the country and the benefits of research in other European Member States are not very well known. It is for this reason that the method I have used in this endeavour has been to allow the two key practitioners and observers of the process to state their opinion as recently as possible in order to allow the reader to gain an overall view as to the status of justice and the method for 'regulating' conflicts in present-day Greece. It is therefore a modest introduction but I hope it will serve as an invitation for scholars in the field to explore such issues in the new millennium.

References

Aubert, V., *Continuity and Development*, Oxford University Press, (1990).

Alivisatos, N., *Political Institutions in Crisis 1922-1974: Facets of the Greek experience*, Athens: Themelio, (1986).

Arlacchi, P., *Mafia, Peasants and Great Estates*, Cambridge university Press, (1983).

Bing, J., 'The Ombudsman and Computerised Administration', in: *Informatica e dirito*, 10, (1984), pp. 83–96.

Baerentzen, et all, *Studies in the History of the Greek Civil War 1945-1949*, Copenhagen: Museum Tusculanum Press, (1997).

Coote & Lenaghan, *Citizens Juries*, London: Public Policy Institute, (1997).

Crouch, C., *Sharing public space: organised interests during the nineteenth century*, Oxford, (1988).

Dean, M., 'A genealogy of the government of poverty', in: *Economy and Society*, Vol. 21, No. 3, (1992), pp. 209-251.

Donzelot, J., *The Policies of Families*, trans. R. Hurley, New York, (1979).

Fotinopoulou, T., 'The social Role of the Public Defender (Ombudsman)', in:*Administrative Review*, No. 11, (1998), pp. 5-12.

Gregory, R., and Giddings, P., *The United Kingdom Parliamentary Ombudsman Scheme*, IIAS, (1997).

Hume, L.J., *Bentham and Bureaucracy*, Cambridge, (1981).

Kofas, J., *Intervention and Underdevelopment*, Pennsylvania State University Press, (1989).

Mavrogordatos, G.Th., *Between Pityokampis and Procrustis: The Occupational Organizations in Contemporary Greece*, Odysseas, (1988) (in Greek).

Mavrogordates, G.Th., 'From Traditional Clientelism to Machine Politics: the Impact of PASOK Populism in Greece', in: *South European Society and Politics*, Vol. 2, No.3 (1997), pp. 1-26.

Mingione, E., 'Underground Economy and irregular forms of Employment: the case Greece', in: *EEC, Program for Research and Actions on the Development of the Labour market. Underground Economy and Irregular Forms of Employment (Travail au Noir)*.

Katrougalos, G., 'The South European Welfare Model: The Greek Welfare State in Search of an Identity', in: *Journal of European Social Policy*, Vol. 6, No. 1, (1996), pp. 39-60.

Knemeyer, F.L., 'Polizei', in: *Economy and Society*, ix, (1980), pp. 172-96.

OECD/LEED, *Local Partnerships and Social Innovation*, Paris, (1996).

OECD/ELSA, *The Public Employment Service: Greece, Ireland, Portugal, Paris*, (forthcoming report).

Olsen, J., *Organised Democracy*, 2nd edition, Oslo: Norwegian University Press, (1987).

Mentzelos, A., 'The Control of public Administration and the Body of Controllers of Public Administration', in: *Administrative Review*, Vol. 1, No. 2, (1995), pp. 95-106.

Pagakis, G., 'Organisational and functional modernisation. The protection of the consumer', in: *Administrative Review*, No. 11, (1998), pp. 26-38.

Pagakis, G., 'Administration, Society, State', in: *Administrative Review*, No. 9, (1997), pp. 9-20.

Papadimitropoulos, D., 'The Body of Public Administration Controllers, the Mediateur, and the Principle of Equite in French Public Administration', in: *Administrative Review*, (1995), pp. 34-52.

Pridham, G., 'Environmental Policies and Problems of European Legislation in Southern Europe', Vol. 1, No.1, (1996), pp. 47-73.

Simeonidou, H., 'Social Protection in Contemporary Greece', in: *South European Society & Politics*, Vol. 1, No. 3, (1996), pp. 67-86.

Thedieck F. & Vilella, G., *Restoring the capacities of government and civil society after an internal or external conflict*, Brussels: IIAS, (1999).

Tzannatos, Z., (ed.), *Socialism in Greece*, Aldershot: Gower, (1986).

Tsobanoglou, G., *The Political Sociology of a Labour Reserve: post-war Northern Greece and the Federal Republic of Germany*, (PhD Dissertation), Michigan: University of Michigan, (1991a).

Tsobanoglou, G.,'Considerations on Modern Absolutist Politics in the Periphery: their historical linkages via an analysis of legal modes of codification: The case of post-war Greece', in: Vincenzo Ferrari and Carla Farali, (eds.), *Laws and Rights*, Vol. II., (1993b), pp. 483-521.

Tsobanoglou, G., 'Organised Interests, State and Civil Society in the transition to the modern liberal era', in: *On Implementation of Impersonal Law in Developing Societies*, Onati Seminar Series, (1995).

Vermeulen, H., 'Urban research in Greece', in: Kertzer, I.D., (ed.), *Urban Life in Mediterranean Europe: Anthropological Perspectives*, Urbana: University of Illinois Press, pp. 109-132.

Waltman J. L. & Holland K.M., (eds.), *The political Role of law courts in modern democracies*, Hong Kong: Macmillan, (1988).

Weingrod, A., 'Patrons, Patronage, and Political Parties', in: *Comparative studies in Society and History*, Vol. 10, No. 4, (1968), pp.377-400.

White, C., *Patrons and Partisans: A Study of Politics in Two Southern Italian Communi*, Cambridge: Cambridge University Press, (1980).

The Challenge of Change for Judicial Systems
M. Fabri and Ph.M. Langbroek (Eds.)
IOS Press, 2000

The Problem of Eradicating Corruption from the Judiciary[1]

Maria Dakolias[2] and Kim Thachuk[3]

States without justice are but
bands of robbers enlarged
Saint Augustine

1 Introduction

In general, the courts are expected to be impartial and fair institutions in a system of good governance. In this regard, the judicial system is intended to be apolitical, its symbol being that of a blindfolded Lady Justice holding balanced scales. Indeed, it is such a judicial system that can uphold the rule of law and protect human rights. Societies aspire to create and enforce laws universally applicable on both public and private individuals without the arbitrary use of power. While the organization of the courts may vary from country to country, this is the basic premise upon which societies seek to construct their judicial systems.

In order to guarantee this judicial system, judicial independence is necessary. Judicial independence is probably the single greatest institutional support for the rule of law. Courts are supposed to be non-partisan in the political process, free to make their decisions unhindered by the political influences of daily life. Put another way, courts that are used by political regimes to further partisan or even private ends cannot be thought of as institutions of good governance and as such are illegitimate. Indeed, law is an element of social control; when the courts apply the law to the settlement of disputes, it is a way to enforce this control. If law or the courts are perceived as arbitrary in their application, then the social control objective may be distorted. This is of major concern to democratizing societies. Thus, the law and those that apply it must be perceived as impartial and equitable at all times if order is to be maintained in society.

In addition to independence, accountability of the judiciary is necessary for ensuring impartial and equitable decisions. Without accountability, there is the danger of judicial corruption or impropriety. The overwhelming question becomes the following: can corruption be eradicated given the necessity of maintaining judicial independence under good governance? Particularly during the planning stages of judicial reform, the issue of corruption should be addressed. However, very often the overwhelming concern is to

---

1 This article is an abreviated version of the article published in the 1999 edition of the *Wisconsin International Law Journal*.
2 Maria Dakolias is counsel in the World Bank's Legal Department.
3 Kim Thachuk is criminologist and political scientist.

improve judicial independence. This may be because judges need independence before accountability so that they may be effective.[4] Although there is tension between independence and accountability, independence will be weak if corrupt behavior is prevalent. Judicial reform aims to improve the quality, efficiency, integrity, and access to the judiciary. It is crucial, therefore, to address corruption if independence is to be truly improved.

This article will first establish the problem corruption poses to the legitimacy of government and the rule of law and then it will discuss the consequences of corruption when it appears in the judiciary. Further, it will describe possible situations that, if allowed to persist, may allow corruption to flourish. Finally, the article proposes possible oversight mechanisms and legal and judicial reform programs designed to address corruption in the judiciary.

2 The problem of corruption

Corruption as a phenomenon unfortunately knows no boundaries. Every country has its competition for the spoils of office, with favours dispensed to the party faithful. Every country, regardless of political tradition, culture or socio-economic status, has experienced bribery, misappropriation of funds and misuse of political position to name but a few of the misdeeds of public functionaries. In fact, the difference in experiences between countries is perhaps one of degree rather than kind. One of the more comprehensive definitions of corruption is the use of public office for private gain. Such a definition can be applied transnationally, and, properly adjusted, also through time.[5]

In addition, it is generally agreed that corruption is rooted in human nature. This nature includes instances of fraud (an act of deception deliberately practiced with the view of gaining unlawful advantage), extortion (exacting money coercively), embezzlement (appropriating fraudulently to one's own use that which is entrusted to one's care), violence and other forms of criminal activity. These all can be added to the above definition. The common thread that runs through all of these forms of corruption is their reliance upon secrecy and collusion.[6] Thus, even major *exposés* of corruption reveal only a part of what needs to be known in order to halt such abuses.

In some states, corruption is pervasive throughout all social institutions, from the political system and into the private sphere. In addition, there is increasing realization that corruption is assuming new forms and dimensions, particularly in connection with

---

4 See Volcansek et al. (1996, 131).

5 Joseph S. Nye proposes that corruption is behavior which deviates from the formal duties of a public role because of private-regarding (family, close family, private clique) pecuniary or status gains, or violates rules against the exercise of certain types of private-regarding influence. This includes such behavior as bribery; use of a reward to pervert the judgment of a person in a position of trust; nepotism (bestowal of patronage by reason of ascriptive relationship rather than merit); and misappropriation (illegal appropriation of public resources for private-regarding uses. See Nye (1989, 967-968).

6 There is a culture of protection in the Chilean judiciary with respect to corruption. To complain one is said to have to be a hero. See Matus (1999, 20-21).

the increasing transnationalization of organized criminal activity. Thus, the effects of corruption that may initially plague one sovereign state are now more frequently becoming a concern in seemingly unrelated and previously unconnected regions.

One of the most prevalent forms of corruption is clientelism or patron-client relationships. This is basically a situation in which individuals use their public offices for personal aggrandizement or to gain favorable advantages for themselves or their friends. This system is largely the result of a complex network of personal or familial affiliations and ties, all of which have a long tradition of personal and/or factional loyalties that take precedence over the commitment to public policies and, indeed, the constitution.[7]

Francisco Thoumi points out that this is an 'illegality and dishonesty trap' in which society's tolerance of illegality and respect for the laws of the country tend to deteriorate as they are increasingly exposed to others' disrespect for the laws. Hence, he argues that, 'in a society where there is a great amount of dishonesty and corruption, it becomes increasingly costly to behave honestly' and '[c]onsequently, a particular individual with a particular set of values could behave honestly in one environment but dishonestly in another.'[8] Further, over time an honest individual working in a dishonest environment will adapt and behave in a more dishonest fashion.

3 The consequences of judicial corruption

3.1 Risk for judicial independence

Such conditions for corruption have adverse effects on the judiciary, putting its independence at risk. In general, the concept of judicial independence rests on three factors: the rule of law, the functional specialization of the judiciary, and the autonomy of the legal profession. More importantly, the judiciary figures significantly in the separation of powers in democratic governments. The concept of the separation of powers was instituted to avoid overwhelming concentrations of power in a single branch of government. Each branch thus serves as a check on the other two branches of government with the purpose of avoiding corruption and despotism. However, to carry out this function the judiciary needs institutional as well as personal independence. Although not all countries follow the separation of powers doctrine they have some system of checks and balances; for example, the constitutions of Germany and Canada do not include a doctrine of separation of powers, rather, their judiciaries have functional independence.[9]

Despite the fact that each branch scrutinizes the others' activities, often there is little real understanding of what the judiciary actually does in terms of specific actions. This misunderstanding occurs because the concept of judicial independence has often gone so far as to be an impediment to open communication, even if it is only for the purpose of constructive criticism. Indeed, it is often the 'other-worldly' nature of judiciaries that

7 See, e.g., Diaz Uribe (1986).
8 Thoumi (1987).
9 See Research Papers (1993, 1423).

shrouds them in mystery and sets the stage not only for much misunderstanding, but for lack of understanding about what is actually transpiring.

Judicial independence, while an important guarantee of impartiality and non-partisanship, can also be the cloak behind which judges may conceal illegal or corrupt acts. Indeed, this problem leaves the door open for corrupt activity to go unnoticed or unchallenged. Thus, while there is the need to guarantee judicial independence, branches of government should cooperate and communicate more effectively in order to ensure that the business of government is being done within the guidelines of the constitution. Independence, therefore, requires safeguards against corruption. If there is no judicial accountability, the cloak of independence may feed corrupt behavior. This, of course, requires a delicate balance between independence and accountability.

Judicial independence is an imperative feature of any justice system. Contrary to common opinion, judicial independence signifies much more than a judge's freedom from political influence. Independence has a number of definitions and dimensions,[10] including structural, organizational and administrative aspects of a judicial system, which all play a role in judicial independence.[11] There are several different types of independence: substantive independence, which is functional or decisional independence in German and American law, respectively (making judicial decisions and exercising official duties subject to no other authority but the law), personal independence (adequately secured judicial terms of office and tenure), collective independence (judicial participation in the central administration of courts) and internal independence (independence from judicial superiors and colleagues).[12]

The judiciaries in Latin American countries, for example, have historically not acted as significant institutional counterforces to legislative and executive abuses of power for a number of historical, political and structural reasons.[13] Judges who may be susceptible to pressure from other branches of government may also be more likely to sell themselves to litigants and lawyers.[14] In Chile, under the Pinochet regime, judges who

---

10 Owen Fiss describes three different types of judicial independence: first, party detachment, which is an independence from the interests of the parties; second, individual autonomy, independence from the bureaucratic judicial structure, i.e. other judges; and third, political insularity, independence from the other governmental institutions. See Fiss (1993).

11 See Proposiciones para la Reforma Judicial (1991) (stating that the public's decreasing respect in Chile for the judiciary results from structural and organizational factors and that transparent mechanisms and mechanisms for public control of the judiciary are as important as the principle of independence).

12 Shetreet (1985, 598-599).

13 One commentator lists seven factors as explanations of the judiciary's traditional role of dependence: a tradition of executive dominance, political instability, the Roman or code law system with little support for judicial activism, the use of precedent and judicial law or policy or policy-making, the highly complex structure and processes of the judicial system itself that prevent a number of issues from coming before the courts, the limited use of judicial review, the lack of popular independent power base in the population and the appointment, tenure and impeachment processes. See Verner (1984, 468-477). Verner then attempts to quantify the levels of independence of the different Latin American judicial systems and provide a typology of the same. See id. at 477-504.

14 See 'Columnist Links Submissive Judiciary', FBIS, (June 21, 1996), available in Daily Report, FBIS-LAT-96-129.

did not obey were fired, persecuted or had their careers frozen.[15] If a government wants to have control of the judiciary it will necessarily appoint more corrupt judges. However, corruption in the judiciary will undermine the government's legitimacy and inevitably lead to injustice.[16]

Methods to ensure independence vary from country to country. Keith Rosenn groups a variety of Latin America's constitutional safeguards protecting judicial independence into two overlapping categories: measures to protect the integrity of judicial decisions, and measures protecting the personal independence of the judiciary.[17] The former includes protecting the judiciary from other branches' interference, jurisdictional monopolies, requirements for a reasoned opinion, and public trials.[18] Among others, the latter includes irreducible salaries, judicial budgets that are fixed percentages of the state budget, and tenure in office.[19] Forms of accountability include elections, criminal prosecutions, commission supervision, collegial supervision, the media, and civil society.[20] It should be noted, however, that the judiciary can never be completely independent since in most countries, the legislature provides the resources by which it functions.[21] In some cases, it is the executive through the Ministry of Justice that even manages its budget.[22]

3.2 Consequences for the administration of justice

Corruption in the justice system thus spawns further corruption which leads to a loss of legitimacy and often violence. A vicious circle of corruption and lawlessness ensues from which it is difficult to extricate society. Indeed, corruption in the judiciary is somewhat distinct from corruption in other sectors of government because the judiciary is most often viewed as the failsafe between constitutionalism and a free-for-all or a Hobbesian state of nature. Corruption undermines political legitimacy and makes citizens become distrusting of government. If corruption is to be addressed it needs, among other things, independent prosecutors and judiciary.[23] However, if the judiciary cannot perform this function, the corruption will never be punished because individuals and other branches of government are confident that they are free to do as they please.[24] The judiciary, then, can be the cause of corruption especially if it is slow and does not accuse the guilty.[25]

---

15 See Gisela von Muhlenbrock, Discretionality and Corruption: The Chilean Judiciary, Presented at the Corruption and Democracy Workshop, North-South Center, University of Miami 6 (May 9, 1995).

16 See 'Procurator General Zhang Jiging on Judicial Corruption', FBIS, (March 9, 1995), available in Daily Report, FBIS-CHI-95-049.

17 See Rosenn (1987).

18 See id. at 14-15.

19 See id. at 15-23.

20 This list of methods is drawn from Noonand and Kennth (1993).

21 See American Bar Association, An Independent Judiciary: Report of the Commission on the Separation of Powers and Judicial Independence 60 (1997).

22 Germany is one example. See e.g. Dakolias (1995, 167).

23 See Colazingari and Rose-Ackerman (1998).

24 See Otis (1997, 52).

25 See Jones (1998, A11).

This will lead to impunity of corrupt activities and if nothing is done to address it, unaccountability of the government.[26]

3.2.1 Quality of jurisprudence

One of the important characteristics of a judiciary is that its opinions be consistent and predictable. Corruption muddies such clarity, for it is difficult to predict bribes and their effects. It becomes harder for a business to calculate its risk of losing a particular potential lawsuit, making investment decisions more fraught with unknown variables.[27] Similarly, it becomes harder for a person to assess the chances of winning or losing a lawsuit. Further, a corrupt decision stays on the record, tainting subsequent decisions. The harms caused by judicial corruption, however, reach far beyond the parties to a particular dispute. Corrupt processes have an effect on how the law is interpreted in other courts and in society generally, on potential litigants, on economic decisions, on the cost of litigation, the pace of reform, and the spread of corruption both within the judiciary and beyond. It creates lack of transparency in the judicial process.

3.2.2 Access to justice and efficiency

Lack of access to justice is a considerable problem in many countries. The above-named harms – unpredictable decisions, low public opinion and inflated transaction costs – all exacerbate this problem by discouraging potential litigants. On an intuitive level, the problem caused by judicial corruption is that a party is deprived of a fair judicial procedure and, thus, there is a higher chance that the case's outcome is unfair. This contradicts the very essence of justice and of the notion, to which all legal systems subscribe, of equality before the law.[28] A person denied access to a just resolution of disputes is arguably denied a basic human right.[29]

Not everyone can afford to engage in corrupt exchanges. The presence of corruption raises transaction costs and can even be seen as triggering a bidding war for judicial services that escalates prices for those who participate.[30] At the same time, it can slow or otherwise deteriorate services for those who do not participate. Judicial staff may be bribed to hurry or otherwise improve certain procedures at the cost of others. As a result, the pace of litigation is driven by corruption rather than legal procedures. This creates inefficiency and delays in the judicial process. Thus bribes raise the cost of litigation so that only some can afford to receive a certain quality level of justice. In addition, the public cost increases as a result of corruption so that the overall cost of justice is effected.

---

26 See von Muhlenbrock, *ibid.* note 12, at 8.

27 Studies on corruption generally show that high levels of corruption are associated with lower levels of investment as a percentage of GDP. See Mauro (1995), (1997); Klitgaard (1991); Buscaglia and Dakolias (1996).

28 See Odrai (1995).

29 See Universal Declaration of Human Rights, Article 10.

30 See Dakolias (1995).

3.3 Consequences for society

In recent years, increasing attention has been paid to the problem of corruption in general and judicial corruption in particular. In a few countries, corruption has been identified as the most important problem in the country. This is true both in Venezuela and Argentina.[31]

Addressing the problem is difficult. Criminalizing bribery, for example, will not necessarily resolve the problem of corruption. If people do not perceive that it is in their best interest to be honest, they will constantly seek to circumvent the rules, whether or not laws exist. In addition, because there is not a built-in incentive, those investigating corruption may themselves be susceptible to looking the other way for a price. This is especially the case when civil servants are underpaid and perceive that the benefits of corruption outweigh the costs of getting caught.

Again, reforming the system, rather than targeting individual cases, will be more beneficial in the long-term. Thus, civil service reform will be easier to effect than will be attempting to detect, apprehend and try smaller corruption cases. However, there are some benefits to making examples of notorious violators of the justice system. Thus, selective exposure of corrupt acts in sensitive areas of government convince the public that the government is dedicated to eradicating the problem. That is, a carefully controlled dose of grand-standing will assist in gaining public support for reform efforts. Public endorsement is an essential ingredient for government success at reform, for it is the sense of justice that needs to be restored to society, not just rules and procedures. Sensitivity to democratic standards that was lost to corruption has to be relearned, not imposed. Campaigns of public outreach that specifically address corruption and the measures being taken to halt it are beneficial, therefore, to overall attempts to eradicate it.[32]

3.3.1 Public opinion

While the courts have an important role, so too does the public. The public must have confidence in the judiciary in order to give it legitimacy.[33] However, in many countries the citizens not only lack such faith in the judiciary, but they complain about corruption, delay, cost, and unfairness. In some cases this perception is deserved and in others it is not. One of the main problems facing Latin America's justice systems is lack of public confidence in the judiciary.[34] Along with slow resolution time, a main cause of this disillusionment is corruption.[35]

Many polls indicate that corruption in the judiciary is a concern among citizens. In Argentina, 57% of those polled by Gallup said that they felt corruption was the main

---

31 See Argentina Gallop Poll *in* Poder Cuidadano (Año 7, No. 61, Mayo de 1997). Also in Luis Pásara, *La justicia en la Argentina* (article on file with the authors). See Manzetti and Blake, at 28.

32 See Esterling (1998, 117).

33 See id.

34 See Dakolias (1995).

35 See Buscaglia and Dakolias, (1996, 1). Slow processing times and corruption are related: the slower a process, the more likely a party will be to try to influence a member of the judiciary to expedite it. See id.

problem with the judiciary.[36] In Honduras, three out of four polled believed the judiciary was corrupt.[37] Even in Costa Rica, 54% of those polled believed that judicial decisions were subject to external 'pressures.'[38] Studies show, too, that these public perceptions are not illusory. In Peru, a study funded by the UNDP found that three of four penal cases were influenced by corruption.[39] By adding to Latin Americans' mistrust of the judiciary, corruption undermines the institution's prestige and effectiveness. However, lack of trust is not concentrated in Latin America; in 1995, only 8% of those polled had a great deal of confidence in the judiciary, though 80% believed that the judges are fair and honest in their decisions.[40]

It is important to note, however, that very often the public gets its information about the judiciary from the media.[41] In one survey, more than 80% of the judges in the United States felt pressure to be directly accountable to public opinion.[42] In order to address this pressure, 84% of those judges felt judges should devote more resources to public relations to educate the public and explain the tension between independence and accountability.[43] Their perception is that the courts should take more direct action and not rely on third parties to defend them. If the courts alienate the public and lose its support and participation, they cannot carry out their appropriate role.[44]

3.3.2 The media

On the other hand, although public opinion is important, judges must be careful to rule based on law and not on public opinion.[45] That is not to say that there is not a need to understand the citizens in order to bring community perspectives to the courts. In the United States, for example, while some judges feel that they cannot speak to the public in the US under the code of judicial conduct,[46] isolation is not possible anymore. Further, the media may over-exaggerate issues in order to sell more publications.[47] In this instance, judges should respond through organized institutional programs to attacks on judicial decisions or inaccurate media reporting.[48] Such programs can also be an effective way of educating citizens and hearing about their needs and perceptions. However, because of the tendency of the media to dramatize issues, judges do not as a rule grant interviews because of fear that impartiality is compromised.[49] Hence, it is often the duty of others to respond on behalf of the courts to untruths or exaggerations.

---

36 See MacLean (1997).
37 See id.
38 See id.
39 See id.
40 See note 18, at 60-61; McCabe (1999).
41 See Esterling (1998, 112).
42 See id. at 116.
43 See id.
44 See note 18, at 61.
45 See Esterling (1998, 114).
46 See id. at 117.
47 See id. at 113.
48 See id.
49 See id. at 114.

If judges do not respond there is no counter-balance of information available to the public.[50] In one survey in the US, over 50% of judges had been publicly criticized in the last 5 years, but less than 10% responded to this criticism.[51] In some cases, the bar or independent lawyers have responded successfully. If not addressed, unjust criticism can destroy public confidence in the judiciary. There is a need for the judiciary itself to become more active in public information and relations. However, there is a delicate balance because judges must not alienate the public; the rule of law depends on public trust.[52] In this way, an effective response mechanism by the judges, the bar and the public is necessary to address criticism.[53]

The role of the media cannot be downplayed, however. It is often an essential element for not only advertising the court's positive work, but also in addressing and uncovering corrupt activities. A free press should make it easier to fight corruption.[54] The media can help to build public support to attack corruption. Part of the fight against corruption is to show the public that something is being done to eradicate it. This means that the fight against corruption is made visible. Because the people know that something is being done and that corrupt behavior is being punished from the very large abuser to the small one, the public will change its cynicism.[55] This means that if a judge is found guilty he/she does not return to the bench to decide cases as occurred in one case in Argentina.[56]

3.4 When judicial corruption comes under foreign scrutiny

When judicial corruption in one country reaches an extreme, the door is often opened to the foreign scrutiny of judicial practices. The issue of corruption often transcends international boundaries in a number of ways. Thus, for example, when criminals are not being brought to justice in one jurisdiction, they are free to continue activities such as drug trafficking that have an effect on other countries.[57] In addition, with nationals living abroad, there are many links to home countries and more sophisticated organized crime.[58] Such organized crime undermines the rule of law and legitimacy through corrupt individuals and judicial proccss.[59]

Judicial corruption can affect the courts not only in terms of their legitimacy within the country but also internationally. For example, US courts reviewed corruption in Bolivian courts to determine the specific public interest factor for the doctrine of *forum*

50 See id. at 113.
51 See id. at 115.
52 See note 18, at viii.
53 See id. at 64.
54 See Heymann (1996, 323, 328).
55 See id. at 331.
56 See Alvarez (1996, 42).
57 See 'European Council Adopts Common Position on Fight Against Corruption', European Report, October 11, 1997, Europe Information Service.
58 See Shelley (1995, 463).
59 See id. at 48.

non conveniens.[60] Although it is not the business of US courts to supervise foreign courts that are sovereign, the Bolivian Minister of Justice himself complained of corruption.[61] In 1991, eight members of the Bolivian Supreme Court were charged with corruption.[62] In addition, the US court indicated that delays may also render a court an inadequate forum.[63] An example of an Indian court was used where a case could take up to 25 years to be resolved. In addition, foreign pressure can be made to reform the judiciary to improve investment.[64]

4 Corruption in the judiciary

Corruption poses the greatest threat to judicial independence; it touches both individual independence and institutional independence. When a judge acts unethically the consequences are far greater than the 'intrinsic moral seriousness.'[65] Representative John Hostettler has noted that there are two types of judicial misconduct. First, is misconduct as a result of improper motives; for example, those decisions and actions which arise from corruption, such as bribery or fraud. A second form of judicial misconduct arises from those judicial actions which are wrongful not because of the judge's motivations, but because of a lack of merit in his decision – such as a judge's clear misinterpretation of the constitution or a judge's legislating from the bench.

Judicial independence is an important concept as long as it does not become judicial license. Like all power, judicial power will grow and threaten individual liberty if left unchecked. Impeachment is a strong 'constitutional check' in the United States. What is important to remember is that the constitution is the law of the land and it is the role of judges to enforce the limits set by the constitution, not to reinvent those limits. Thus, the constitution gives judges 'judicial power' to be exercised.

So the question then becomes: can corruption be addressed without disrupting the balance of independence? It may be the case, perhaps, that it cannot be done and that we must accept that corruption will inevitably mean that there will be greater intrusion into independence. However, it is clear that independence must not protect judges from discipline investigation.[66]

4.1 Changing the legal system and judicial reform

As a result of widespread corruption or a weak rule of law, many countries are embark-

60 See *Carballo* v. *Kavlin and Kavlin*, No. 96-2219-CIV-RYSKAMP, 1997 U.S. Dist. LEXIS 13808, at *7 (D. Fla. Sept. 9, 1997).

61 See id. at *7-8.

62 See id. at *8.

63 See id. at *9.

64 See Matus (1999, 64).

65 William Thomas Braithwaite, *Who Judges the Judges?*, Chicago: American Bar Foundation (1971), 9, cited in Volcansek (1996).

66 See Wallace (1998, 341, 344).

ing on judicial reform. Many of the judicial reforms being launched across the different regions attempt to make judicial procedures more efficient and transparent, in part by redistributing responsibilities. they also seek toimprove access, efficiency and quality of the delivery of justice.[67] Where there is an entrenched network of corruption, the players will clearly oppose such reforms; judges or staff members may resent losing control over procedures that are a source of illicit income.[68] These players could slowreform by openly opposing it, or by interfering in a more covert way.[69]

Corruption scholars have often argued that corruption slows reform by providing band-aid solutions, and thus detracts from the urgency of repairing the underlying structural problem.[70] If companies are effectively able to bribe their way through certain procedures, they will have less inventive to lobby for change. Corruption, then, can be an obstacle to reform at a time when governments across the region are busily trying to mend or reconceive their judicial systems.[71]

Many judicial reform programs aim at increasing independence but they should also aim to reduce and prevent corruption. Independence will be improved only if it has legitimacy. There is a clear danger of only ensuring independence, which some say is the cause of some of the problems in Italy. However, even in countries where the emphasis is on independencerather than on accountability, like the US,[72] there are increased efforts to address accountability. There is a danger, therefore, in supporting independence without considering anti-corruption strategies. Those people with vested interests in the current operations of a corrupt judiciary will adapt the reforms aimed at improving independence to the old ways of operation. In this way, the reforms are rendered largely ineffective.

Rather, the reforms should aim to instill loyalty in the institutions and not in individuals. In this way, a two-stage reform might be considered. The first stage should, as some countries have done, remove those people that are corrupt from the judiciary. Cleaning house is important to rid the judiciary of vested interests that will attempt to use the reforms to benefit themselves and adapt the reforms to enhance their corrupt behavior. New people should be utilized to assist in the reform process; they can help to build loyalty in the institution and the institution-building process. Incentives will also need to be considered to avoid situations such as the one that occurred in Sri Lanka when typists objected to photocopiers being used in the courts because they receive payment by the page.

The second stage of the reform should consider the periodic rotation of staff as is being done in Sri Lanka. Such rotation may assist the judiciary in spreading the reforms,

67 See generally Dakolias (1995), (1999).

68 See Buscaglia (1997).

69 Experience has shown that where those implicated in a reform effort do not support that effort, success is less likely. See Dakolias (1995).

70 See Robin Theobald, *Corruption, Development and Underdevelopment*, Houndmills, Basingstoke, Hampshire: Macmillan.

71 Jorge Correa writes that at no other time in history have there been so many efforts to reform judicial systems. See Correa (1997, 173).

72 See Volcansek (1996, 87).

building teams, as well as improving loyalty to the judiciary and its principles. The President of Ukraine suggests that there is a need for preventive measures as well as certifying state employees and firing those employees who do not meet certification. In addition, he adds that there should be rapid response to citizen and mass media reports where employees or state bodies are accused of unlawful acts.[73] This two-stage process, together with efforts to improve appointment, promotion, discipline, salaries, pensions and ethics codes for judges and judicial employees, should improve case management, public education, and accountability and provide some relevant lessons in the judicial reform process.

When planning the reform of a corrupt judiciary, the focus should be on: (1) training and education, (2) selection, advancement and salaries, (3) monitoring and removal, (4) transparency in procedure and decision-making, and (5) participation of civil society. These categories are not meant to be exclusive or exhaustive, and they tend to focus on strategies that have already been attempted.

5 Conclusion

Although the tension between accountability and independence is not new, it needs to be taken into consideration in the discussion of corruption. The balance of independence and accountability are critical when anti-corruption measures are considered in any country. Each country has tipped the balance differently and within each country the balance will change within a given time period. Therefore, a constant analysis of the tension is necessary.[74] Re-evaluation of the country-specific circumstances will determine how the balance should be tilted at any given time. In such an analysis greater independence may be advocated when there is evidence that the legislature is encroaching on judicial independence. For example, a legislative policy of initiating impeachment proceedings against activist judges as scare tactics should be considered as a factor in the evaluation.[75]

Legal and judicial reform programs should take such issues into account from the start. Efforts should be made to analyze whether corruption exists in a given judicial system and to assess the degree of existence. At the very least, additional information is needed during program design. To achieve these ends, the commitment and openness of the government and the judiciary are required, as well as more research in the area of corruption.

As a complement, such reforms should be monitored and researched. As reforms proceed throughout the world, it would be helpful to assess and compare their performance, considering which measures work under what circumstances, and which do not.[76]

---

73 See id.

74 Interview with Giuseppe Di Federico, in Sounion, Greece (Sept. 4, 1999).

75 A booklet was circulated in the US Congress on promoting such a policy. 'Restraining an Overactive Judiciary' (1996). See *supra* note 18, at 15. Robert Dole and Newt Gingrich threatened to initiate impeachment proceedings against Judge Bear if he did not change his ruling. See id. at 16.

76 See Dakolias (1999).

Such information could be crucial for future reformers.[77] This could be especially helpful in the area of judicial corruption. Corruption is an elusive topic for quantitative research because those involved do their best to cover their tracks.[78] Documents are destroyed, allegations denied, and opinions written in such a way as to obfuscate the real reasons for the decision. Despite these difficulties, several books have come out examining the workings of corrupt judiciaries.[79] One example is '*El Libro Negro*' which describes corrupt behavior in the Chilean judiciary, but was banned soon after being released.[80] Still missing, however, is a more systematic, quantitative study of the problem.[81] How common is judicial corruption? Are most judges corrupt, or only a small percentage?

Another line of study that could shed light on this topic is a comparison of the different methods for managing judges and judicial careers.[82] Even countries that have implemented evaluation programs are not foolproof.[83] Such research might be able to reveal why some judiciaries, despite being fraught with problems of delay and mismanagement, are perceived as relatively corruption-free.[84]

There is still much to learn, then, about the dynamics of judicial corruption. General corruption scholarship provides some of the basic theory about the phenomenon, and, further, scholars have filled in a few of the gaps by looking directly at corruption on a case-by-case basis. As reformers begin to confront judicial corruption, however, they would benefit from a richer body of scholarship. The recent example of the Russian Federation is a clear example of the pressure of corruption within a country. Economic development depends on a functioning judiciary.[85] As corruption is an obstacle to development,[86] there is a need for the judiciary to provide the institutional checks that guarantee accountability and oversight.[87] Moreover, without this oversight and consultation, economic reforms may be unstable and subject to reversal.[88] With fewer checks and balances, there is less of an opportunity for corrupt behavior.

---

77 On the importance of monitoring reform programs, see Golub (1993).

78 See Katz (1985).

79 See, e.g., Verbitsky (1994). See also Ojeda (1995).

80 The publisher was arrested and a warrant is out for the arrest of the author. The book was banned as a result of a case filed by one of the judges identified in the book. See Matus (1999). See also La Nacion, *Chile: Detuvieron al Editor del Libro Negro de la Justicia Chilena* (last modified June 18, 1999) <http://63.78.200.196/aaaflash/ busca.asp?ID_AAAControl=1232>.

81 See Buscaglia and Dakolias (1996). Example of using complaints in the media as a means to measure corrupt behavior.

82 A study like Volcansek's comparison of judicial discipline in Italy, France, England and the US would not need to rely on a great deal of quantitative data. See generally Volcansek (1996).

83 The Chilean judiciary evaluates its judges' responsibility, capacity, knowledge, human relations, and public relations. One of the best rated judges in Chile was recently convicted of corruption, 'Juez exonerado estaba entre los mejores de 1998', *La Tercera*, (Oct. 10, 1999).

84 See Rosenn (1998), (affirming that Brazil's judiciary does not seem to suffer from rampant corruption); Deflem (1995).

85 See Dakolias (1995).

86 Fifty-five percent of those polled agree that the greatest obstacle to development is corruption. See Prensa Libre, *Guatemala: Morelli Senala Justicia mas propicio a Corruption* (last modified Nov. 23, 1998) <http://63.78.200.196/aaaflash/busca.asp?ID_AAAControl=129>.

87 See Haggard and Kaufmann (1994).

88 See Dakolias (1995).

References

Alvarez, Gladys, 'Hay Buenas Noticias que no se Llegan a Conocer', *Exposiciones Y Debates*, Aug., 1996.

Braithwaite, William Thomas, 'Who Judges the Judges?', Chicago: *American Bar Foundation*, 9, (1971).

Clifford Wallace, J., 'Resolving Judicial Corruption While Preserving Judicial Independence: Comparative Perspectives', 28 *Cal. W. Int'l L.J.*, (1998).

Colazingari, Silvia and Rose-Ackerman, Susan, 'Corruption in a Paternalistic Democracy: Lessons from Italy for Latin America', 113 *Pol. Sci. Q.*, (1998).

Correa Sutil, Jorge, 'Modernizacion, Democratizacion y Sistemas Judiciales', in: Edmundo Jarquin and Fernando Carrillo, (Eds.), *La economia political de la reforma judicial*, (1997).

Dakolias, Maria, 'Court Performance Around the World: A Comparative Perspective', 2 *Yale Hum. Rights & Dev. L.J.*, (1999).

Dakolias, Maria, 'A Strategy for Judicial Reform: The Experience in Latin America', 36:1 Va. *J. Int'l L.* 167 n.100, (1995).

Deflem, Mathieu, 'Corruption, Law and Justice: A Conceptual Clarification', 23*J.L. & Crim. Just.*, (1995).

Diaz Uribe, Eduardo, *En clientelismo en Colombia*, Bogota, Colombia: Ancora Editores.

Esterling, K.M., 'Public Outreach – The Cornerstone of Judicial Independence', 82 *Juridcature* 114, (1998).

Fiss, Owen M., 'The Right Degree of Independence', in: Irwin P. Stotzky (Ed.), *Transition to Democracy in Latin America: The Role of Judiciary*, Boulder: Westview Press, (1993).

Golub, Stephen, 'Assessing and Enhancing the Impact of Democratic Development Projects: A Practitioner's Perspective', 28 *Stud. Comp. Int'l Dev.*, (Spring 1993).

Haggard, Stephan and Kaufmann, Robert, 'Democratic Institutions, Economic Policy and Performance in Latin America', in: Colin I. Bradford, Jr. (Ed.), *Redefining the State in Latin America*, (1994).

Heymann, Philip, 'Democracy and Corruption', 20 *Fordham Int'l L.J.*, (1996).

Jones, Bart, 'Graft: the Lingua Franca of Latin America', *Wash. Times*, May 24, (1998).

Katz, Stanley N., 'A Historical and Social Perspective on Judicial Corruption', 16*Loy. U. Chi. L.J.*, (1985).

Klitgaard, Robert, 'Adjusting to Reality: Beyond State vs. Market in Economic Development', *ICS*, (1991), in: Edgardo Buscaglia and Maria Dakolias, *Judicial Reform in Latin American Courts: The Experience in Argentina and Ecuador*, (1996) (World Bank Technical Paper No. 350).

MacLean, Roberto, 'Algunas consideraciones sobre los efectos de la administracion de justicia en la propiedad y los contratos', in: Edmundo Jarquin and Fernando Carrillo, (Eds.), *La Economia Politica de la Reforma Judicial*, (1997).

Manzetti, L. and Blake, C.H., 'Market Reforms and Corruption in Latin America; New Means for Old Ways', *Rev. Int'l Pol. Econ.* 5.

Matus, Alejandra, *El Libro Negro de la Justicia Chilena 20-21,* Santigo, Chile: Planeta, (1999).

Mauro, Paulo, 'Corruption and growth', 110 *Q.J. ECON.* 681, (1995).

Mauro, Paulo, 'The Effects of Corruption on Growth, Investment, and Government Expenditures: A Cross-Country Analysis', in: Kimberly Ann Elliot (Ed.),*Corruption and the Global Economy* 83, (1997).

McCabe, Kathryn, 'And the Survey Says ... American Public is Polled for Opinions on Justice System', 82 *Judicature,* (1999).

Noonan, John T. and Kenneth, Winston, (Eds.) *The Responsible Judge: Readings in Judicial Ethics*, (1993).

Nye, Joseph S., 'Corruption and Political Development: A Cost-Benefit Analysis', in: Arnold Heidenheimer et al. (Eds.), *Political Corruption: A Handbook*, New Brunswick, U.S.A.: Transaction Publishers, (1989).

Odrai, Alberto Borea, 'Corrupcion y Justicia en America Latina', *Contribuciones* 4/95, (1995).

Otis, John, *Law and Order,* Latin trade, (1997).

Research Papers of the National Commission on Judicial Discipline & Removal, 1423, (1993).

Rosenn, Keith S., 'Judicial Reform in Brazil', 4 Nafta: *Law and Business Review of the Americas,* (Spring 1998).

Rosenn, Keith S., 'The Protection of Judicial Independence in Latin America', 19*Inter-Am. L. Rev.*, (1987).

Shelley, Louise I., 'Transnational Organized Crime: An Imminent Threat to the Nation-State?', 48 *J. Int'l Aff.,* (1995).

Shetreet, Shimon 'Judicial Independence: New Conceptual Dimensions and Contemporary Challenges', in: Shimon Shetreet (Ed.), *Judicial Independence: the Contemporary Debate,* (1985).

Theobald, Robin, *Corruption, Development and Underdevelopment*, Houndmills, Basingstoke, Hampshire: Macmillan.

Thoumi, Francisco E., 'Some Implications of the Growth of the Underground Economy in Colombia', 29 *J. Interam. Stud. & World Aff.* 35, 44, (1987).

Verner, Joel G., 'The Independence of Supreme Courts in Latin America: A Review of the Literature', 16 *J. Lat. Am. Stud.*, (1984).

Verbitsky, Horacio, Hacer la Corte: *La contruccion de un poder absoluto sin justicia nu control*, Editorial Planeta, (1994). (Linking corruption to public disillusionment with judiciary).

Volcansek, Mary L. et al., *Judicial Misconduct: A Cross-National Comparison*, Gainesville: University Press of Florida, (1996).

Part IV

Governance and Change of Courts and Public Prosecutors' Offices

The Challenge of Change for Judicial Systems
M. Fabri and Ph.M. Langbroek (Eds.)
IOS Press, 2000

On the Quality of the Administration of Justice, Judges and Courts

Frans C.J. van der Doelen[1]

1 Introduction

For a long time, the administrators of justice in the Netherlands operated quietly in the background. But times have changed and the media and the public have 'discovered' legal proceedings. Whether it concerns the speed of procedures, the provision of services or uniformity of law: more than ever, the judiciary are held accountable for the quality of their actions.

The judiciary will have to respond to this development by permanently reflecting upon their performance. Clearly, the Government plays a vital role, while at the same time it must refrain from interfering in the administration of justice. In fact, the degree of independence of the judiciary determines the quality of a state governed by law. At the same time, the term independence might result in defensive behaviour, even in cases where the essence of judicial independence does not necessitate it. It is therefore important always to analyse carefully what this independence should lead to and in which cases the term is being misused.

More systematic and external accountability for the quality of the administration of justice does not impede the preservation of judicial independence in any way. The United States in particular have had much practical experience in this area, as is shown by the emergence of more empirical analyses of the administration of justice (paragraph 2), the systematic judicial evaluation of judges (paragraph 3) and the development of Trial Court Performance Standards for courts (paragraph 4). A great deal is happening in the Netherlands as well. In September 1998, the project entitled Reinforcement of the Judicial Organisation Project (*Versterking Rechterlijke Organisatie*, abbreviated as pVRO) which is supported by the Presidents' Meeting, suggested a number of initiatives (paragraph 5). This development toward improving quality is not an isolated incident. The pVRO responds to the increasing pressure from the press, the public and the political body to account for the quality of the administration of justice, judges and courts more systematically and externally.

---

1 Head of the Policy and Instrumentation Division of the Administration of Justice Department, Ministry of Justice, the Netherlands. This article has been written in the author's private capacity.

2 Well-defined quality

In general, quality may be defined as 'meeting the standards'. Inevitably, the next question will be 'which standards?'. The (minimum) standards of quality of the administration of justice are found in Article 6 of the ECHR. It concerns independent, impartial judges, who are accessible to anyone, who conduct fair and public hearings and pass judgment within a reasonable time. Already, several measures have been taken to stimulate professional quality (public hearings, written grounds for sentences, three-judge closed sessions, consultations on legal precedents, appeal and cassation, complaint handling procedures, etc.). However, these measures are directed inwardly for the most part, they are not easily accessible and they are of a casuistic nature. It is relatively difficult for the outside world to get a clear picture of the quality of the administration of justice in the Netherlands. Not much systematic and useful information is being collected. No specific data to reveal patterns regarding appeals, cassation, the handling of complaints, challenges, etc., is being collected. However, there are two factors which force the judiciary to account for the quality of the administration of justice on a broader, more accessible and external basis: political forces and the social context.

Judges and their representative organisations are increasingly better at manipulating the political agenda and, at regular intervals – given the problems, not entirely illogically – come up with warnings about the imminent loss of quality of the administration of justice. No doubt, these concerns are legitimate and they have resulted in a considerable financial injection to the judicial organisation and capacity in the recent Government Agreement. However, for these repeated alarm signals to the political circuit to remain credible in the long run, the judiciary should be able to account to the outside world for what should be and actually is an acceptable quality level of the administration of justice in the future. If the quality dimension is overshadowed by quantitative production figures, simply because they can be based upon hard figures, there is only one thing left to do. Next to the quantified production, the quality level of the administration of justice must be presented in a more reliable, verifiable and systematic manner.

In addition, there is increasing social pressure on the judiciary to collect and study more systematic information regarding the developments of the administration of justice. Society computerises and large-scale databases emerge. In the event that lawyers or other interest groups should start to use Internet sites and create their own databases to assess, for example, the consistency of judgment in order to use the possible lack thereof in their arguments, the judicial organisation would simply be at risk. This tendency, noticeable in the United States, toward types of so-called 'actuarial justice' will not fail to affect the administration of justice in the Netherlands in the future. In the future, lawyers' clients will increasingly ask the following type of questions: 'what are my chances in the proceedings?' and 'how much will it cost me?'. Information technology provides the tools to answer these questions. Thanks to legal-data collections, several measurements can be carried out from which verifiable quantitative conclusions can be drawn. Three examples to illustrate that – in more epistemological terms - a critical, empirical and analytical approach of the administration of justice may provide new ideas about the future in an area that is traditionally dominated by a dogmatic, normative and hermeneutic approach (compare Albert, 1976).

In an unorthodox plea, Barendrecht (1978) analyses the role of civil cassation in supervising and guarding the quality of the administration of justice. The three core tasks of the Supreme Court - guarding legal rights, uniform interpretation of law and the development of law - are analysed on the basis of figures. A random survey showed that approximately two-thirds of the workload of the Supreme Court concerns legal rights. Around one in twenty of the complaints regarding legal rights is successful. Barendrecht concludes: 'Much effort is put into handling the complaints regarding legal rights and often to no avail' (ibid, p. 15). One year of the development of law results in 432 paragraphs with 156 clear rules, 16 rules of thumb, 9 rules of consideration and 61 other directions. It was shown that new rules and justification requirements lead to more appeals in cassation, resulting in an unexpected overload of cases in certain legal areas: 'It is therefore a drastic policy measure to decide to extend the development of law in such an area. Other problems are left aside and we must therefore make the right decision' (ibid, p. 40).

The need for a reliable insight into the quality of the administration of justice may also be covered by a more systematic collection of available data within one's own circle, as was shown by the following study of the quality within the Tax Division of the Amsterdam Court of Appeal: 'One might view the degree of acceptation of the judgment as one quality factor. One criteria is the number of appeals in cassation that are lodged. The number of appeals in cassation rendered in a percentage of the total number of judgments hovers between fourteen and fifteen. Of those appeals, approximately 25% result in an allowance.' (Groeneveld, 1996, p. 31). If the judiciary were to collect such and other data more systematically, it would undoubtedly be easier to establish a standard (perhaps different standards for the various divisions and types of court) and to provide an insight to others on how the quality of the administration of justice is by now threatened by an increasing pressure to speed up the legal procedures.

After all, the need for a more reliable insight into the quality of the administration of justice may be met by carrying out social research. For example, studies by the WODC (Centre for Scientific Studies and Documentation) showed that in 1995 the district with the longest prison terms on average imposed penalties that were twice as high as those with the shortest average prison terms for similar offences. Such research shows that it is necessary to develop a consistent policy on penalties and a system for determining these penalties in order to enable the judge to impose similar penalties in similar cases.

3 Judicial evaluation

In the reports of *Toekomst ZM*, the quality of the administration of justice is referred to as a significant intrinsic value, which may act as a mobilising catalyst for the necessary changes within judicial organisation. In the development of quality systems there is a tendency towards intervision and peer review. In this area, much has already been accomplished, for instance in 1990 the promising NVvR (Netherlands Judges' Association) conference on peer review and intervision. In subsequent years, a system of evaluations for judges has been developed. Work pressure and the labour-intensive character are important reasons for judges not to participate in intervision projects. Another factor is that there is no clear personnel policy for the judiciary, and as a result, the confidential nature of such a far-reaching project is insufficiently guarded. (Koers et al., 1998, 54). In the meantime, the above-mentioned pVRO has paid more attention to the prerequisites, people can build on the experiences and it might be possible – as was argued in the project *Toekomst ZM* – to establish a set of generally accepted standards of quality within three to four years.

Practices abroad provide interesting experiences in the area of intervision projects. In particular, the United States and Canada have had a great deal of experience with quality projects for individual judges, normally referred to by the term 'judicial evaluation'. These systems were originally developed in the 1970s. Anxious citizens appointed themselves as a 'court watch' and published overviews of the performance of judges in order to influence the possible re-election of the judge. The media was quick to react by publishing lists of the ten best and worst judges. Subsequently, the judiciary itself initiated the creation of quality systems. Currently, in some states, evaluation results are published of judges performing badly, three months before the elections (Röhl, 1993, p. 109). Without wanting to glorify the American legal system, it is interesting to examine the way in which they have developed the external accountability of the quality of the judiciary.

In a pilot project in the Canadian Nova Scotia in Canada, the judicial evaluation was developed by asking lawyers to assess individual judges on a number of characteristics by completing an anonymous, written questionnaire. Lawyers were asked to assess the following five items: 'legal ability, impartiality, judicial management skills, disposition practices and comportment'. Judges received, often for the first time in their life, systematic information on their own performance as a judge, and in three ways. Firstly, they were given the opportunity to assess themselves by filling in the questionnaire were given and, after that, they could compare themselves with the average. In addition, they were given an impression of the opinion of 50 lawyers. Finally, the participating judges were given the opportunity to discuss the complete overview with an experienced – often retired – judge selected by themselves, who acted as a mentor.

A noticeable element of the description of the pilot project is the considerable number of precautions taken to safeguard the confidentiality of the information, both with regard to the judge and the lawyers. Measures were taken to ensure that the information could not be requested within the context of the Canadian Government

Information (Public Access) Act, the research was carried out separately on a 'stand alone' computer and forms and data bases were destroyed following the end of the research. Another important success factor of the project was that judges and lawyers participated on a voluntary basis and that their anonymity was guaranteed. As a rule of thumb, a minimum of 50 lawyers had to assess a judge in order to attain reliable results.

The results of the pilot project were satisfactory. The quality of the judges was adequate. Lawyers rated 80% of the judges as being good to excellent. The overall project was also judged favourably. The judges were positive about the set-up of the project, they were of the opinion that the independence of the judiciary had not been threatened at all *and* they were in favour of the continuation of the project. The research also showed that the participating judges believed that the individual discussion of the questionnaire with their personal, selected mentor to be the most effective method. The pilot project also improved the learning processes of the entire judiciary, since the questionnaires were analysed to further direct the general training policy of judges. The analyses showed that the individual differences among judges are larger than the differences between the courts. This is another argument in favour of specific training of individual judges. The importance of the link between the judicial evaluation and the education policy cannot be overstated. After all, the organisational sociologist Mintzberg has made it clear that courses are the only way to implement changes within professional organisations. The autonomous 'stubborn' professionals are relatively immune to other types of direction, such as administrative routines imposed centrally or financial incentives.

4 The performance of the courts

The Prisma Agency fulfils an important role in the development of the quality policy of the Dutch courts. A summary of six studies carried out by Prisma between October 1994 and May 1996 (at six District Courts, twenty-one Subdistrict Courts, six District Public Prosecutor's Offices and six staff organisations) showed that the quality of the courts' organisation is relatively weak and that result-based management and the orientation upon the environment is fairly limited. As of 1997, Prisma supports quality projects within judicial organisations according to the model by the Dutch Quality Institute (*Instituut Nederlandse Kwaliteit,* abbreviated as INK). An essential element of this approach is that the organisation itself is responsible for quality assurance. Courts have to examine themselves in future. The INK method assists courts in the development of a coherent vision of organisational aspects (such as leadership, strategy, personnel management, resources policy) and the end results pertaining thereto (such as the endorsement by clients, personnel and society).

The introduction of quality management according to the INK model is a step-by-step development, i.e., awareness, training, position determination, self-evaluation and audit. The realisation of quality management in terms of these steps at the various components of judicial organisation is outlined in Table 1.

Table 1 – Numbers of Prisma products for types of courts in 1998

Court	Subdistrict Courts	District Courts	Appeal Courts
Presentation	6	13	3
Training	9 pers	129 pers	16 pers
Position determination	3	6	
Self-evaluation		1	
Audit			

The table shows that the majority of courts are still at an exploratory stage as regards quality assurance. By means of presentations by Prisma staff members, they have acquainted themselves with the philosophy and working methods of the INK model. In addition, the management of the court participates on a large scale in the courses and training provided by Prisma. A minority of courts have already moved to position determination, in which a court assesses its strong points and weak points on the basis of a systematic method and initiates improvement projects. The next stage, i.e., compiling a self-evaluation report – in which the weak points that were discovered have been corrected by the improvement projects – has only been carried out by one District Court. An assessment of the efforts by a team of (external) auditors has not been realised as yet. So there is still a long way to go for the courts. It should be pointed out that the activities of Prisma only focus upon improving the quality of the organisation. The quality of judicial decisions is given as a fact. Only at the explicit instigation of the courts themselves does Prisma take into account, in the position determination and self-evaluation stages, how management-oriented support services might contribute to the further professionalisation of the judges' work and the realisation of the quality standards pertaining thereto.

In the future, the primary process (the judges' work) will inevitably be included systematically in the self-evaluations, so that the artificial distinction between legal and organisational quality may be abandoned (Ten Berge, 1997). Courts in the United States developed from a mere administration-oriented (production) management to a quality-oriented management around ten years ago. Originally, the emphasis in the United States (where the workload of the judiciary exploded in the 1970s, just as it happened in the 1980s in the Netherlands) was also put on the productivity and processing times and improvements were sought mostly in the area of management, centralisation and organisational structures. However, gradually there was a growing awareness that leadership and the local culture of a court are much more important to the quality of the administration of justice. As a result, the results of the judges' work was given a more prominent role in the discussion. In 1986, a working group composed of judges, academics and public servants was set up which, following on from the discussion, elaborated the so-called system of 'Trial Court Performance Standards' (TCPS).

In TCPS, five diverse items of the quality of a court are measured: accessibility; duration and timeliness; equality, fairness and integrity; independence and accountability; public trust. The crux of the system is that it defines exactly which aspects/indicators there are and how they should be measured. A broad spectrum of methods of collecting data is used: observations, surveys, statistical data, experiments, etc. TCPS is not merely a technocratic system without an underlying vision of how a court should ideally perform. The underlying notion is that the independence of the judiciary should not result in a situation where they do not co-operate with other government bodies, where they are not held accountable externally or provide services that are below average. After all, it is obvious that the environment (the judges, lawyers, public prosecutors, etc.) determines to a large extent the quality of the administration of justice. Courts need the co-operation and support of citizens, lawyers, the Child Care and Protection Board, the Public Prosecutions Department, and the Probation and After-care Service in order to be able to perform well.

All in all, the content-related objective of the TCPS is oriented more toward the judges than toward staff members of the judicial organisation. It focuses on systematic measurements rather than on reputation. The systematic method seeks to improve the courts themselves. Participation is voluntary, the results are not public and the system is not deemed to be suitable for court to court comparisons. It has taken quite a long time to turn it into a workable and accepted system. Between the development of indicators, gaining support, followed by carrying out pilot projects and finally by the recent step of broader distribution and further reaching institutionalisation through manuals and courses, lie around ten years (Bureau of Judicial Assistance, 1997).

Lastly, an entirely different approach to improve the quality of American courts may be found in the 1990 Civil Justice Reform Act. This Act focuses upon reducing costs and delays at the federal courts. This Act, *inter alia,* stipulates that regular clients of federal courts write a public report from time to time concerning the extent in which courts may be improved in specific areas. They then report on the extent to which a court has, in the subsequent year, succeeded in improving the weak points that were signalled. This (external) type of accountability on the performance of a court has proven to be one of the most effective measures to implement the desired organisational changes and to improve the efficiency, effectiveness and customer-friendly attitude of courts. Another most effective measure has been the regulation that courts should report to Congress annually on how many cases the individual judges had on the shelf and how many of these were approaching the critical limit of a reasonable processing term.

5 The Reinforcement of the Judicial Organisation Project: 'On the Quality of the Administration of Justice'

If the Dutch, Canadian and American experiences show anything, it is that the quality of the administration of justice, judges and courts can be properly measured. Of course, whether the American systems described above will come to the Netherlands remains to be seen. The American trial culture differs considerably from the Dutch system. American courts have more room to manage the course of the proceedings and the organisation in their own way. Furthermore, the recruitment, selection and training of judges is less rigidly regulated, there are less three-judge sections and, in many cases, no appeal can be lodged. Naturally, in such a context it is logical to seek other ways in which to safeguard quality (judicial evaluation, TCPS). The lack of faith on the part of American citizens in the Government and the emphasis upon accountability in the public sector are also two important, general forces that may explain why the United States are so far ahead in this area.

The emphasis upon the various national differences might lead to the idea that the Netherlands does not need a systematic quality policy at all and that the current situation is satisfactory. That is probably a misconception given the consequences of such a standpoint in the end. Or, as the German legal academic Röhl broadly formulates it in response to an extensive study of management and control of the American administration of justice: *'Wenn die Richter sich weiter darauf beschränken, ihre Belastung zu bejammern und sich im übrigen hinter der richterlichen Unabhängigkeit zu verschanzen, geraten sie in die Gefahr, (vollends) zu inferioren Massendienstleistern zu werden, denen früher oder später auch die Unabhängigkeit beschnitten wird. Es gibt nur einen Ausweg. Die Justiz muss ihre Verwaltung selbst in die Hand nehmen und ihre Unabhängigkeit durch ein agressives Quantitäts- und Qualitätsmanagement rechtfertigen.'* (Röhl, 1993, p. 16).

The judiciary in the Netherlands have taken note of Röhl's warning, given the pVRO which has already been initiated. In various pVRO sub-projects, the various aspects of the judiciary's quality (administration of justice, judges and courts) have been examined in different ways.

For example – also with a view to improving the quality of the administration of justice – a start has been made with the national development of penalty systems, publishing judicial decisions on the Internet (*ELRO*) and an integrated, national disclosure of legal precedents (George). Such computerised systems provide important incentives to an overall, systematic and transparent collection of judicial decisions.

The quality of the individual, judicial professional has already been put on the agenda by the steering group *Toekomst ZM* by making a case for the introduction of more systematic types of peer review. Within the context of pVRO, a start has been made with the modernisation of personnel management, whereby the essential characteristics and performance of judges will be defined. Perhaps they can use the results of the American approach of 'judicial evaluation'.

Finally, the promotion of quality on the organisational level of courts is carried out through the sub-project 'Evaluation research of clients and personnel' ('*Waarderings-*

onderzoek klanten en personeel'). The courts in Haarlem and Alkmaar have some experience in this area. In addition, the development of quality indicators has been started, which might provide a basis for a well-balanced system of quality assurance.

Based upon the experiences abroad as described above, the conclusion may be drawn that it is of the utmost importance that the development of a system of quality is carried out under the responsibility of the judicial professionals themselves. It is also clear that the development and actual implementation of an operative system of quality assurance is a process of many years duration. The fact that the first steps have been taken with the self-evaluations under the supervision of Prisma*and* the fact that much may be learned from the experiences in the administration of justice in other countries might possibly accelerate the process of large-scale institutionalisation. Only then will it become apparent whether the contrasts that are often emphasised between quantitative production, responsible professional quality and judicial independence are in actual fact artificial contrasts. After all, a policy of quality results in fewer mistakes, less reparative activities and ultimately in a higher productivity. Would it not be nice and easy if everyone would have the entire file at their disposal and in time from now on, if hearings would start on time, if recent case law could be easily disclosed in a systematic way, etc.? Increasing the quantitative production and professional quality is not contradictory. Both are necessary if we are to ensure the support of the public, the press and politics for an independent judiciary in the near future.

6 Professionals, the public, the press and politics

The programme of the pVRO is ambitious, but it is also a sign of the times, given the developments within other Dutch professional groups, the increasing pressure of the press and the public and the political demand for more external accountability.

6.1 Professionals

Over the past years, the Netherlands has been catching up in the area of external accountability by professionals (such as medics, academics, lawyers, accountants). Since the mid-1980s, the academic world has been dominated by top-ten lists of economists that are quoted most and public reports of external visitation commissions are also published regularly. In the medical world, the reports of visitation commissions are not public. However, the weekly magazine *Elsevier* does publish a top thirty of the Dutch hospitals on the basis of a survey among GPs. (De Hen, 1998), invites a hospital director to publish in annual reports how many times a surgeon carries out a specific type of operation (since this is closely related to the death rate) and there is a lawyer who asks people on the Internet to report complaints of bodily injuries and such like. It might be some time before we – as, of course, they already do in the US – publish the Adjusted Mortality Rate of individual surgeons on the Internet.

6.2 *Public*

Such developments are also taking place within the judiciary. Citizens put pressure on the judiciary for more openness. For example, the Foundation Data Base of the Netherlands (*stichting Databank Nederland*) has already put all additional functions of judges on the Internet. It is expected that judicial sentences will be made available anonymously within the near future, which will no doubt influence future judicial decisions. We must be careful not to take the administration of justice 'report mark' to extremes. Above all, the privacy of judges and justiciaries must be guarded. In addition, expertise with regard to content is necessary to form a proper, well-balanced and fair opinion on the basis of protected information and isolated data bases. Citizens rightly demand insight into the performance of the public administration and questions will have to be answered. Discussions on other issues suggest that public reports with specific aspects of secrecy may be a useful compromise. For example, by anonymous, comparative overviews (of judicial decisions, judges or courts) or by taking the context into account in the reported results (compare quality lists of elementary schools or the aforementioned Adjusted Mortality Risk of medical specialists).

6.3 *Press*

The press have by now discovered that judges are a potential source of news. In December 1998, an article was published in the monthly legal magazine *Amice* in which anonymous lawyers give their opinion of the Netherlands judges in interim injunction proceedings. 'Lawyers: 10 out of the 64 judges in interim injunction proceedings are below par' was the headline of the newspaper *Trouw* before the official publication of the article. The article in *Amice* contained hardly any in-depth reflection and confined itself to a sensationalist review of individual judges, mentioned by name. Obviously, such an unreliable newspaper survey fails to provide a basis for a well-founded improvement of quality. Given the trend in the media, the judiciary would be wise to carry out the 'judicial evaluation' themselves. Then, they could have replied that it takes 50 lawyers to obtain a reliable picture of a judge (instead of 3 to 4); that the quality of a judge depends for an important part upon his environment, for example upon the level of the local bar (compare *Trouw*'s observation that judges in interim injunction proceedings in the rich, urban west of the Netherlands generally obtain better results); that the American examples show that judges in traffic cases are generally rated lower by lawyers; and that lawyers render a harsher judgment the more they appear before a particular judge (the interpretation should therefore take the systematic distortions of this type of research into account).

6.4 *Politics*

Before quality assurance is introduced within the judicial organisation, a structure of accountability toward the political body should be developed, in line with the independent nature of the administration of justice. The specific institutionalisation and regulations of quality assurance within the academic world might be a source of inspiration. The academic world also has an area of tension between important conflicting values such as academic freedom on the one hand, and, on the other hand, the necessity of accountability in view of ministerial responsibility and the parliamentary right of budget. By law, quality assurance is a matter for the universities themselves, they have to provide a basis for comparative studies. The supervision of quality assurance is carried out by means of visitations by broadly composed commissions which publish their findings regularly in a public report. The visitations include both education and research. The implementation has been laid down in a protocol. The Ministry of Education, Culture and Science supervises by means of meta-evaluations, carried out by an independent Inspectorate. The Inspectorate visits the departments with the visitation report in hand and reports to the Minister. Both the Inspectorate and the Association of Co-operating Netherlands Universities (*Vereniging van Samenwerkende Nederlandse Universiteiten*) monitor the follow-up of the visitations (Weusthof, 1994). Such a quality system would seem most appropriate within the context of judicial professionals and their organisations. The contours memorandum is in favour of an integral policy of quality, summarising the most important characteristics in the following sentence: 'Periodic self-evaluations and (external) visitation commissions in conjunction with a public report, might be part thereof.' (Contours Memorandum, p. 17).

7 In closing

Increasing pressure from the public, press and the political body forces the judiciary to concern themselves on a more systematic basis with the issue of quality. The existing quality guarantees are insufficient, especially in view of the increasing demand for more systematic and external accountability by the public, press and the political body. At the moment, it is important to define clear and measurable criteria, indicators and standards as a basis on which the judiciary may account more systematically and externally for the quality of the administration of justice, judges and courts, in the future.

Practices abroad are evidence that it is certainly possible to outline the quality of the administration of justice, judges and courts. The American TCPS project shows how legal standards of a court (accessibility; duration and timeliness; equality, fairness and integrity; independence and accountability; public faith) can actually be measured. The Canadian Nova Scotia project shows which aspects are important for the quality of a judge (legal ability, impartiality, judicial management skills, disposition practices and comportment) and works out how the lawyers' opinions might provide a useful tool for improvements.

Experiences abroad show that the development and implementation of such initiatives take some years. That is hardly surprising. After all, it is not a mere technical operation in which only criteria, indicators and standards have to be defined. At least as much thought must be put into the institutional integration. There is a considerable difference between whether the information regarding the quality of the administration of justice is used by a central Inspectorate (France), is made public (some American States) or functions within a visitation type of system (the Netherlands academic world). Only where judicial professionals start taking responsibility for quality initiatives will a more structural integration of a quality system be possible. An important step has been taken in the Netherlands by setting up the pVRO.

References

Albert, H., 'Kennis en recht: De rechtswetenschap in the licht van het kriticisme', in: H. Albert, *Rationaliteit in wetenschap en samenleving. Opstellen over wetenschap, ideologie en politiek*, edited and introduced by Friso D. Heyt, Alphen aan de Rijn, 1976, pp 174-190.

Barendrecht, J.M., *De Hoge Raad op de hei. Kwaliteitsbewaking en leiding over de rechtspraak door de civiele cassatie: een analyse en denkrichtingen voor de toekomst,* (Tjeenk Willink), 1998.

Bureau of Justice Assistance, *Planning Guide for using the Trial Court Performance Standards and measurement system*, Monograph US Department of Justice, July 1997.

Bureau of Justice Assistance, *Trial Court Performance Standards and measurement system implementation manual,* Monograph US Department of Justice, July 1997

Groeneveld, Th., 'Kwaliteit in de belastingsector', in: *Studieweekend gerechtshof Amsterdam, Kwaliteitsperspectief in de rechtspraak,* Prinsengrachtreeks 1996/2, Amsterdam, 1996, pp 29-33.

Hen, Paul de, 'De ranglijsten van het jaar 1998, Academisch Ziekenhuis Utrecht blijft de ranglijst aanvoeren', in: *Elsevier*, 5-9-1998, pp 116-140.

Kat, Micha, 'KG-rechters beoordeeld', in: *Amice*, November 1998, pp. 7-13.

Koers, A.W., Ph.M. Langbroek, J.A.M. Venniz, J.M.M. Austen, M. Hiemcke, *Rechtspreken en Rechterlijke Organisatie anno 2005, Denkrichtingen voor de toekomst,* 1998 (Steering group *Toekomst ZM*).

P.M. Langbroek, K. Lahuis, J.B.J.M. ten Berge, '*Kwaliteit van rechtspraak op de weegschaal, bijdragen aan het congres over kwaliteit van rechtspraak',* held on 25 September 1997 in Zutphen, Utrecht/Zutphen, 349 p.

Poel, Dale H., *The Nova Scotia judicial development project. A final report and evaluation,* Halifax, 1997, 67 p.

Röhl, Klaus F., *Gerichtsverwaltung und Court-Mangement in den USA. Von Efficienzmanagement zum Qualitätsmanagement. Beiträge zur Strukturanalyse der Rechtspflege,* Köln, Budnesanzeiger, 1993, 142 p.

Trouw, 'Rechters langs de meetlat. Advocaten: 10 van de 64 kort-gedingrechters beneden de maat', 24 November 1998.

Weusthof, Peter, J.M., *Interne kwaliteitszorg in het wetenschappelijk onderwijs*, diss. University of Twente (CHOB), Enschede, 1994, 244 p.

The Challenge of Change for Judicial Systems
M. Fabri and Ph.M. Langbroek (Eds.)
IOS Press, 2000

Measuring Performance in Criminal Justice:

An Initial Evaluation of the Application of the New Public Management to Criminal Justice Agencies in England and Wales

Barry Loveday[1]

1 Setting the scene

Over the last two decades, as part of the 'Thatcher revolution', all public services have been subject in England and Wales to increased demands to improve efficiency and effectiveness, and to provide Value For Money [VFM]. Reflecting their commitment to the private provision of goods and services, the Conservative Governments of Thatcher and Major encouraged either privatisation of services or the introduction of private sector management techniques into the public sector. In the Health Service, such was the then Government's commitment to private provision, it was to establish an 'internal market' which it believed could be expected to improve efficiency by introducing a purchaser/provider split. Although this particular innovation was not to survive the change in government in 1997, other elements of the 'new public management' approach have survived and are (to the evident surprise of 'old Labour') now being as (or more) rigorously pursued by New Labour as the predecessor Conservative Government.

This is perhaps best reflected in the evident commitment of the current Government to the introduction and pursuit of performance management in the public services and the universal application of performance measurement to these services. One consequence of this has been that while 'New Labour' have invested more money in the public services they expect,in performance terms, to get much more out of them as a return on their investment. In the Health and Education services comparative performance data are given as much, if not more importance, as by the Conservatives. In the Education sector an Inspectorate (and Chief Inspector) established under the Conservative Government continues to apply a 'blame culture' to teaching staff whose schools are deemed to be 'failing'. The comparative assessment of performance based on performance indicators has a now near universal application in public services. It remains the case, however, that reservations continue to be expressed as to both their utility and purpose in the public services. Setting objectives and targets for services may be appropriate where that service has almost complete control of the 'product' but may be more problematic where it does not. In the latter

---

1 University of Portsmouth, Great Britain.

case many other extraneous factors may fatally undermine the value of the measurement undertaken when the service measured has little ability to influence those extraneous factors which may impact on the service delivered.

Pertinent examples would continue to include education and health services for example. In education family background and family expectations can impinge substantially on what the child seeks to achieve. In relation to health it is clear that factors such as diet and housing may have a significant influence in terms of health 'outcomes'. The Health Service has, of course, no influence over either of these. The impact of factors external to the public services have been long recognised in the literature and have been the subject of ongoing comment (Pollitt, 1990; Flynn, 1997; Horton and Farnham, 1999; Carter et al., 1992). As has been argued by one commentator, the application of performance targets and performance goals to public services may ultimately fail if only because the use of essentially private sector management techniques overlooks the very real differences which pertain to public as opposed to private sector provision.

In his highly enlightening study of performance measurement Dilulio argues that the essential differences between public and private management are 'rooted in the nature of their respective goals' and that there are,in general terms, two types of goals (Dilulio, 1993). These he describes as operational and non-operational goals, where an operational goal is an image of a desired future state of affairs that can be compared unambiguously to an actual or existing state of affairs. This contrasts with non operational goals which he argues is an image of a desired future state of affairs that cannot be compared unambiguously to an actual or existing state of affairs. As Dilulio argues in relation to this:

> 'Generally speaking, public managers have non-operational goals, while private managers have operational goals. Moreover, public managers often work in the context of multiple and contradictory non-operational goals' (Dilulio, 1993, 146).

The desire of General Motors or Exxon to increase sales by 20% in a foreign market would, for example, clearly constitute an operational goal which can be clearly compared to an actual state of affairs (low or no sales). A commitment to 'making America's welfare system work' would be identified as a non-operational goal being an image of a desired future state of affairs that cannot be compared unambiguously to an actual or existing state of affairs. Moreover, the absence of a 'bottom line' in public management makes the application of private sector goal achievement even more problematic. As Dilulio observes, quoting Allison, 'there is little if any agreement on the standards and measurement of performance to appraise a government manager, while various tests of performance-financial return, market share, performance measures for executive compensation are well established in private business. (...) Governmental managers rarely have a clear bottom line,while that of a private business manager is profit, market performance and survival' (Dilulio, 1993, 144).
One consequence of recognising the reality of differences between operational and non-operational goal setting between types of organisation may impact on the

determination or measurement of efficiency within organisations. As Dilulio has also noted in relation to efficiency measurement:

> 'Efficiency refers to a relationship between valued inputs and desired outputs: maximising outputs from a given set of inputs, or minimising the inputs necessary to achieve a given level of outputs. In many, perhaps most, government agencies, the relationship between valued inputs (people, money) and desired outputs (less crime, better public health) is ambiguous. Where goals are nonoperational and the technologies to achieve them are either uncertain or completely unknown or simply unavailable, the quest for a 'bottom line' is a fool's quest. To the extent that goals are vague or inconsistent, the concept of efficiency is irrelevant. The concept of efficiency is thus irrelevant to many, if not most, public management tasks' (Dilulio, 1993, 146).

While the same commentator was to argue that limited and specific operational goals could be identified within the public services the primary difference between public and private sector goal setting had to be acknowledged. One additional factor that also pertained to this problem, he concluded, was that Government agencies 'must serve goals not of the organisation's own choosing'. Moreover, control over 'revenues, productive factors and agency goals is vested to an important degree in entities external to the organisation – legislatures, courts, politicians and interest groups' (Dilulio, 1993, 144). This again only further highlighted the differences between the private sector and public agencies. It was, presumably, for this reason that Dilulio was to conclude, in relation to the application of private sector performance criteria to public bodies, that:

> 'Because public management and private management are alike in all unimportant respects, it makes little sense to lament that 'government is not run like a business' or to assume that government agencies are inherently less 'efficient' than private firms' (Dilulio, 1993, 149).

He was also to note that the 'multiple and contradictory non operational character of most public management goals,particularly the lack of a market test of output, was a further barrier to the application of private sector performance evaluation to public bodies. The arguments presented by Dilulio while important and persuasive in their own terms are also significant if only because the author belongs to an important and influential school of thought in America which is led by James Q. Wilson and which has traditionally espoused market solutions to many problems identified within the US Criminal Justice system. The clear limitations identified by this leading commentator concerning the application of measurement of performance within the public sector have, however, been highlighted by others. Perhaps the most prominent critique of the push toward performance measurement made recently has come from Carter, Klein and Day. In their highly informative study 'How Organisations Measure Success. The Use of Performance Indicators in Government' (Carter et al., 1992), the authors note that a number of problems surround the application of PIs (Performance Indicators) to public agencies.

2 The complexity of performance measurement

As has been succintly argued by Carter et al., a range of questions arise in relation to the use of PIs in the public sector and while it is unnecessary to explore their case in great detail it may be useful to summarise the salient issues they identify as problematic in the use of performance criteria. As they argue in the first instance, a problem may well arise in terms of performance 'ownership' in that it is often very difficult to specifically identify single agency performance when there is, for example, a high degree of interdependence between agencies in the delivery of services. As the authors note, for example, one question in relation to ownership is the following:

> 'The degree to which performance ownership is constrained by the interdependence of different units, services or activities within an organisation: if the ability of a unit manager to deliver a good service is constrained by or dependent upon what others do, how far does the individual manager own his or her performance?' (Carter et al., 1992, 31).

This issue is, however, more than outweighed by a further constraint in the use of PIs. This concerns the extent to which performance can be expected to be affected by environmental factors beyond the control of the organisations concerned. In relation to the criminal justice system it will be clear that enviromental factors can be of critical importance in determining levels of input, resource demand and to a significant extent levels of output (Carter et al., 1992, 133). Additionally, public organisations may vary in the degree of uncertainty about the relationship between means and ends, that is 'the causal relationship between the input of resources and the achievement of stated objectives' (Carter et al. 1992, 33). As the same authors go on to argue:

> 'In many organisations, objectives are by no means self evident. As [Cyert and March] pointed out long ago organisations are rarely oriented towards the achievement of any specific goal. Indeed objectives are often absent or ambiguous or phrased in a very general way as to be not "operational". More likely there will be multiple objectives that are often in conflict' (Carter et al., 1992, 33).

To these important limitations on the application of PIs can be added others which also demonstrate the difficulties and complexity surrounding their use. In relation to public agencies 'even if objectives are clear and precise' it is often difficult to establish the relationship between the activities of a service and its impact and the extent to which performance depends on external actors. As is argued by Carter et al., for example:

> 'If a police force is charged with reducing crime but is uncertain whether the number of bobbies on the beat, the density of neighbourhood watch schemes or the local level of unemployment will have the greatest impact on crime levels (...) then it is difficult to construct a useful PI of police performance. Or if the objective of the NHS is to improve the health of the nation, is this objective best achieved by the provision of a good health service or by improving housing and diets? In short does the service actually own the product for which its performance is being assessed?' (Carter et al., 1992, 33).

3 Assessing performance

The application of PIs, as has been argued, presents particular problems for public agencies. While this is so it is also clear that any evaluation or assessment of performance presents equally formidable barriers to overcome particularly when there is no clear consensus on the role and function of the agency. As has also been argued by Carter et al. in relation to assessment the most common feature of performance evaluation (in the UK at least) has been by reference to the now well established '3Es' of Economy Efficiency and Effectiveness. The 3Es, which became the mantra of Thatcherite reform of the public services in the UK, had however the unintended (or perhaps even the intended) effect of identifying performance gains in terms of cutting costs rather than reflecting concern about the quality of the service provided. Effectually the 3Es could be best summed up for the public sector as designed to procure 'more for less' from the public services and particularly public service workers.

In highlighting the term 'economy' the Conservative Governments of 1979-1997 encouraged all public managers to identify and assess economy 'exclusively in terms of cost' (Carter et al., 1992, 37). As the same authors were however to note, this approach only reflected a desire to minimise resource consumption by public agencies. Moreover, by focusing on inputs (resources provided) this process 'completely ignored the quality of the output whether it was of an acceptable standard (Carter et al., 1992, 37).

Linked to the very limited purpose given to the economy Carter et al. were also to note that in relation to the application of 'efficiency' the primary aim became an emphasis on cost-cutting in the public services. Yet nothing better illustrated the limited intentions of Government in relation to the evaluation of PIs than its assessment of effectiveness. With a term that is particularly difficult to clearly define, apply and measure and one that is 'fraught with ambiguity and confusion' the practical assessment of effectiveness became (and remains) the extent to which output achieved government (or other) objectives. As has been argued by Carter et al. in relation to this:

> 'Indeed, in practice effectiveness may mean no more than the achievement of targets. These definitions limit effectiveness to an evaluation of outputs of specific

programmes; there is no attempt to link outputs and outcomes and no assessment of the overall policy aims' (Carter et al., 1992, 38).

The very limited evaluation of effectiveness may, however, be easily explained. For as Pollitt has argued, by subordinating outcomes to outputs would accurately reflect a government interest in cost-cutting rather than performance evaluation (Pollitt 1986). Yet such an emphasis on output has also traditionally allowed the Government to sidestep the 'enormous technical difficulty of establishing the causal relationship between outputs and outcome'. As will be argued in relation to PIs, for criminal justice the problem of identifying 'outcome' in relation to individual agencies remains almost insurmountable. This is in part because of the very interdependence which characterises the operation of the criminal justice 'system' and agencies within it. Finally, Carter et al. have identified to two futher problems with performance assessment. The first pertains to issues of 'quality of service' where it becomes clear that in terms of the 3Es the quality aspect of service delivery has been usually subsumed under the imperative of efficiency gains. As has been argued, however, for those who ostensibly espouse the value of performance measurement, any improvement in efficiency should not be at the expense of quality of service (Carter et al., 1992, 140). Finally, the same authors argue that the most important attribute of any PI is the credibility of the information upon which it is built. As is argued: 'If the information is unreliable then many of the criteria of PIs will be impossible to achieve'. In this sense, the accuracy and comprehensiveness of the information provided becomes of critical importance, as does, of course, the integrity of personnel within the agency providing that information.

As the foregoing summary of the work of Carter et al. demonstrates, there are a multitude of problems surrounding the use of PIs in public agencies. These are of course to a great extent diminished if the primary purpose of performance measurement is the reduction in costs. It may well be that in the past the use of PIs has indeed provided a camouflage for cost-cutting rather than improved provision of service. This approach did, of coure, largely characterise the approach of the Thatcher-Major Governments where 'compulsory competitive tendering' became the ultimate goal in cost-cutting across the public sector.

It is also clear however that where the Government wishes to approach the application of PIs with greater integrity major problems in terms of evaluation will necessarily have to be confronted. As will be argued, such is the complexity of such an evaluation in relation to criminal justice agencies that there is little likelihood of exact performance criteria being discovered to enable meaningful performance measurement to be conducted.

4 New Labour and performance measurement

In what has proved to be something of a surpise to many of its more traditional supporters, rather than abandoning the previous government's commitment to performance measurement 'New Labour' has embraced this approach with even greater fervour. As has been demonstrated in a series of Government Strategy Documents and White Papers, New Labour appears to be more committed to this approach to assessing the work of the public services than its predecessor Government which initiated this approach in the 1980s. As has been demonstrated, perhaps most clearly in its 'Best Value' initiative the current Government is committed to furthering the use of PIs across the public sector, including criminal justice.

It should be stressed at once that this approach, identified in detail within the White Paper entitled 'Modernising Local Government. Improving local services through best value', represents a qualitative change in terms of the performance criteria developed by the previous Conservative governments. For the first time, for example,a clear emphasis is placed on the quality of service provision. This is best demonstrated in the decision, much welcomed within the public services, to end compulsory competitive tendering which as the same White Paper notes, when operational often meant that service quality was neglected (Department of the Environment and Transport 'Modernising', 1998, para. 1.5). Nevertheless, this approach does in no sense diminish the overall importance New Labour attaches to PIs in the public sector. As, for example, is argued within the same White Paper, the key principles underlying the approach to Best Value emphasise that:

> 'The quality of services as well as their cost matters and although there will be no compulsion to put services out to tender there should be no presumption that services should be delivered directly if other more efficient and effective means are available. Setting performance targets, as part of regular service reviews and reporting achievements publicly against those targets in Local Performance Plans will be fundamental in demonstrating whether best value is being obtained' ('Modernising', 1998, para. 2.1).

Within the same document detailed outlines as to how public agencies will conduct performance reviews and to what purpose are identified. As is argued within the White Paper 'the review process is designed to ensure that demanding targets for efficiency and quality improvement are set' ('Modernising', 1998, para. 4.19). This can now be expected to embrace:

> 'a. annual efficiency targets which would represent a year on year improvement;
> b. service targets for the longer [5 year] term;
> c. annual service targets which are consistent with the longer-term target' (Modernising, 1998, para. 4.21).

Within the same document it is also stressed that local performance plans and planning and performance management systems 'are likely to develop in tandem. Each of these provides an opportunity for authorities to advance specific performance improvements, typically on an annual basis' ('Modernising', 1998, para. 4.23).

As can be readily ascertained from the above, the approach taken to improving service demonstrates a remarkable similarity to that initiated by the old Conservative Government. Moreover, despite the expression of concern over the application of such criteria from numerous commentators, New Labour appears to be more committed to the use of PIs in the public sector (even if as a Government it is as interested in the quality of service as much s competition) than its predecessors. This commitment is manifested across the public sector but for the purpose of this paper it is the remarkable commitment to close performance measurement within the criminal justice system which is of particular interest. Irrespective of all the apparent dangers of applying performance criteria and PIs to public agencies New Labour has given fresh impetus to performance management in a recent official publication outlining its strategic plan and 'business plan' for the Criminal Justice System 1999-2002.

5 New Labour's strategic and business plans for criminal justice

As is stated within the Strategic Plan the Government has set out the 'aims and objectives for the criminal justice system together with a range of performance measures and targets monitoring performance across the criminal justice system as a whole. Within the Business Plan the Government has set out the 'the ways in which the criminal justice system will be working to meet the aims during 1999-2000'. Within the document highly detailed measures and targets are clearly identified and are detailed below.

Figure 1 – Performance Measures and Targets: Programme

Measure	Supporting data	Target
The long-run rate of the growth of crime	British Crime Survey data on the growth of crime[2]	A reduction in the growth of crime relative to its long-run rate by 31 March 2002
The level of disorder	Current British Crime Survey data on perception of disorder	Level to be reduced by 31 March 2002
Vehicle crime	Current recorded crime data on theft of and from vehicles	30% reduction in the level of vehicle crime within 5 years

2 Details of this measure and target wil be finalised by 31 October 1999.

Fear of crime	Current British Crime Survey data on fear of crime	Fear of crime to be reduced by 31 March 2002
The economic cost of crime	New measure to be developed by 31 March 2000	Economic cost of crime to be reduced by 31 March 2002
Rate of re-convictions of offenders	Current data on actual and predicted reconviction rates from the Offenders Index	Rate to be reduced by 31 March 2002
Rate of re-convictions of persistent young offenders	New measure to be developed by 31 March 2000	Rate to be reduced by 31 March 2002
Measure(s) of just processes and outcomes, *to be formulated*	New measure to be developed by 31 March 2000	To be set by 31 March 2001 for improvement by 31 March 2002
Time from arrest to sentence for persistent young offenders	Measurement introduced 1 October 1998	Halving from 142 to 71 days by 31 March 2000
Time from arrest to sentence or other disposal for all offenders	Interim measure of time from charge to sentence or other disposal[3]	Interim target of reduction by at least 2 days by 31 March 2000
The satisfaction level of victims, witnesses and jurors with their treatment in the criminal justice system	New survey measures to be introduced by 31 March 2000	To be set by 31 March 2000 for improvement by 31 March 2002
Measure on the rights of defendants, *to be formulated*	New measure to be developed by 31 March 2000	To be set by 31 March 2001 for improvement by 31 March 2002
Level of confidence in the criminal justice system	New measure to be developed by 31 March 2000	To be set by 31 March 2001 for improvement by 31 March 2002

3 A measure from arrest to sentence or other disposal is to be developed by 31 March 2000 with a new target them set for a further reduction by 31 March 2002.

As is argued in relation to them the Government reiterates its commitment to improve performance management throughout the criminal justice system [CJS]. As is stated:

> 'This will be taken forward collectively and by depertments, agencies and services individually. A priority task is to complete a suite of performance measures and targets for all eight criminal justice system objectives' (CJS Strategic Plan 1999, para. 1.4.2).

The strategy adopted by the Government will also require a more integrated approach in the delivery of justice. Agencies are encouraged to develop a more coordinated response to the delivery of service, which will be achieved by the development of a new 'strategic approach for more effective and efficient working between different parts of the system at national and local levels' [CJS Strategic Plan 1999, para. 1.1.1]. At a local level there will be a determined move to establish wherever possible, coterminous boundaries between respective agencies. The first step in this direction has already been reflected in the decision to decentralise the Crown Prosecution Service by creating CPS boundaries based on existing local police force boundaries. This probably useful development is, however, more than matched by the very elaborate performance and strategic management structures which are to be created to oversee the implementation of the Strategic and Business Plans. As the same document goes on to argue the creation of a new 'strategic Planning Group' consisting of senior officials and a new Criminal Justice Joint Planning Unit will be made responsible for improving joint planning and 'performance management'. To this will be added a 'cross-departmental Integrating Business and Information Systems [IBIS] Board to maximise 'whole system' benefits from information and business systems to encourage inter-agency cooperation' (CJS Strategic Plan 1999, para. 3.4.2).

To further facilitate an integrated approach, Joint Performance Management arrangements will also be extended. Involving the CPS and police forces, currently the Government intends to involve other agencies at a later date. Embracing all of this will be, however, a 'new performance management approach' which will identify statistical data to set targets, to ensure that measures for the CJS and each agency and service are consistent and to 'show the contribution each is making to overall performance at national and local level'. This initiative will also require regular monitoring of performance against 'targets', comparative performance information and the development of the capacity to 'assess the performance of the criminal justice system as a whole'. The latter will, it is expected, 'provide assurance' that the CJS is operating 'economically and efficiently' is achieving its 'aims and objectives effectively' (CJS Strategic Plan 1999, para. 3.5.3).

6 The way forward?

In developing its new approach to integration and performance the Government argues that there is an immediate need to ' complete development of the first batch of CJS performance measures and establish data collection systems to report on performance' and also to complete a review of audit and inspection arrangements to provide 'an assurance on the efficiency and effectiveness of the CJS as a whole' (CJS Strategic Plan 1999, para. 5. 4). It concludes its strategic review by emphasising that this initiative heralds a new approach to the delivery of justice by agencies that will be required to view the CJS 'as a whole'. As is stated within the Plan:

> 'This is not a one-off plan to be filed and forgotten; it is the start of a developing process. More work is needed, but this document sets out the principles that will be applied in assessing future priorities' (CJS Strategic Plan 1999, para. 6.1.1).
> For the first time a report on the performance of the criminal justice system as a whole [covering 1999-2000] will be published in 2000and further reports ... thereafter. These reports will demonstrate what has happened in the year and indicate what needs to be done to improve future performance' (CJS Strategic Plan 1999, para. 6.2.2).

The Government's Strategic Plan would appear to provide only further evidence (if this was needed) as has been succinctly argued by Horton and Farnham that:

> 'Labour continues to promote performance management which it advocates even more zealously than its predecessors (...) it is clear that Labour has retained the public quality systems set up under the Conservatives and strengthened its attachment to performance management. Labour is determined to use targets and performance indicators as a means of increasing not only productivity and performance but also accountability of ministers for their departments' (Horton and Farnham, 1999, 255).

It would therefore appear to be the case that New Labour, perhaps more than its predecessor Government has decided to put its faith in the expanded use of performance management, despite its rather questionable pedigree. A number of issues arise from this very questionable approach and relate to the extent to which any measurement beyond the most banal can realistically be made of the performance of individual agencies and the degree to which the coordinated approach to the criminal justice system can be effected by way of a performance-management approach identified by the Government within its Strategic Plan. Moreover, it may well be the case that given the significance of 'extraneous' factors over which the CJS has little or no influence the Government may have created a 'hostage to fortune' particularly in relation to the performance measures and targets set for the CJS as a whole.

As is demonstrated below (see Figure 2 below) a very sizeable responsibility has been given to the CJS in terms of, for example, effecting a reduction in the long-run rate of the growth of crime along with a reduction in the fear of crime.

Figure 2 – Performance measures and targets

The following performance measures and targets will be used to assess achievement against objectives.

Objectives	Performance measures and targets
1. To reduce the level of actual crime and disorder	• a reduction in the long-run rate of the growth of crime • a reduction in the level of disorder • a reduction in vehicle crime by 30% within 5 years
2. To reduce the adverse impact of crime and disorder on people's lives	• a reduction in the fear of crime
3. To reduce the economic costs of crime	• a reduction in the economic cost of crime
4. To ensure just processes and just and effective outcomes	• a reduction in the levels of reconvictions for offenders • a reduction in the rate of reconvictions of persistent young offenders • measure(s) of just processes and outcomes *to be formulated*
5. To deal with cases throughout the criminal justice process with appropriate speed	• halving the time from arrest to sentence for persistent young offenders from 142 to 71 days • a reduction in the time from arrest to sentence or other disposal (for all offenders)
6. To meet the needs of victims, witnesses and jurors within the system	• an improvement in the satisfaction level of victims, witnesses and jurors with their treatment in the criminal justice system
7. To respect the rights of defendants and to treat them fairly	• measure on the rights of defendants *to be formulated*

8. To promote confidence in the criminal justice system	• an improvement in the level of confidence in the criminal justice system

To what extent is it possible for CJS agencies even if working in a coordinated fashion to actually be able to achieve either of these objectives? There has, for example, been a long-term shared view as to the very limited influence of the CJS and individual services on the problem of crime. This conclusion was of course reached earlier and addressed in official publications on the role of the CJS in terms of crime control. One notable characteristic identified within these publications was the large volume of offences that are on a regular basis never dealt with by the CJS because they are never reported by the victim (British Crime Survey 1992, 1997). Additionally, the attrition rate which is the percentage of offences which are committed but which are either not reported or recorded when added to the number of cases not pursued or prosecuted,remains alarmingly high and is a further reminder that Government expectations of criminal justice in terms of performance may hugely exaggerate the ability of the CJS to significantly effect a reduction in criminal behaviour. As Home Office data demonstrate, for crimes against individuals and their property, 3 in 100 offences resulted in a criminal conviction or a police caution (see Figure 3 below).

Figure 3

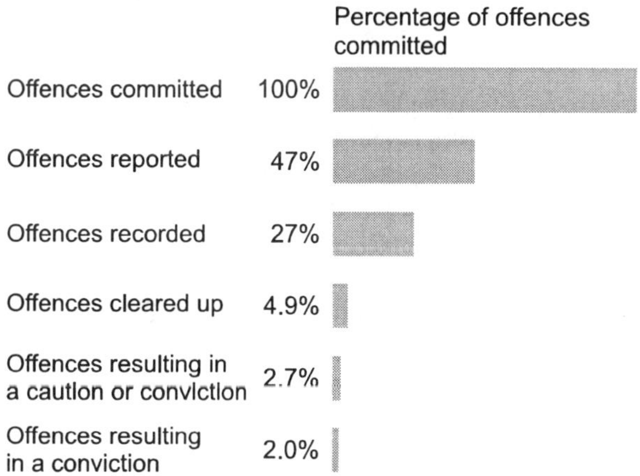

Source: Barclay - Home Office 1995

Nor is it possible to ignore the significance of the those who collect the data upon which,presumably, judgements as to performance of an agency will be based. One good example of this problem has traditionally arisen with police forces. Perhaps reflecting organisational doubts about the intrinsic value of crime figures as an indicator of efficiency, police forces have often unofficially exercised considerable discretion over what offences are recorded. and how they are recorded (Young,

1991). The tendency to record offences that reflect well organisationally while 'losing those that do not', has a long history and can be expected to assume a higher salience if crime figures are viewed as indicators of efficiency. This point has been well made by Coleman and Moynihan, who argue that :

> 'Especially important [in the collection of crime data] is the way in which such data are regarded by those who have a role in producing them. Any measures that are seen as reflecting on the capacities and qualities of those involved present particular difficulties: those that are seen as productivity measures or success rates require much more subtlety in their interpretation. The figures used to measure police performance, for example, are often not created independently but produced by the organisation. They are not only social constructions but are also open to manipulation and disputes about interpretation' (Coleman and Moynihan, 1996, 136).

The identification of the limited value of the official crime data upon which the CJS is to be at least in part judged in terms of performance immediately highlights one of the limitations identified earlier. This of course relates to the credibility of th information which forms the basis of the assessment of the measurement of performance. As was noted by Carter et al, if the information is unreliable then many of the criteria of Performance Indicators will be impossible to achieve. Moreover, as was also to be discovered by Carter et al., the very application of performance measures could significantly influence what the agency did therafter. As was to be argued by Carter et al.:

> 'There is a widespead feeling [within the policeservice] that the pressure on the police to increase productivity and display value for money has resulted in an excessive and undesirable interest in the 'measurable aspects of police work'. This trend can be seen in operational terms with the spread of techniques such as graded response and crime screening (...) it is widely held within the service that the focus on the quantifiable has occurred at the cost of the unquantifiable preventative and service functions that are essential ingredients of traditional policing' (Carter et al., 1992, 63).

As will also be seen in relation to another agency, the identification of productivity targets, besides seriously skewing the activity of the organisation towards the measurable, may also begin to undermine both the purpose and overall integrity of the agency. As again was to be discovered by Carter et al., 'goal displacement' may lead personnel to do whatever is thought appropriate to achieve set objectives and targets. As they note:

> 'More specifically, critics point to the 'goal displacement' caused by the pursuit of measurable targets rather than essential objectives; a response that in its extreme manifestation led to the case of Kent officers who persuaded convicted prisoners to

> 'confess' to unsolved crimes for which they were innocent, thereby improving the clear up rate of the individual officers' (Carter et al., 1992, 63).

The potential dangers of performance measurement undermining the integrity of the organisation subject to it has been manifested within other agencies. Perhaps the most interesting example to date has been provided by the Crown Prosecution Service. As was to be discovered by the Glidewell Inquiry, the impact of performance management was to be severe within the organisation in which the Inquiry was to find over 80% of respondents to a staff survey believed that the CPS was 'one of the worst organisations in which to work' (Loveday, 1999, 23). While much of the discontent arose from CPS lawyers who at this time were heavily involved in monitoring performance within the CPS rather than 'frontline prosecuting' it was also clear that to achieve performance targets local discretion supposedly exercised by CPS prosecutors was effectively overridden by central directives. As can be seen from the the Key Targets set for the CPS for the year 1995-96, the aim to reduce unit costs and to increase 'year on year' the percentage of cases discontinued before the first hearing 'as a percentage of all cases discontinued' may have created the very crisis which was to later engulf the entire Service (see Figure 4).

Figure 4 - Key Targets 1995-96

The key targets against which performance will be measured in next year's Annual Report are:

- To achieve a reduction in unit costs in real terms, whilst preserving value for money.
- To achieve a 5% reduction in the proportion of cases resulting in all non-jury acquittals and bind overs in the Crown Court.
- To increase year on year the percentage of cases discontinued before the first hearing as a percentage of all cases discontinued.
- To despatch payment of prosecution witnesses' expenses within a period of between 5 to 10 working days of receiving a correctly completed form.
- To increase by 5% per year the proportion of complaints replied to within 10 days of receipt.
- To respond to Parliamentary correspondence within 15 days of receipt in 80% of cases.
- To introduce prosecution team working to all Areas by autumn 1996.

As again was to be argued by Carter et al. there has been certainly in the immediate past an assumption that economy was effectively linked to cost-cutting and this has more recently been reinforced by the Government requirement for all public sector bodies to achieve a 2% efficiency gain year on year for around five years. As costs were cut the administrative load placed on prosecutors within the CPS increased. One quite unintended consequence of this, however, was ever increasing pressure to discontinue cases which were judged to be 'borderline cases ' in terms of prosecution outcome. As the Glidewell Inquiry was to note:

> 'We could not fail to recognise the volume of doubts and on occasion criticisms expressed to the effect that the CPS is thought to discontinue cases judged as borderline in an effort to ease the pressures on hard-pressed lawyers. We consider that there may be some validity in these criticisms' (Glidewell, 1998, Chap. 4, para. 32).

The same Inquiry was to discover that rates of discontinuance appeared to be high in offences against the person and of criminal damage and that 'those categories showing the highest percentage rates of cases terminated were often the most complicated or sensitive and therefore the most difficult to prosecute' (Glidewell, 1998, Chap. 4 para. 44). The Inquiry was to also find that there was evidence that the CPS also regularly downgraded charges and that while there were no published statistics it was clear that where the CPS altered charges 'most of these were the same categories of offence as those in which rates of discontinuance were particularly high' (Glidewell, Chap. 4, para. 44).

Evidence from Glidewell suggested that the drive for efficiency within the service (measured by internal targets) appeared to have undermined that agency's effectiveness. Discontinuance was most likely to occur with offences of violence against the person and least likely to involve motoring offences. Yet in terms of both the public interest and public confidence in the CJS the decision to so frequently discontinue the most serious cases while pursuing the least serious may be viewed as one consequence of having committed the CPS to organisational goals which it was required to achieve. Downgrading of offences may also have been cost-driven. As has been argued by Rose, public interest considerations used by the CPS as a defence for non prosecution probably hid a deeper reality where 'the pre-eminent public interest was not justice but cost' (Rose, 1996, 136). As Rose was to argue, CPS decision making appeared to be influenced by a:

> 'Further cost driven factor which exerts a powerful influence on prosecutors' decisions. Under pressure from the Treasury the CPS has, since 1992, set its staff annual 'performance indicator' targets aimed at getting the cases which are to be dropped thrown out at the earliest possible stage' (Rose, 1996, 136).

One consequence of the drive for economy and efficiency rather than effectiveness was that while the resource to output relationship appeared to be successful in that targets were met, the final outcome proved to be increasing failure. As the graph below demonstrates while crime continued to rise at this time, the number of prosecutions steadily fell (see Graph 1 below).

Graph 1

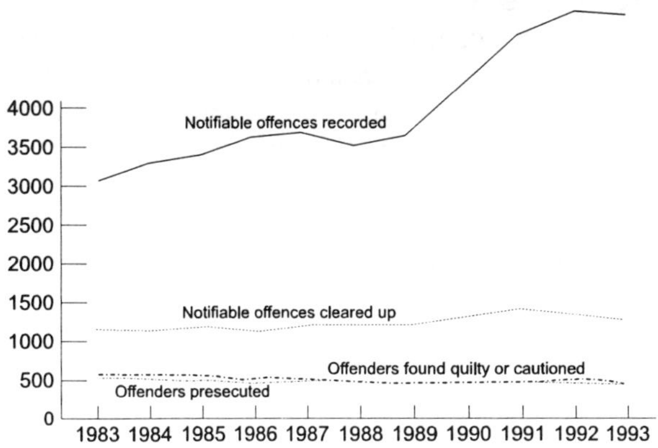

Source: Home Office 1994

7 Coordinating criminal justice and the application of joint performance measures

The Government's objective to seek closer integration between different agencies within the criminal justice system must be considered laudible if not highly desirable. Yet without seeking to question the general purpose and aims of the Government it is clear that its early insistence on the use of joint performance management may generate some problems. This may arise from the fact that, despite the laudable objectives set by it, the Government may not have fully appreciated the difficulties that are bound to arise when a multi-organisational system exhibits high levels of discretionary power usually jealously guarded by professional independence and organisational culture. As has been argued in relation to the CJS, its structure:

> 'Is what we might call muli-organisational, that is, it is a system of densely interconnected but largely autonomous organisational units. They do not operate as a single organisation for two main reasons: [i] there is a strong and justified belief that the advantages of decentralised control outweigh those of control from the centre and [ii] the parts pre-date the whole and often have a strong wish to remain independent (as in the case of the judiciary) (Moxon, 1985).

Moreover, in addition to the independence exhibited by each agency there are a multitude of what might be described as 'sub-systems' each of which can be expected to have differing views as objectives and priorities within the CJS. One example of this might be the police service where within it three professional groups seek to seperately identify organisational issues which are of interest to its members (ACPO; the Police Federation and Superintendents Association). Besides this there are two governmental bodies, each of which may have differing views as to current policing priorities; centrally the Home Office and locally the police authority. Nor can the

Police Complaints Authority be ignored which has had an increasingly important part to play in the effective government of the police. As can be seen, subsystems within the operational purview of individual agencies suggest that achieving high levels of coordination could prove to be problematic. It remains, however, the discretionary areas exercised by agencies that makes the development of an 'integrated system' within the CJS most unlikely. It is of interest here that for the 'system' to work at all it has been felt that the exercise of professional discretion is essential. Whether this is the case the Judiciary, the CPS and the Police have traditionally exercised a high level of professional discretion. Whether in terms of sentencing, the decision to prosecute or the decision to arrest these decisions have and continue to remain within the professional discretion of discrete agencies, none of which would wish voluntarily (or otherwise) to surrender such clear independence.

8 Conclusion

The very nature of the structure of the CJS would suggest that the Government's aim to achieve the better integration of business processes to improve the efficiency of the CJS could meet with only limited success. This issue is of course only compounded by the division of responsibility at central Government level between the Home Office and the Lord Chancellor's Department. There is no Ministry of Justice to attempt to coordinate the desired integration. In the absence of any immediate facility to encourage integation there is the evident threat of greater central intervention in the 'local' delivery of service. Setting objectives and targets centrally and thereafter enforcing them will inevitably encourage such intervention. This may be even more likely when the Government wishes to impose its vision of an integrated and coordinated system on what is a disparate and often conflicting collection of agencies and sub-system which may often be in conflict with each other in terms of purpose and priorities. Yet the Government's wish to see a smoothly operating criminal justice 'system' may overlook the fact that for reasons of, amongst other things, equity and liberty the very disparate nature of the CJS could, ironically, be one of its real strengths. Performance management within 'joined up' Government could ultimately lead not just to failure, because of the problems of evaluation within an interdependent system which encourages a high degree of professional autonomy and discretion, but may encourage significant central intervention as the Government 'encourages' criminal justice agencies to achieve the goals and targets set for them by it. For the New Labour Government which is ostensibly committed to greater decentralisation the 'performance management' approach threatens to generate the very centralising policy which in opposition it so frequently condemned. As has been demonstrated within the CPS the pursuit of a performance 'results' culture can create serious dysfunctions which ultimately undermine the effectiveness of the organisation. The application of the same performance culture across the criminal justice system in the pursuit of elusive targets may also emphasise the 'mechanistic' perception apparently held by New Labour in relation to criminal justice. There is within the managerialist approach the real danger identified by commentators that the pursuit of efficieny gains and performance measures may ultimately only serve to reinforce pragmatic expediency (Rutherford, 1996,134). For as has been succinctly argued by Carol Jones:

> 'The virtue of managerialism is that it is divorced from any substantive normative or political values. Indeed, it transforms the absence of principled policy (for example along the lines of justice and fairness) from a vice into a virtue' (Jones, 1993).

Within the context of improving performance within criminal justice it is to be sincerely hoped that in its search for improvements in the delivery of justice that 'New Labour' does not become merely the agent of 'old vices'!

References

Barclay, G.C., *Digest. Information on the Criminal Justice System in England and Wales*, Home Office, (1995).

Carter, N., Klein, R., and Day, P., *How Organisations Measure Success. The Use of Performance Indicators in Government*, Routledge, (1992).

Coleman, C. and Moynihan, J., *Understanding Crime Data. Haunted by the Dark Figure*, Open University Press, (1996).

Dilulio, J. Jnr., 'Measuring Success when there is no Bottom Line [in] Performance Measures for the Criminal Justice System', Discussion Papers from the BJS-Princeton Project, US Department of Justice, (1993).

Flynn, N., *Public Sector Management*, 3rd ed, Prentice Hall, (1997).

Home Office, Digest 3, *Information on the Criminal Justice System in England and Wales,* (1995).

Home Office, *Criminal Justice System Strategic Plan and Business Plan* (1999).

Home Office, *British Crime Survey 1992,* (1997).

Her Majesty's Stationary Office, *The Review of the Crown Prosecution Service Chairman Rt. Hon. Sir Iain Glidewell,* (1998).

Her Majesty's Stationary Office, *Modernising local government. Improving Local Services Through Best Value*, Department of the Environment and Transport, (1998).

Horton, S. and Farnham, D., *Public Sector Management in Britain*, Macmillan, (1999).

Jones, C., *Auditing Criminal Justice*, British Journal of Criminology, (1993).

Loveday, B., *The Impact of performance culture on Criminal Justice Agencies. The case of the Police and CPS*, ICJS University of Portsmouth, (1999).

Moxon, J., *Managing Criminal Justice. A Collection of Papers*, Her Majesty's Stationary Office, (1985).

Rose, D., *In the Name of the Law. The collapse of Criminal Justice*, Jonathan Cape, (1996).

Rutherford, A.,*Transforming Criminal Policy Spheres of Influence in the United States, the Netherlands and England and Wales During the 1980s*, Waterside Press, (1996).
Young, M., *An Inside Job*, Oxford Clarendon Press, (1991).

The Challenge of Change for Judicial Systems
M. Fabri and Ph.M. Langbroek (Eds.)
IOS Press, 2000

Selected Issues of Judicial Administration in a Comparative Perspective

Marco Fabri[1]

1 Introduction

> '(...) this study has been undertaken in the belief that there is no valid reason why the judicial work of a government should not be performed with the same efficiency, economy, and dispatch that is demanded of the conduct of legislative and administrative affairs' (Willoughby, 1929, 8).

Willoughby in 1929 had already recognized that courts are complex organizations and that they can be analyzed in terms of the characteristics they share with other public organizations, even if they still have some peculiarities. Many judicial systems are suffering from a high volume of cases and they are often considered ineffective and inefficient in their performance, while there is a general disagreement between judicial and administrative responsibility. This seems particularly true in Europe where a judicial administration movement has never started and, as far as I know, very little attention has been paid to organizational studies of courts and prosecutor's offices, that have always been an exclusive ground for legal studies.

This article should be read as a very short list of issues that have been affecting the courts and that need to be much better analyzed and studied in Europe. The ultimate goal is to stimulate the debate on issues that, as far as I know, have often been neglected by public administration scholars but that are very important for the independence of the judiciary as well as for the improvement of the performance of European justice systems. To do so, in these few pages, I will briefly describe the institutionalization of the discipline of judicial administration in the United States and the genesis of the judicial administrator or court manager. Then, I will deal with some selected issues of judicial administration such as: caseflow management, forecast caseload and evaluation and planning of judicial needs. Originally, I wanted to dedicate a few words to alternative dispute resolution and information technology in the justice systems, since this latter is in particular a very important 'means of change', but the

1 Senior Researcher at The Research Institute on Judicial Systems on the National Research Council (IRSIG-CMR), Bolgona, Italy.

page constraint has not allowed me to do so.[2] The concluding remarks will claim a need for a mind shift, or a *second order change* (Watzlawick, Weackland and Fish, 1974), in the justice systems, as a breakdown from rooted dysfunctional assumptions.

2 Judicial administration and the role of the court manager

> 'An inefficient court does less with its resources than an efficient court – fewer people get justice' (Wheeler, 1988, 13).

As Wheeler and Whitcomb (1977, 7) note, judicial administration 'is a slippery concept'. It is easy to find plenty of definitions, it depends on the point of view of the actor of the legal system. As a broad definition, judicial administration can be thought of as the environment in which the justice system acts. This environment is composed of several aspects, the judicial administration tries to coordinate, to manage in an efficient and effective way all these different elements. The discipline was certainly born in the United States and it has a spiritual father: Roscoe Pound, whose address entitled 'The Causes of Popular Dissatisfaction with the Administration of Justice' delivered at the annual meeting of the American Bar Association (ABA) in 1906, is still considered the first manifesto of judicial administration. In this address, he enumerated several issues which are still debated today such as: the multiplicity of courts, waste of judicial manpower, archaic and rigid procedural rules, no overall authority, responsibility and accountability for judicial operations. As Wigmore (1937, 177) notes 'the seed of judicial administration, the importance to manage courts, to divide the judicial function from the administrative one had been launched'.

At that time in the Unites States 'Courts tended to operate as feudal kingdoms with no centralized authority with no centralized coordination, let alone management. The situation was made worse in most jurisdictions by the election of the clerk of the court (...) whose office was usually supported by fees collected for services or paper filed' (Lawson, 1982, 5). Some of the consequences of this situation were the lack of judicial branch accountability, the difficulties in having a flexible system to transfer judges and other personnel according to caseload needs, the lack of professional administrators based on the assumption that judges could control clerical staff, and that administrative matters would be properly attended under the judges' direction.

A few years after the Pound address, in 1913, the American Judicature Society was founded, an organization of lawyers and non-lawyers concerned with the administration of justice (Lawson 1982, 14). Between 1920 and 1930, several Judicial Councils were created following Pound's idea. These councils were generally composed of

---

2 The *Research Institute on Judicial Systems* of the Italian National Research Council is currently carrying out, with other partners, a research project on court technology in Europe. The project, sponsored by the European Commission, the Grotius Programme, is still in progress and the final event, the *First European Seminar on Court Technology*, is due to be held in Bologna, Italy, in September 2000. Its aim is to give a first broad overview of the state and use of information and video technologies in courts and prosecutor's offices in the European Union.

judges, lawyers, academics, and public members. Their functions were to collect statistics on court dockets and caseflow, and to carry out studies and to make recommendations for the improvement of the administration of justice.

The first court manager was created in Boston in 1924. A position of executive clerk to the chief judge, with duties very close to those which are generally considered appropriate for trial court administrators.

The Administrative Office of the United States Courts was established in 1939, notwithstanding that 'there were no specifications as to education and other qualifications for the position (of judicial administrator). Also the position continued to be viewed in the context of providing administrative assistance to the chief justice in carrying out the duties of that office' (Lawson and Howard, 1990, 13). National associations of court administrators were created in the mid-1960s. Many judges, during a survey in the mid-1960s showed an awareness that the business of the trial courts should be administered like a business under the experienced supervision of someone whose sole job it is to administer, because the administrative judge or presiding judge is bound by time-consuming, non-judicial work (Klein, 1967, 179).

So, slowly but progressively, the judiciary of the United States began to internalize the concept of judicial administration as something that has to be managed by people who have particular skills and competence. The court managers should be trained in business, but should also have the necessary know-how related to the peculiar needs of the judicial environment. It is a question of accepting the idea that it is one thing to dispense justice and another to manage, to run the courts which are complex organizations. 'Judges are now aware that there is more in management of the court than one learns in law school (...) management, is like law, a profession, and it is almost as inappropriate for a manager to try a lawsuit as it is for a lawyer - without the benefit of long orientation - to efficiently manage a complex organization such as a court' (Gallas, 1968, 334).

In the 1970s there was the explosion of the judicial administration issue thanks to Chief Justice Burger who strongly asked for the creation of court administrators or court managers 'to manage and direct the machinery so that judges can concentrate on their primary professional duty of judging' (Burger 1969, 108). After that address, substantial federal grants by the Law Enforcement Assistance Administration were invested in the judiciary. Two national conferences on judicial administration were held in 1971 and 1978. The first led to the creation of the National Center for State Courts (NCSC) - a non-profit organization committed to improving the administration of justice - and of the Institute for Court Management that would merge with the National Center some years later. During the 1970s several states enacted new judicial articles in order to unify and simplify the trial court structure as well as establishing a judicial college for training judges (ABA, 1981).

In the following years there has been an institutionalization of the court manager's role. Massive amounts of literature in the United States have been produced during these years about delay reduction, caseflow management, jury management, court facilities, performance evaluation, technological innovation, and the core functions of the court managers (Baar and Perry, 1981; Mahoney, Solomon, 1981; Reinkensmeyer, 1990).

The creation of these new management positions in the courts has been an answer to the growing caseload, court congestion, and to the complexity of the system that needs professional and specific expertise and skills quite different from the classical juridical knowledge (Solomon, 1981a, 1981b, 1990; Friesen, 1984; Röhl, 1993).

3 The workflow and caseflow analysis

'(...) everyone is entitled to a fair and public hearing within a reasonable time' (art. 6 European Convention on Human Rights, Rome, November 4, 1950).

In this section I will explore some changes that have commenced in judicial offices after the judicial administration discipline was recognized as valuable and profitable for the improvement of court operations. In this article it will not be possible to treat extensively the issues that I will raise, and so I hope that they will provide some stimulus for further discussion and analysis.

Basically, it is possible to single out quite a few areas in which the internal organization of work has affected or should affect courts. One certainly deals with the better management of the workflow and in particular of the paperflow. As is known, courts are considered to be organizations which are labour-intensive and they are still characterized by an enormous production of paper. To manage the paper workflow, to reduce the paper that goes through the court, to diminish overlaps, redundancy of operations, and data entry, are some of the aims that a programme of caseflow management tries to pursue (Solomon M., 1973; Clifford, 1983).

Court caseflow can be considered the process by which cases go through the court from filing until court jurisdiction is ended (Clifford and Jensen, 1983, 59; NCSC, 1989a). Caseflow management is the active monitoring, supervising and managing of caseflow so that each case moves through the court without undue delay. The concept of delay is difficult to define. In common language, to delay means to postpone and to put off, and it has a bad connotation. In the court environment it means that a case does not move as fast as it could, because of problems that are generally recognized as court problems. Usually delay deals with expectations and subjective perceptions of the 'local legal culture' (Goerdt, 1987; Mahoney, 1988), which is different in every environment. A delay that could be acceptable in one community could be unacceptable in another (Mahoney and Sipes 1985; Melcher, 1984). The level of compliance is different in each area and for each person but it has to be recognized that there is a certain *critical threshold* beyond which aversion and dissatisfaction for the administration of justice can be very dangerous for a country that bases its legitimacy on popular consensus.[3]

The implementation of a programme of caseflow management should coincide with a programme of delay reduction and it should be the basis from which to express evaluations on the performances of the different components of the court (Ostrom and Hanson, 1999). The fundamental elements involved in a caseflow management programme are: (a) judicial commitment, leadership and the mechanism of accountability; (b) involvement of the different actors in the system; (c) court supervision of case progress; (d) definition of goals and standards; (e) monitoring of cases by an information system; (f) a firm trial date; (g) a policy against unjustifiable continuances; (h) an assignment system; and (i) education and training (Mahoney, 1988).

There is no single model of successful delay reduction or delay prevention programme. For each programme six areas of interesting data can be identified which have to be considered: (1) measures of activity; (2) measures of inventory; (3) measures of delay; (4) measures of scheduling accuracy; (5) evaluation measures; (6) individual case progress information (Clifford and Jensen, 1983; Solomon and Somerlot, 1987). Inside each of these large categories it is possible to breakdown the analysis on the basis of the capability of the information system and the needs of the courts. It is fundamental at least to monitor the number and the age of pending cases globally, per type of case and per judge.

If there are standards (ABA, 1990, 1992) the following step is to determine the backlog, that is the number of cases that have not been disposed of within the established time-limits. It is also useful to know the length of the backlog for each case and for the entire caseload: the time between events, the number of continuances, the number of dispositions for each stage of the proceeding (Sipes and Mahoney, 1985).

Among the different techniques that an effective caseflow management can contain, there is the *assignment* of cases to the judges and consequently the kind of calendar adopted. The assignment is the moment at which each case is given to a judge or to a pool of judges. The calendar, in this context, is the way in which the work of judges is organized.

After the case has been assigned it can be handled by an *individual*, a *master* or a *hybrid* calendar. In an *individual calendar*, a judge is responsible for a case from the beginning to the end, for all the steps that will occur from the moment of assignment until disposition. In a *master calendar*, each judge has a particular function to conduct in the different stages of the proceedings. There is a functional specialization based on the assumption that because of the increasing complexity of the law, it is necessary to have judges who specialize in a particular stage of the proceedings. The *hybrid calendar* can assume different forms. As the term suggests, it is a mixture of the individual and the master calendar applied during one or more stages of the proceedings. There are pros and cons for each of the calendars mentioned, even if some

3 Italy has probably the largest backlog and the slowest pace of litigation, both criminal and civil, among all the Western countries. For the excessive duration of trials Italy has been repeatedly condemned by the European Court of Human Rights.

empirical research has shown that an individual calendar seems to be a little bit more expeditious than the other methods for civil cases (Goerdt, 1987; Mahoney, 1988).[4]

Some courts are also experimenting with a particular kind of caseflow management called: *Differentiated Caseflow Management* (DCM) (Cooper and Solomon, 1993). It changes the chronological concept of handling the cases in the courts. In other words, the system 'first-in, first-out' is substituted by a system which takes into account the complexity of each case and assigns it to a particular track of procedure. In this way, simple cases can be disposed of quickly. They do not wait for cases filed before them which may be much more complex in nature, therefore taking longer to dispose of. If DCM is adopted, there is an early court intervention in each case. The screening criteria to assign each case to the correct track involves the parties and is based on established variables. There is a different way to process each case in each track, with predetermined events and time standards for each track. The court has to monitor and supervise the progress of the cases. The case assignment system can be suited to each track. The workload as well as the calendar of the judges are better managed as well as the eventual use of alternative dispute resolution because it is only concentrated in certain tracks. The courts have much substantive information about cases at an earlier stage. Court personnel can be better allocated on the basis of the caseload for each track.

I do not know how many courts in Europe have utilized these techniques, or maybe similar other ones, that have been useful for better managing the courts. As far as I know, there are no studies in Europe that have addressed these issues. If there would be, it would be worth sharing the information among scholars and practitioners in order to explore what has been developed in the European courts.

4 Forecast caseload and planning judicial needs

> 'Before adding more judges or more courts, we should be sure we are making the best and fullest use of those we have' (Pound, 1940).

Another major reorganization of the work concerns an accurate evaluation of the needs and their best allocation inside the office (Lawson and Gletne, 1980, 1987; Flango and Ostrom, 1996). Here, there is emphasis on measures of productivity, efficiency, and the effectiveness of both administrative and judicial work. The means used in an attempt to determine reliable measures are mainly the determination of the caseload and different methods by which to forecast it. Subsequently, there is an allocation of resources by some quantitative criteria.

This is extremely important in a period such as this resulting in a constant limitation of resources; to determine as precisely as possible the needs of the court or

4 It is important to notice that the calendar system is affected by the procedural law (e.g. adversarial or inquisitorial) used in a country. As far as I know, there are no studies that have related the calendar systems with the kind of procedure adopted.

prosecutors' offices and to allocate resources where they are required is one of the most difficult tasks. Workload measures try to figure out and forecast, when possible, the caseload that can be handled by the court. Workload measures provide quantitative support to the request for more resources, as well as to their allocation inside the court. In the courts that have their own budget, workload measures can be very useful to justify a request for funds from the Ministry of Justice or the Legislature.

Another scope of workload measures is the measurement of productivity. Once the study concerning the workload has been conducted, it is possible to create standards which can be used for performance appraisal. On the other hand, these measures can be adopted by the managers of the court to set goals and objectives for the future.

Among the different possible methods of measurement adopted, I will briefly consider: (a) *the weighted caseload*, (b) *the delphi method*, (c) *historical data*, (d) *the unit cost method*.

With a *weighted caseload* the goal is to compile a caseload that can be comparable but, at the same time, that takes into account the different case types or case events. Generally, some time measurement is calculated for case types or case events. Once the factor of time for each type of case has been determined, it is applied to each case of that particular kind. With the sum of the different caseloads for the kind of case now weighted in favour of a determined factor, it is possible to calculate a number which determines the overall caseload of a judge or of a court.

In order to calculate the time quantification, it is possible to carry out a *time study* which is a classic observation of employees performing work. Another method is to consider only a work sample in order to estimate the time necessary to finish a particular function. This sample has to be representative, because it will be inferred to apply to all types of cases. The last method which I think is worthy of mention is the definition of standard data. They are, basically, determined by surveys of the existing situation; then, there is a standardization of tasks by method engineering and the calculation of the standards based on the two analyses just mentioned.

The *delphi method,* substantially calculates the time necessary to complete a specific job by several interviews with experts. The essential objective of this method is to reach consensus on workload measurement.

Historical data are probably the most popular. They are based on the number of cases concluded and the number of employees or the number of judges. A simple division allows one to calculate a ratio between the cases concluded and the number of judges and/or employees.

The *unit cost* indicates the quantity of resources required to produce an unit of output. It is calculated by dividing the total resources by the number of dispositions in a given period.

Some of these methods discussed take into account the different mix of cases that characterize a caseload, a very crucial point, while some others do not. All of them have, anyway, some elements in common. They are affected by the availability of data and by the reliability of their collection. They inevitably create a certain degree of judicial and staff resistance. They have to be monitored and updated periodically.

Once a reliable measure of the workload has been determined, it is necessary to estimate the number of cases expected in the future so that it is possible to identify future judicial needs. In order to foresee the total caseload or the caseload for the type of case in question the most used forecasting method is Multiple Regression Analysis. Several independent variables are taken into account for civil, criminal and juvenile cases in order to build a quite reliable multiple regression. By dividing the number of cases foreseen by the numbers determined with the workload studies discussed above, it is possible to estimate the numbers of judges and clerical employees that will be required during the following year.

After having obtained the resources, they have to be allocated. They can be allocated taking into consideration some different criteria or measures. *Direct measures* such as the number of filings or the number of active pending cases: *Indirect measures* such as: the number of dispositions, number and rate of jury trials, case processing times, the use of outside judicial assistance, time spent by each judge. *Surrogate measures* such as: population growth and density, the number of attorneys, presence of a state institution locally, economic situation of the area, new local law, some particular political factors (National Center for State Courts, 1983).

These techniques, when they have been adopted, have greatly changed the way in which work is conducted in the courts. First of all, they help to introduce concepts of efficiency and productivity in the judiciary, concepts that are often considered a menace to judicial independence. Secondly, they have allowed a better evaluation of judicial needs and a more rational and fair allocation of them, both statewide and inside the courts. Thirdly, they have been a powerful tool to establish the position of the court administrator, who can undertake a performance evaluation, set goals and objectives, and create a reporting system (Feeney, 1987).[5]

5 Concluding remarks

> 'It is not easy to remain optimistic after trying reform that fails. Often the conclusion is it is safer and easier to do nothing. This nothing-works explanation has a great deal of power. At a minimum it is a highly useful reminder that problems are not always what they seem and that our solutions, particularly if we are too simplistic, can themselves become part of the problem' (Fenney, 1987).

While writing this paper I discovered how little seems to be known about the functioning of the European courts, particularly in comparison with the huge amount of literature on the courts in the United States. Many questions require an answer and I think that it would be helpful if public administration scholars would start dealing with

---

5 I am aware of the fact that this section of the article could sound quite deterministic. The point that I would like to stress is that some simple but reliable data about the functioning and the performance of the judiciary must be collected and also made available to the public. Too often the inaccurate argument that judicial performance cannot be evaluated has been taken for granted.

judicial administration issues, too, as they do for other government sectors. 'Of all the branches of public administration that of the administration of the law is the most defective' (Willoughby, 1929, 3).

It is about time that a movement in judicial administration should also start in Europe, as it is quite embarrassing to see the difference between the number of empirical researches that have been conducted in the United States, Australia, Canada, in comparison with the few available in Europe.

The study of the administration of justice in continental Europe, with maybe a few exceptions in Northern Europe although it is merely an hypothesis, seems to be still dominated by a traditional legal approach, with very little attention paid to organizational and institutional aspects.

The European judicial systems seem very rooted in a false conflict between an efficient administration and a good quality of justice. Information technology along with management techniques are often perceived by judges as a menace to their autonomy and independence, meaning that all the management positions in the courts as well as in the Ministry of Justice are too often held by members of the judiciary.

Generally, judges are not trained in management tasks, they do not have a system approach but rather a legal approach to problem solving, meaning that they tend to implement reforms with their traditional professional legal skills (Schön, 1983). They have a rooted skilled incompetence (Veblen, 1954; Argyris and Schön, 1992) in dealing with organizational matters, innovation processes and change. Their behaviour is embedded in an outdated legal framework.[6] Their major concern is still judicial independence as an objective, rather than judicial independence as a means for a better administration of justice, generating a typical case of goal displacement.

Judicial professionals are not able to overcome organizational defence (Argyris, 1990), and as a consequence judicial reforms and innovation processes are very hard to implement and quite often they do not provide the expected results. The Italian case is a typical example of the failure of judicial reforms governed by legal professionals. In the last twelve years the Italian judicial system has endured several important and traumatic reforms such as: a Code of Criminal Procedure,[7] major changes in the Code

6 In this case it is more than a framework: 'a social script embedded in a work organization: it influences work practices, but also ways of reflecting on that organization and its possible alternatives. A formative context can be defined as the set of institutional arrangements, cognitive frames and imageries that actors bring and routinely enact in a situation' (Ciborra, 1993, 28; Ciborra and Lanzara, 1989).

7 Among the several reforms that have taken place in the Italian judiciary during the last twelve years the Code of Criminal Procedure is worth mentioning. In 1988, the Italian Parliament enacted a new Code of Criminal Procedure, entering into force on October 24, 1989. The new Code superseded the 1930 Code that was originally drafted under the Fascist *regime* and was amended several times after the Second World War, to adapt it to the post-war Constitution. The structure of the first code (known as *codice Rocco*, after the Minister of Justice who signed and played a major role in its preparation) was based on a non-adversarial or inquisitorial model and hierarchical officialdom (Damaska, 1986). The Code was an attempt to move toward an adver,sarial model of criminal procedure, a model that has its distinctive source in liberal ideology and it is considered the more appropriate system for liberal democratic states (Damaska, 1983). A reform was also considered necessary, because of the huge backlog of cases and the length of procedures. Therefore, the decision to move from a non-adversarial model to an adversarial one was based on two major concerns: (1)) the idea that an adversarial proce-

of Civil Procedure, a different geographical distribution of the courts and prosecutors' offices, an increasing number of justices of the peace, massive investment in information technology, the recruitment of hundreds of judges and prosecutors and thousands of administrative personnel. Even if to evaluate these reforms is very difficult, and it is certainly beyond the scope of this brief article, it is still possible to say that, generally speaking, these reforms are perceived as a failure by citizens, policy makers and by the same legal professionals. All the reforms have been generated under the inaccurate impression that backlogs, delays and poor judicial performance could be addressed with law reforms and more resources. This is a just too simplistic approach which is typical of legal professionals, in particular of judges and prosecutors, who have, on the one hand, a skilled incompetence in managing innovation processes and, on the other, a strong commitment to defend their organizational privileges.

The intricacies between management issues and judicial activities are so strong that it is necessary to exploit new ways to preserve judicial independence as well as an adequate performance. Needless to say, in democracies the independent discretion of a judge in deciding a case is an inviolable principle but the increasing role of the courts in our societies requires a certain standard of performance that can be attained only if court structures, court procedures, technology, and resources are updated and professionally managed (Conti and Lipscher, 1990). Courts cannot escape from some form of accountability concerning their performance. Administrative and judicial activities have to be welded together to tackle with success the backlogs, delays and the always increasing problems that courts and prosecutors' offices have to deal with.

Judicial independence cannot be a defence for judicial unaccountability or an excuse to stop any managerial innovation, including the introduction of professional managers within the justice systems. The change of courts toward the improvement of the administration of justice encompasses the acknowledgment of the need for court managers. They can bring a different perspective both in dealing with day to day court operations and implementing reforms and innovation projects.

If in public administration sectors such as health, education, and local government, the need for managers has been recognized as fundamental to change old habits and bring into the organization new ideas, then this should be true also for the justice system. Even considering all the peculiarities of the justice system, the stubborn defence of legal professionals to have a monopoly in the definition of judicial policies and in the management of the courts has affected court performance too negatively to

dure fits better in a democracy; and (2)) the need to regain some effectiveness and efficiency in the administration of criminal justice. After more than 10 years of application of the code, we can safely say that these goals have not been fulfilled at all. The assumption that the oral process by itself accelerates the pace of litigation and increases the efficiency and the effectiveness of the administration of justice is simply wrong. The oral process reform is just one important step of the many that have to be taken to really affect the quality of the administration of justice. For example, it makes no sense to change the criminal procedural rules without reforming the institutional role of prosecutors and judges, as well as giving defence attorneys equal opportunities to carry out investigations. The legal formalism that pervades the Italian legal culture has saddled the new code with rules that do not work in practice.

be able to continue. A change in court management cannot be postponed any longer.[8] The role of court administrators is to provide management expertise, in a context of judiciary independence in the adjudication process, to improve efficiency and performance as a fundamental part of the ultimate goal to implement justice. As organizations, justice systems have to learn how to balance the trade-off between independence and performance accountability. The balance of the system is deeply affected by the way in which the tensions generated by this trade-off are dealt with (Touraine, 1973).

In this framework an important role can be played by European scholars in public administration. The lack of empirical research on judicial administration should be filled. The study of court administration should draw concepts and models from organization theory as well as management and policy analysis in order to integrate the traditional legal approach used to tackle the justice system's problems.

In continental Europe judicial distinctiveness seems to have kept public administration scholars at arm's lenght with the judiciary who have a prejudice towards judicial reforms and innovations. Of course there are no prescriptive solutions in any absolute sense, but there is certainly the need to find new ways to deal with old problems. Buzz-words such as management, efficiency, effectiveness, benchmark, learning organization, and knowledge management should not lead to superficial 'turn key' solutions (Friedberg, 1993) but should rather be of help in starting a process of change in the justice systems toward a real modification of the actors' behaviour, and thereafter performance.[9] I hope public administration scholars in Europe will take up this challenge.

References

American Bar Association, *Standard Relating to Court Organization,* Chicago, IL., ABA (1990).

American Bar Association, *Standard Relating to Trial Court,* Chicago, IL., ABA (1992).

American Bar Association, *The Improvement of the Administration of Justice,* Chicago, IL., ABA, (1981).

Argyris, C., *Overcoming Organizational Defence*, Allyn & Bacon, (1990).

Argyris, C. and D. Schön, *Organizational Learning*, Reading, MA., Addison Wesley, (1992).

---

8 In 1929 Willoughby wrote: 'In large part responsibility for existing unsatisfactory conditions is due to the fact that consideration of the judicial branch has been confirmed almost wholly to the legal profession, the members of which are not primarily interested in matters of administrative organization and technique, or fitted by their training and studies to handle such matters in a competent matter'.

9 This is the ultimate goal of organizational learning, which should take place in three steps. A cognitive one where people become exposed to new ideas and knowledge and they then begin to think in a different way. The internalization of these new ideas change their behaviour. These changes should result in an improvement to organizational performance and results (Garvin, 1993; Senge, 1990).

Barr, C. and M. Perry, *Judicial Administration in Canada*, Montreal, McGill, Queen's University Press, (1981).
Burger, W., 'Court Administrators-Where Would We Find them?', *Judicature* 53 (3), (1969), pp. 256-257.
Church, T., *The Old and the New Conventional Winsdom of Court Delay*, 'The Justice System Journal', 7, (1982), pp. 395-408.
Ciborra, C., *Teams, Markets and Systems*, Cambridge, University Press, (1993).
Ciborra, C. and G.F. Lanzara, 'Change and Formative Contexts in Information Systems Development', in: Klein, H. and K. Kumar (eds.), *System Development for Human Progress*, New York, NY., Wiley and Sons, (1989).
Conti, S. and R. Lipscher, *Changing Roles and Relationship of Judicial Branch Leaders in Court System Administration and Ways to Develop Productive Working Relationship Between those Leaders*, Conference Papers: Second National Conference on Court Management, Phoenix, AR, (1990).
Cooper, C., Solomon, M and H. Bakke, *Differentiated Caseflow Management*, Washington D.C., U.S. Department of Justice, (1993).
Damaska, M. R., *Adversary System*, in, *Encyclopedia of Crime and Justice*, New York, Free Press, vol. I, 25, (1983).
Damaska, M. R., *The Faces of Justice and State Authority*, New Haven, Yale University Press, (1986).
Feeney, F., 'Evaluating Trial Court Performance', in: *The Justice System Journal,* 12, (1987), pp. 425-434.
Flango, V. and J. Ostrom, *Assessing the Need for Judges and Court Support Staff*, Williamsburg, VA., NCSC, (1996).
Friedberg, E., *Le pouvoir et la règle. Dynamiques de l'action organisée*, Paris, Edition du Seuil, (1993).
Friesen, E., 'Cures for Court Congestion', in: *The Judges' Journal*, 23 (1), (1984), pp. 4-8.
Gallas, E., 'The Planning Function of the Court Administrator', in: *Judicature*, 50 (8), (1967), pp. 268-271.
Gallas, E., 'The Profession of Court Management', in: *Judicature*, 51 (9), (1968), pp. 334-336.
Garvin, D., *Building a Learning Organization*, 'Harvard Business Review', July-August, (1993), pp. 78-91.
Goerdt, J., *Examining Court Delay. The Pace of Litigation in 26 Urban Trial Courts,* Williamsburg, VA., NCSC, (1986).
Hewitt, W., *Videotaped Trial Records. Evaluation and Guide,* Williamsburg, VA., NCSC, (1990).
lzbiky, J., Savage C., 'ADR: Explanation, Exaples and Effective Use', in: *The Colorado Lawyer*, 18 (5), (1989), pp. 825-1062.
Klein, F. , 'The Position of the Trial Court Administrator in the States', in: *Judicature*, 50 (8), (1967), pp. 278-280.
Lawson, H., *Court Reform in State Courts. Issue-Procedure-Results,* Photocopy, (19-82).

Lawson, H. and B. Gletne , *Workload Measures in the Court,* Williamsburg, VA., NCSC, (1980).
Lawson, H. and B. Gletne, *Planning in the Court Environment,* Sacramento, CA., The EMT Group Inc., (1987).
Lawson, H and D. Howard, *Development of the Profession of Court Management: A History with Commentary*, Photocopy, (1990).
Mahoney, B., *Changing Times in Trial Courts,* Williamsburg, VA., NCSC, (1988).
Mahoney, B. and L. Sipes, 'Zeroing in on Court Delay: The Powerful Tools of Time Standards and Manged Information', in: *Court Management Journal*, 8, (1985).
Mahoney, B. and H. Solomon, 'Court Administration', in: Klein F. (ed.), *The Improvement of the Administration of Justice*, 6th edition, Chicago, IL., American Bar Association, 35-60, (1981).
McDermott, J. And S. Flanders, *The Impact of the Circuit Executive Act.* Washington, D.C., Federal Judicial Center, (1979).
Melcher, F., 'Setting Time Standards: How Much delay is Too Much?', in: *The Judge's Journal*, 23 (1), (1984).
National Center for State Courts, *Assessing the Need for Judicial Resources,* Williamsburg, VA., NCSC, (1983).
Ostrom, B. and R. Hansom, *Efficiency, Timeliness, and Quality: A New Perspective from Nine States Criminal Trial Courts*, Williamsburg, VA. NCSC, (1999).
Pound, R., 'Principles and Outline of a Modern Unified Court Organization', in: *Journal of the American Judicature Society*, (1940), pp. 225-233.
Reinkensmeyer, M., 'A Profile of Court Managers. Findings of a Nationwide Survey', in: *The Court Manager* 5 (1), (1990), pp. 4-15.
Röhl, K., *Gerichtservewaltung und Court-Management in den USA*, Köln, Bundesanzeiger, (1993).
Schön, D., *The Reflective Practitioner. How Professionals Think in Action*, New York, NY, Basic Books, (1983).
Senge, P., *The Fifth Discipline. The Art and Practice of the Learning Organization*, New York, NY, Doubleday Currency, (1990).
Sipes, L. and B. Mahoney, 'Zeroing on Court Delay', in: *Court Management Journal*, (1985), pp. 8-14.
Solomon, H., 'The Training of Court Managers', in: *Brigham Young University Law Review*, 3, (1981a), pp. 683-693.
Solomon, H., 'Reflection on Wingspread II. Looking Back and Assessing the Future', in: *The Justice System Journal*, 6, (1981b), pp. 165-175.
Solomon, H., 'Court Management Training', in: *The Court Manager*, 5 (2), (1990), pp. 4-6, 16.
Solomon, M.., *Caseflow Management in the Trial Court*, Chicago, American Bar Association, (1973).
Solomon, M. and Somerlot, *Caseflow Management in the Trial Court,* Chicago, IL., ABA, (1987).
Touraine, A., *La production de la Société*, Paris, Edition du Seuil, (1973).

Veblen, T., *The Higher Learning in America; a Memorandum on the Conduct of Universities by Business Man, Stanford*, Academic Reprints, (1954).

Watzlawick, P., Weakland, J.H. & Fisch, R., *Change: Principles of Problem Formation and Problem Resolution*, New York, Norton, (1974).

Wigmore, J., 'Rosco Pound's St. Paul Address of 1906. The Spark that Kindled the White Flame of Progress', in: *Journal of the American Judicature Society*, 20 (5), (1937), pp. 176-187.

Willoughby, W.F., *Principles of Judicial Administration,* Washington, D.C., The Brookings Institution, (1929).

The Challenge of Change for Judicial Systems
M. Fabri and Ph.M. Langbroek (Eds.)
IOS Press, 2000

Le ministère public: l'évolution d'une bureaucratie

Thibaut Duvillier [1]

1 Introduction

Nous nous proposons de présenter, sous une approche essentiellement socio-organisationnelle du système judiciaire, l'analyse de la structure interne du parquet de Bruxelles.[2] Cette étude découle d'une enquête sociologique de terrain qui demeure une première au sein de cette institution judiciaire particulière.
Cet exposé se structure autour de deux axes.

1. Dans le cadre de notre étude, la pertinence analytique des travaux d'Henry Mintzberg nous a offert une meilleure compréhension du fonctionnement du parquet de Bruxelles. Les différentes composantes de l'organisation interne au parquet présentent les traits caractéristiques d'une configuration de type 'bureaucratie professionnelle'. Cependant, à l'instar du concept d'idéal-type de Max Weber, il ne faudrait pas perdre de vue l'aspect théorique des configurations mintzbergiennes. Ainsi, Henry Mintzberg évite de porter le flan à la critique en affirmant qu'*il est clair que chaque configuration reste une simplification qui ne rend pas justice à la réelle complexité de toutes les structures organisationnelles.*[3]

2. L'analyse de la motivation et de la satisfaction au travail des parquetiers bruxellois en tant que moteur de toute gestion du personnel nous a permis de confronter les théories classiques de sociologie des organisations au fonctionnement d'une institution judiciaire particulière.

Avant d'aborder les réflexions sociologiques que l'on peut tirer de nos recherches, il convient de se pencher brièvement sur la méthodologie utilisée. Nous avons procédé à une collecte de données empiriques sous la forme d'entretiens semi-directifs avec des magistrats de différents niveaux afin que l'échantillon respecte au mieux les caracté-

---

1 Thibaut Duvilier est aspirant du Fonds National de la Recherche Scientifique de Belgique, Assistant volontaire à l'Université Libre de Bruxelles, et Chercheur au Centre d'Etudes et de Recherches en Administration Publique.

2 Cette contribution s'inspire largement de notre communication à la Conférence Annuelle du Groupe Européen d'Administration Publique prononcée le 02 septembre 1999 (Cape Sounion, Greece, 01-04 september 1999) d'une part et d'un article à paraître dans la Revue de l'Institut de Sociologie de l'Université Libre de Bruxelles d'autre part.

3 Mintzberg (1987, 237).

ristiques fonctionnelles du parquet (35 magistrats au total). Il nous faut aussi différencier les concepts à la base de notre étude. Le sens commun introduit une confusion regrettable entre la motivation au travail et la satisfaction au travail c'est-à-dire entre l'investissement au travail et le bonheur au travail. La motivation se traduit par une disponibilité intellectuelle et pratique au travail. La satisfaction se définit *comme toute représentation de soi - de sa situation au travail - au moyen d'une comparaison sociale favorable que la personne élabore et transmet aux autres.*[4]

De manière générale, il ressort de l'enquête non pas la constatation d'une démotivation mais plutôt celle d'une tendance croissante à l'insatisfaction au travail.

Les magistrats consacrent toujours autant de temps à leur travail qu'avant l'affaire Dutroux. Une raison toute simple explique cet état des choses: les magistrats remplissent une fonction d'utilité sociale, de service public à la communauté. L'état de leur motivation réside, en grande partie, dans l'existence d'une conscience professionnelle presque inébranlable. Cependant, si les magistrats ne sont pas démotivés, ils manifestent clairement de l'insatisfaction.

Outre le manque de confiance et de considération à l'égard de l'institution judiciaire depuis la mise en lumière de 'ses dysfonctionnements' lors de l'éclatement de l'affaire Dutroux et les conditions matérielles de travail déplorables, il est un des facteurs d'insatisfaction qui, au regard de son importance aux yeux des magistrats, attire toute notre attention. Il s'agit de la nature des contacts que les magistrats entretiennent avec les employés administratifs d'une part et les justiciables d'autre part. Cette source d'insatisfaction peut se comprendre à la lecture de la théorie des configurations d'Henry Mintzberg et plus particulièrement à la lecture de notre hypothèse relative à la catégorisation du 'ministère public' dans la configuration de type 'bureaucratie professionnelle'. Nous utilisons le terme d'organisation professionnelle. Mais quelle réalité recouvre exactement ce concept?

2 Le parquet de Bruxelles: une bureaucratie professionnelle

D'après Mintzberg,[5] toute organisation comporte au moins quatre éléments indispensables à son fonctionnement: le sommet stratégique, le centre opérationnel, la technostructure et la fonction de support logistique. Dans le cas du parquet de Bruxelles, la technostructure est quasi inexistante et la fonction de support logistique très développée. Cette partie de la configuration regroupe l'ensemble du monde administratif gravitant autour des magistrats. Ces derniers, membres du centre opérationnel, sont des professionnels hautement qualifiés. Les logiques managériales différentes de ces deux parties, support logistique et centre opérationnel, ne se combinent pas toujours de manière très harmonieuse. La bureaucratie professionnelle trouve donc son expres-

4 Eraly (1997, chapitre IX, 23). En outre, le lecteur peut se raporter à l'article du même auteur. Eraly (1983, 61-79).

5 Nous nous rapportons aux deux principaux ouvrages Mintzberg (1982), (1990). Pour une lecture plus critique de la pensée mintzbergienne, nous conseillons le livre de Jean Nizet et de François Pichault. Nizet, Pichault (1995).

sion dans la coordination d'un support logistique s'apparentant davantage à une bureaucratie mécaniste au sens traditionnel du terme avec un centre opérationnel professionnalisé.

Plusieurs caractéristiques du parquet de Bruxelles correspondent à la configuration mintzbergienne de la bureaucratie professionnelle.[6]

1. *Une structure décentralisée, dépendante de la formation de standards de qualification (diplômes) de bon nombre de ses opérateurs professionnels*[7] qui travaillent au sein d'unités spécialisées (sections dans notre cas) et de manière autonome tout en étant sujets au contrôle de la profession, constitue une des premières caractéristiques des bureaucraties professionnelles. De manière à insister d'une part sur le contrôle horizontal du travail par les pairs et d'autre part sur le caractère professionnel des opérateurs et sur le principe d'autonomie qui régit leur profession, Olgierd Kuty emploie, pour désigner les parquets, le concept de 'modèle professionnel collégial horizontal'.[8]

2. *Des buts relativement imprécis, trop généraux, de l'organisation ou plutôt*, dans le cas qui nous occupe, de l'absence d'une politique criminelle claire et cohérente, naissent des conflits de pouvoir entre collègues, eu égard notamment au système de sélection des dossiers et de l'allocation de ressources humaines supplémentaires.

A l'instar des bureaucraties professionnelles telles que les hôpitaux et les universités, les ressources limitées des parquets tendent à renforcer les jeux de pouvoir inhérents à toute organisation. Certes, une pyramide hiérarchique existe. Mais, des stagiaires judiciaires aux premiers substituts du procureur du Roi, des médecins stagiaires aux chefs de service et des assistants aux professeurs ordinaires, les luttes d'influence sont légion dans ce type «d'administration publique». Ces ressources stratégiques font, elles aussi, l'objet d'une intense mobilisation. Le système de classement des dossiers judiciaires au parquet de Bruxelles, la prise en charge des patients dans les hôpitaux et la recherche d'heures d'assistanat à l'université provoquent régulièrement des conflits, ou du moins des tensions, entre des personnes au statut équivalent. La standardisation des qualifications et des compétences, propre à la bureaucratie professionnelle, induit des comportements de concurrence entre des personnes hautement qualifiées, de formation équivalente mais travaillant au sein d'unités autonomes. L'indépendance dans l'exercice de la profession constitue un autre trait marquant de cette configuration. En ce qui concerne le ministère public, une nuance s'impose toutefois au regard du droit constitutionnel. 'La plume est serve, mais la parole est libre'. En d'autres termes, *dans ses actes écrits, le ministère public est l'agent du gouvernement auprès des juridictions.(...) le pouvoir exécutif possède un pouvoir hiérarchique à l'égard du parquet uniquement pour ordonner des poursuites, non pour les interdire. (...) Lorsque le ministère public intervient oralement à*

6 Mintzberg (1990, 255-284).
7 Mintzberg (1990, 257).
8 Kuty (1997, 57-65).

l'audience (...) il est organe du pouvoir judiciaire. (...) Il n'est plus lié par les prescriptions de ses supérieurs hiérarchiques.[9]

Au sein du parquet de Bruxelles, comme dans les autres bureaucraties professionnelles, l'autonomie des opérateurs rend difficile l'application par le sommet stratégique d'une politique déterminée. A défaut de pouvoir prétendre à une stratégie d'ensemble totalement cohérente, chaque section du parquet formule ses propres objectifs. De ses différentes stratégies peuvent naître des conflits relatifs à l'allocation des ressources matérielles et humaines entre les différentes unités de l'organisation.

En termes mintzbergiens, les bureaucraties professionnelles sont confrontées à deux types de pression: celle des citoyens qu'ils soient patients, étudiants ou justiciables d'une part et celle des autorités officielles (ministères de la Justice, de la Communauté française...) d'autre part. Ce dernier groupe de pression représente un type de coalition externe considérable puisque ce sont ces instances qui approvisionnent les organisations en ressources humaines et matérielles. Afin de pouvoir bénéficier des ressources les plus indispensables à l'exercice de leur profession (par exemple un timbre ou une farde jaune), les magistrats doivent remplir un nombre incroyable de papiers. Les contacts entre cette coalition externe, fonctionnant plutôt sur base du modèle de bureaucratie mécaniste, et les bureaucraties professionnelles amènent presque inévitablement des frictions. Cependant, il est un bien auquel les experts attachent beaucoup plus d'importance, c'est leur indépendance au travail. Tant le corps scientifique tend à résister à l'instrumentalisation de l'université, tant les magistrats ne voudraient subir du ministère de la Justice des pressions dans le cadre de l'exercice de leurs fonctions. En effet, au risque d'être caricatural mais explicite, l'autonomie, l'excellence professionnelle et le prestige figurent en tête de liste des objectifs fonctionnels de 'ces bureaucrates professionnels'.

3. *Un environnement complexe et plus ou moins stable figure parmi les autres caractéristiques des bureaucraties professionnelles.* Si Henry Mintzberg utilise ce terme pour qualifier une organisation, c'est que cette dernière présente encore certains traits caractéristiques de la bureaucratie traditionnelle. De fait, les réponses apportées par le gouvernement depuis l'affaire Dutroux, la marche blanche et les conclusions de la Commission d'enquête parlementaire sur les disparitions d'enfants confirment un des traits caractéristiques de la bureaucratie tels que définis par Michel Crozier.[10] En effet, *le rythme essentiel qui caractérise l'organisation bureaucratique, c'est l'alternance de longues périodes de stabilité et de courtes périodes de crise et de changement.*[11] Cependant, le parquet de Bruxelles, en privilégiant certaines procédures issues en partie des travaux du Plan de la Pentecôte,[12] n'a pas attendu la crise actuelle en vue d'adapter ses structures internes à l'évolution de la criminalité environnante. Faut-il voir dans cette plus grande capacité d'adaptation d'une administration à son environ-

9 Uyttendaele (1997, 508).
10 Crozier (1963).
11 Bolle de Bal (1965, 194).
12 Cartuyvels, Mary (1997, 97-127).

nement un élément particulier aux bureaucraties professionnelles? Au stade actuel de nos recherches, nous ne pouvons répondre à ce type de questions.

4. *Un autre aspect récurrent aux structures bureaucratiques professionnelles mérite d'être souligné*. La coexistence de mondes différents (celui des magistrats, des justiciables, des employés administratifs,...) influence sensiblement leur satisfaction au travail. En d'autres termes, l'analyse du degré de coopération des magistrats avec les employés et le type de contacts entretenus avec les justiciables nous paraît judicieuse.

3 La rencontre de deux mondes: les magistrats et les employés administratifs...

La cohabitation sur un même lieu de travail de 'fonctionnaires' relativement peu qualifiés, aux horaires rigides et aux tâches quotidiennes répétitives et monotones d'une part, et de magistrats hautement qualifiés aux horaires plus flexibles et aux tâches plus variées d'autre part, n'est pas toujours aisée. Pour les premiers, une obligation de moyens et pour les seconds, une obligation de résultats.

L'absence de hiérarchie entre magistrats et employés administratifs permet à ces derniers de contrôler une large zone d'incertitude, au sens Crozier du terme, puisque les magistrats, dans l'exécution de leur travail dépendent directement de la bonne volonté des employés. Au sein du parquet, la coexistence de deux hiérarchies distinctes, celle des magistrats et celle des employés, nous paraît inopportune.

L'extrait suivant, issu d'un entretien avec un magistrat du parquet, illustre parfaitement le problème posé par Crozier: *J'avais demandé à des employés de faire des copies urgentes et ils lisaient leur journal. (...) Quand des avocats ou des particuliers se présentent au guichet, il n'est pas rare que les employés les fassent attendre 15 minutes avant de se lever. Et si vous réagissez, ils savent que nous n'avons aucun pouvoir sur eux, bien au contraire c'est plutôt eux qui en ont sur nous pour l'exécution de notre travail...il vaut donc mieux parfois se modérer devant des situations pourtant inadmissibles au risque que cela se retourne contre vous. En fait, s'ils veulent vraiment nous emmerder, ce n'est pas les occasions qui manquent.*

Nous n'imputons pas cette situation à une incompétence généralisée au sein du monde des employés administratifs mais plutôt à un manque de communication tant latérale (avec les magistrats de la hiérarchie parallèle) que verticale (avec le chef des employés) et à une politique de sanction déficiente. Au regard de ces deux stratégies de management, nous verrons que l'évaluation des performances constitue un outil précieux en matière de gestion des ressources humaines. Quant aux raisons qui motivent les individus à agir de la sorte, nous pouvons nous référer à la théorie de l'école française de sociologie des organisations. En effet, comme l'ont souligné Crozier et Friedberg, l'absence officielle de pouvoir des employés telle que définie dans l'organigramme de l'institution ne signifie pas nécessairement une absence de pouvoir à un niveau plus informel. Ce pouvoir-là est conditionné par les marges de liberté dont bénéficient les employés disposant de ressources stratégiques.[13]

Pour régler ce type de problème inhérent à toute bureaucratie professionnelle, nous avons pu remarquer que l'attribution d'employés par magistrat (ce qui est arithmétiquement possible au point de vue des effectifs) permet une collaboration plus fructueuse entre les deux parties. Le sentiment de former une équipe renforce le dynamisme au travail et la confiance de l'un envers l'autre. Et surtout, élément très important que nous avons pu observer lors d'un travail de consultant à la société aéronautique belge S.A.B.C.A., sensibiliser les employés aux dossiers qu'ils manipulent les rendrait plus attentifs au travail indispensable qu'ils effectuent chaque jour. En reprenant les termes d'Ackermann et Mouhanna,[14] nous pouvons affirmer qu'il devrait exister autant de binômes de confiance entre magistrats et employés que de binômes de confiance entre magistrats et services de polices. Par ailleurs, la mise en oeuvre d'un système d'évaluation des performances permettrait au magistrat et à l'employé d'engager un réel dialogue sur le travail réalisé. Tant au niveau méritocratique qu'au niveau communicationnel, l'évaluation des performances présente de nombreux avantages en matière de motivation et de satisfaction au travail. Un tel système ne peut s'avérer efficace que s'il s'accompagne d'une politique de sanction versus gratification performante. Or, il faut bien constater que dans beaucoup d'administrations publiques belges, en ce compris le parquet de Bruxelles, cette technique de management ne rencontre pas les attentes que l'on serait en droit d'espérer. N'est-il pas logique que certains employés ne soient plus motivés ni impliqués dans leur travail dès lors que la qualité de ce dernier ne se voit pas reconnu à sa juste valeur par le magistrat? N'est-il pas encore plus démotivant pour un employé assidu au travail d'observer que pour un même salaire et pour un même type de travail un autre employé preste le minimum voire moins que la charge de travail qui lui incombe au regard de son contrat? Dans cette perspective, une situation de travail où certains agents qui ne respectent pas les obligations contractuelles ne se voient nullement sanctionner conduit inévitablement à développer un sentiment d'impunité chez certains avec pour corollaire un sentiment de démotivation chez d'autres. L'évaluation des performances et du mérite devrait permettre notamment de changer le système actuel et obsolète de promotion en fonction de l'ancienneté. Dès lors que l'on admet que l'ancienneté ou la couleur de la carte politique de l'employé ou du magistrat ne constitue pas un facteur objectif de distribution des gratifications et des promotions, il paraît plus censé de prendre en considération la performance de la personne. Evaluer la performance d'un individu, c'est juger de la qualité de son travail. On ne met pas en cause la personnalité de l'agent mais le travail tel qu'il est effectué. En dehors de cet aspect méritocratique, il importe de mettre en évidence l'objectif communicationnel de l'appréciation du rendement. L'entretien d'évaluation permet à l'employé et au magistrat de dialoguer de manière constructive sur le travail accompli, sur les manquements constatés et sur les moyens à mettre en oeuvre pour y remédier. Cette responsabilisation des

13 Crozier, Friedberg (1977). Crozier, Friedberg (1987, 377-397).
14 Ackermann, Mouhanna (1995, 137-148).

agents du système judiciaire par le biais de la communication permettrait de diminuer l'imperméabilité existante entre le monde des magistrats et celui des employés.

4 ...Ou la rencontre de deux autres mondes: les experts et les citoyens

L'utilisation d'un langage ésotérique contribue à mystifier la sphère judiciaire.[15] Les magistrats sont, surtout ces dernières années, montrés du doigt pour leur attitude suffisante voire arrogante envers les justiciables. A y regarder de plus près, ce type de constatations se retrouve dans toutes les organisations professionnelles. En fait, le caractère extrêmement complexe et inaccessible que revêt le langage de ces opérateurs professionnels renvoie, en partie, au système de valeurs de notre société. Tant le rôle qu'ils remplissent dans cette société que le statut que leurs relations leur confèrent tendent à véhiculer l'image de personnes imbues d'elles-mêmes. La légitimité de leur fonction sociale et la crédibilité de leurs propos en dépendent. Ce langage relativement abscons pour le commun des mortels demeure une des lignes de conduite des opérateurs au sein des bureaucraties professionnelles. La coordination des tâches dans ces organisations ne pouvant, principalement, s'effectuer que par standardisation des qualifications, il paraît vraisemblable d'affirmer que des changements radicaux relatifs à la simplification du langage judiciaire ne peuvent être impulsés que par les formateurs de ces professionnels. Cependant, que ce soit via la loi Franchimont ou par le biais de la médiation pénale et des nouvelles techniques d'audition au sein de la cellule de justice accélérée pour bandes organisées, les tentatives de rapprochement entre les 'initiés' et les 'profanes' se multiplient.

Même si magistrats et justiciables ne s'expriment pas de manière identique, l'écart à la règle permet bien souvent de (ré)concilier les deux parties en présence. De l'avis de la plupart des magistrats rencontrés, cet écart s'impose dans une certaine mesure comme une évidence dans un contexte d'aspirations et d'exigences croissantes à une justice plus 'humaine'. Strauss insistait, dans sa 'théorie de l'ordre négocié',[16] sur la manière dont une règle peut être mise en oeuvre. Selon lui, une règle sur papier n'existe pas en tant que telle. Ce qui est importe, c'est la négociation autour de la règle qui permet son application. En cela, le sociologue fonctionnaliste Peter Blau qui étudiait, lui, le fonctionnement du système judiciaire, rejoint la pensée de Strauss.
Blau affirmait non seulement que certaines bureaucraties ne fonctionnaient pas selon leurs propres règles mais qu'en plus c'était cet écart à la règle qui permettait à l'administration judiciaire américaine de poursuivre ses objectifs.[17]

La règle, en l'occurrence, la loi, prescrit à chaque magistrat de poursuivre tous les délits de vol. Mais, dans les faits, lorsque un individu au casier judiciaire vierge commet un vol à l'étalage, vu le nombre de dossiers et l'absence de gravité des faits,

15 A ce sujet, une enquête de chercheurs de l'Université Laurentienne (Ontario) rapporte des conclusions surprenantes quant à la lisibilité des lois. Ribordy, Laflamme, Cazabone (1986/87, 223-245).

16 Strauss (1984).

17 Blau (1955).

il ne sera vraisemblablement pas poursuivi. Ce type d'écart à la règle est donc plus que souhaitable...en attendant un renforcement des effectifs administratifs et judiciaires. De même, l'assouplissement de la loi sur le bilinguisme légal constitue un autre exemple d'écart à la règle souhaité tant par les magistrats francophones que néerlandophones afin de diminuer l'arriéré judiciaire. La politique tatillonne menée par les deux derniers ministres de la Justice est plus qu'idéologiquement orientée et ce, au détriment de l'adéquation entre les ressources humaines disponibles au parquet de Bruxelles et ses besoins. Idéalement, il faudrait 50 magistrats supplémentaires et surtout des secrétaires polyvalents pour permettre aux magistrats de consacrer l'entièreté de leur temps à leur fonction de base. Ici encore, les professeurs d'université, en tant qu'agents de bureaucraties professionnelles, connaissent presque tous ce type de problèmes relatifs à la gestion du temps. Enfin, certains magistrats n'ont pas attendu l'accélération donnée par le gouvernement à la mise en oeuvre du projet Franchimont. Leur attitude par rapport aux justiciables en ce qui concerne les informations délivrées sur l'état d'avancement du dossier et les pratiques d'autopsie par exemple dénote un certain écart à la règle. Tout en respectant certaines règles déontologiques comme le secret de l'instruction, cet écart paraît humainement compréhensible à l'égard des justiciables. De plus, dans le cadre des procédures de médiation notamment, la rencontre et le dialogue entre l'auteur des faits et la victime et la prise de conscience par ce dernier de l'acte qu'il a posé, prennent une importance considérable et invitent les magistrats à changer leur manière de travailler; à adopter un comportement, un rôle plus adéquat aux attentes formulées par les justiciables.

Mais pour que cet écart à la règle revête toute son efficacité, il faut que le système de classement des dossiers, les procédures de renvoi de ceux-ci chez des collègues et l'établissement d'une liste de priorités soient fixés d'un commun accord entre les magistrats afin de mener une politique criminelle cohérente. A ce niveau, il nous faut bien constater que le mur se lézarde.

5 En guise de conclusion

Au sein d'une bureaucratie professionnelle, toutes les rencontres, entre magistrats d'une part et services de police, avocats, employés administratifs, collègues et justiciables d'autre part, contiennent en elles les germes de conflits latents. Le langage, la tenue vestimentaire, le décor, la distance émotionnelle requise à l'égard du justiciable tendent à éloigner, voire à séparer, deux mondes qui se côtoient quotidiennement. Tous ces éléments sont les composantes d'une même culture professionnelle. Face à cette culture professionnelle inadaptée aux attentes citoyennes, il convient de s'interroger sur les changements les plus appropriés à apporter en termes de rôle de magistrat. Même si la médiation pénale et la procédure accélérée ne peuvent prétendre à la totale adéquation entre la fonction de 'juger' et les souhaits, relativement vagues voire confus, des justiciables, il nous faut bien reconnaître que ces procédures ont le mérite d'exister et de ce fait, dénotent une certaine évolution des mentalités judiciaires. La traduction la plus significative demeure, à nos yeux, la volonté d'ouverture vers l'extérieur d'une structure traditionnellement caractérisée par un corporatisme aigu.

Références

Ackermann W., Mouhanna, C., 'Une justice à deux: la procédure pénale au quotidien' in *Cahier de la Sécurité Publique*, n°22, 1995, pp. 137-148.

Blau, P.M., *The dynamics of Bureaucracy*, Chicago & London, The University of Chicago Press, 1955.

Collectif, *L'Affaire Dutroux. La Belgique, malade de son système,* Bruxelles, Ed. Complexe, 1997.

Crozier M., *Le phénomène bureaucratique,* Paris, Ed. Seuil, 1963.

Crozier M., Friedberg, E., *L'acteur et le système*, Paris, Ed. Seuil, 1977.

Crozier M., Friedberg, E., 'Le pouvoir comme fondement de l'action organisée' in Chanlat J-F., Séguin F., *L'analyse des organisations. Une anthologie sociologique. Tome II Les Composantes de l'organisation*, Québec, Ed. Gaëtan Morin,, 1987.

Dejemeppe, B., 'La gestion des parquets: du modèle administratif au modèle managérial' in *Juger*, n° 11-12-13, 1997, pp. 70-74.

Eraly, A.., 'A propos de la satisfaction au travail. Nouvelles perspectives' in*Annales de l'Institut de Sociologie*, Bruxelles, Ed. de l'ULB, 1983, pp. 61-79.

Eraly, A., *Gestion sociale des entreprises*, Bruxelles, P.U.B., 1997.

Kuty, O., 'Gestion des parquets:une analyse sociologique' in *Juger*, n° 11-12-13, 1997, pp. 57-65.

Mintzberg, H., *Structure et dynamique des organisations*, Paris, Ed. d'Organisation, 1982.

Mintzberg, H., 'Structure en 5 points: une synthèse de la recherche sur les formes organisationnelles' in Chanlat J-F., Séguin F., *L'analyse des organisations. Une anthologie sociologique. Tome II Les Composantes de l'organisation*, Québec, Ed. Gaëtan Morin, 1987.

Mintzberg, H., *Le Management. Voyage au coeur des des organisations*, Paris, Ed. d'Organisation, 1990.

Nizet, J., Pichault, F., *Comprendre les organisations: Mintzberg à l'épreuve des faits*, Paris, Ed. Gaëtan Morin, 1995.

Ribordy F-X., Laflamme, S., Cazabon, B., 'Les textes de lois sont-ils lisibles et compréhensibles?' in *Revue de l'Institut de Sociologie*, n°1-2, 1986/87, pp. 223-245.

Strauss, A.L., Negotiations: varieties, contexts, processes, and social order, San Francisco, Jossey-Bass, 1984.

Uyttendaele, M., Regards sur un système institutionnel paradoxal. Précis de droit public belge, Bruxelles, Ed. de l'U.L.B. & Bruylant, 1997.

The Challenge of Change for Judicial Systems
M. Fabri and Ph.M. Langbroek (Eds.)
IOS Press, 2000

Good Judges Are Not Born But Made

Recruitment, Selection and the Training of Judges in the Netherlands

Odette Buitendam[1]

1 Introduction

The above title is partly derived from a special issue of *Trema*, the Dutch magazine for the Judiciary. By means of personal anecdotes a depiction was sketched in the magazine for recent graduates as to the manner in which the training for becoming a judge originated and developed. Prior to the 1950s there was nothing: no entrance examinations, no (structured) training and no assessment. Gradually, recruitment and training became more structured and a training institute was established.

In 1996,[2] after the Dutch Lower House had expressed its concern in respect of whether the judicial authorities were sufficiently equipped in both the management and qualitative aspects for their tasks, a commission of experts was requested to advise the Government in this regard. The recommendations from this report have in the meantime led to the start of an extensive campaign to modernise the judicial organisation.[3] This operation has as its objective to effectuate administrative reorganisation and to improve the administration of justice. A large part of this modernisation will be undertaken by the judicial organisation itself (under the title of *programma Versterking Rechterlijke Organisatie*). Through nationally initiated projects and local 'teams for change' within the judicial sphere, in the coming years work will be embarked upon to realise four programmes, namely a) the strengthening of the administration; b) the development of the external orientation towards society; c) the optimalization of the work processes; and d) improvement in personnel management.

The last mentioned project was started in September 1998. This project has to stimulate, support and co-ordinate the introduction of a new personnel management policy witin the Judiciary. For this purpose it directs itself towards the development of a contemporary personnel policy whereby objective aims and development on the basis of competency management form the point of departure.

Instruments for this purpose are position profiles and central competences, integrated formation planning, career policies and other personnel methods such as recruitment, mobility and assessments. The results of this project will, as is expected, provide an important basis and starting point for the enrichment of the structure and

---

1 Ministry of Justice, The Hague, the Netherlands.
2 *In preparing the budget*, Ministry of Justice on 10 December 1996.
3 See the contributions by Cleiren and Brommet, and by Eradus in this collection.

cohesion for the training of judges. This enrichment will over a period of time allow for more specific points of contact for the further professionalisation of the labour-market policies in favour of the judicial organisation.

With regard to his responsibility to create a role for creating the necessary framework and conditions in respect of recruitment, selection and the training of judges, the Minister of Justice in June 1999 of this year sent a note to the Lower House in which he hinted at a policy change with regard to the recruitment, selection and training policy for members of the judiciary. The justification for this was, amongst other things, questions tabled by Members of Parliament regarding the quality of the training of judges, as well as the current capacity problems within the judiciary. These problems are closely allied to the recruitment, selection and training of future judges.

Provisionally, the impression is that the demand for judges will increase in relation to increased policy on different levels, under which is the law concerning aliens. But also, the already referred to modernisation operation will, in the coming years, demand a great deal of capacity on the part of the courts.

In this article, I will give an outline of the current recruitment, selection and training policy for judges whereby, firstly, I will deal with the state of affairs regarding competency management for the judiciary (section 2). Subsequently, current recruitment, selection and training will be discussed (section 3); the bottlenecks in the described routes will be elaborated in section 4; the new training model and the announced (policy) measures will be highlighted in section 5, followed by a conclusion (section 6).

2 Competency management for the judiciary

In 1997, the Ministry of Justice decided to introduce competency management as a management tool. Since 1997, different pilot studies have taken place in several judicial areas. The judiciary project entitled 'Competences & Performance' has defined 39 competences. The earlier project entitled 'Personnel policy' by the judiciary itself also employs this competency list but has also added to it. This seemed to be necessary on account of the special position occupied by the members of the judiciary in view of their independent status. Meanwhile, within this project of competency profiles for different judicial and non-judicial functions, result areas and achievement criteria have been formulated. Competency profiling has begun in a number of court circuits.

At the Public Prosecutions Department, for that matter, steps have already been taken for competency management to play a role in the training activities. At this moment, there is already a project up and running whereby each function is coupled with a package of training and courses.

This means that per field the necesarry knowledge and proficiencies are charted. This knowledge and proficiency is subsequently translated into training and courses whereby activities such as practical training and working visits are also provided.

An interesting foreign example of the coupling between competences and training policy is to be seen in a Canadian trial project wherein judges are assessed by lawyers with respect to five aspects namely legal ability, impartiality, judicial management skills, disposition practices and comportment.[4] The completed lists of questions were also analysed in order to provide a more specific direction to the general training policy for judges.

3 The current recruitment, selection and training route

One can be trained to become a judge in two ways. Firstly, there is a training programme to become a judge or a public prosecutor for young academics (the so-called *RIAO* training programme). This training is for a maximum duration of six years. In order to be able to follow this training, one may not be older than 30 years of age.

The training consists of two routes: the inner practical training and the outer practical training. During the inner practical training, one acquaints oneself with all sectors of the court and the public prosecutor's office. This period is supported by theoretical courses which are provided by the *Stichting Studiecentrum Rechtspleging* (*Study Centre for the Judiciary and for the Administration of Justice*), an independent foundation appointed by the Minister to carry out the training activities.

Independent of which choice one makes, the inner practical training is completed in a court or at a public prosecutor's office. The outer practical training is for a period of two years and is often spent within the legal profession (the Bar) but practical training in the corporate sector or by public bodies (Government) is also possible. Where one has relevant work experience, a dispensation of up to a maximum of two years is provided. Reductions are usually given for the outer practical training.

The application procedure is a long process and takes about 8 months (including the placement period in the court where the training will take place). Entry to the training is dependent on the selection procedure results and the number of available places, which are determined on a yearly basis by the Minister. Over the last five years, the average number of available places has amounted to about 50 per year. After a brief selection procedure, two psychological tests follow by means of which analytical capacity, intelligence and personality are tested. Finally, an interview takes place before a selection commission. Entry to the different stages of the selection procedure is dependent on the results of the preceding programme. If all stages have been completed satisfactorily, the person in question is temporarily appointed for service at one of the nineteen District Courts.

If the training has been successfully completed, there follows, dependent on the choice one makes, nomination as a trainee judge/deputy(assistant) judge or substitute officer. After one year appointment as a judge or officer can take place.

---

4 EGPA 1-4 September 1999, workshop entitled 'Justice and Public Trust', at which this project was discussed.

The second possibility is the so-called external candidate training. The recruitment of lawyers with experience in advocacy, academic study, trade and industry or the public authorities contributes to a more open administrative legal system and is also conducive to expertise being brought in-house, which would otherwise be conspicuous its absence or insufficiency.

Persons older than 30 years of age and with a minimum of 6 years relevant legal experience can be considered for the training of external candidates scheme. A Commission comprising of members appointed by the Minister advises on the suitability of candidates who are active outside the judiciary for the position of a judge. This selection procedure is of considerable duration and is similar to the selection procedure for the *RAIO* training. Initially, an interview takes place with several members of the Commission on the basis of which an assessment is made as to whether the applicant has a reasonable opportunity of succeeding in the selection procedure. Where this is the case, a psychological examination will follow which will address intelligence, analytical capacity, communicative qualities, mental stability, social conduct and decision-making qualities. Contiguous to this, discussions are held with the members of the Commission on the basis of which a provisional opinion is reached. After viewing the results of the psychological examination, a second deliberation takes place followed by a final determination. The decision can conclude that someone is considered to be immediately suitable for a judicial position and can therefore be directly nominated to the post.

It can also be the case that the candidate is considered to be primarily suitable but that in the first instance, more experience should be gained in a position of training at an appointed court. During such a training position, one can take part in the three-judge section of the court, make personal appearances and lead the hearing of witnesses, and pronounce judgements whereby one is supervised by experienced judges. Usually, the duration of this training is about one year but it may also be longer.

If the training has been completed satisfactorily, one can in principle be appointed as a judge.In as much as the result of the training remains uncertain and likewise there is no guarantee of an appointment upon the completion of the training, the candidate continues with his/her current employment outside the judiciary.

4 Bottlenecks in the current routes of recruitment, selection and training

4.1 Capacity requirements and prognosis

Earlier, a connection was highlighted between capacity problems and the directional course of the recruitment, selection and training routes. At this moment in time, there is no acceptable model in order to be able to determine concretely the influx of judges. For the inflow via the *RIAO* training, a number amounting to 50 has in practice been the case for many years. After the training which takes from 4 to 6 years, these persons end up, depending on their choice, in the judiciary or the Department of Public Prosecutions of the Ministry of Justice. The remaining employment vacancies are filled by the recruitment of outsiders. Table 1 depicts the requirement estimates against the expected inflow whereby the expected inflow is determined by, on the one hand, the natural 'decay' and, on the other, the growth. The choice of *RAIOs* for 1999 and 2000 is known.

For the years thereafter, an equal division of preferences for the judiciary and the Department for Public Prosecutions of the Ministry of Justice has been made. This prognosis is relative to a tentative estimate. A number of developments have not been included such as, for example, the effect of growth and the steadily increasing of aliens and criminal cases.

Table 1

	Estimated inflow	Inflow via *RAIO* training	Required inflow via outsiders
1999	144	18	126
2000	78	16	62
2001	65	20	45
2002	84	20	64
Total	371	74	297

Source: Advice Note by the Working Group on 'Recruitment, selection and training for members of the Judiciary', The Hague, May 1999.

4.2 Bottlenecks in the recruitment, selection and training of **RIAOs**

The first bottleneck can be found in the duration of the selection procedure. The selection procedure for *RAIO* training takes up a great deal of time. There are specific reasons for this. After all, the desired objective is in the selection of sufficient candidates for a training period of (a maximum) six years, whereby the scope for interim drop-outs is required to be kept to a minimum and a high degree of quality has to be guaranteed.

Given the current scarcity in the employment market for lawyers and in the legal sector as a whole, the increasing demand for judges, the diminishing interest for the *RIAO* training and the increasing number of potential candidates who withdraw in the interim (partly because of accepting employment elsewhere), is too expensive and the selection procedure too lengthy. A more competitive recruitment and selection policy is required. In 1998 a start was made in this respect and the selection procedure for the *RAIO* training was shortened from 9 months to 6 months (excluding the placement period at a court where the training will take place). Currently, possibilities are being sought to further shorten this to three months including the placement period.

A second bottleneck concerns the age criterion. Above the age of 30, one cannot be considered for entry to the *RIAO* training. Persons exceeding the age of 30 but who still do not have a minimum of six years relevant legal experience (required in order to be considered for the external candidate training) are on the grounds of the current criteria refused entry to the training to become a judge. The Equal Opportunities Commission has recently on two occasions tabled a question to the Ministry of Justice concerning whether the age criterion contravenes the equal opportunities legislation. The Commission determined and replied in both cases that by upholding the age criterion, no gender differences were applicable such as those stated in Article 3 clause 1 of the Equal Opportunities Act, but that the statutory dispensation policy does allow for a gender difference and is therefore incompatible with the above-named article.

A third bottleneck is the duration of the *RAIO* training. The 6-year training course has the consequence that the inflow over the short term cannot be increased in view of the fact that the training lasts for six years. The question is whether, considering the current capacity problems, this is a desired state of affairs.

Finally, the decreasing interest among *RAIOs* to choose for the judiciary can also be seen as a bottleneck. After the third year of the *RAIO* training, a choice has to be made between 'sitting' and 'standing'. More than fifty percent of the course members currently decide, after the completion of the third year, to seek employment at the Department of Public Prosecutions of the Ministry of Justice. If this tendency continues, then the shortage in judges will further escalate. A more active recruitment policy for the judiciary is therefore desired.

4.3 Bottlenecks in the recruitment, selection and training of external candidates

The problems concerning the recruitment, selection and training of external candidates in the judiciary have already for some time been the subject of discussion. The bottlenecks mainly relate to the long selection procedure, the diversity of the training programmes, the legal status of external candidates in training and the high drop-out percentage among external candidates during training. The structure of the training itself erects many barriers to the commencement of training and the completion thereof.

The training is not structured and is almost totally left to the courts. The duration and content of the training differs from court to court. It is plausible that the variation in training is a cause of the differences in the norms of assessment applied by the courts. Moreover, although the courts also have an internal agreement concerning the training, as regards national policy there is practically no mutual co-ordination. Understandably, the courts have become somewhat attached to the current external trainee route. One is free to choose candidates and besides, this structure allows for the possibility of creating a specifically applied training route for the external trainee. The duration of the *RIAO* training is in principle from four to six years, therefore there can only be an adapted form of the external trainee route for the short and medium-term requirements for judges.

In the past several attempts had already been made to improve the selection procedure and the training of external candidates.[5] In 1995 a Working Group drafted a

5 Here, Working Group under the auspices of the management of the Study Centre for Administrative Justice (S.S.R.) in January 1993 published a Training Plan Pertaining External Candidates by the Courts of Law. In May 1994 there appeared the Note 'Training External Candidates Sitting as Magi-

Model Training Statute on behalf of external candidates at the courts of law. Many echelons have endorsed this model but this has not led to any actual implementation by the courts.

The selection commission has no responsibility for finding a training position. This is still left to the candidate's own initiative. In other words, where a candidate is deemed to be suitable by the Commission, that does not mean that a training position has been reserved. From the point of view of the candidate, there is an actual expectation that prior to the application, contacts are made by a court of law. Though a candidate has successfully completed the training and can be nominated to a permanent judicial position, the nomination is actually dependent on the available placement possibilities at the court of law where the candidate has undergone his/her training. Such is the case with the *RIAO* training, that the successful completion of this training does not automatically result in a (guaranteed) appointment. One can ask whether this is indeed a reasonable state of affairs. After all, a not insubstantial financial investment is required of the candidates.

On account of the uncertain outcome of the training, the candidate generally retains his/her current position. This means that the training is in the candidate's own time or with the permission of the current employer, and therefore is unsalaried.

Despite initiatives to provide uniformity and an improvement of the training for external candidates, there is to date at the national level scarcely any minimum requirements for the training of external candidates. There is a small degree of support for the courses in the training of external candidates by the Study Centre for the Judiciary and for the Administration of Justice. The content of the training is for the large part left to the courts. This subsequently gives rise to an uncertain legal status.

Behind the specific bottlenecks referred to, there is also a problem of a more general nature. For the judiciary the current recruitment, selection, training and placing are separate routes where no policy is being applied. Because of this, a total overview is lacking as to the manner of recruitment, the number of external candidates in training, the number which do not complete the training or are not placed, the training programme, the available training capacity in the courts and the actual use of appointed means by the judiciary. Moreover, there is a lack of any insight as regards local and regional recruitment problems and in capacity problems, which arise through internal promotion to the Courts of Appeal and the national bodies. With this lack of any national overview, a cohesive policy can scarcely develop. From the annual reports of the judiciary (dating from 1998) it is apparent, for example, that a number of courts have problems in filling vacancies, that the local approach is lacking and that from this perspective a stronger national direction is called for. A systematic yearly collection of data would provide an insight into the origins of the capacity

---

strates'. This Note was prepared by a Working Group made up of representatives of the Nederlandse Vereniging voor Rechtspraak (Dutch Association for Legal Administration), the S.S.R. (see above) and the Ministry of Justice. After endorsement by the sector's consultative judiciary body a second Working Group was established which was assigned the task to further develop the recommendations made in the preceding Note.

problems, which could then can be the subject of anticipatory analysis and intervention.

For the development of a cohesive policy there is likewise an accepted prognosis model which is necessary in order to be able to calculate the necessary influx. At the moment, this is not the case. It is expected that capacity problems will increase because of factors such as policy intensity and the ever-increasing ageing population. It is certain that this last mentioned generally accepted problem on the labour market will hinder recruitment results in this area. A more intensive recruitment and active employment market approach will be necessary in order to be able to realise an optimal inflow for the judiciary.

The current prognosis provides a sufficient insight to be able to take the necessary (policy) measures. In order to be able to take into account the specific factors in the future, on the basis of which a more exact capacity requirement policy for the (medium to) long-term can be established, the necessary investment in the development of a more secure prognosis model for the intermediate term has to be ensured. Such a model in combination with knowledge of the labour market for lawyers must provide a basis for a more concrete recruitment policy for both the inflow via the *RAIO* training as well as the external candidate training.

In the case of several courts of law, the capacity prognosis to be developed at the local level will have to be tested for, amongst other things, the capacity data and the internal promotion to the bodies of appeal. On the basis of this testing, a prognosis model for all courts of law can be established for the recruitment, training and in and (in)outflow within the judiciary.

5 The new training model and policy measures

In this section, the main points will be reiternated and discussed as regards the desired future and, subsequently, the measures which the Minister has intimated at in relation to this will be outlined.

The Minister has in mind over a period of time a training route whereby the selection of candidates takes place on the basis of central competences and a modular build up of the training will be developed which can be directed towards the various proficiencies and knowledge of candidates. In this respect, the training will be more clearly coupled with and implanted into personnel policy. Within a set period of time, the differences between the training routes will be consigned to history which will mean that a substantial inflow of judges will have enjoyed training linked to their university studies. The character and the structure of the current *RAIO* training will at the same time remain as it is and will be the norm as regards the content and level of the training requirements for the other training routes.

The modules to be developed must be attuned to the different functions prevalent within the judicial organisation. Offers will therefore be more attuned to demand. The developing function differences in functions is a consequence of the increasing interest within the administrative courts in, for example, quality policy, integrated management, alternative arbitrary settlement and legal economic questions. In the future, each function will be considered to a list of training modules which will be seen to belong to the 'standard baggage'.

Given, on the one hand, the attempt to implement this ultimate model and, on the other, to resolve in the short term the highlighted bottlenecks, the following measures and activities have been hinted at and which will be carried out over the coming two years.

1. Within a year dependable prognosis models for the mid to long term will be required to be developed for both the national and local levels in order to allow a better insight into the requirements of judges.
2. A national employment market strategy will be required to be developed so that target groups will be able to be approached in a timely and adequate manner. This will at the same time contribute to an improvement of the national image of the judiciary.
3. The curtailment of the selection procedure should prevent candidates from dropping out during training merely because of the fact that they can gain employment elsewhere.
4. In view of the duration of the *RAIO* training, in the short term there will be the necessary increased inflow of external candidates. Therefore, local recruitment activities will be intensified and must be supported, possibly supplemented, by a national recruitment campaign. It goes without saying that the selection commission must be strengthened so that candidates can be selected more quickly and in greater numbers.
5. The training capacity at the courts will be increased.
6. A specially developed method of education for external candidates will be implemented in the short term and will be obligatory.
7. The legal status of external candidates will be improved in that a temporary full-time position will be offered and the satisfactory completion of the training will result in a permanent appointment.
8. A new target group will be allowed entry to a specially developed training programme: this category is for persons older than 30 years of age but as yet with insufficient relevant work experience for external candidate training.
9. A national examination and education programme will examine the collaboration possibilities between universities and the judicial organisation. This must result in an improved integration of the training and will also provide an insight into the possibilities to apportion parts of the curriculum to the universities by means of introducing a gown year/dual study routes in the differential phase of the legal studies.
10. The valid age criteria will be abolished.
11. Within a determined period of time, possibilities will be sought to bundle or intensify co-operation on the part of the select commission for the mutual benefit of the judiciary.

6 Conclusion

If one wishes to change an established organisation, then homo erectus will also have to be changed.

The changes which the judicial organisations in the Netherlands are undergoing (such as a new management structure, the implementation of integrated management and competency management) make the training of judges an important instrument in bringing these changes into effect. The future training policy therefore plays a critical role and it will be because of this that a strategic training policy must form part of the organisation policy.

Assuming that the desire for the recruitment, selection and training of judges should meet extensive quality requirements and that these routes, as such, should be constructed in such a manner that personnel requirements and outflow are better attuned to each other, then the combination of the above-mentioned measures must lead to a more oriented recruitment, an improvement in the training and a strengthening of the desirable facets inherent in the judicial function as a whole. Likewise, the results of this soon to be implemented policy will be coupled with the personnel policy sub-project of the programme entitled Reinforcement of the Judicial Organisation Project (pVRO). The added insight of a sound prognosis and training places make a more oriented national policy possible.

The value of competency management will in the future become evident from the applications for recruitment, selection, training, functionality and assessment interviews and discussions, career pathways and mobility.

The development of competency management forms an indispensable part of the modern recruitment, selection and training policy. After all, before the required competences can be established, it must be mapped out what sort of contribution can be expected from a judge directed towards the (changing) organisation.

As the competences become more permanent then the content of the training can be duly attuned and by means of these competences, candidates can be assessed as to their suitability to take up legal office.

References

Adviescommissie Toerusting en Organisatie zittende magistratuur (the so-called Leemhuis Committee), *Rechtspraak bij de tijd*, (January 1998).

Doelen, F.C.J. van der, *Over kwaliteit van rechtspraken, rechters en gerechten* (About the quality of judgements, judges and the courts).

Poel, D.H., *The Nova Scotia Judicial Development Project*, Halifax, (1997).

Trema (*Tijdschrift voor de rechterlijke macht*), (September 1997).

The Challenge of Change for Judicial Systems
M. Fabri and Ph.M. Langbroek (Eds.)
IOS Press, 2000

Managing Juvenile Criminal Justice in Italy

Anna Mestitz[1]

1 Introduction

The organization and management of juvenile criminal justice might be considered only a marginal sub-area of the judicial system, but this sub-area often does play a role as a laboratory where innovations and new ideas may be tested and sometimes transferred into the adult judicial system. In this regard I may quote Damaska who stressed that in Germany 'The move toward the welfare state was accompanied by a new approach to crime, emphasizing social policy at the expense of legal considerations, with attitudes toward crime committed by minors often playing the role of the Trojan horse in the citadel of the classic legal system' (1981, 126). Such a statement is certainly valid for most modern judicial systems.

In the following pages I shall first provide a general overview of the organizational and functional features of the Italian juvenile justice system, by stressing both those shared with other Western systems of juvenile justice and those connected with the main problems of managing juvenile judicial cases - problems I shall then try to summarize in the second part of my presentation. Although I can only provide general information in this brief article it is worth pointing out that my contribution is based on our research activities over the last decade in different Italian juvenile courts (of the Northern and Southern regions), through participant observation, interviews and an analysis of official documents.[2]

2 Structural and functional features of the Italian juvenile justice system

The actual working of the juvenile justice system is influenced by decisions taken not only by the courts and prosecution offices, but by a plurality of agencies. Thus its organization and management are very complex, involving many subjects and institutions both internal and external to the administration of justice. At the top of the judicial system there are two central bodies: the Higher Council of the Magistracy (HCM) and the Ministry of Justice (MJ).[3] Moreover, the juvenile courts and prose-

---

1 Research Director at the Research Institute on Judicial Systems of the Italian National Research Council (IRSIG-CNR), Bologna, Italy.

2 I must say that I feel somewhat uneasy in quoting myself and my collaborators so often, but unfortunately no other research in the field of organization and management of the juvenile justice system is available in Italy.

3 The *Consiglio Superiore della Magistratura* and the *Ministero di Grazia e Giustizia*.

cution offices collaborate with the national welfare agencies (*Servizi sociali minorili*) and the correctional institutions, which are dependent on the same MJ. They also collaborate with groups and subjects external to the administration of justice, such as the police, the welfare units of local government and/or administrations, volunteer associations and communities. I shall first describe the structure of the jurisdiction, then the central bodies and the subsystem composed of both the internal and external network of different agencies.

The 1st level of juvenile jurisdiction is concerned with judgment in fact and law, and it is quite separate from the adult system. It includes 29 juvenile courts (*Tribunali per i minorenni*) spread over the country and an identical number of prosecution offices (*Procure della Repubblica per i minorenni*). Both are generally located in the same buildings. Cases are reported to the prosecution offices (by citizens, the police, welfare agencies etc.) and the treatment of cases is governed by the principle of mandatory criminal action. The juvenile courts deal with civil, criminal and administrative matters, but not with family matters (separation and divorce are decided in ordinary tribunals).

The interconnections among civil, criminal and administrative measures, provided for by law, are a functional feature of the juvenile courts that deserves to be mentioned. Criminal competence is concerned exclusively with crimes committed by offenders aged from 14 to 18 (offenders under than 14 years of age cannot be charged), and before charges are brought courts must evaluate whether each offender is responsible and in full possession of the 'capacity to understand and consciously act' (*capace di intendere e volere*). Administrative competence is concerned with so-called 'social maladjustment' (*disadattamento sociale*), i.e. juveniles in danger of becoming delinquent. In these cases the court may intervene with supportive and rehabilitative measures such as social service supervision or placement in institutions for children. Civil competence is concerned with the protection of mistreated and neglected minors, mainly without a family or with manifestly inadequate or incompetent parents. In these cases the court intervenes with protective measures such as adoption or by moving the child from his/her family to another family temporarily or definitively (or to institutions for children). So the juvenile criminal court may adopt civil measures in order to help or protect the offender if his/her family is inadequate or physically absent.[4]

In the Court of Appeal, at the 2nd level of jurisdiction, there are special 'juvenile sections' (*Sezioni minorili di Corte d'appello*) which are concerned with reviewing the judgment in fact and law. Finally, the sentences delivered by the 'juvenile sections' of appeal may then be revised before the Supreme Court of Cassation only as regards aspects of law, but this happens very rarely. In fact the first level of jurisdiction is the

---

4 It is interesting that, notwithstanding the fact that such interconnections are foreseen by law our own research in the juvenile court in Bologna did not show any interconnection but rather a clear separation: in fact the civil measures were very rarely used in the criminal preliminary hearing, only one case in 1992, none in 1993, one in 1994 (Mestitz, Cocchini and Nicolì, 1996, 133).

main seat where juvenile justice is delivered and managed. For this reason I shall focus only on this level.

The decisions of both the juvenile courts of 1st instance and the sections of appeal are made by panels of a variable number of professional and lay judges sitting in camera (in order to protect the accused juveniles from the curiosity of the public). It is important to note that the Italian career judges and public prosecutors belong to the same corps: they are both indicated by the term 'magistrates' (*magistrati*) and share the same recruitment, training and career. They can even move easily from the position of judge to that of public prosecutor and vice-versa in the course of their long career. The sub-group of 'juvenile magistrates' includes also the lay judges who, as in many other European countries, have to be recruited among 'experts' in disciplines relevant to the juvenile phenomena, such as psychology, criminology, sociology, psychiatry etc. They are appointed temporarily for three years and may serve three or more terms in office.

With respect to the different phases of the criminal proceedings we may distinguish four different judging forums as follows:

- judge of the investigative phase (*giudice dell'indagine preliminare, g.i.p.*): a single career judge;
- judge of the preliminary hearing (*giudice dell'udienza preliminare, g.u.p.*): a panel composed of three judges, including one career judge and two lay judges (one male and one female);
- juvenile criminal court (*tribunale minorile penale*): a panel of four judges, including two career judges and two lay judges (one male and one female);
- juvenile section of appeal (*sezione minorile di Corte d'Appello*): a panel of five judges, including three career judges and two lay judges (one male and one female).

Most criminal cases are dismissed by the judge of the investigative phase and/or decided by the judge of the preliminary hearing, thus only a minority of cases proceed to trial. For example, our research findings in the juvenile court of Bologna show that only 4% out of the total cases in 1994 were decided by the criminal court and 66.5% were dismissed by the judge of the investigative phase (Mestitz, Cocchini and Nicolì, 1996). It should be noted that in Italy juveniles cannot be transferred to adult criminal courts as happens, more and more frequently, with serious offenders in the United States (Champion and Mays, 1991; Fritsch and Hemmens, 1995). In Italy, in fact, the treatment of young offenders is much more benevolent.

I shall now focus my attention on the two central bodies responsible for the organization and personnel of the juvenile courts and prosecution offices.

(1) The HCM is a body composed of a two-thirds majority of magistrates (judges and public prosecutors) elected by their own colleagues. It makes all decisions concerning the magistrates from recruitment to retirement, being responsible for their recruitment, training, career, discipline and distribution in the different positions and places on the national territory. It is also responsible for the appointment of the lay judges, whose candidatures are proposed by the Presidents of the juvenile courts.

(2) The Central Office for Juvenile Justice[5] is a department of the MJ (COJJ-MJ) which is headed by a magistrate assisted by colleagues. It is responsible for the recruitment, training and career of the non-judicial personnel such as the social workers serving in the units of the MJ and other personnel serving in the juvenile correctional institutions. It must manage the centralized budget and provide for the organization, technologies and other resources needed by the following institutions: 29 juvenile courts, 29 juvenile prosecution offices, 29 juvenile social services units (each of them connected to the various juvenile courts), juvenile correctional institutions operating on the national territory: that is 26 *Centri di Prima Accoglienza* (CPA) – where the offenders stay during the first days following arrest – and 21 *Istituti Penali Minorili* (IPM).

The centralization deriving from these two bodies (HCM, COJJ-MJ) leads to a high degree of bureaucratization and both centralization and bureaucratization strongly influence the effectiveness of the system.[6]

For analytical purposes I distinguish between two functional subsystems in the organizational structure of the juvenile justice system, one 'internal' to the administration of justice and the other 'external'. In both, the courts and prosecution offices occupy the central position.

The 'internal subsystem' is composed of the above mentioned institutions (juvenile courts and prosecution offices, social services, correctional institutions) managed by the MJ, which are very closely interconnected. Very often the same buildings where juvenile courts and prosecution offices are located also host one or both of the two correctional institutions (CPA, IPM) and the national social service units of the administration of justice. These units collaborate with public prosecutors and judges in collecting information about minors and their families, assist them during the criminal proceedings and carry out many other tasks often concerned with the execution of the sentences.

As mentioned above, the juvenile justice system is functionally connected and in various ways dependent on the 'external subsystem' which includes a network of other subjects and institutions necessary for the working of the system. The first group included in the external subsystem is that of defence lawyers, who are private practitioners providing legal aid and defence for the minors and interacting with the prosecution offices and the juvenile courts. In turn these latter institutions interact with the following external groups: the judicial juvenile police, the social services of the local government and/or administrations (municipality, province, region), and the volunteer associations and communities, where the juvenile offenders may be taken for the execution of different sentences (probation, rehabilitation, placement outside the home, etc.).

As far as the most relevant functions of both the national social service of the judicial administration and the social services of the local governments are concerned

---

5 The *Ufficio Centrale per la Giustizia Minorile*.

6 For example, each court and prosecution office has to ask the COJJ-MJ to satisfy its needs for buying furniture, vehicles, computers etc. and each request must be written and fully justified.

I may recall that the public prosecutors acquire the necessary information from internal and external institutions: the judicial juvenile police, the national and local social services. Note that the judges do not use the juvenile police but acquire the same information from both the national social service of the judicial administration and the social services of the local governments. Thus both social services may strongly influence the decision-making of juvenile magistrates because they collaborate with the magistrates to collect information, to assist the juvenile during the proceedings, to execute most judgments and other tasks.[7]

This summary description has perhaps provided a general idea of the complexity of the juvenile justice system but I must also underline the complex organizational and functional connections among the groups and individuals serving in the network of different juvenile justice institutions. One central aspect is that the groups functionally led by the magistrates in their daily activities are composed of persons serving in different departments of the public and local administrations. It will be recalled, for example, that the magistrates collaborate with social workers belonging both to the MJ and to the local governments and/or administrations. Moreover, each unit of juvenile police officers serving in the prosecution offices, is composed of members of three different corps: the police (*Polizia di Stato*), the *Carabinieri* and the finance police (*Guardia di Finanza*), each of whom belongs to three different Ministries (Interior, Defence, Finance) and has its own hierarchical senior officers.

A natural consequence of the above mentioned structural and organizational features is that the magistrates perform a dominant overbearing role not only in the courts and prosecution offices, but also in the two central bodies (HCM and COJJ-MJ) as well as leading all groups which collaborate in the working of the juvenile justice system. Therefore they are the most powerful and authoritative group representing juvenile justice in our country; they also represent the point of reference for the media in describing juvenile deviation and concomitant social problems. As a matter of fact, in Italy juvenile problems have been primarily considered a judicial rather than a political or social concern as in other countries. One reason is that for many decades juvenile social problems were traditionally entrusted to the juvenile justice system because of the lack of a welfare system. In fact the social services were only introduced in the 1960s and are, still at present, understaffed in many regions of the country. As a result, this gap was necessarily filled by the judiciary without any opposition even by defence lawyers, who have been traditionally very marginal in the inquisitorial legal system and particularly in juvenile jurisdiction.

7 For example, they look for placement outside the home, they supervise the work and school activities that minors have to carry out in the cases decided by the court, they play the role of probation officers by supervising the minors on probation, they seek collaboration from religious and volunteer associations, rehabilitation communities etc.

3 Main problems in managing the Italian juvenile justice system

Problems in the management of the juvenile justice system may be classified into three main categories: (i) the above mentioned structural and organizational features (centralization, bureaucracy, complexity and magistrates' leadership); (ii) some problems which have been observed in other Western systems of juvenile justice (Klein, 1984); (iii) the specific functional problems of the Italian juvenile justice system (which may also be connected to some external influences varying according to the different regions of the country).

First let us briefly recall the trends shared with other juvenile justice systems and then move on to focus on the main problems emerging from our researches in different juvenile courts of the Italian Northern and Southern regions.

3.1 Problems shared with other Western systems of juvenile justice

Our researches have shown quite striking differences in the working of the juvenile justice systems in the various regions of Italy, basically confirming the high variability which has emerged from many cross-cultural comparisons. Hackler stressed that 'juvenile justice systems, like many bureaucratic structures, display great diversity in achieving their goals. The formal rules and laws that prescribe how things should be done are almost always modified somewhat in local situations. This happens within the same countries, or provinces, or states, where we assume that the uniformity of rules should lead to more uniformity in behavior' (1984, 231-232). Also in Italy the juvenile justice system is to a wide extent, in this sense, informal; judges and prosecutors, who in general are very motivated, are often so committed as to bend the application of the law and procedures in order to promote what in their view is in the best interest of the minors.

With respect to the distinction made between the 'due process' model and the 'traditional' or 'family' model (Ito, 1984), certainly Italian juvenile courts can be classified in the second category where 'juvenile judges retain a good deal of discretion in adjudicating offenders' (Champion and May, 1991, 107). Although the crimes committed by minors are governed by the principle of mandatory prosecution (a typical feature of our legal system), in fact the application of laws and procedures in handling the cases and treating juveniles is highly discretionary, as in other countries. In criminal cases this discretion can be observed on the part of the police, the public prosecutors, the judges and even the social workers. These groups and individuals may choose among several options, but they all appear to assume that in principle the juvenile criminal proceedings should be governed by the goal of imparting some sort of moral education to people under age.

By examining the trends in the treatment of offenders we may also distinguish between 'welfare' and 'justice' methods of dealing with juvenile offenders,[8] or between legalism and paternalism, categories adopted in comparative research. Actually the cross-cultural studies which have tried to identify common trends in the management of juvenile justice, have stressed that the 'inevitable tug of war between welfare and justice approach, between paternalism and legalism may provide the single most pivotal dimensions along which to array and assess different juvenile justice systems' (Klein, 1984, 13). They indicated that in the 1980s the United States, Great Britain and Canada were more justice oriented, and in Israel, the Netherlands, Sweden and Italy a welfare orientation prevailed; the German system appeared more ambivalent (*ibidem*).

In fact in Italy the treatment and the processing of juvenile offenders have always alternated between punishment and welfare in the traditionally paternalistic, informal and confidential style of the juvenile judiciary, historically influenced by socio-economic conditions and other cultural and socio-political pressures by individuals and groups (the Catholic culture was certainly the most influential). The 1970s and 1980s witnessed a long period of welfare policies where the majority of juvenile courts considered the punishment of deviant juveniles as a last resort, where the treatment of offenders was (and still is) inevitably unequal because it depends on what judges consider to be an offender's best interests.

This benevolent and tolerant ideology permeated the first juvenile code of criminal procedure enforced in 1989 (DPR 448/88), which introduced a quasi-accusatorial model and was strongly concerned with the rights and the protection of the accused juvenile. But paradoxically the new legislation opened a more punitive trend in the treatment of offenders (Mestitz, 1997a), by following the same orientation observed in other countries such as Great Britain, where a new emphasis in crime control and punishment has emerged (Leng, 1994) and the United States, where the numbers of juveniles in detention centres increased by 46% from 1983 to 1991 (Snyder and Sickmund, 1995, 144).

In the period 1990-1996 the numbers of minors sentenced have increased nearly four times, notwithstanding the fact that in the same period the number of cases reported to the prosecution has remained constant (Table 1). On the other hand, the minors in custody are very few and decreasing, but Table 2 shows a noteworthy phenomenon: in the period 1991-1997 about 2/3 of the total 'entrances'[9] into custody

---

8 I make reference to the widely accepted English classification of 'justice' and 'welfare' models, as described in Farrington (1984, 71-72). According to this author, in a 'justice system' it is assumed that people are responsible for their behaviour; and that crimes are committed as a result of conscious and rational decisions; there is an emphasis on deterrence and retribution; it is held that punishment should be proportional to the seriousness of the crime committed and there is the idea of equality before the law. Instead, in a 'welfare system' people are assumed to be greatly constrained by their background and, to some extent, not responsible for their actions; the emphasis is on rehabilitative treatment, which is chosen according to the social background of offenders rather than according to their offences, and it is inevitably unequal because it is tailored to unequal needs.

9 The official statistics do not calculate the numbers of minors in prison by year but only the numbers of entrances into custody by year.

concerned preventive detention. In this regard it may be noted that about 45% of the total population in preventive detention are foreign juveniles, although their total number in Italy is very limited. This phenomenon does not seem entirely due to the increase of immigration in our country; I argue that a discriminating pre-selection of cases – operated by magistrates, social workers and/or police officers – might play a relevant role in the more severe treatment of foreign young people, mainly gypsies or irregular immigrants from Albania or the former Yugoslavia (Mestitz, 1999).

Table 1 – Comparison between the number of complaints presented to the juvenile prosecution offices and the number of juveniles sentenced (1990-1996).

years	*complaints*	*juveniles sentenced*
1990	41,051	1,244
1992	44,788	2,448
1994	44,326	3,688
1996	43,975	4,252

Source: Istituto Nazionale di Statistica

Table 2 – Comparison between the number of complaints presented to the juvenile prosecution offices, the 'entrances' into custody, and Italian and foreign juveniles in preventive detention (1991-1997).

		total entrances	*preventive detention*		
years	*complaints*	*into custody*	*total*	*Italian*	*foreign*
1991	44,977	1,954	1,731	1,035	696
1993	43,375	2,314	1,824	1,131	693
1995	46,051	2,013	1,493	725	768
1997	43,341	1,888	1,401	618	783

Source: Ministero di Grazia e Giustizia (1998)

Moreover, in the first half of the 1990s the more punitive trend emerges from the increase and the lengthening of the criminal proceedings.

(i) Increase of criminal proceedings. At the national level the massive expansion in the number of young people involved in trials emerged from our research findings by considering two joint indicators: first, the decrease in the dismissal of cases before and during the preliminary hearings; second, the constant increase in the number of cases which proceed to trial (by nearly six times in the central regions, and three times in the South and islands), a factor which also contributes to the lengthening of the proceedings (Mestitz, 1997a).

(ii) Lengthening of criminal proceedings. Our research findings and the interviews with juvenile magistrates indicate that they often use the long criminal process itself as a punishment and the lengthening of the proceedings is a traditional strategy used for 'informal aims' such as to threaten or to teach 'proper' behaviour to less serious juvenile offenders (Mestitz, 1997b).

In conclusion, similar to other Western juvenile justice systems the Italian one is characterized by: a 'traditional' or 'family' model, high variability, informality and discretion, and more recently a shift from welfare policies to a more punitive trend in the treatment of offenders.

3.2 The specific functional problems

I shall now indicate only five of the crucial variables influencing directly or indirectly the treatment of offenders, as they have emerged from our research in different juvenile courts.

3.2.1 Close interaction between judges and public prosecutors

In the adult judicial system strong criticisms have been raised against the location of courts and prosecution offices in the same buildings which – among other dysfunctional effects – gives rise to informal contacts and *ex parte* communications between judges and public prosecutors, leading the latter 'to acquire de facto the control and definition of a consistent share of public policy in the criminal sector' (Di Federico, 1998, 383). In the juvenile justice system the physical vicinity of courts and prosecution offices has the same dysfunctional effect, but they are in some way mitigated since the accused are almost always confessed criminals. The magistrates stress that vicinity is a positive feature because they may easily meet and discuss the cases, plan their specific judicial actions and more general policies. In my view it is a negative feature since these ties end up by reinforcing even more the very strong leadership exerted by juvenile career magistrates on all other internal and external groups and subjects (including lay judges and defence lawyers) who cooperate in the working of the juvenile justice system. The general attitude of submissiveness to the juvenile career magistrates appears to be a major dysfunction, also for the protection of juvenile rights.

3.2.2 Marginal role of the defence lawyers

The role of defence lawyers has been traditionally very marginal in the inquisitorial legal system and particularly in juvenile jurisdiction. If, in the past, few legal rights and little protection had been granted to the juvenile defendants by the previous inquisitorial Code of Criminal Procedure, at present with the quasi-accusatorial Code of Juvenile Criminal Procedure (enacted in 1989), the role of defence lawyers has formally changed. Nevertheless, far too often they do not fully exercise the defensive role that the law provides for. They tend, more often than not, to entrust the case to the magistrates. Among other reasons, this happens also because of their lack of knowledge and specialization in juvenile laws and procedures. This explains why, *de facto,* magistrates consider themselves as the real defenders of young offenders and use their great discretionary power for what they consider to be the best interest of minors (the definition of which is left to any single judge or public prosecutor).

3.2.3 Strong influence of social workers

Juvenile judicial decision making is strongly influenced by the structure, organization and functioning of social workers, both those internal to the administration of justice and those of the local governments. This appears to be relevant in the unequal treatment of offenders on the national territory. I mentioned above that welfare units carry out many essential tasks, thus it is easy to understand that the judicial system may be negatively influenced when these units are lacking in personnel or do not collaborate willingly with the magistrates. In fact in the welfare units of the administration of justice, often severely understaffed, the social workers have a huge workload. Moreover, in some Southern regions the workload cannot be shared with the local social workers since the local governments have not created a welfare service (Mestitz and Colamussi, 1997). Sometimes judicial decision making is influenced by the presence/absence of institutions for residential placement as well (open home-like settings, rehabilitation communities etc.). In other regions where local welfare agencies exist, the collaboration may be difficult because of two main reasons: (i) social workers do not share the court decisions or judicial policies with regard to juveniles; (ii) they have to attend to a massive non-judicial workload (i.e. they have to take care of other groups such as the old, the poor, the physically and mentally handicapped etc.) (Mestitz, 1997b). Often the social workers resent the dominant role that the juvenile magistrates expect to play even in areas outside their professional competence, that is areas in that welfare services consider to be their own. As a consequence, a great deal of variability in the treatment of offenders in juvenile courts derives from the structure, organization and staff of both the national welfare units and the local ones.

3.2.4 Centralization and leading role of the two central bodies

During the last 30 years the HCM has progressively widened its competence in regulating important features of court organization and management. For instance, it decided the general criteria for distributing the case-load both in the courts among the judges and in the prosecution offices among public prosecutors. Conversely the powers of the heads of courts and prosecution offices have been consistently reduced. These regulations may be quite dysfunctional: in one juvenile court we found that they have created remarkable rigidity precluding a rational distribution of cases (Mestitz, Cocchini and Nicolì, 1996). On the other hand, the organizational rigidity deriving from HCM regulations must be added to that deriving from the centralization of the budget, organization and non-judicial personnel management in the COJJ-MJ. Moreover other dysfunctional effects derive from centralization and bureaucracy:[10] the many and complex regulations of public administration expenditures very often do not permit the speedy supply of requested resources and sometimes the expenses and the

10 I am currently undertaking research in all 29 prosecution offices and courts, in order to explore the flow of communications among the different units which cooperate in the working of the juvenile justice system. Our preliminary findings (Faccioli and Mestitz, unpublished paper) confirm that 70-80% of the interactions among the magistrates and the internal and external units take place through written communications, an empirical indicator confirming both bureaucracy and rigidity. It appears that even the external institutions which are either lacking in a bureaucratic structure, or have a less pronounced bureaucratic structure (such as the defence lawyers, the volunteer associations and communities, the social workers of the local administrations), do end up by adopting the predominant bureaucratic communication style.

innovations decided by the COJJ-MJ are considered useless by the courts. The latter occurred, for example, when a videotape recording system was introduced in a juvenile criminal courtroom where our group was conducting participant observation of the first experiment regarding the introduction of the videotape recording equipment (Di Federico, Lanzara and Mestitz, 1993).

3.2.5 Inadequate specialization of both career magistrates and lay judges and the small degree of independence of lay judges

The above mentioned general attitude of submissiveness to the magistrates is closely connected with the problem of their poor professional qualifications due to inadequate selection, training and specialization. It must be underlined that the HCM has for many years disregarded some of its most important tasks like those concerning the training of magistrates. Only in the last few years have a limited number of continuing education programmes have been enacted by the HCM.

In recent decades many European countries have introduced reforms aimed at improving the education, selection and training of judges, public prosecutors and lawyers (France, Germany, Spain, Portugal etc.) in order to cope more effectively with the growing complexity of legal practice. Unfortunately Italy cannot be included in that group. Our comparative researches have shown that the professional qualifications of Italian magistrates are very low and so unsatisfactory as to become a major problem (Mestitz and Pederzoli, 1995). Suffice it to recall that recruitment by means of a national competition is by no means reliable and a mere 12-month on the job training period after recruitment is deemed sufficient to build up the professional skills of our magistrates for all the many tasks (judicial and administrative) to which they may be assigned in the course of their lifelong career. As a consequence, juvenile magistrates, as other groups in the judiciary, are neither specialized nor trained in the specific field in which they operate. It must be stressed that the on the job training is not compulsory in the juvenile courts and prosecution offices; only newcomers who choose to serve initially in the juvenile justice system undertake this specific on the job training. Moreover, any magistrates from the ordinary courts (criminal, civil, financial, etc.) and prosecution offices who wish to move during their career to a vacant place in a juvenile court or prosecution office (as to any other court, position etc.) must present their request to the HCM, which usually decides with little or no consideration of the actual professional qualifications of the candidates (seniority considerations usually prevail).

This situation is made even worse by the lack of specialization of both the defence lawyers (above mentioned) and the lay judges. The latter, according to the law, should be recruited from 'experts' in disciplines such as psychology, criminology, sociology, psychiatry, etc., but they are basically recruited through a system of co-optation which does not guarantee in any way either their specialization or their independence. Our research findings (Faccioli and Mestitz, 1995) have shown that recruitment is, to a large extent, based on a patronage system: only one third of all the lay judges in service in 1991 in the juvenile courts had the qualifications requested by law while the majority was composed of school teachers (often retired) in literature, mathematics, etc., or even persons with a university law degree (*ibidem*). We argued that the guarantees for their independence are lacking basically for two reasons: (i) the lack of specialization of the majority causes them to be closely dependent on the career judges' opinions and knowledge; (ii) the co-optation procedure is dominated by the magistrates, since the HCM appointment has to be preceded by the formal proposal of the President of the court (generally agreed with other career magistrates of the court and prosecution office). As a rule the proposal is accepted by the HCM. Furthermore, the magistrates are against any change in the norms (dating from 1934!) and the regulations concerning the recruitment of the lay judges. We have argued that since the lay judges number about three times the number of juvenile career magistrates and help to carry out various non-judicial tasks in the courts, the magistrates are resistant to change because the present system appears functional mainly to provide for human resources necessary to carry out routine tasks (*ibidem*).

4 Concluding remarks

The aim of this summary presentation has been to give a general idea of the structure and management problems in the Italian juvenile justice system. I hope at least to have shown that the effectiveness of the system is adversely influenced, on the one hand, by the centralization of the Italian judicial system and, on the other, by the complexity of the juvenile subsystem deriving from the collaboration of many groups and institutions. The effectiveness of the system is also influenced by the dominant role performed by magistrates, the marginal role of the defence lawyers, the lack of independence and competence of lay judges, the lack of social workers and other issues mentioned above. Obviously the effectiveness might be improved by changing the law and/or the procedures at least in order to have a less unequal treatment of offenders on the national territory. But organizational change is never easy and most of all in complex, bureaucratic and strongly centralized organizations (moreover, the justice system is, above all, a fundamental institution of social life – like the Army, the Church, the Synagogue or other religious institutions – deeply rooted in tradition, history and the past). For these reasons, in the judicial system organizational change is particularly difficult and a change in the legislation is usually not sufficient for changing individual behaviours. This is clearly shown by the case of defence lawyers, who notwithstanding the new legislation are still as marginal as in the past. On the other hand the difficulties in organizational change due to the strong centralization were confirmed, some years ago, by research (Di Federico, Lanzara and Mestitz, 1993) which entailed the observation of experiments on the introduction of videotape recording systems in some Italian criminal courtrooms. That research clearly demonstrated that the centralization (bureaucratization, rigidity etc.) of the judicial system together with the habit of introducing the innovations from top down (that is by law) has scarcely affected at the operational level (*ibidem*).

The implementation of innovations, and more generally organizational change, are better attained in decentralized and flexible organizations through some bottom-up strategies in order to deal more effectively with the social-psychological system (since change implies coping with the stress and other well-known variables concerning the individuals and the groups). Up to now the most successful way to change individual behaviours is a combination of three bottom-up strategies: information, participation and training. In other words all the groups involved in a plan of organizational change must be widely informed, must participate and discuss the plan and must then be trained in order to adopt/implement the innovation, be it a new law, a videotape recording system, social workers' policy, a computer program etc. Unfortunately these strategies have never been adopted in Italy unlike the United States, where a lack of centralization has permitted the successful adoption of organizational and technological innovations in the courts *(ibidem)*.

References

Champion, D.J., G.L. Mays, *Transferring Juveniles to Criminal Courts*, Westport CT: Praeger, (1991).

Damaska, M., 'The reality of prosecutorial discretion: comments on a German monograph', in: *The American Journal of Comparative Law*, XXIX, no. 1, (1981), pp. 119-138.

Di Federico G., Prosecutorial independence and the democratic requirement of accountability in Italy. Analysis of a deviant case in a comparative perspective, in: *British Journal of Criminology*, no. 3, (1998), pp. 371-387.

Di Federico, G., G.F. Lanzara, A. Mestitz,(eds.), *Verbalizzazione degli atti processuali, tecnologie video e gestione dell'innovazione nell'amministrazione della giustizia*, Roma: Consiglio Nazionale delle Ricerche, (1993).

Faccioli F., A. Mestitz , 'Indagine sui giudici onorari minorili in Italia', in: *Minori giustizia*, no. 2, (1995), pp. 70-140.

Farrington, D., 'England and Wales', in: M.W. Klein, (cd.), *Western Systems of Juvenile Justice*, Beverly Hills/London/New Delhi: Sage, (1984), pp. 71-95.

Fritsch, E., C. Hemmens, 'Juvenile waiver in the United States 1979-1995: a comparison and analysis of State Waiver Statutes', in: *Juvenile and Family Court Journal*, (1995), pp. 17-35

Hackler, J.C., 'Implications of variability in juvenile justice', in: M.W. Klein, (ed.), *Western Systems of Juvenile Justice*, Beverly Hills/London/New Delhi: Sage, (1984), pp. 213-233.

Klein, W.M., (ed.), *Western Systems of Juvenile Justice*, Beverly Hills/London/New Delhi: Sage, (1984).

Ito, J.A., *Measuring the performance for different types of juvenile courts*, Williamsburg VA: National Center for State Courts, (1984).

Leng, R., 'Alternative penal sanctions in England and Wales', in: J.W. Bridge, E.K. Banakas, J.P. Gardner, D.L. Carey Miller, (eds.), *United Kingdom Law in the Mid 1990s*, Part 2, London: United Kingdom National Committee on Comparative Law, (1994), pp. 618-638.

Mestitz, A., Politiche giudiziarie minorili tra mafia, media e nuovo codice di procedura penale,in: *Polis*, XI, 2, (1997a), pp. 193-211.

Mestitz, A., (ed.), *La tutela del minore tra norme, psicologia ed etica*, Milano: Giuffré, (1997b).

Mestitz, A., 'Détention des mineurs et médias en Italie', in: P. Mary, T. Papathéodorou, (eds.), *La surpopulation pénitentiaire en Europe*, Bruxelles: Bruyant, (1999), pp. 75-86.

Mestitz, A., A. Cocchini, A. Nicolì, 'Organizzazione e funzionamento dei tribunali per i minorenni. Analisi di un caso', in: *Working papers IRSIG-CNR*, 6, Bologna: Lo Scarabeo, (1996).

Mestitz, A., M. Colamussi, 'Processo penale minorile: l'irrilevanza del fatto e la messa alla prova. Criteri interpretativi e prassi applicative', in: *Working papers IRSIG-CNR*, 8, Bologna: Lo Scarabeo, (1997).

Mestitz, A., P. Pederzoli, 'Training the legal professions in Italy, France and Germany', in: C.N. Tate, T. Vallinder, (eds.), *The global expansion of judicial power*, New York: New York University Press, (1995), pp. 155-179.

Ministero di grazia e giustizia, Ufficio Centrale per la Giustizia Minorile, Rapporto statistico sulla criminalità minorile (IV Conferenza Nazionale di Statistica, Roma), (1998).

Snyder, H.N., M. Sickmund, *Juvenile offenders and victims: a national report*, Washington DC: Office of Juvenile Justice and Delinquency Prevention, (1995).

Part V

Courts, Public Prosecutors' Offices and ICT

The Transparent Judge

Will Lady Justice Lose Her Blindfold?

Wim B.H.J. van de Donk[1]

1 Introduction

Jan Leijten, a former Advocate-General of the Dutch Supreme Court, regularly writes novels and short stories. In a collection of short stories, published as *de Verschikkelijke Eenzaamheid van de Inbreker* ('The Terrible Loneliness of the Burglar'), he repeatedly talks about judges. In one of these stories, entitled 'This secret is not so great, or the judge an ass', he focuses on judicial decision-making in general and on the judges' discussions behind closed doors in particular. Leijten seems not to be very enthusiastic about the quality of these deliberations. He approvingly quotes from a novel by Pitigrilli; *L'espirimento di Pott*. Pott is a judge, the President of a panel of three-judges in a criminal court. Leijten quotes the following final lines of the judgement that followed extensive deliberations *in camera*: 'In the name of the people of France, etc., etc., (...) the court considering that, (...) etc., etc., and especially because the judge sitting on my left is an ass, and because the judge who is sitting on my right is also an ass, you, Maria Larson, will be sentenced to three years imprisonment. You will have three days to lodge an appeal, and I really advise you to do so because, happily enough, not all judges are like these two' (Pitigrilli, quoted in Leijten, 1992, 141). Leijten continues the story with his own experiences in three-judge divisions and the deliberations *in camera*. He concludes that the 'quality' of these deliberations is one of the best reasons for the subsistence of their confidential character.

1 Centre for Law, Public Administration and Informatization, Tilburg University. The authorwould like to expresses his gratitude to Mrs. Lucinda Mos for her help in the preparation of this contribution and to Mrs. Ineke Sijtsma for her corrections and suggestions regarding the use of the English Language.

As a highly experienced insider, Leijten is in a much better position to give his opinion on these deliberations than those who only have access to the outcomes of judicial decision-making processes. The judicial system is, to a large extent, a 'closed shop', characterised by all kinds of barriers that guarantee its institutional independence.

This independence has largely contributed to a limited openness of judicial decision-making processes and the relative isolation of their institutional neighbours. These characteristics of reticence and separateness have been, in the last decades, one of the reasons for political and societal critique. In many European countries this critique has been developing on the basis of one or more serious incidents. The general image of the judicial system is nicely portrayed in the cartoons that Plantu recently published in his *Le petit Juge Illustré*: old-fashioned organisations that use antique technologies – such as typewriters – that originated at the beginning of the 20th century. These organisations have not been able to adapt to a profoundly changed society. The image of old-fashioned organisations that use old-fashioned technologies, however, might become outdated in the next decade. Not the typewriter, but the use of modern information and communication technology (ICT) in the judicial system is considered to be a strategic answer to many of the external and internal critiques. Several kinds of computer systems (that support administration, documentation, registration, decision-making and communication) are being introduced in judicial organisations.

The 'managerial revolution' that has so profoundly inspired and changed the organisations of the executive branch of government has now also reached the judicial branch. And, as has been the case in the executive branch, ICTs are the most important instruments used to implement radical reforms. These reforms not only concern managerial and organisational dimensions of judicial organisations such as the Public Prosecutions Department and the judiciary. They also concern the 'core business' of these judicial organisations: decision-making by public prosecutors and judges.

2 A verdict on change: new ambitions for the judiciary

Proposals for a more 'uniform' sentencing policy are cornerstones for a modernised judicial system in the Netherlands. Both the Public Prosecutions Department and the judiciary are confronted with a series of initiatives (from within and outside their organisations) that aim at the development and implementation of guidelines for claiming and sentencing. ICTs play a crucial role in these initiatives. Apart from this, both the Public Prosecutions Department and the Judiciary are the objects of a major effort to modernise their organisational and decision-making structures and processes. In both policy trajectories, the (further) development of ICT is a *conditio sine qua non* for the success of these operations.

The Leemhuis Committee, which advised the Dutch Government on the future organisation of the judiciary, explicitly mentioned the use of ICTs as an important vehicle for modernisation strategies. ICTs are considered to be powerful tools for implementing a new managerial (steering) philosophy for the judiciary that aims to introduce new budgeting methods, the measurement of workloads, planning and control, and performance indicators.

In the major policy papers that have been published in the last two years, an ambitious mission to reform the judiciary is formulated.[2] The Dutch Government (or more specifically the subsequent Ministers of Justice) is aiming at:

- improvement of the flexibility and pace of the judiciary organisation and the several judicial (decision) processes,
- modernisation of its equipment and procedures, especially by using more applications of information and communication technology,
- rationalisation and a more uniform sentencing policy, aimed at improvedequality before the law and greater uniformity of the judiciary branch of government,
- improvement of the openness and transparency of the judicial institutions towards their societal and political environment.

When reading these documents (and, indeed, an observation of the emergent projects within the organisation of the judiciary *anno* 1999), one cannot but conclude that some of the key elements of the new public management paradigm have finally reached the judicial branch of government. This might explain why the EGPA's annual conference last year was devoted to this branch. Neither public administration science nor public administration practitioners have devoted very much attention for the judicial branch of government (at least in the Netherlands, this was the case until a few years ago). De Montesquieu's separation of powers has also meant, to a large extent, a mutual blindness, and a separation of *Esprits*.

Indeed, these new ambitions and ideas for managing and rendering justice are often introduced into the judicial system by people who are from outside the organisation. The average judge did not have a tremendous interest in management and organisation, let alone computer-supported administration and decision-making. Yet, exactly these aspects of the functioning of the judicial organisations represent an important opportunity to make sure that the judicial system will be able to cope with the tremendously increasing workloads. People who were knowledgeable about organisational and managerial aspects, like Dato Steenhuis (one of the first Dutch Attornies-General who came in from the outside), were given major positions and

2 'Rechtspraak bij de tijd. Rapport van de Adviescommissie toerusting en organisatie zittende Magistratuur' (The Judiciary Up to Date. Report of the Advisory Committee for Equipping and Organising the Judiciary), 'Verantwoording in onafhankelijkheid, naar een verantwoorde besturing van de rechterlijke organisatie' (Accountability in Independence. Towards a Responsible Management of the Judicial Organisation), 'Rechtspraak in de 21e eeuw. Contourennota Modernisering Rechterlijke Organisatie' (Administration of Justice in the 21st century. Policy Paper for the Modernisation of the Judiciary) and 'Recht van Spreken'. Interdepartementaal Beleidsonderzoek Bedrijfsvoering Rechtspraak' (The Right to Speak. Interdepartmental Study into the Management of the Judiciary).

responsibilities. The committees mentioned earlier were formed by experienced people from outside the judicial organisation.

Culturally, systematic thinking about work processes and the administrative organisation of the judiciary was not institutionalised, it was indeed almost completely lacking. Judges were independent functionaries who prepared their 'files' at home, one at a the time. Only because their workload increased drastically in the 1980s and 1990s has the question of management and organisation of the judiciary system become accepted (although reluctantly) as a relevant question that affected them, too. Since the beginning of the 1990s, because of the societal annoyance with its functioning (speed, quality, carefulness), the organisation of the judicial system has been rapidly ascending the political agenda. Great pressure was put on the police, the Public Prosecutions Department, the prisons, and the judiciary. It became clear that it would be very difficult to tackle new developments in crime with old-fashioned organisations. Something had to be done. The first thing these organisations came up with was, of course, asking for more money.

The major increases in budgets that they demanded from the political decision-makers also increased the justification of the latter to want to know everything that went on. The members of the judicial branch of government quickly discovered that politicians and policy makers did not - any more - simply accept their requests and allocate the extra money they asked for. They had to get used to the fact that the policy makers, instead, began asking all kinds of nasty questions. Moreover, these questions were asked in a kind of 'language' they considered a very strange and threatening one for their traditional and independent status.

Within the general framework of the mega-policy outlined above, all kinds of policies and trajectories have become operative. A new system for the measurement of the outputs of each court has been developed. The heart of the system is formed by an information (registration) system, that enables and supports extensive forms of *bench-marking*, management of workloads and (re)allocation of resources.

This new steering philosophy and managerial approach is now reflected in the proposals for a new institutional arrangement for steering and managing. One of the major innovations is a 'Raad voor de Rechtstpraak' (National Council for the Judiciary) that will have to assume important tasks and responsibilities in the management of the judicial system. This national Council will be positioned between the regional courts and the Ministry of Justice. The courts are transformed into 'largely autonomous business units', that will have a large degree of freedom to manage their own business. In the figure below, it is clear how individual judicial organisations are becoming embedded in a steerable judicial system:

Figure 1

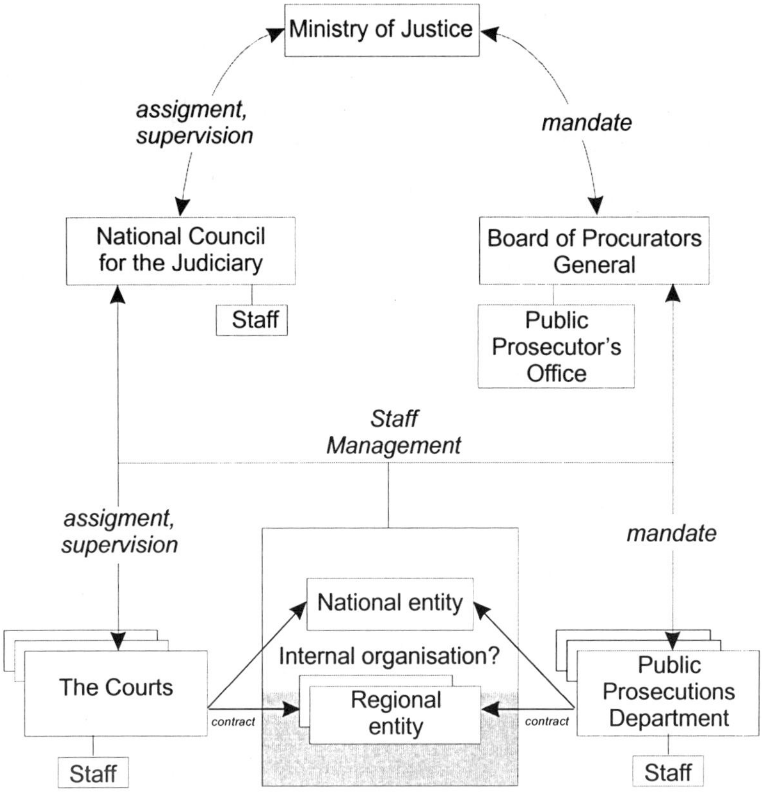

Source: 'Recht van Spreken'[3]

The decentralisation of managerial competences and annual budgets to the court level is taking place at exactly the same time in which the Ministry is developing a much more extended and effective framework of central and uniform information systems and policies. Higher degrees of autonomy and freedom[4] are developing in a context of higher degrees of digital transparency. And higher transparency as we have seen in public administration history (Finer, 1997) and other policy domains (Zeef, 1995; Van de Donk, 1997, 1998a and b), enormously reinforces the possibilities and opportuni-

3 One of the documents mentioned in footnote 1. On the left, we see the judiciary, on the right, the Public Prosecutions Department. In the middle, we see the central staff, which is responsible for the information infrastructure, which can easily be viewed as the techno-structure of the information viewed organisation. Like the Public Prosecutions Department, the judiciary will have its national steering committee. The council of the Procurators General, that has become more active in the last decade (although in constant competition with the Minister of Justice), gets its counterpart for the judiciary in the newly proposed Council for the Judiciary. Much more than the traditional paradigm of an independent judicial system, the figure shows the paradigm of new public management.

4 Courts will even have some possibilities to put aside a certain part of the annual budget (e.g. the money they have 'earned' by being more productive and/or efficient).

ties for external control. In the public domain, this seems to involve in most of the cases, most of the time, all kinds of vertical control.

3 Informatization: decision support and management

As I said before, the further development and use of ICTs support the renewal and reorientation of both the managerial and the claiming and sentencing policies.[5 6] In this section, I will focus on the strategic significance of ICTs for claiming and sentencing. Before I reflect upon the meaning of informatization in this field, I will proceed with a short description of some of the major systems in the Dutch judicial system: Polaris/Bos, IVS, and Nostra.[7]

1. Polaris/Bos: a system designed in and for the Public Prosecutions Department. The project was started a few years ago to improve the implementation of national sentencing guidelines. It is aimed at an improvement of the equality before the law. Some 35 guidelines have been incorporated in the system that enables both implementation and critical evaluation of these guidelines. The system (Bos) incorporates a scoring system (derived from the Polaris guidelines) that supports public prosecutors in formulating their demanded sentences. It was introduced nationally in 1999. Besides the support of the public prosecutors and their assistants, it enables the systematic registration of claims, and the number of decisions that did not follow the advice of the scoring system (for both the regional level and the national level, Boss will be implemented at a national level). The system will enable one to determine, for each of the offences that are programmed in it, the demanded sentence that should be formulated by the public prosecutor according to the Polaris guidelines. Proponents of the system are convinced that digital guidelines are much more effective than those that are only printed on paper.

2. IVS is a database system that has been developed by researchers at the Law and Information Technology Department of Leiden University. The roots of their endeavour lie, again, in the great variety in sentencing behaviour of judges. The system has been developed as a kind of monitoring system. Its application will be made available to judges, who seem to appreciate information about motivation and decisions in earlier cases that can help them to make decisions. The system not only describes in a statistical sense, but also helps to make good decisions, in a normative sense. Both objective and subjective (and inductive) criteria can be taken into account in the cases that are brought together in the database. The

5 In the Netherlands, when the prosecutor requests a conviction on the basis of the available evidence he also asks for a specific punishment to be imposed.

6 They also drastically reinforce the capacity to execute sentences, as Stavros Zouridis showed in his contribution to this meeting.

7 In this draft, these systems are briefly introduced on the basis of some documents and Oskamp and Schmidt (1998).

system is designed for providing the necessary justification for sentences in more complex cases, and helps to bring about a kind of virtual co-ordination and communication between judges in different courts. It is a kind of database that mentions and illustrates complex cases. Oskamp and Schmidt, who have developed the system, think that its application should remain restricted to these cases, since the harmonisation of simple cases can more easily be attained by regular forms of co-ordination. The designers emphasise that the system only supports debate and discussion between judges, in a general and non-compelling way. New information and sentencing grounds which the judges want to include in the database can be added to the system. The system has been developed according to what Tata (1998, see also Tonry, 1987) has described as the paradigm of 'Neutrality, Ownership and Choice' in the construction, use, and adaptation of judicial decision support systems. This paradigm reflects a kind of second-generation thinking about these systems, and tries to counter the criticisms that have been formulated, in theory and practice, against the less flexible systems that have been developed in the 1970s and 1980s (from guidelines to guidance). Justice would be turned into an inflexible machine, in which only very limited, formalistic aspects of the case could be considered, making decision-making a kind of artificial activity. The discretion of the judges would be transferred to the public prosecutor, who would have more possibilities to frame the initial conditions of the decision. Second-generation applications were also a recognition of the judge's ability to circumvent these systems by an increased knowledgeability about the way they 'decide' (Tata, 1998, 149).

3. Nostra is a database system that has been developed by three district courts in the north of the Netherlands (Assen, Groningen, and Leeuwarden). Its development has been supported by the Ministry of Justice. The system enables a transparent overview of sentences per offence, at the level of both individual cases and higher levels of aggregation. It makes an inventory that can help to achieve more consistency in sentencing, but, as the project documentation emphasises: the system does not prescribe decisions. Up until now, the system has only been accessible in these northern courts, but not for the northern public prosecutors and lawyers (Oskamp & Schmidt, 1998; Otte, 1998).

The three examples mentioned above are just three examples from the Netherlands. I want to stress that I have introduced them only briefly. A fuller description is not my aim, and would also be outdated the moment I wrote it down. Still, these examples adequately reflect the trend that can be seen in the judicial branch of government. Informatization is more than an instrument. It is, indeed, a kind of strategy that earlier guided forms of business process re-engineering in other sectors. The use of protocols in the field of health care, the use of Decision Support Systems in the Tax Division, the use of automated systems for policy implementation in the domain of social security and many other things: these are comparable sets of evolving practices and norms (as well as the same kind of controversial issues, see Frøkjær, 1989).[8]

The computer systems mentioned above are especially designed to facilitate and encourage a systematic registration and a comparative analysis of huge amounts of judgements and sentences (between courts, between judges, between types of offences). Some of them are developed to actively guide and support judicial decision-making by public prosecutors and judges. In a technical sense, these systems are really hybrid systems. Technically speaking, the differences between registration and decision support, and between decision support and management information, are rather arbitrary.

Some of the systems are also used to train new judges. Decisions can be evaluated with the help of the system. Systematic registration (and a limited form of analysis) of the results of judicial decision-making processes was, of course, very well possible in the pre-computer era (that for most judicial organisations ended only a few years ago). Such an analysis/evaluation was – at an earlier stage – usually carried out by academic researchers and cunningly calculating law firms. Since the time has now arrived that policy-makers and judicial managers are using computers more skilfully, these analyses and evaluations can and are being made in a much more comprehensive way and on a more regular basis. Moreover, they are used to suggest, develop, and implement all kinds of policies that aim at a rationalisation of judicial organisation and decision-making.

This shift in the use of these systems (out of the field of inquisitive researchers into the domain of judicial policy-makers and managers) has contributed to an important difference. Where researchers were especially focused on an *explanation of the differences* in sentencing, policy-makers and managers are, in the first place, inclined to develop policies *to reduce them*. Support for these policies can be 'organised' rather easily: civil commotion about striking disparities and asinine judges can be dextrously used, as a *policy window,* to put their proposals on the political agenda.

In the 1970s and 1980s, these systems were still very rare, and could only be used by proficient users. At the beginning of the 1990s, these systems were in most of the cases installed on stand-alone computers, which enabled the systematic registration and analysis of one or two offences for one or two courts. The advent of the network computer and data communication, and the development of user-friendly interfaces stimulated the further development of these applications. We are now witnessing the first steps to integrate these systems with the administrative and managerial information systems. This integration is especially fuelled by the new managerial approach, which is characterised by performance indicators and the allocation of budgets that are related to these performances.

---

8 See Snellen, Van de Donk, and Baquiast(1989). Since this book has been published, expert systems and other kinds of decision support systems have become more effectively integrated and embedded in larger information infrastructures and systems.

All this brings up the question of whether the use of Judicial Decision Support Systems will indeed be limited to the aims for which they were initially developed: a more uniform practice of criminal prosecution and execution of sentences. All kinds of other possibilities for using these systems can and are being thought of. Notably ICTs constantly seem to generate new ideas about the expanded use of these systems. Grapendaal and Van der Linden (1998), for instance, describe how these systems could also be used in the planning and forecasting of penitentiary capacity. This idea reflects the general trend of integrating and co-ordinating information infrastructures within what is called the judicial chain. New possibilities for informational integration challenge, to say the least, existing kinds of organisational differentiation and specialisation. Nobody is challenging the specific role and independence of the judiciary, of course. Even when the police and the Public Prosecutions Department are trying to co-ordinate their activities by linking up their information systems, the special position of the judiciary in the judicial chain is stressed repeatedly with many fine words.

On the other hand, the forthcoming possibilities of integrating information systems and – infrastructures within the judicial chain raises all kinds of questions regarding the possibilities to improve the overall quality of its functioning. It is not certain that the ideas of work flow management will stop on the doorstep of the judiciary. ICTs are constantly tempting policy-makers and managers to cross existing borders.

3.1 Taking off the blindfold: ICT as a seducer of Lady Justice?

Both the management of the judicial organisations and the processes of judiciary decision-making, that until now were conducted behind the thick walls of the Hall of Justice, are becoming more and more 'informated' and more transparent. Transparency is a precondition for control and discipline. More control and discipline are also very important words in the documents and policy papers that reflect the new steering philosophy (although the adjective 'new' must be taken with a pinch of salt, because, in fact, these documents reflect old-fashioned ideas of cybernetic thinking, that, in the light of the new technological possibilities, seems to be enjoying quite a revival!).

In order to improve the further use of these systems, they are integrated in a more or less systematic way. Again, ICTs play a crucial role. This role can be described as an 'attractor'. Following a line we have set out earlier (Snellen, 1994; Van de Donk, 1997; Van de Donk and Snellen, 1998), we do not think that a technology in one way or another 'determines', in a causal sense, the implications we are and will be seeing. These implications are formed in an interplay with other developments in the context of the judicial system.

Further research into the meaning of informatization in the judicial system will have to avoid the trap of technological determinism: ICTs do not cause developments in public administration. The (partially autonomous) technological developments change the production functions within public administration. The possibilities of a technology function as attractors for aims that have been recently formulated in the context of the new steering philosophy for the judicial system (like the cybernetic dream).

Earlier, Snellen and I formulated an approach which we find appropriate to show the mechanisms behind ICT developments and applications in public administration. By combining a causal and a functional form of explanation, this approach makes it possible to show how and why the existence of a technology as a field of potentialities 'attracts' certain social (and technological) reactions in the form of socio-technical realizations (see the model that is based on Van Parijs' work in Van de Donk and Snellen, 1998).[9]

This way of looking into the meaning of informatization might very well be applied to the developments we have described for the judicial systems. A causal relationship exists between autonomous ICT developments and the cost structure of information and communication on the one hand, and possible cost savings, e.g. through replacement of personnel or the design of procedures, on the other. Summarizing, ICT developments change the production functions in the organisations and institutions of the Judicial Branch of government. At the same time, a causal relationship exists between cost profiles and the cost-saving possibilities of ICT and the cost, service, and decision-making (equality) within the judicial system. ICT developments improve the best practices of different types of activity in the Judicial Branch as they have done in the Executive Branch. The consequence of these two causal links is that ICT exerts a constant attraction (acts as attractor) on the practices of the judicial system. Ideas about the possibilities of ICT (*technologische Leitbilder* or guiding images) as an 'attractor' incite, on the one hand, a further development of ICT and, on the other, an increase in the level of efficiency, service provision, and all kinds of standards within the judicial system (regarding management as well as decision-making). Utilization of the possibilities created by ICT to enhance efficiency, the level of service provision and common/uniform standards often requires institutional adaptations. For example, administrative processing of traffic offences (see Zouridis, 1999), which has become attractive because of ICT developments, requires adaptations of legal regulations (and may be of our opinion about due process).

A way of reasoning that would only bring to the fore the causal and functional relationships of ICT with the judicial system would suffer from a one-sided technological orientation. The research into the meaning of informatization for the judicial system has to account for the more or less autonomous political, legal, economic, and professional developments of the judicial system as well. The developments we have mentioned before (e.g. the Leemhuis Committee) may also cause changes in the levels of efficiency, of quality decision-making and of (other) standards in the judicial systems, and at the same time cause institutional changes. The initiatives regarding the

---

9 In explanations of social developments, a combination of a causal and a functional line of reasoning may be detected. The causal line of reasoning connects prior situations with later consequences. In this line of reasoning, causes are prior conditions that are a necessary and sufficient condition for the appearance of a later state of affairs. The functional line of reasoning connects later states of affairs to prior situations in such a way that the (continuance of the) existence of the prior situations is made understandable by the improvement they entail in later states of affairs. These kinds of reasoning are thus each other's mirror image in as far as the direction of explanation is concerned. Causal reasoning explains later occurrences by former ones, while functional reasoning explains former occurrences in the light of later ones (see Van de Donk and Snellen, 1998).

new mission and ambitions of the judicial system are, in this respect, as important as the technological developments (e.g. the design of more effective procedures, a more uniform sentencing and claiming behaviour on the part of individual judges, a more open and responsive attitude towards society, a more cost-effective way of budgeting and a new steering philosophy that requires forms of bench-marking and performance indicators). Therefore, as we concluded for public administration, the meaning of ICTs for the judiciary should be discussed in terms of 'implications' and not about causal consequences etc. Autonomous developments in and around the judiciary and the Public Prosecutions Department, and the changes in ideas and ideals in that respect, are as important for the effects of ICT applications on public administration as the technological developments themselves.

3.2 Transparency and integration: discipline or dialogue?

An intriguing question is whether (and how) these increased potentialities for transparency, discipline, control, and integration of all kinds of information[10] will be used. A further question is how this will eventually affect the independence of individual judges and judicial institutions. It is far too early to give an answer to these questions, but we cannot be too early in our effort to find ways of appropriately formulating these questions. In this respect, one could be rather worried about the technical and isolated focus on Judicial Decision Support Systems. As the approach outlined above makes clear, the questions and answers that are provided by people who develop these systems are often not very adequate. Simply stating that the individual judge or a lay person will have opportunities to dispute the 'suggestions' that are put forward by the system will not be enough. Decision-making behaviour, even that of the judges, is embedded in the institutional and cultural context of the judicial system and the judicial organisation at large. These contexts are changed, maybe even more profoundly than by the use of ICTs, by the new managerial paradigms and steering philosophies.

Like the doctor, the judge is a highly trained professional, who is used to working individually, without managerial forms of supervision. A more extensive use of decision support systems at managerial levels might very well change this situation. Digital forms of inter-vision (between professional colleagues) are vulnerable to central forms of super-vision (by court managers, sentencing-policy makers and so on). The mere availability of actual and complete information (about approved sentences in comparable cases) is changing the information environment, and, hence, the decision environment of the professional judge and public prosecutor. Of course, the proponents of these systems say judiciary decisions will remain independent. As far as the public prosecutor is concerned, the sentencing guidelines that are programmed into the administrative systems he uses to prepare his cases are nothing but guidelines. The proponents of an extended use of these systems do not stop to repeat that they will continue to respect the independence and freedom to decide of the judges and prosecutors.

10 E.g. about workloads, tempo, claiming and sentencing behaviour.

The question is whether they will really continue to do so. Read the lines that Steenhuis (the Attorney General we mentioned before) wrote in the booklet that introduced the '*P*roject *O*ntwikkeling *La*ndelijke *Ri*chtlijnen *S*trafvordering' (the project for the development of national sentencing guidelines), which is about to implement the already existing guidelines into the information systems that are used in the public prosecutor's office: 'Up to now, the efforts of the Public Prosecutions Department to realise a more uniform prosecution have not been a complete success. With Polaris, we will be ultimately able to realise the harmonisation we have been aiming for for so long.'[11] The acronym of the project, *Polaris*, is well chosen. It does not hide the ambitions of the project: all the noses of the mulish, self-willed and 'independent' public prosecutors should be pointing in the same direction. Although the digital guidelines are, for the time being, limited to the most frequent types of criminal offences, the ambition is to broaden the regime of the Polaris system towards the less frequent ones. More important than the broadening of the project towards other kinds of offences, however, is the aim to be able to actually implement the guidelines that have already been developed. The fact that they can be integrated into the systems that are installed at the desktops of the public prosecutors and their assistants increases their significance. The fact that they are incorporated in computer programmes is crucial. The guidelines are now an integral part of the decision environment of the public prosecutor, much more effectively than before, when they were only sitting in the window-sill, bound in a nice dust jacket.[12] Bossystem (just one more *s* is missing to understand its meaning) is also becoming an almost indispensable 'aid' for public prosecutors. Bos (a Decision Support System) is a system that almost completely 'guides' the decision-making by the individual public prosecutor who must demand a specific punishment to be imposed. The grounds for the requested punishment, it seems, become especially important when the prosecutor decides not to follow the 'advice' formulated by the system. Besides the fact that the system leads him or her through the process step by step, all decisions are registered, which enables a complete registration of the decision process per prosecutor, per offence, and so on.

When we compare the meaning of these systems within the domain of the judicial system with those that have been implemented in other domains that also involve highly trained and skilled professionals (like decision-makers in some domains of policy implementation or medical doctors), we see some interesting similarities (Berg, 1998).

One of the most striking ones is that these systems limit and discipline the informationdomains of professionals, as well as their room to manoeuvre (at least the room they have to do this unnoticed). Normally transparency and registration are soon followed by ('attracting' forms of) evaluation. Evaluation in many cases provokes a kind of steering. Like other professionals, public prosecutors and judges gradually discover that they are part of larger systems and arrangements in which their actions

---

11 Source: *Introduction of Polaris*, Public Prosecutors Office, p. 3.

12 'This does not necessarily place any constraints on the sentencing decision of the judge, it merely provides the judge with information which can help the pursuit of consistency' (Tata, 1998, 145).

are co-ordinated in a more or less systematic way. These developments are not only observable at the level of individual professionals, but also at the level of professional organisations.

The 'informating capacities' of the systems these professionals and their organisations use[13] are (sur)rendering their (information) domains amenable to systematic forms of (external) control and evaluation more than they have ever been before. This control and evaluation can be executed, moreover, on the basis of reliable (their own), systematic, and recent information. These characteristics are increasingly facilitated by explicit (usually) information policies, that contribute to a further harmonisation and a more uniform definition and use of data. The decision-making processes of individual public prosecutors and judges is becoming embedded in these information policies more than ever before. Independence presupposes a certain degree of autonomy and variety. ITS seem to reinforce just the opposite: disciplined processes and uniform data.

3.3 Will Lady Justice lose her blindfold?

The judiciary might very well be the next 'victim' of the information revolution, which earlier successfully enabled external and mainly vertical strategies of control in hospitals, schools, municipalities, and different kinds of individual professionals as well as their organisations. Of course, these strategies can be predominantly vertical and/or horizontal in nature. In the public domain, ICTs especially seem to attract a further development of vertical and centralised strategies of external control. Whole sections of society, even those parts that have been the domain of independent professionals for ages, are becoming embedded in all kinds of rather centralising planning and control systems. One might very well ask whether this is a development that, after all, realises forms of technocratic utopias in public organisations at a time that society at large seems to be less and less suitable for that kind of central-rule approach.

The Public Prosecutions Department and the judiciary seem to be affected by a larger strategy that is 'suggested' by informatization developments. This is a 'strategy' that highlights characteristics of transparency, discipline and control. It is a strategy that is also developing in other domains of public administration. The application of rules can be more and more transparent and disciplined at the same time. These characteristics of transparency and discipline are seized upon rather greedily by all kinds of 'managers' who, up until now, had to accept higher levels of discretion of the professionals than they, all in all, were prepared to accept. The public annoyance with the functioning of the judicial system was a circumstance cunningly seized upon to expand the technological means to know and to control. ICTs are an important attractor and seem to convey a very specific steering philosophy.

Whether or not Lady Justice will lose her blindfold is difficult to predict. Perhaps she will only use a blindfold of a more translucent nature. The informatization deve-

13 In some cases, they already share them with others, like the police or other actors in the *judicial chain*.

lopments in the judicial system have only just started. Here again, however, ICTs seem to have strategic potential, and may even change our image of the law. Like the chess computer did, judicial decision support systems may very well show that they, much more than human beings, are able to sentence in a consistent and uniform way. The question is, of course, whether we really value such consistency and uniformity as the main characteristic of judicial decision-making. It might very well be that the need for openness and control of the judiciary must be understood much more in a horizontal, regional direction than in the managerial verticalism that now seems to be dictating the developments.

Of course, an individual judge will be very well able to reject the ICT paradigm that informs many of the reforms in the judicial system. He will be much less able to counter the societal trend of openness and horizontal forms of accountability (e.g. Frissen, 1996). Of course a judge can remain as stubborn as a donkey and refuse to accept the limits to his authority. Much more than before, however, he will very quickly be known as such by people who have access to the data that are registered in the system. For the future autonomy of the judicial branch, it is therefore important to monitor the way and the extent to which these systems will be embedded in the institutional and organisational dynamics of judicial organisations.

4 Some questions to conclude

The research agenda of the institutional meaning of the introduction of ICT in the Judicial System is in many ways an unfinished one. I have only tried to develop some ideas about an approach to the study of informatization in the judicial system. The main point that I want to illustrate with this contribution is that it is necessary not to study informatization in an isolated way. The study of informatization should, morover, not be restricted to the micro level and technicalities of the many applications that are developed for the different parts and organisations of the system. Instead, it should reflect the broader contexts and developments that surround the introduction and use of these intriguing artefacts.

To conclude, I will point out a few questions for further research and debate.

- Will public prosecutors and judges be confronted with a decreased level of discretion, and if so, who will be gaining the kind of power that is associated with it?
- Will the extensive use if ICTs significantly change the character of judicial decision-making and the institutional and organisational characteristics of the judicial organisations? What does this mean for the character of the law?
- How will the use of ICTs and the related steering philosophies affect the institutional position of the judicial system, and how will this affect the relationship with the other powers (politics, bureaucracy, other actors in society)?
- Will the concept of an (ICT-supported) judicial chain be a feasible concept without indeed using these chains to bind together previously autonomous organisations (will the use of ICTs at a mainly administrative level affect the politico-strategic dimensions of the organisations that are involved?

References

Berg, M., et al., *De nacht schreef rood. Informatisering van zorgpraktijken* The Hague, Rathenau Instituut, (1998).
Donk, W.B.H.J. van de, *De arena in schema. Over de betekenis van informatisering voor beleid en politiek inzake de verdeling van middelen over verzorgingshuizen*, Lelystad, Koninklijke Vermande, (1997).
Donk, W.B.H.J. van de, 'Beyond Incrementalism?', in: I.Th.M. Snellen & W.B.H.J. van de Donk, (Eds.), *Public Administration in an Information Age*. Amsterdam/Tokyo/New York, IOS Press, (1998).
Donk, W.B.H.J. van de, & I.Th.M. Snellen, 'Towards a Theory of Informatization in Public Administration?', in: I.Th.M. Snellen & W.B.H.J. van de Donk, (Eds.). *Public Administration in an Information Age*. Amsterdam/Tokyo/New York, IOS Press, (1998).
Frissen, P.H.A., *De Virtuele Staat*, Schoonhoven: Academic Press, (1996).
Grapendaal, M. & B. Van der Linden, 'Naar een nieuw straftoemetingsbeleid, in: penitentiaire capaciteitsproblemen en Amerikaanse oplossingen', in: *Justitiële Verkenningen*, Vol 24, no.5, (1998), pp. 8-26.
Leijten, J.C.M., 'De verschrikkelijke eenzaamheid van de inbreker', in: *Balans*, (19-92).
Oskamp, E.W. & A.H.J. Schmidt, 'De opmars van de informatietechnologie', in: Een vergelijkend warenonderzoek van drie strafmaatsystemen, *Justitiële Verkenningen*, Vol 24, June 1998, pp. 39-61.
Snellen, Van de Donk, and Baquiast, *Expert Systems in Pulic Administration. Evolving Practices and Norms*, Amsterdam, Elsevier Science Publishers, (1989).
Tata, C., 'Neutrality', 'Choice', and 'Ownership' in the Construction, Use, and Adaptation of Judicial Decision Support Systems', in: *Journal of Law and Information Technology*, Vol. 6, no. 2, (1998), pp. 143-166.
Tonry, M., 'Sentencing Guidelines and Sentencing Commissions: The Second Generation', in: Wasik & Pease, (Eds.), *Sentencing Reforms: Guidance or Guidelines?*, Manchester, Manchester University Press, (1987).
Zouridis, S., 'There is no escape!', in: *Informatization and the enforcement of trafffic regulations*, Paper voor EGPA conferentie in Athene, (1999).

Reinventing the Docket, Discovering the Database

The Divergent Adoption of Information Technology in the Italian Judicial Offices

*Francesco Contini**

1 Introduction

In this work we will explore and analyze the organizational dynamics that cause difficulties and pitfalls in innovation processes but at the same time we can determine the conditions for their successful adoption. We will consider four Italian judicial offices, organizations that show remarkable difficulty in the adoption of technology, rules, procedures and organizational arrangements. In the Italian judicial system, political reasons play a major role in the failure of the innovation process and sometimes lead to the rejection and sabotage of rules and technology (Di Federico, 1993). In the cases we have studied, however, the political dimension of organizational life seems to have played a minor role. We will consider here the introduction of a computerized case management system, called Re.Ge., that was intended to replace the 'paper dockets' and to represent the basic tool for office automation. The innovation was quickly adopted but, through a reinvention process (Rice and Rogers, 1980), it was transformed into a perfect functional equivalent (Merton, 1957) of the original technology which it replaced. In this way the innovation lost possible new meanings, uses and, in conclusion, its potential for change.

To some extent, this kind of replacement is frequent in judicial organizations where it is common to observe cases in which the organization shows a remarkable capability to destructure the innovation object. In the course of our analysis we will attempt to explain the reasons for this phenomenon. At the same time we will illustrate how the organizational factors that destructure the innovation might lead to a different kind of adoption capable of exploiting the resources of the innovation.

The research team observed the adoption of a computerized case management system in four judicial offices as participant observers, adopting a research interven-

---

* Researcher at The Research Institute on Judicial Systems of the National Research Council (IRSIG-CMR), Bologna, Italy.This article is based on research developed by the Research Institute on Judicial Systems of the Italian National Research Council within a formal cooperation agreement with the Minister of Justice. I thank Marco Fabri and Davide Carnevali with whom I carried out the fieldwork and the data analysis.

tion strategy.[1] The innovation process (Re.Ge.) was introduced to replace the 'old' paper dockets used by the courts and by the Prosecutors' Offices, and to automate some paperwork procedures.

From a theoretical point of view we have considered the interrelations between the organization and the innovation object, starting from three basic assumptions. First of all, we do not only consider the innovation as a tool characterized by a predefined set of functions and instruction but a social object with an undetermined possibility of actions (Barley, 1986, 1988). Second, the process of adopting the innovation is seen as the development of a network of cognitive, institutional and practical interrelations between the innovation object and the receiving organization. Third, the elements taken for granted by the organizational actors play a decisive role in the process of adoption. We will consider, therefore, the cognitive and institutional elements taken for granted and which are included in the formative context (Unger, 1987; Ciborra and Lanzara, 1989, 1990; Contini, 1999). We will focus on context making, and on the evolutionary processes enacted by the introduction of the innovation process in the organization. Through these processes a new order might be generated, but it might also occur that the existing organizational arrangement is reproduced.

In the following pages we will introduce the basic elements of our theoretical approach and the idea of context making. Then we will describe the context making processes observed in the case studies in order to focus and analyze the dynamics of change. To conclude we will address the institutional, cognitive and practical factors that have affected the adoption of innovation in the judicial offices in the four case studies presented here.

2 The receiving and the formative context

Our theoretical background is widely influenced by Gregory Bateson's works (1972, 1984). We focus on the relationships between the actors and the organizational context, seeking to describe and understand their reciprocal influences during the processes of change as well as during the day by day operations.

The innovation process is seen as the introduction of a new element (the innovation object)[2] into a receiving context. This enacts processes that can lead to its adoption, rejection or reinvention. At the same time the organizational context is reshaped because the innovation object – adopted or reinvented by the organizational actors – has structuring properties (Orlikowsky and Robey, 1991) that might deeply modify the organization.

To analyze these dynamics of change we distinguish between the *receiving context* and the *formative one*. The former is the wide frame that embodies and shapes the milieu and the space in which the actors operate and the innovation is introduced. The

1 The complete results of the research are published in Carnevali, Fabri and Contini (1993).

2 It does not matter if the innovation object is a complex piece of technology or a simple material tool, a formal rule or a procedure.

receiving context is formed by a wide set of elements: the material tools and the procedure used by organizational actors, the structure of tasks and roles, the mechanism of the division of labour and its coordination, the formal and the informal rules, the 'codes of meaning' that the actors use and reproduce to make sense of organizational life.

This bundle of factors and relationships define (in space and time) the organizational situation in which an innovation is introduced. Therefore it represents the organizational stage on which the innovation process takes place. We use the word 'context' to highlight the fact that these organizational features are interrelated into a web of functional, cognitive and institutional relationships that delineate a microecology of actions (Bateson, 1972, 1984; Lanzara, 1993).

The formative context can be considered as the hidden subset of the receiving context. The elements of the receiving context and their relationships may be visible and well known to the organizational actors but also hidden, unknown and taken for granted. While those which are visible are perceived and can therefore be discussed and modified, those which are hidden, being deeply-ingrained and invisible to the actors, are not immediately accessible. This subset of the receiving context constitutes the *formative context*: 'a deep-seated texture of relations, rules, habits, cognitive frame and institutional arrangements which agents bring and routinely enact in a situation of action' (Unger, 1987; Lanzara, 1998). It constitutes a background condition for action, enforcing constraints, giving direction and meaning, and setting the range of opportunities for undertaking action (Ciborra and Lanzara, 1990; Blackler, 1992).

In comparison with the wider receiving context, the formative context generates a deeper influence on everyday actions as well as on innovation processes. It constitutes the second level (implicit and tacit) of organizational knowledge. Therefore it deeply informs individual and organizational action, both strategic (Crozier and Friedberg, 1978) and routinized (Pentland and Reuter, 1994), and it plays a relevant role also in the design process (Lanzara, 1993).

For these reasons it is embedded in artifacts, routines, organizational structures, and microecology of actions. Basically, it constitutes the ground where the social construction of organizational life takes place (Berger and Luckmann, 1966). Through evolutionary processes or breakdowns, the formative context traces the shifting boundaries between not only the known and the unknown, but even between the knowable and the inconceivable.

3 Adoption process as context making

Several studies illustrate the discrepancy which may occur between a planned approach to the design of technologies and formal rules and the realities of the implementation (Fabri, 1994), where trial and error, negligence, chance and serendipity seem to be the major forces (Ciborra and Lanzara, 1994). The path of implementation can lead to a rejection of the innovation (which may even be forgotten, like the videotape recording systems in the Italian courts),[3] but also to speedy adoption, such as for the use of the fax machine. We have frequently noticed cases in which the innovation object, its technological features and the functionality defined through the *ex ante* design, are reinvented during the adoption process (Rice and Rogers, 1980).

The idea of *context making* can help us to understand these findings. Context making takes place when the innovation is tested, and is somewhat related to the elements of the receiving context. The tool, such as a computerized system, ends up being a 'box' characterized only by the functional properties defined by the designer: it becomes an artifact, a social tool, integrated into a web of practical, cognitive and institutional relationships – a tool in context. In this way the new technology receives a specific organizational meaning, it begins to be regulated also by informal rules and starts to be inserted into the microecology of activities.

The adoption, the rejection and more frequently the reinvention of the innovation pass through its interplay with the formative context. During the adoption process, a major role is played by the deployment of the relationships between the innovation object and the elements of the formative context which are taken for granted. They drive the adoption process, saturating the innovation with acceptable meanings and uses. But the interplay between the innovation object and the formative context can also result in the lack of available functions and in tensions or conflicts until the rejection of the innovation. Through these dynamics, the innovation may become a new, fully integrated element of the formative context. For example, a material tool could become an artifact used in an automatic way, a procedure designed through a BPR could become a natural routine, a formal rule could become a set of instructions habitually followed by organizational actors. It is interesting to observe that, through these processes, the innovation and the formative context are reciprocally shaped. This means that the constraints and the original features of the innovation object, but also the properties, the elements and the relationships of the formative context are mutually formed. For these reasons, observing the context-making is a useful approach to the analysis of the innovation processes.

4 The receiving context: prosecutors' offices and *preture*

The four case studies involved are two *preture* and the two related prosecutors' offices[4] located in two cities in the north of Italy which we will call Luni and Velleia to respect the confidentiality of the people involved.

---

3 For a wide analysis of this case see Di Federico, Lanzara and Mestitz (1993).

4 In the Italian judicial system the *pretura* (analogous to a Magistrate's Court) was a limited jurisdiction court of first instance where single judges dealt with both civil and criminal matters, handling cases involving up to 50 million Lira in civil matters, and up to 4 years imprisonment in criminal cases. A sentence of up to ten years could be passed in cases specified by the law. The prosecutors' offices are in charge of initiating criminal actions, conducting investigations and supervising the police.The preture merged with the first instance courts of general jurisdiction (*tribunali*) in June 1999.

To replace the 'old fashioned' paper dockets with a computerized system, or to move from the conventional paper form to an up to date electronic form might seem a simple task. The old tool is replaced by a new one that (at the very least) performs the old functions in a quicker, more reliable and complete way. But the study confirms that the adoption of innovation in the judicial administration is extremely difficult.

Before the introduction of the innovation the receiving contexts at Velleia and Luni were similar. Paper dockets and paper forms widely characterized the microecology of actions in the judicial offices. Their use was governed by the Code of Criminal Procedure, by several decrees of the Minister of Justice and by formal organizational rules.

Essentially, the paper dockets are used to keep track of the criminal proceedings. Specified procedural events in each criminal proceeding (from complaint to judgment) must be recorded there. Thus, the administrative personnel (both at the prosecutors' office and at the court) write by hand events such as the date and a summary of the criminal complaint, the names of the victims and of the indicted persons, the formal charges, the date of the trial, the judgment etc. Occasionally the data stored in the paper dockets are retrieved in order to answer lawyers' or citizens' questions.

In our case studies the most common judicial documents were prepared by filling out paper forms. While the paper dockets contained all the information necessary to complete these forms, the administrative staff, the prosecutors or the judges retrieved the data directly from the case files. The reasons for this are, first, that unlike the paper dockets, the case files are generally updated. Second, the paper dockets are cumbersome, difficult to manage, and the time that must be dedicated to the recording of the crime reports and to the updates of the data frequently takes an entire day. Consequently, they were very rarely used to retrieve the data necessary to write the judicial documents. Even the statistical data were collected from the paper dockets during the afternoon, when the ordinary office work diminished somewhat.

This microecology action, shaped by tools, routines, rules and (as we shall see) meanings, shows clear limits and difficulties in functioning. Nevertheless, it constitutes a well-known pathway for action, and an appropriate way of doing the work in each of our case studies.

5 The formative context of the paper dockets

To identify the elements of the formative context we gathered and compared three types of data: the description (*expost*) of the microecology of actions centred on paper artifacts (dockets and forms), interviews with expert witnesses concerning the adoption of the innovation object, and participant observation concerning the use of the innovation.

The first elements taken for granted are the *unit of action* and *the unit of place*, following Aristotle's drama. These two elements are embedded in the design and physical constraints of the artifact. The docket is placed in the clerks' offices (not in those of the judges and prosecutors) and just one office worker at a time can work with it. But the very physical constraints of the artifact delimit a visible and clear object: the embodiment of the history of the office, the bureaucratic 'book of memory' of the life of the organization (Carnevali, 1995). The dockets and the paper forms are coherent and integrated with the *conventional layout* of judges' and prosecutors' offices: large tables to manage the dockets, chests of drawers to collect the paper forms, huge bookshelves for the case files. This layout reflects both the bureaucratic and material control of the clerks over the dockets and the (social) division of labour between judges (or prosecutors) and the office workers (Rosen, Orlikowski and Schmahmann, 1990). The latter still play an ancillary role: they copy judicial documents, help judges and prosecutors in writing out by hand or typewriting judicial documents, but they have little control as regards the organization of the workflow and the management of the office.

Another relevant element of the formative context is the visibility and consequently the *accountability* of judges' and prosecutors' work. Since it is difficult to access the data collected in the paper dockets, even the Chief Prosecutor (or the Chief Judge), the prosecutors (or judges), and office workers may find it problematic to know what their colleagues are doing.[5] In other words, especially in the larger offices (Mele, 1994), the paper docket deters coordination based on mutual adjustment of organizational actors and on hierarchy (Mintzberg, 1983).

The problems related to the external visibility and accountability of the offices are still more relevant. For example, it is very difficult to get the information that might be necessary to evaluate the actions of prosecutors, or to discover a lack (or an excess) of investigations (Di Federico, 1995; Zagrebelsky, 1994; Maddalena, 1997; Fabri, 1997), or, at least, to judge the equal treatment of citizens made by courts and prosecutors' offices. Even the statistical data, present in the paper dockets, are frequently unreliable and ambiguous.

6 The parallel use of paper dockets and Re.Ge.

The *innovation process* (Re.Ge.) is a case management system based on a client-server layout. The application and the data archives remain on the server while magistrates and office workers, using their own clients (e.g. personal computers connected into a LAN), can access, update, and search the data. Access to application is restricted to authorized users. Different levels of password are needed to read the information, to add new data or to revise the existing data. The data can be transmitted from the prosecutors' offices to the judges' offices (*pretura*) and viceversa. Finally, the system can elaborate statistical data and execute simple text editor functions.

5 It can happen in prosecutors' offices that two or three prosecutors are carrying out parallel investigations on the same case without even knowing it.

6.1 The 'analogic adoption'

Since the introduction of Re.Ge., the four case studies have demonstrated several common elements. For a long time they used both the new computerized system and the old paper dockets. Consequently the redundancy of artifacts and procedures was slowing down the functioning of the offices, reducing their performances.

The first problem was the training, since it took place exclusively 'on the job'. Furthermore, while the paper docket was an artifact immediately visible and accessible, well known by the office workers and by the magistrates, Re.Ge. was (and indeed still is) a strange, 'esoteric' object. When opening a page of the paper docket everything is clear: the data regarding a specific case are stored in lines, while columns specify the types of data that have to be filled in. Opening Re.Ge. on the monitor a dos-window appears for the data entry or for information retrieval, and the relationship between the records or the automatic procedure embedded in the system is nottransparent. The personnel found Re.Ge. ambiguous, difficult to understand and to control. Consequently this cognitive decoupling between the artifacts and the organizational actors made the change extremely difficult (Weick, 1990; Norman, 1990).

Ultimately the decision to discontinue the paper dockets faced a legal constraint as well: the offices were awaiting the application of a decree of the Minister of Justice that authorized the discontinuance of the paper dockets and the sole use of Re.Ge. Another institutional assumption of the formative context is that 'any object with a juridical relevance can not be forsaken or replaced without a formal rule that authorizes it'.

The judicial offices began to use Re.Ge. and to develop new routines. During this stage, in which the official dockets were still the 'old paper books', the parallel use of Re.Ge. and of the paper dockets facilitated the development of routines in a 'protected' environment.

While the parallel use of two technologies is a recurrent event in innovation processes, it was necessary to move from this situation and to discontinue the paper dockets. To postpone this decision would have worsened the organizational problems related to the adoption of the new Code of Criminal Procedure (enacted in 1989). In fact, the waste of time resulting from the duplication of the procedures would have slowed down office productivity, and therefore would have led to an increase in the number of pending cases both at prosecutors' offices and at the courts (Fabri, 1994). But the absence of a specific formal governmental decree made it impossible to abandon the paper dockets and to use Re.Ge. exclusively until, finally, a decree by the Minister of Justice authorized the use of the so-called '*sistemi di registrazione automatica*' (literally 'automatic recording systems' commonly called databases) on condition that they could follow the data set of the paper dockets. This means that the databases must retain the same structure as the paper dockets and that, if necessary, the software application must be able to reproduce the dockets on paper. In other words the new electronic artifact must be able to reconstruct the abandoned paper dockets.

This decree, closely linking the innovation (Re.Ge.) with the pre-existing artifacts, points out another element of the formative context which is an institutionalized rule that specifies a hidden property of the innovation object: to be acceptable, the innovation object must be transformable into an exact duplicate of the artifacts that are supposed to be substituted. Precisely in accordance with this assumption the old paper docket has been replaced by its 'modern duplicate'. Therefore even the path dependency (David, 1985) is taken for granted and becomes an element of the formative context.

Besides this *institutional aspect*, the links between the paper dockets and Re.Ge. embrace the *symbolic dimension*. The name of the application (Re.Ge.) is an abbrevation of the main dockets called *Registri Generali*. The organizational actors commonly call Re.Ge. '*registro automatizzato*' (automated docket). This analogy eased the making of sense and drove the context making. The fact of considering Re.Ge (technologically a data base) as an 'automated docket' facilitated the discovery of analogies with the paper artifact: the complexity of the electronic system was simplified, and the new artifact was placed in a well-known domain.

The choice of the name, underlining the fact that Re.Ge. was still a docket, even if automated, could be considered an effect of the formative context. The formative context of the paper docket could have deployed its influence in two directions. On the one side, it might have limited the capability of the developers of the application to figure out the potentiality of change of the artifact. On the other, the same group of developers might have decided to create a product acceptable to the judicial offices (or 'formative context-oriented'). Indeed, to explain to an old- fashioned organization that a data base would replace the paper dockets would have puzzled the organizational actors, and probably generated a cognitive decoupling - or even a collapse in the making of any sense (Weick, 1993a) - as well as institutional and organizational break down (Lanzara, 1998). Conversely, the cognitive analogy between the paper and the automated docket eased the making of sense.

Coherent with these cognitive and institutional assumptions, the organizational actors also found *practical similarities* between Re.Ge. and the pre-existing artifacts. The routines centred on the paper dockets were quickly transferred to Re.Ge.

Therefore the discontinuance of the paper dockets and the adoption of the innovation passed through the strong analogy between Re.Ge. as an 'automatic recording system' and the paper dockets. This helped the growth of institutional, cognitive, and practical links between the innovation object and the formative context. Through this 'analogic adoption', Re.Ge. not only took the place of the paper dockets but became a perfect functional equivalent of them (Merton, 1957).

6.2 The analogic trap

The analogic adoption speeds up and eases the adoption of the technology, because the old meanings and routines of the paper dockets can be transferred to the 'automatic docket' (Douglas, 1986; Hofstadter, 1995). Nevertheless, at the same time it reduces the opportunity to discover any new possible meanings and functions of the innovation object.

Three years after the introduction of Re.Ge., when we began participant observation in the offices, the routines, the meanings and the institutionalized rules of the paper dockets were simply transferred to the 'automated docket' in three of the four case studies. Only one office was trying – with limited results – to use Re.Ge. not only as an automated docket but also for simple office automation procedures (such as to print the cover page of the case files) or to collect statistical data. However, the four offices did not adopt the innovation as a database – that is a 'shared collection of interrelated data designed to meet the needs of multiple types of end users' (Martin, 1983) – but 'simply' as an automated docket. In this way they discovered neither the office automation concept (and functions) embedded in the notion of a database nor the 'informating power' of computer technology (Zuboff, 1988). In conclusion, the analogy focused on the idea of an automated docket that eased the adoption which was (and is still for many judicial offices)[6] a hidden trap.

Consequently, an innovation object in a state of tension with the features of the formative context can freeze the making of sense and contrast with organizational routines or institutionalized norms, with a consequent rejection of the innovation itself. But, on the other hand, an innovation object that perfectly matches the cognitive and institutional assumption of the formative context will not produce a deep and relevant process of change. This dilemma between stability and change can explain both the rapid learning (Hedberg, 1981) of the use of Re.Ge. and its superficial and careless adoption.

7 From the automated docket to office automation

During our participant observation only the Luni prosecutors' office was able to escape from the trap of the 'automatic docket'.

The process started with the acquisition of new computers. All the office workers and the prosecutors received new personal computers connected to a LAN in order to access Re.Ge. and to share resources. Every PC was provided with a new set of applications (word processor, spreadsheets, database). If this new technological platform (Ciborra, 1983) is taken as the starting point of the new process and the same technological improvements took place in every case study, the different situations and outcomes which we have observed cannot be explained. More than the resources themselves, the relevant factor has been the *resourcefulness* (Weick, 1993b), the capability to deal with new problems and resources.

With this technological platform, three organizational actors – a prosecutor, a clerk and a software technician – began to develop new software tools and to generate new organizational routines. The prosecutor developed an application based on the

6 Recently we have made some observations which clearly demonstrate that this situation is still diffused in many judicial offices.

function of the new word processor to ease the data entry in standard documents (e.g. the decree of indictment). He created electronic forms with blank spaces to be filled with data such as the name of the indicted person and of the victims, or the charge. The new functions of the word processor (macros, glossaries, and automatic modules) speeded up the entire process. Basically it was a quasi-automated system for the editing of standard judicial documents. Then he made the application available to the office. The clerk, with the help of the prosecutor, began to develop and expand the application. This individual learning by the prosecutor quickly took the form of organizational learning (Argyris and Schön, 1978, 1996). Within a few weeks the office had changed its way of functioning. A new artifact was regularly used and adopted. Thanks to this system, the personal computers and the network became a new effective working tool.

The speedy adoption of this new artifact is a clear evolution of the traditional paperwork of the prosecutors' offices. The handwriting of the paper form is now performed using the PC and an electronic format. If the analogy between Re.Ge. and the automatic docket was strong, then the analogy between the electronic and paper formats was the driving force behind the adoption process. Routines, institutionalized rules, and meanings moved quickly from the paper to the electronic format. The tool was connected with the institutional arrangements and the cognitive assumption of the formative context of the paper docket.

While the prosecutors and the office workers tested (and adopted) the electronic form, the software technician developed a new program to download the data collected on Re.Ge. and to upload these data on the electronic forms. This new software, called *Decise,* was capable of automatically assembling documents (indictment decrees, lists of witnesses, requests for hearings), which merged the data collected on Re.Ge. with the electronic forms. Therefore it simplified the prosecutors' work and automated a large area of the clerks' activities, radically changing their work. For the first time the huge amount of data collected on Re.Ge. was usable for office automation.

The development of Decise is a typical case of software *bricolage* (Lanzara, 1998) through which a new artifact and its related organizational routines are created using *second hand resources* (Levi-Strauss, 1962) such as common software originally designed for other purposes. Frequently, in this process, the users of the innovation play a major role, for example in the design of the tool, and its concrete realization. Furthermore, these *bricoleur* are *not professionals* of computer technology - in our case they are a prosecutor and a clerk - and therefore they do not use their primary organizational knowledge. The prosecutor and the clerk who realized the process of change, explored these systems' possibility for action, and designed and developed the new software keeping the functional needs of the office constantly in mind.

We must point out that the prosecutor, the clerk and the technician were frustrated by the idea that the large amount of data collected by Re.Ge. was not used for office automation purposes. For these *bricoleur* Re.Ge. was not an 'automated docket', but a database, an idea that (as we have shown) does not belong to the judicial world. This means that, unlike the adoption of Re.Ge., the sensemaking was based on an analogy with something distant from the everyday life of judicial and prosecutors' offices.

But the creation of this new tool and the 'office automation experience' immediately generated a problem. For the first time the data collected on Re.Ge. were systematically used in office work. Frequently the administrative personnel, downloading data from Re.Ge., discovered mistakes, inaccuracies and incompleteness. In these cases it was necessary to update the data collected on Re.Ge. with a visible waste of time. To put it succinctly, the use of Decise demonstrated the poor quality of the data entry made with Re.Ge. Therefore to appreciate completely the automatic functions of Decise it was necessary to redefine the data entry routine.

8 Making a new formative context

The problem raised practical, cognitive and institutional implications and finally originated a context-making cycle. As we mentioned, due to the analogy between Re.Ge. and the automatic docket, the data entry routine was still that which had been developed for paper. But the 'office automation experience' pointed out that the data entry must be *more standardized* on Re.Ge. than in the paper dockets.

The office worker involved in the use of Decise understood that a perfect correspondence between the data collected on the case file and the data gathered on Re.Ge. was necessary. The automatic use of the data showed that Re.Ge. was something different from an automated docket. The closeness of the analogy, taken for granted until then, started to deviate.

Also the meaning of the artifact changed. Re.Ge became not only a tool to keep track and control the history of the criminal proceedings, but a *database for office automation*. Consequently its institutional position in the taken for granted hierarchy of organizational artifacts established itself. Decise and Re.Ge. became the central artifacts of the prosecutors' office.

It is important to point out that – for the first time – the problem has not been solved simply with an improvement in the data entry procedure. The disalignment between Re.Ge., Decise and the formative context gave rise to a new making of sense and new institutionalized rules. The organizational actors directly involved in the use of Re.Ge. and Decise started to understand that to work with the automated procedures a different approach is required. New rules to standardize the data entry were quickly drafted, new routines were generated. The traditional meaning of the automated docket, the microecology of action based on 'paper', became immediately outdated. As the technician accurately pointed out 'they understand the meaning of the database only when they start to use the data that they have collected'.

9 Concluding remarks

In this work we have tried to analyze the context-making emanating from the interactions between the innovation object and the formative context. In three cases the formative context resisted the 'destabilizing effects' (Unger, 1987, 7) generated by the innovation object. Re.Ge embedded the routines and the assumptions taken for granted, therefore the paper docket was reinvented.

Only at the Luni prosecutors' office have we observed a context-making cycle that simultaneously shaped both the formative context and the artifact. In this case, the organizational actors, through the use of Re.Ge and the electronic form, discovered some taken for granted assumptions of the formative context and began to perceive them as constraints. But this cognitive decoupling is not enough to complete a context-making cycle. It is necessary to transform the new meaning of the artifact (Re.Ge. is a database) into a new and accepted microecology of action consistent with the institutionalized rules.

Here we can briefly summarize the elements that enabled the context-making cycle. First of all, the *analogy* (Hofsdatter, 1995) played a major role in the making of sense. Fundamental, in particular, was the capability of making analogies with elements that did not belong to the formative context, such as the database. While an analogy based on the taken for granted cognitive scheme tend to reproduce the existing formative context, an analogical thought based on elements that do no belong to the formative context can drive the 'sense-making' to discover new meanings and a new potential for action. Relevant in this respect can also be the creation of *transitional objects* (Winnicot, 1953) such as the electronic forms. They are artifacts rooted in the existing formative context but, through their use, the organizational actors might generate a new making of sense or discover some hidden constraints of the formative context. The third element is *resourcefulness:* the capability to use the available assets, to discover and remove obstacles that still obstruct the process of change. Finally, organizational actors are also crucial for their *bricolage capability*, which is relevant not only to create or modify artifacts and routines, but also, to drive the change through the 'syncretic blending' of existing artifacts, routines, institutional assumptions and cognitive frames.

In this article we have tried to analyze the hidden side of the adoption of a case management system, to show its traps and difficulties as well as to point out the risk of a simple replacement of 'old technology' with a 'modern surrogate'. In the Italian judicial system this risk is very high, and the large-scale consequences for the functioning of the judicial system are clear. In is known that computer technology can automate the office work in judicial organizations, with an expected positive impact on the effectiveness and on the quality of justice. Furthermore its 'informating power', improving the internal and external visibility of judges' and prosecutors' work, could ameliorate both the peer control and the accountability of the system. But these results are achievable only through an extensive process of change, capable of modifying the cognitive and institutional assumptions of the formative context. We think that these potentialities for change will only become realizable in a long term. In the meanwhile, the adoption of computer technology cannot basically consist of the replacement of paper tools with their modern functional equivalents, or the massive introduction of information technology as this would simply be a ceremonius adoption of a technological myth (Meyer and Rowan, 1977), with a minimal impact on the concrete functioning of the organization.

References

Argyris, C. and D.A. Schön, *Organizational Learning. A Theory of Action Perspective*, Reading, Mass.: Addison-Wesley, (1978).

Argyris C. and D.A. Schön, *Organizational Learning II*, Reading Mass.: Addison-Wesley, (1996).

Barley S.R., 'Technology as an Occasion for Structuring: Evidence from Observation of CT Scanners and the Social Order of Radiology Departments', in: *Administrative Science Quarterly*, 31, 1, march, (1986), pp. 78-108.

Barley S.R., 'The social construction of a machine: ritual, superstition, magical thinking and other pragmatic responses to running a CT Scanner', in: Lock M. and D. Gordon, (eds.) *Knowledge and Practice in Medicine: Social, Cultural and Historical Approaches*, Hingham, Mass.: Reidel Publ. Co, (1988)

Bateson G., *Steps to an Ecology of Mind,* New York, NY: Chandler Publ. Co, (19-72).

Bateson, G., *Mind and Nature. A Necessary Unity*, Glasgow: Collins, (1984).

Berger, P.L. and T. Luckman, *The Social Construction of Reality*, Garden City, NY: Doubleday and Co, (1966).

Blackler, F., 'Formative Context and Activity Systems: Postmodern Approaches to the Management of Change', in: Reed, M. and M. Hughes, (eds.), *Rethinking Organization: New Direction in Organizational Theory and Analysis*, London: Sage, (1992).

Carnevali, D., 'Dal sistema per l'automazione dei registri generali al database dell'-ufficio giudiziario', in: Working Papers IRSIG-CNR, n. 4, (1995), pp. 76-116.

Carnevali, D., F. Contini e M. Fabri, *Office automation e organizzazione degli uffici giudiziari penali*, in: Working Papers IRSIG-CNR, n. 4, (1995).

Ciborra, C.U., *Teams, Markets and Systems - Business innovation and Information Technologies*, Cambridge, U.K.: Cambridge University Press, (1993).

Ciborra, C. and G.F. Lanzara, 'Change and Formative Contexts in Information Systems Development', in: H. Klein and K. Kumar, (eds.), *System Development for Human Progress*, New York, NY.: Wiley and Sons, (1989).

Ciborra C.U. and G.F. Lanzara, 'Designing Dynamic Artifacts: Computer Systems as Formative Contexts', in: Gagliardi P., (ed.) *Symbols and Artifacts. Views of the Corporate Landscape,* New York, NY.: Walter de Gruyter, (1990), pp. 147-165.

Ciborra C.U. and G.F. Lanzara, 'Formative Contexts and Information Technology: Understanding the Dynamics of Innovation in Organizations', in: *Accounting, Management, and Information Technology*, Vol. 4, no. 2, (1994), pp. 3-27.
Contini, F., 'Processi d'innovazione e context making', in: Ciborra C.U. and G.F. Lanzara, (eds.), *Labirinti dell'innovazione. Tecnologia, organizazione, apprendimento*, Milano: ETAS, (1999).
Crozier, M. and E. Friedberg, *L'acteur et le systeme*, Paris: Editions du Seuil, (1977).
David, P.A., 'Clio and the Economic of QWERTY', in: *American Economic Association Papers and Proceedings*, (1985), pp. 332-337.
Di Federico, G., 'Proposte per la modernizzazione dell'apparato giudiziario italiano', in: Di Federico, G., G.F. Lanzara, and A. Mestitz, (eds.), *Verbalizzazione degli atti processuali, tecnologie video e gestione dell'innovazione nell'amministrazione della giustizia,* Roma: Consiglio Nazionale delle Ricerche, (1993), pp. 383-416.
Di Federico, G., G.F. Lanzara, A. Mestitz, (eds.), *Verbalizzazione degli atti processuali, tecnologie video e gestione dell'innovazione nell'amministrazione della giustizia,* Roma: Consiglio Nazionale delle Ricerche, (1993).
Douglas, M., *How Institutions Think*, Syracuse, Syracuse University Press, (1986).
Fabri, M., 'Theory versus practice of Italian criminal justice reform', in: *Judicature,* Vol. 77, No. 4, (1984), pp. 211-216.
Fabri, M., 'Discrezionalità e modalità d'azione del pubblico ministero nel procedimento penale', in: *Polis*, anno XI n. 2, pp. 171-192, Hedberg, (1981).
Hedberg, B., 'How Organizations Learn and Unlearn', in: Nystrom P.C. and H. Starbuck, (eds.), *Handbook of organizational Design*, Vol. 1, Oxford: Oxford University Press, (1981).
Hofstadter, D.R., *Fluid Concepts and Creative Analogies Computer Models of the Fundamental Mechanism of Thought*, Basic Books, (1995).
Lanzara, G.F., *Capacità Negativa. Competenza progettuale e modelli d'intervento nelle organizzazioni,* Bologna, Il Mulino, (1993).
Lanzara, G.F., 'Self-desctructive processes in institution building and some modes countervailing mechanisms', in: *European Journal of Political Research*, vol 33, (1998).
Lévi-Strauss, C., *La pensée sauvage*, Paris: Edtion Du Seuil, (1962).
Maddalena, M., *Meno grazia più giustizia,* Roma: Donzelli, (1997).
Martin, J., *Managing the Database Environment,* Englewood Cliffs, N.Y., Prentice Hall, (1983).
Meyer J.W. and B. Rowan, 'Institutionalized Organizations: Formal Structure as Myth and Ceremony', in: *American Journal of Sociology*, Vol. 83, no. 2, (1977), pp. 340-363.
Mele, V., 'Rapporti tra procuratore capo e sostituti: una circolare del C.S.M. da rivedere', in: *Documenti Giustizia*, n. 12, (1994).
Merton, R.K., *Social Theory and Social Structure*, Glencoe: III Free Press, (1957).
Mintzberg, H., *Structure in Fives: Designing Effective Organizations*, Englewood Cliffs, NJ: Prentice Hall, (1983).

Norman, D., *The Psychology of Everyday Things,* New York, NY, Basic Books, (1990).
Orlikosky, W.J. and D. Robey, 'Information Technology and the Structuring of Organizations', in: *Information Systems Research*, Vol. 2. n. 2, (1991), pp. 143-169.
Pentland, B.T. and H. Reuter, 'Organizational Routines as Grammars of Action', in: *Administrative Science Quarterly*, 39, (1994), pp. 484-510.
Rice, R.R. and E.M. Rogers, 'Reinvention in the Innovation Process', in: *Knowledge,* Vol. 1, no. 4, (1980), pp. 499-514.
Rosen, M., W. J. Orlikowski and K.S. Schmahmann, 'Building Buildings and Living Lives: A Critique of Bureaucracy, Ideology and Concrete Artifacts', in: Gagliardi, P., (ed.), *Symbols and Artifacts: Views of the Corporate Landscape,* Berlin: Walter de Gruyter, (1990), pp. 69-84.
Unger, R.M., *False Necessity,* Cambridge, UK: Cambridge University Press, (1987).
Weick, K.E., 'Technology as Equivoque: Making of sense in New Technologies', in: P.S. Goodman, L.S. Sproull and Associates, *Technology and Organizations,* San Francisco: Jossey-Bass Publ., (1990).
Weick, K.E., 'Organizational Redesign as Improvisation', in: G.P. Huber and W.H. Glick (a cura di), *Organizational Change and Redesign*, Oxford: Oxford University Press, (1993a).
Weick, K.E., 'The Collapse of Making of sense in Organizations: The Mann Gulch Disaster', in: *Administrative Science Quarterly*, 38, (1993b), pp. 628-652.
Winnicott, D.W., 'Transitional Objects in Transitional Phenomena', in: *International Journal of Psychoanalysis*, 34, (1953).
Zagrebelsky, V., 'L'organizzazione delle procure della Repubblica presso le preture', in: *Documenti Giustizia*, (1994), pp. 741-770.
Zuboff, S., *In the Age of the Smart Machine. The Future of Work and Power*, New York: Basic Books, (1988).

The Challenge of Change for Judicial Systems
M. Fabri and Ph.M. Langbroek (Eds.)
IOS Press, 2000

Les technologies de l'information au service de la modernisation du service public de la justice en France

François Staechelé[1]

1 Introduction

Le ministère de la Justice français[2] a fait ses premiers pas sur l'Internet vers 1995-96. Le seul objectif visé était alors de présenter la justice française au monde et au justiciable français en particulier. Il n'était pas question de recourir à ce nouveau moyen de communication pour améliorer le fonctionnement interne de l'administration. Les propositions faites dès cette époque par certains praticiens de créer un groupe de travail pour étudier les conditions de son utilisation au sein de l'institution judiciaire n'ont même pas été examinées. Plusieurs facteurs expliquent cette attitude. Le principal est sans doute la méconnaissance de l'intérêt technique de l'Internet en tant que moyen de communication interactif. Il était alors considéré comme un gadget dangereux dont l'administration ne pouvait attendre que des inconvénients. Une circulaire en a d'ailleurs interdit l'usage, aussi bien dans les palais de justice que dans les services du ministère, circulaire qui est restée en vigueur pendant plusieurs années.

Il faut reconnaître que la réputation sulfureuse que la presse française faisait à l'Internet, les risques réels que pouvait générer pour les réseaux locaux des juridictions et de l'administration centrale un dispositif dont les règles de sécurité n'étaient pas encore clairement définies, le sous-équipement chronique des juridictions en matériel informatique, la faiblesse du budget du ministère de la Justice, la difficulté de faire comprendre les bénéfices que l'institution pouvait retirer de la communication électronique, et l'attentisme, voire l'inertie de l'encadrement judiciaire, pouvaient difficilement conduire à la révolution des esprits que suppose le recours à l'Internet dans une administration.

Le changement de gouvernement, le discours d'Hourtin[3] de Monsieur Jospin, premier ministre, puis la redéfinition complète et concrète des objectifs du gouvernement en la matière exprimée dans un remarquable document intitulé le 'Plan d'action du gouvernement pour la société de l'information' (PAGSI),[4] ont profondément bouleversé le paysage de l'Internet français et ont donné aux administrations une

1 François Staechelé est premier vice président au Tribunal de grande instance de Metz, France.
2 http://www.justice.gouv.fr/
3 http://www.internet.gouv.fr/francais/index.html
4 http://www.internet.gouv.fr/francais/index.html

impulsion sans cesse réactivée depuis lors. Comme tous les autre ministères, celui de la Justice a décrit les efforts particuliers qu'il a faits pour le développement de l'Internet dans son secteur, dans un document appellé 'Programme d'action ministériel pour la société de l'information' (PAMSI).[5]

Cette impulsion gouvernementale au plus haut niveau avait cependant été précédée par des initiatives des praticiens, magistrats notamment, lesquels accompagnent aujourd'hui la mise en place du réseau des réseaux dans l'administration judiciaire et participent activement aux instances mises en place pour définir le contenu, l'objet et les méthodes qui doivent gouverner le développement pratique du PAMSI.[6]

Cet exposé reprendra ces éléments en analysant successivement les changements apportés grâce à l'Internet aux modes de communication avec les citoyens, aux modes de communication internes de l'administration judiciaire, avant d'évoquer les perspectives à court terme lesquelles engloberont les partenaires de la justice et les autres administrations dans le cadre d'un extranet.

2 Des nouveaux modes de communication avec le citoyen

2.1 L'accès à l'information juridique

L'arrivée de l'Internet dans le paysage judiciaire français a coïncidé avec une nouvelle stratégie de la gestion des conflits dans la société civile. Jusque là, l'un des axes majeurs de la politique judiciaire était de développer aussi largement que possible l'*accès au juge*. Cette politique a cependant rapidement trouvé ses limites du fait de l'engorgement des juridictions. Désormais, une priorité est donnée au développement, non seulement de l'accès au juge, mais surtout de l'accès au droit,[7] priorité qui doit avoir pour effet de prévenir les conflits et de faciliter des règlements non juridictionnels,[8] et de permettre ainsi l'accès au juge sans asphyxier le service public de la justice.

L'Internet se prête évidemment merveilleusement à cette nouvelle politique. Cette volonté de mettre en ligne les données publiques essentielles comporte plusieurs volets:

- l'enrichissement du corpus d'informations juridiques pratiques mis à la disposition des citoyens, non seulement par le site Web du ministère de la Justice,[9] mais aussi par les autres ministères (par exemple le ministère des Finances[10] dont la Direction générale de la concurrence, de la consommation et de la répression des fraudes[11]

---

5 http://www.justice.gouv.fr/publicat/pamsi1.htm
6 http://www.justice.gouv.fr/publicat/pamsi1.htm
7 http://www.justice.gouv.fr/actua/gipoffre.htm
8 http://www.justice.gouv.fr/publicat/note5.htm
9 http://www.justice.gouv.fr/publicat/note5.htm
10 http://www.finances.gouv.fr/
11 http://www.finances.gouv.fr/pole_ecofin/consommation/index.html

diffuse de nombreuses pages d'information des consommateurs, ou celui du médiateur de la République);[12]

- une présentation de l'histoire,[13] de l'organisation[14] et du fonctionnement[15] de la justice, que vient compléter une riche documentation journellement actualisée sur des sujets de société intéressant la justice,[16] les projets développés par le garde des sceaux, les expositions[17] organisées par le ministère, des éléments statistiques,[18] le tout étant facilement accessible grâce à un moteur de recherche[19] et un plan-guide:[20]
- la mise en ligne du journal officiel de la République française,[21] à la fois dans des pages Web (mise en ligne du J.O. du jour ainsi que les cinq derniers numéros) et par une liste de diffusion[22] privée très intéressante d'Adminet[23] permettant de recevoir dans sa boîte aux lettres les articles dudit journal officiel filtrés selon les mots clés définis par l'utilisateur;
- la création d'un site public d'accès aux textes essentiels[24] qui met en ligne une quantité considérable de codes et lois (mis à jour), ainsi que les arrêts fondamentaux du Conseil constitutionnel,[25] du Conseil d'Etat,[26] de la Cour de cassation[27] et de la Cour des comptes;[28]
- le soutien technique et financier à la création de pages Web[29] par les juridictions et les services extérieurs du ministère, pages destinées à donner aux justiciables les informations qui leur sont nécessaires pour l'exercice concret de leurs droits et la connaissance de leurs institutions locales;
- la création d'une mission de recensement et la mise en oeuvre d'un plan de numérisation permettant à terme de mettre à la disposition du public l'ensemble des circulaires, ainsi qu'une part importante de ce qu'on appelle communément la 'littérature grise',[30] c'est à dire essentiellement les travaux de recherche et les rapports commandés par le ministère;

---

12 http://www.mediateur-de-la-republique.fr/
13 http://www.justice.gouv.fr/minister/histo.htm
14 http://www.justice.gouv.fr/justicef/intro.htm
15 http://www.justice.gouv.fr/justicef/intro.htm
16 http://www.justice.gouv.fr/actua/actuaref.htm
17 http://www.justice.gouv.fr/reportag/expos.htm
18 http://www.justice.gouv.fr/reportag/expos.htm
19 http://recherche-justice.fth.net/
20 http://www.justice.gouv.fr/navig.htm
21 http://www.justice.journal-officiel.gouv.fr/
22 http//www.admi.net/
23 http://www.admi.net/
24 http://www.legifrance.gouv.fr/LEGIFRANCE
25 http://www.legifrance.gouv.fr/citoyen/conscons.htm
26 http://www.legifrance.gouv.fr/citoyen/conseil.htm
27 http://www.legifrance.gouv.fr/citoyen/cass.htm
28 http://www.legifrance.gouv.fr/citoyen/comptes.htm
29 http://www.justice.gouv.fr/reportag/rouen.htm
30 http://www.justice.gouv.fr/publicat/parution.htm

- l'implantation de bornes interactives dans les palais de justice et les maisons de la justice et du droit.[31]

Il est cependant un domaine où la diffusion à l'intention du grand public de l'information juridique a progressé moins rapidement: celui de la diffusion de la jurisprudence.

Les décisions du Conseil constitutionnel[32] sont certes offertes au grand public, mais on peut douter de l'utilité pratique de cette décision pour le commun des justiciables dès lors qu'en France le juge ne peut contrôler la constitutionnalité des lois. Les arrêts essentiels de la Cour de cassation[33] ou du Conseil d'Etat[34] sont mis également en ligne sur le site Legifrance.[35] Cependant la diffusion des bases de données juridiques crées par l'administration faisant l'objet d'un monopole attribué à un concessionnaire (la société O.R.T.), par application d'un décret très controversé du 31 mai 1996;[36] il n'y a que fort peu de décisions mises en ligne en accès gratuit. Les professionnels et notamment les magistrats (ces derniers aux frais du ministère de la Justice) peuvent en revanche avoir accès à la jurisprudence complète de la Cour de cassation et à plusieurs autres bases de données juridiques très fournies en accès payant sur le site Jurifrance[37] géré par la société O.R.T.. Un mouvement se dessine actuellement qui a pour objectif de permettre à la justice de se 'réapproprier sa production' pour les besoins de son fonctionnement habituel, dans le cadre de son réseau privé virtuel dont il sera question ci-après. Des études sont en cours pour mettre à la disposition de tous les magistrats la jurisprudence de la Cour de cassation et pour favoriser la création d'ateliers de jurisprudence régionaux.

La Cour de cassation publie cependant sur son propre site[38] le contenu de son bulletin d'actualité[39] qui recense régulièrement les sommaires de ses arrêts les plus intéressants. Une fois que le fond de ces bulletins sera accessible par un moteur de recherche, la haute juridiction sera en mesure d'offrir au justiciable et au praticien du droit un panorama incomparable de sa juriprudence, bien plus utile et plus exploitable qu'une collection exhaustive de ses décisions en texte intégral.

2.2 *La communication interactive avec les citoyens*

Les services de l'Internet vont bien au-delà de la simple mise à disposition d'informations. Ils permettent aussi des échanges interactifs. Le site du ministère de la Justice permet ainsi à chaque justiciable d'adresser un message au ministère.[40] Mais ce n'est

31 http://vosdroits.admifrance.gouv.fr/ARBO/140106-fxjus260.html
32 http://www.conseil-constitutionnel.fr/decision.htm
33 http://www.courdecassation.fr/
34 http://www.conseil-etat.fr/
35 http://www.legifrance.gouv.fr/
36 http://www.telecom.gouv.fr/francais/activ/techno/bdjurid.htm
37 http://www.jurifrance.com/wjuridiq/index.ow
38 http://www.courdecassation.fr/
39 http://www.courdecassation.fr/_Annuaire/_ BICC/bicc.htm
40 http://www.justice.gouv.fr/minister/courrier.htm

là qu'une forme de communication embryonnaire. Le gouvernement a des ambitions bien plus importantes. Les voici résumées.

2.2.1 La généralisation du courrier électronique

Conformément aux dispositions générales du PAGSI[41] applicables à l'ensemble des administrations, chaque juridiction, chaque service déconcentré a été pourvu d'une adresse électronique et des moyens matériels pour s'en servir. Il a été décidé de façon concomitante que chaque magistrat et chaque fonctionnaire en relation avec le public serait doté d'une adresse électronique, de manière à permettre l'instauration d'une pratique aussi générale que possible d'échanges électroniques, non seulement à l'intérieur des services mais encore avec le public (30.000 postes répartis en 1900 sites à l'horizon 2000). L'ensemble de ces adresses a donné lieu à un plan d'adressage normalisé. Un annuaire des correspondants publics du ministère est en cours d'élaboration, il sera complété à brève échéance par des annuaires des instances représentatives des professions juridiques et judiciaires et interfacé avec les annuaires des autres ministères. L'ensemble formera la base d'une infrastructure assurant la délivrance et la gestion des clés nécessaires à l'authentification des messages et à leur chiffrement.

Ces avancées technologiques seront accompagnées de réformes du droit de la preuve (authentification, signature électronique, force probante des documents numérisés, nouveaux supports de stockage, etc.) indispensables pour permettre à ces nouveaux moyens de communication de donner toute leur mesure. Un projet de loi en ce sens est en cours d'élaboration.

Ces perspectives donnent lieu à une réflexion méthodologique sur le traitement du courrier électronique menée au sein de chaque entité en vue d'élaborer une charte générale d'utilisation de ces nouvelles technologies et de parvenir à une définition concrète et évolutive, service par service, des processus de distribution, de traitement et de validation des messages administratifs ainsi que règles d'archivage du courrier.

2.2.2 Dématérialiser les procédures administratives et développer les téléprocédures

Le ministère de la Justice a procédé à la mise en ligne de formulaire administratifs[42] numérisés au format pdf sur le serveur Admifrance.[43] On y trouve les rubriques suivantes:

- actions en justice: demande d'aide juridictionnelle,[44] frais de justice, surendettement, injonction de payer;
- casier judiciaire: demande d'extrait;[45]

41 http://www.internet.gouv.fr/francais/index.html
42 http://www.cerfa.gouv.fr/vigueur.nsf/Html/Accueil/$File/Index.htm
43 http://www.admifrance.gouv.fr/
44 http://vosdroits.admifrance.gouv.fr/ARBO/14020205-NXJUS130.html
45 http://vosdroits.admifrance.gouv.fr/ARBO/1410-fxpap149.html

- contraventions routières:[46] avis, carte-lettre;
- état civil:[47] fiche individuelle ou familiale et acquisition de la nationalité française.

L'usager peut ainsi afficher les formulaires sur son écran et les imprimer. Il ne lui est est cependant pas encore possible de réexpédier les formulaires renseignés par la voie électronique. Les réflexions menées notamment par le groupe de travail constitué au sein de la Direction des services judiciaires et les expériences réalisées par certaines juridictions en liaison avec les professionnels du droit permettent néanmoins d'envisager un développement plus ambitieux des téléprocédures concernant des démarches simples se rapportant à des contencieux de masse. Les développements futurs devraient progressivement permettre au justiciable de renseigner le formulaire à l'écran et de le renvoyer par l'Internet, puis à l'administration de le traiter de manière aussi automatique que possible. D'ores et déjà, tout nouveau formulaire utilisé dans les rapports entre le public et un service relevant du ministère de la Justice est systématiquement mis en ligne. Ces orientations supposent la mise en place de serveurs locaux ou régionaux permettant une relation directe entre le justiciable et les juridictions. L'orientation probable, compte tenu de la nature particulière de l'activité judiciaire, sera sans doute de privilégier la dématérialisation des procédures proprement dites, c'est à dire les relations entre l'institution judiciaire et les professionnels du droit dans le cadre sécurisé d'un extranet. Une telle entreprise appelle de lourds investissements préalables en câblage des bâtiments, en renouvellement de matériel et de logiciels, et en personnels. Elle exige aussi une concertation approfondie avec les professionnels du droit, eu égard à la disparité des outils informatiques selon les professions et les régions, ainsi qu'à l'enthousiasme très inégal avec lequel lesdits professionnels accueillent ces nouvelles technologies.

En dehors de l'activité proprement juridictionnelle, les téléprocédures peuvent être développées sans restriction pour les démarches à caractère strictement administratif. Ainsi l'administration pénitentiaire (APNET) s'est elle engagée dans l'élaboration de formulaires permettant de faire acte de candidature aux concours ou de réclamer des autorisations ou des pièces justificatives de situation, comme par exemple les certificats de présence dans les établissements pénitentiaires, les demandes de permis de visite (pour les familles de détenus), les demandes de mutation du personnel, etc.

De la même manière le Service de l'information et de la communication[48] a intégré sur le site Web du ministère une page permettant de se procurer un formulaire[49] de demande d'extrait de casier judiciaire que les utilisateurs pourront imprimer et renvoyer au casier judiciaire national.[50] La mise en ligne de ce formulaire réduit notablement le nombre de rejets résultant de demandes incomplètes.

---

46 http://vosdroits.admifrance.gouv.fr/ARBO/14080401-NXJUS147.html
47 http://vosdroits.admifrance.gouv.fr/ARBO/2104-NXPAP102.html
48 http://www.justice.gouv.fr/minister/minsicom.htm
49 http://www.cerfa.gouv.fr/vigueur.nsf/Html/Accueil/$File/Index.htm
50 http://www.justice.gouv.fr/cjn/index.htm

2.2.3 *Une gestion électronique des concours administratifs*[51]
Avec le développement du chômage, les candidats qui se présentent à des concours administratifs sont extrêmement nombreux et posent de sérieuses difficutés d'organisation à l'administration judiciaire. La présentation des concours,[52] la gestion des inscriptions et de la notification des résultats[53] par l'Internet apportent une notable simplification.

3 Transformer les modes de communication interne

L'accessibilité aux services et au droit offerte au justiciable grâce à l'Internet est appréciable, mais plus précieux encore sont les services qu'il rend au fonctionnement interne de l'administration judiciaire. Si le ministère de la justice français a rapidement compris l'intérêt de l'Internet en termes d'image pour la justice, il a été cependant été beaucoup plus réticent à l'intégrer dans ses schémas directeurs. A cet égard, il a été précédé par les initiatives mises en œuvre par les magistrats eux-mêmes.

3.1 Les listes de discussion des magistrats

Deux listes de magistrats ont ouvert la voie de la communication électronique dans le monde judiciaire. La première en date est une liste internationale de magistrats francophones du nom de Jugenet,[54] hébergée à Montréal et administrée par un juge de la cour municipale de cette ville (Denis Laliberté).[55] Créée en 1995, elle compte actuellement plus de 430 membres, issus d'une trentaine de pays différents du globe. Les français y sont majoritaires. Cette liste permet des échanges conviviaux, la découverte au jour le jour des législations et des pratiques des autres pays, l'organisation de rencontres, la coopération entre magistrats, etc. De nombreux magistrats du ministère de la Justice français en font partie.

La seconde liste, du nom de Thémis-France, est une liste consacrée d'une part au développement de l'internet judiciaire français, et de l'autre aux échanges relatifs au droit applicable sur le sol français. Elle compte environ 270 membres de tous grades et de tous horizons: magistrats de l'ordre judiciaire, de l'ordre administratif, des juridictions financières, magistrats en détachement dans des juridictions internationales comme la Cour de justice des communautés européennes[56] ou le Tribunal Pénal International pour l'ex-Yougoslavie de La Haye,[57] magistrats en fonction au ministère de la Justice ou détachés à l'étranger comme magistrats de liaison ou coopérants. On peut ajouter qu'il existe d'autres listes nationales de magistrats de par le monde,

51 http://www.legifrance.gouv.fr/actua/concours.htm
52 http://www.publicat/magistra.htm**/**
53 http://www.justice.gouv.fr/actua/concours.htm
54 http://www.jugenet.org/
55 mailto: Laliberté@JUGENET.ORG
56 http://europa.eu.int/cj/fr/index.htm
57 http://www.un.org/icty/index-f.htm

notamment en Belgique (Thémis-Belgique), en Amérique du sud, au Portugal, en Allemagne (Iudex) et bien sur aux Etats-Unis et dans le Canada anglophone (Jurist L) auxquelles appartiennent souvent les membres non-français de Jugenet. Des représentants de l'Union internationales des magistrats et de l'Association européenne des magistrats sont membres de Jugenet et tiennent ainsi les magistrats informés de leurs travaux.

Ces listes présentent des avantages considérables pour la mise en place d'un intranet judiciaire national:

- elles permettent à leur membres de se familiariser avec les outils informatiques et les programmes de communication dans un climat détendu et dédramatisé, l'entraide y est bien sûr de rigueur;
- elles procurent à tous un flux de courrier abondant et régulier, indispensable pour pouvoir intégrer l'Internet à son environnement de travail quotidien et pour en banaliser l'utilisation et la maîtrise;
- elles permettent à la réflexion sur l'utilisation de ces nouvelles technologies de mûrir dans un contexte particulièrement fertile, à la fois pratique et théorique, national et international.

De nombreux membres de ces listes font d'ailleurs partie des groupes de travail et de réflexion qui ont été constitués au ministère de la Justice pour réflechir au développement de l'intranet judiciaire.

Ces listes de discussion ont aussi donné lieu à la diffusion d'un certain nombre de pages Web présentant des organismes professionnels et leur production, tels que l'Association nationales des juges de l'application des peines,[58] l'Association nationale des praticiens de la Cour d'assises[59] ainsi que des syndicats professionnels de magistrats. On peut penser qu'elles préfigurent celles que l'on verra bientôt sur le RPVJ dont il va être question maintenant.

3.2 Le réseau privé virtuel du ministère de la Justice (RPVJ)

3.2.1 Structure

Organisation et définitions[60]

Il s'agit d'un réseau privé mis à disposition du ministère de la Justice aux termes d'un marché public, par l'un des plus grands fournisseurs d'accès à l'Internet de France, la Société Oléane, filiale de la société France Télécom.

Cet intranet permet non seulement l'utilisation des outils standards de l'Internet dans le cadre sécurisé des échanges administratifs, mais aussi l'accès à l'Internet public, les serveurs étant protégés par des pare-feu et divers dispositifs destinés à interdire les intrusions et les piratages en tous genres. L'ensemble des flux électroni-

58 http://interlex.droit-eco.u-nancy.fr/RAP/
59 http://juripole.univ-nancy2.fr/ANAPCA
60 http://justice.gouv.fr/chancell/cc42intr.htm

ques transite par les serveurs de l'intranet. Les documents attachés font l'objet d'un traitement anti-viral actualisé en permanence. L'ensemble des serveurs est installé dans les locaux du ministère de la Justice. La confidentialité des échanges entre magistrats est assurée par chiffrement, la réglementation française[61] ayant été récemment libéralisée sur ce point.

Les connexions à ce réseau privé se font selon trois modalités principales, qui correspondent à des tarifs et à des coûts de fonctionnement différents:

- les connexion individuelles 'Dial'se font par modem, à un tarif proche de celui pratiqué par les autres fournisseurs d'accès. Ce mode de connexion est adapté pour les postes isolés, les agents fonctionnant en 'travail déporté' (télétravail) ou en déplacement;
- les connexions 'Call' raccordent un réseau local plus ou moins important à l'intranet, via une connexion RNIS à 64 kbps. Il s'agit encore de connexions temporaires, mais leur coût n'est plus fonction du nombre d'agents en ligne;
- les connexions permanentes offrent un accès illimité et fixent à un réseau ou à un ensemble des réseaux interconnectés. Elles supposent un serveur local et des agents de maintenance spécialisés. C'est la solution la plus économique et la plus confortable pour connecter un grand nombre d'agents sur un site important. Plusieurs sites pilotes fonctionnent déjà sur ce modèle.

A terme, toutes les cours d'appel devraient être dotées d'une connexion permanente et d'un serveur local gérant messagerie et pages Web selon un modèle répliquant le serveur actuel de la Chancellerie.

Les services offerts par l'intranet

Les services offerts sont ceux, classiques, de l'Internet. Leur originalité ne réside que dans les contenus.

1. Le courrier électronique, les forums et les listes de discussion

a. Les services de messagerie

Chaque agent en relation avec le public sera doté dans l'année d'une adresse électronique personnelle. D'autres adresses sont créées, de deux types: les adresses structurelles (adresse des entités administratives) et les adresses fonctionnelles (adresses de services – ou de serveurs – essentiellement à l'usage des partenaires institutionnels de la justice).

Ces adresses permettent une libre communication aussi bien dans l'intranet qu'-avec l'internet public. L'objectif visé est de pouvoir supprimer, à tous le moins fortement réduire, le recours aux modes classiques de transmission du courrier et de réaliser des économies substantielles en frais postaux et téléphoniques, ainsi que de télécopie, de déplacement et de photocopie, tout en accélérant notablement l'échange des messages.

---

61 http://droit.org/cgibin/affiche_page.pl?lien=19990319/PRMX9903477D.HTML&requete=CRYPTOLOGIE

b. La diffusion des circulaires et des notes administratives: les listes de diffusion
Les frais d'expédition des circulaires et des notes internes à l'administration seront réduits de manière drastique par le recours à des listes de diffusion, lesquelles permettront d'adresser pour un coût dérisoire et de manière instantanée la masse considérable des documents de service, tant entre l'administration centrale d'une part, et les cours d'appel et les services extérieurs d'autre part, qu'entre les cours d'appel ou les services extérieurs et les juridictions et services locaux.

Dans le même temps sera constituée pour être mise en ligne sur le Web une base de données des circulaires du ministère actuellement publiées dans un 'bulletin papier'. Cette diffusion vient compléter le nombre considérable de documents, rapports et discours publiés sur les sites Web des ministères. La diffusion des rapports de recherche[62] commandés par le ministère (littérature grise) suivra le même sort.

c. Les listes de discussion thématiques ou fonctionnelles
Alors que les listes de diffusion (encore appelées listes de distribution), univoques par nature, ont pour fonction de prendre en charge les flux d'information descendants, les listes de discussion et les forums permettent des échanges interactifs, soit thématiques (discussions autour de problèmes juridiques), soit fonctionnels (listes composées d'agents remplissant les mêmes fonctions), ou bien encore axés sur des projets (groupe de travail chargé de réflechir à des réformes ou de suivre la réalisation d'un projet). La Direction de l'administration générale et de l'équipement du ministère[63] s'est pourvue d'un serveur de liste auquel les autres directions confient progressivement les listes qu'elles créent.

Il existe ainsi actuellement une liste de discussion utilisée par la commission Internet de la Direction des services judiciaires[64] et deux forums de discussion (bogue de l'an 2000, introduction de l'Euro). La Direction de l'administration pénitentiaire[65] a lancé une liste consacrée au 'plan d'exécution des peines' découlant d'une réforme récente; la Direction des affaires criminelles et des grâces[66] élabore les outils permettant une lutte plus efficace contre la délinquance économique et financière; le Service des affaires européennes et internationales[67] organise de cette manière la communication avec ses correspondants à l'étranger et les magistrats de liaison.

2. Les page Web

L'intranet offre une liberté de création et d'accès à l'information impossible sur l'Internet public, en raison notamment du monopole de diffusion des bases de données juridiques reconnu à la société O.R.T. et du caractère nécessairement confidentiel de certaines informations en matière judiciaire.

---

62 http://www.msh-paris.fr/cesdip/
63 http://www.justice.gouv.fr/minister/mindage.htm
64 http://www.justice.gouv.fr/minister/mindsj.htm
65 http://www.justice.gouv.fr/minister/mindap.htm
66 http://www.justice.gouv.fr/minister/mindacg.htm
67 http://www.justice.gouv.fr/minister/minsaei.htm

a. Les bases de données
L'intranet permet la libre diffusion des bases de données judiciaires. Il suscitera sans doute aussi la création de nouvelles bases, comme celle des experts judiciaires ou des auxiliaires de justice, et de réservoirs d'information spécialisés dans certains domaines: délinquance économique et financière, lutte contre les trafics en tous genres, bases de données des ressources pour le placement des mineurs en difficulté, fichier national des prévenus, etc. Tous ces outils rendront indiscutablement la justice plus rapide et plus efficace.

b. Les magazines électroniques
Chaque direction de l'administration centrale peut présenter ses orientations de politique judiciaire, les illustrer sous la forme de gazette électronique interne aux services. C'est ce qu'a déjà commencé à faire l'administration pénitentiaire.

Chaque structure présente sur l'intranet a la possibilité d'y développer ses propres pages Web, soit dans une perspective locale, soit dans une perspective nationale. Les maîtres mots restent cependant *le décloisonnement* des services de l'administration centrale et *la mutualisation* des ressources.

c. Les pages de service
L'intranet est un outil tout indiqué pour tenir au courant les magistrats et les fonctionnaires de toutes sortes d'informations relatives notamment à la sécurité sur le Web, aux virus, aux nouveautés en matière de matériel et de logiciels, etc.

d. Les pages de convivialité (initiatives culturelles, services sociaux)
Une place sera réservée aux organismes à caractère social comme la Mutuelle des personnels du ministère de la Justice. La question de l'allocation d'un espace disque aux syndicats n'a pas encore été abordée. Certains d'entre eux se présentent pour l'instant sur des sites extérieurs: l'Union syndicale des magistrats[68] (USM) sur le site du Juripole,[69] le Syndicat de la magistrature[70] sur le site personnel de l'un de ses membres, le Mouvement des magistrats européens pour la démocratie et les libertés[71] (MEDEL) sur un site international hébergé au Portugal, l'Association européenne des magistrats[72] (AEM), l'Union internationale des magistrats[73] (UIM) sur le site Jugenet[74] au Québec et sur son site miroir au Juripole de Lorraine.

68 http://juripole.univ-nancy2.fr/USM
69 http://juripole.univ-nancy2.fr/
70 http://www.alpes-net.fr/~hbalmain/
71 http://www.cidadevirtual.pt/asjp/medel/novos/geral3_fr.html
72 http://space.tin.it/edicola/goberto
73 http://jugenet.org/uim
74 http://jugenet.org/

3. File Transfer Protocol (FTP)

L'intranet offre également une base de téléchargement de textes, de logiciels, de 'patches' réparant des bogues, de signatures de virus, de textes, de formulaires, de documents de formation, etc.

4. Les visioconférences

Le caractère très éclaté des institutions judiciaires contraint souvent magistrats et fonctionnaires à des déplacements nombreux et onéreux, parfois pour des réunions fort brèves. L'intranet permettra de les réduire au minimum incompressible en ouvrant la possibilité de 'rencontres virtuelles' en visioconférence, notamment entre les responsables de l'administration centrale et les chefs de services déconcentrés. Des salles et des postes spécialisés seront équipés à cet effet.

Cette technique pourrait également être utilisée moyennant quelques modifications législatives:

- pour permettre aux juges d'instruction d'assister à distance à certains actes d'instruction, pour entendre de manière non traumatisante des enfants victimes d'abus sexuels, voire pour interroger à distance des personnes détenues à l'étranger ou posant des problèmes de sécurité. Il n'est cependant pas encore question d'audiences de jugement virtuelles comme il est parfois suggéré dans d'autres pays;
- pour développer des formes nouvelles de formation continue avec les écoles relevant du ministère et pour organiser des 'congrès virtuels' regroupant des spécialistes dans certains domaines du droit.

Les responsabilités dans la société de l'information
Lorsqu'il est question de diffuser des informations officielles, surgit nécessairement la question de la responsabilité du contenu des messages. Se pose aussi la question de savoir quels mécanismes de contrôle il convient de mettre en place.

En matière de *courrier électronique*, est responsable du contenu d'un message soit le chef de service lorsque le message a été diffusé sous son autorité, soit celui qui l'a rédigé lorsqu'il est diffusé en son nom propre et avec son adresse personnelle, ou encore en cas de faute détachable du service .

En ce qui concerne les *pages Web* le responsable de la structure est responsables de ce qu'il publie, une validation préalable est donc impérative.

Pour les *listes de diffusion* est reponsable celui qui a ordonné la diffusion du document, et le cas échéant celui qui aurait procédé à la diffusion.

S'agissant des *listes de discussion et des forums* chacun est responsable de ses propres contributions. L'administrateur a la possibilité de désabonner l'un de ses membres en cas de manquement aux règles préétablies gouvernant la liste, mais il n'assume pas pour autant la responsabilité des contenus. Il pourrait cependant en être autrement dans les listes ou les forums 'modérés', c'est à dire les listes dans lesquelles aucun message n'est diffusé sans l'accord du modérateur.

Ces nouveaux outils conduiront nécessairement à une réflexion sur l'organisation des nouveaux circuits de décision, encore qu'il n'existe pas de raisons particulières de ne pas appliquer les principes de responsabilité traditionnels.

S'agissant du contrôle, il a été décidé de laisser à chaque agent le libre accès aussi bien aux services offerts par l'intranet que par l'Internet public. Ce choix, fondé sur la confiance dans le sens de la responsabilité des agents, a été motivé par la nécessité de permettre à chacun d'avoir accès aux inépuisables ressources documentaires offertes par le réseau des réseaux et de se familiariser aussi rapidement que possible et de manière évolutive avec les nombreux outils de cette nouvelle technologie. Il favorisera le initiatives locales et la créativité des services.

3.2.2 Fonctionnement

a. Le dispositif de formation professionnelle

Sans un dispositif de formation adapté, la création d'un intranet serait d'une efficacité illusoire. Les grandes écoles du ministère: l'Ecole nationale de la magistrature[75] (ENM), l'Ecole nationale des greffes[76] (ENG), l'Ecole nationale d'administration pénitentiaire[77] (ENAP), et le Centre national de formation des éducateurs de la protection judiciaire de la jeunesse[78] (CNFEPJJ) se sont dotées des équipements nécessaires et mettent en oeuvre un plan de formation dans trois directions: formation initiale des agents recrutés, formation continue des agents en place et formation des formateurs.

L'Ecole nationale de la magistrature a ainsi installé une salle multimédia d'une vingtaine de postes dont la moitié raccordés à l'Internet par le câble, a embauché trois techniciens spécialisés dans l'Internet et a défini un véritable schéma directeur pour réaliser les objectifs du ministère. Non seulement elle forme les auditeurs de justice aux NTIC, mais à très court terme elle se dotera en plus d'un serveur autonome et publiera les travaux de ses enseignants et des auditeurs. Son installation permettra d'offrir des stages de formation continue aux magistrats en juridiction.

L'Ecole nationales des greffes a elle aussi aménagé des salles permettant l'enseignement des NTIC. Son objectif est de former tous les personnels des greffes à l'utilisation de ces nouvelles technologies. La priorité est cependant donnée, ce qui est naturel, à la formation des formateurs qui dans chaque ressort de cour d'appel seront un appui local au développement de ces technologies, ainsi qu'aux responsables de la gestion de l'informatisation et à leurs adjoints.

Beaucoup d'espoirs sont placés dans le recours à l'autoformation grâce aux listes de discussion, aux forums, à la visioconférence et aux instruments de formation qui seront diffusés. Sur le plan pédagogique un CD-ROM de formation à l'Internet est en cours de réalisation. Il est aussi probable que la pression des enfants des agents et la

75 http://juripole.univ-nancy2.fr/ENM/index.html
76 http://juripole.univ-nancy2.fr/ENG/index.html
77 http://www.justice.gouv.fr/minister/enap.htm
78 http://www.justice.gouv.fr/minister/cnfepjj.htm

vulgarisation du commerce électronique seront de puissants moteurs d'apprentissage pour tous.

b. Courrier électronique et structures hiérarchiques
Il n'a échappé à personne que l'extraordinaire souplesse offerte par la messagerie est de nature à modifier profondément la circulation de l'information et par voie de conséquence d'affecter le cloisonnement des circuits hiérachiques.

S'il est évident que ce nouvel outil n'est pas une justification pour contourner les règles hiérarchiques fixées par le Code de l'organisation judiciaire, il est cependant vain, voire préjudiciable de vouloir brider autoritairement la 'circulation horizontale' de l'information. Il apparait donc nécessaire de fixer les règles d'une déontologie de la communication qu'il appartiendra à chacun de respecter dans l'intérêt bien compris d'un fonctionnement optimum du service. Une utilisation intelligente des facilités de la messagerie, qui permet les envois en copie et les transferts de messages avec une extrême facilité, devrait permettre aux responsables hiérarchiques d'être parfaitement informés du fonctionnement de leur service et même de se constituer des dossiers électroniques permettant de mobiliser beaucoup plus facilement qu'actuellement les renseignement qui leur sont nécessaires.

c. Incidence sur l'organisation des services
Le fait que les services seront en relation par l'Internet tant avec le public qu'avec les professionnels du droit et les autres membres de l'intranet, conduira à mettre en place de nouvelles structures propres à gérer convenablement ces communications. Il est ainsi probable qu'à court terme il faille créer des emplois de 'cybervaguemestres' qui auront la responsabilité le filtrer le courrier en provenance du public, de le réorienter et de répondre aux questions les plus simples, comme le font déjà les services d'accueil. Il conviendra sans doute aussi, après un temps d'expérimentation, de multiplier l'implantation de bornes télématiques permettant aux justiciables arrivant au palais de justice d'obtenir les renseignements diffusés sur les pages Web du ministère.

Chaque service devra par ailleurs s'organiser pour être en mesure de gérer sa boîte aux lettres électronique, définir à cet égard le rôle du magistrat et de son secrétariat. On assiste en réalité à la naissance d'une nouvelle culture professionnelle, qui trouvera son plein emploi dans les outils beaucoup plus performants encore qui verront le jour dans les années à venir et qui permettront un traitement automatisé des messages électroniques.

3.3 L'Internet et la justice administrative

La stratégie des juridictions administratives est très différente de celle des juridictions judiciaires. Le service informatique du Conseil d'Etat exerce en effet un contrôle hiérarchique total sur l'ensemble des juridictions de l'ordre administratif, ne laissant aucune place à l'initiative locale. Le parc applicatif des juridictions est homogène et est géré par télémaintenance.

Il faut préciser que le Conseil d'Etat a déjà une longue expérience de la communication électronique, puisque depuis 1985 il a mis en place un serveur minitel accessibles aux avocats au Conseil par mot de passe. Ce serveur sera basculé sur l'Internet et deviendra l'unique mode de communication avec lesdits avocats.

Un projet d'interconnexion de l'ensemble des juridictions administratives est à l'étude, toujours sous la houlette du Conseil d'Etat qui a pour objectif:

- de permettre l'accès à un service de documentation commun; les magistrats disposent déjà de l'application Ariane qui recense toute la jurisprudence administrative et qui est couplée avec un traitement de texte et un moteur de recherche. Ils disposent aussi d'un outil de gestion et de suivi des dossiers;
- de mettre en place une messagerie et un serveur de forums;
- de permettre le transfert électronique des dossiers et leur consultation entre les différents niveaux de juridiction.

4 Les perspectives

La puissance de l'Internet tient principalement à l'uniformisation des protocoles de communication qui permet une circulation de l'information affranchies des limitations imposées par les disparités de matériels, de sytèmes d'exploitation, de logiciels, etc. Cette standardisation va entraîner un profond bouleversement des réseaux locaux qui, à terme, fonctionneront pour l'essentiel au standard TCP/IP. On se rend compte que dans ces conditions, l'intranet va bouleverser l'organisation interne du travail juridictionnel, en développant les performances des réseaux internes et en permettant leur interfaçage avec les réseaux professionnels partenaires de la justice.

4.1 Développer les performances des services en termes d'utilisation du réseau

Une fois que les services auront pris l'habitude de travailler quotidiennement avec l'Internet, que les bases de données internes seront disponibles pour tous, les ressources documentaires à la disposition des magistrats se développeront, et les possibilités de travail en réseau: gestion administrative des ressources humaines et financières des juridictions et services extérieurs, gestion électronique du tableau de service, des salles d'audience, des documents, workflow, etc, envahiront progressivement tout l'espace judiciaire. Les circuits que suivent actuellement les dossiers se simplifieront et les procédures de décision se clarifieront dans la mesure où l'ensemble des éléments décisoires pourra être réuni en un dossier électronique accessible instantanément à l'ensemble des responsables de la chaîne décisoire, même largement disséminés du point de vue géographique.

La standardisation des protocoles de communication aura peut-être des effets plus importants encore sur les réseaux locaux et sur l'organisation du travail bureautique dans les palais de justice, que sur les communications entre les diverses structures de l'institution judiciaire. La modification en profondeur des méthodes de travail imposera un renouvellement complet de la réflexion sur l'organisation des services et les circuits de procédure.

4.2 Moderniser les méthodes de communication avec les partenaires de la justice

Si l'introduction des standards de l'Internet modifie nos habitudes de travail, la création d'un extranet incluant nos partenaires habituels sera, s'il se fait, une révolution bien plus fondamentale encore. Dans les entreprises, nord-américaines surtout, existe depuis longtemps une normalisation des échanges de données informatiques (EDI). Mais nulle part, sauf peut-être en Australie, les standards de l'EDI ne semblent avoir pénétré le monde judiciaire. La complexité et surtout la spécificité des procédures de chaque pays ne poussent sans doute pas à une normalisation internationale des échanges judiciaires, et moins encore le fait que les partenaires des juridictions soient très nombreux, structurés en unités de tailles très variées et d'une mentalité très individualiste.

L'arrivé de l'Internet va cependant changer cet état de choses. Jusqu'à présent, les juridictions (plus exactement les ministères de la justice) et les professions libérales qui s'étaient informatisées avaient fait élaborer à grands frais des logiciels 'verticaux' spécialisés. Puis l'on s'est avisé que tous y gagneraient si ces logiciels pouvaient communiquer. On a donc, à grands frais encore, tenté de les rendre communicants. Mais cette manoeuvre s'est avérée difficile et pour de multiples raisons: fragilité des sociétés informatiques travaillant avec les ministères (le marché est étroit), incompatibilités logicielles, inexistence de standards d'échanges, évolution rapide des techniques de communication, etc.

Les nouveaux outils de l'Internet invitent à inverser la problématique: plutôt que d'essayer de rendre communicants des logiciels judiciaires, il s'agit de judiciariser les logiciels de communication et de profiter ainsi d'une interface très évoluée, adaptable à moindres frais aux particularités de la justice et surtout à l'hétérogénéité de nos partenaires, peu familiarisés avec l'informatique pour l'essentiel. Il donc possible d'envisager:

- soit une interface 'littéraire' qu'apprécient des juristes en froid avec les opérateurs booléens;
- soit de concevoir des échanges de formulaires préétablis dont l'utilisation permet la création de dossiers électroniques offrant toutes les garanties de fiabilité, de sécurité, d'authentification, de non-répudiation, etc, qu'un professionnel du droit peut attendre d'un outil de travail qui prend en charge non une gestion comptable de stocks, de client ou de facturation, mais celle d'un suivi et de gestion d'une procédure judiciaire;
- soit des échanges respectant les exigeantes normes internationales EDIJUSTICE.

5 Conclusion

L'Internet peut être la clé qui permettra le décloisonnement de l'institution judiciaire, tant dans son fonctionnement interne que dans ses relations avec les autres administrations et qu'avec le public. Une chance à saisir pour la justice. La saisira-t-elle?
Des moyens importants (au regard du budget de la justice), une mobilisation considérable des professionnels du droit et des services des ministères de la justice sont nécessaires pour parvenir à des résultats significatifs en termes d'économie et d'interopérabilité. Une révolution des mentalités sera nécessaire: prendre la mesure de l'importance de la communication dans la 'maison justice'... Il faudra une patiente maïeutique pour une difficile gestation...

The Challenge of Change for Judicial Systems
M. Fabri and Ph.M. Langbroek (Eds.)
IOS Press, 2000

La publication électronique des informations juridiques suisses

Vers un service universel

Christine Poupa[1]

1 Une situation de monopole (années 1987/1997)

1.1 Contexte

Pendant des siècles, la Suisse n'a été qu'une Confédération d'Etats, faite d'alliances assez lâches entre cantons souverains. En 1848, la Suisse est devenue un Etat fédératif doté d'un Tribunal fédéral formé de 11 juges, non permanent et sans siège fixe (son président le convoquant en séance dans le lieu de son choix). Ses attributions consistaient surtout à trancher des contestations entre cantons, entre la Confédération et un canton, entre des particuliers et la Confédération.

La révision totale de la constitution fédérale de 1874 fait du Tribunal fédéral un organe permanent, avec un siège fixe à Lausanne, et élargit considérablement ses attributions. Ses tâches ont augmenté: la Confédération a de plus en plus de compétences dans de multiples domaines du droit. Alors qu'en 1848 le droit fédéral ne comprenait que la constitution et quelques lois fondamentales, il s'étend aujourd'hui pratiquement à l'ensemble du droit civil et pénal, ainsi qu'à une grande partie du droit administratif.

Le Tribunal fédéral reste une autorité de recours chargée essentiellement de veiller à l'application du droit fédéral, n'examinant l'interprétation du droit cantonal que sous l'angle restreint de sa conformité au droit fédéral. Sauf exceptions, le Tribunal fédéral rend son jugement au terme d'une procédure purement écrite, sans instruire à nouveau, donc sans audition des témoins, expertises, etc...

Parallèlement à l'extension de ses compétences juridictionnelles, le Tribunal fédéral a dû faire face à un accroissement de ses effectifs: de 1875 à nos jours, l'effectif des juges est passé de 9 à 30, celui des rédacteurs de 2 à 76 (46 greffiers et un collaborateur personnel pour chacun des 30 juges) et celui du personnel administratif et de chancellerie de 8 à 89.

Du point de vue de la procédure, le Tribunal fédéral occupe une place particulière: les cantons sont demeurés, dans une large mesure, souverains. Il existe donc 26 lois

---

1 Institut de Hautes Etudes et Administration Publique, Chavannes-près-Renens, Suisse.

d'organisation judiciaire et 26 codes de procédure différents, qui se démarquent parfois considérablement, sur des points importants, suivant les courants juridiques qui les ont inspirés. Les voies que doivent emprunter les justiciables avant de pouvoir s'adresser au Tribunal fédéral peuvent être très différentes, selon le for juridique.
La circulation des informations est donc primordiale en Suisse, dans le domaine juridique. La Confédération s'en est préoccupée.

1.2 Politique fédérale: une claire répartition des tâches entre l'Etat et l'économie privée dans la publication électronique des données juridiques

Nous reproduisons ci-dessous un passage du communiqué de la Chancellerie fédérale et du Département fédéral de justice et police proposant au Conseil fédéral (le gouvernement fédéral suisse) une nouvelle politique de diffusion des données juridiques (ce communiqué, daté de février 1997, est disponible sur Internet):[2]

> 'Les auteurs proposent une claire répartition des tâches entre l'Etat et l'économie privée dans la publication électronique des données juridiques... Concrètement, une telle diffusion comprend avant tout la législation (Constitution, lois, ordonnances, droit international) et la jurisprudence fédérales qui devraient être rendues accessibles au public dans toutes les langues officielles. Toutes les autres publications juridiques sur support électronique (doctrine, commentaires, manuels de droit etc.) devraient par contre être laissées au libre marché. La Confédération mettra toutefois à disposition des entreprises privées... les données juridiques sous forme électronique dont elle dispose.'

Cette prise de position s'explique en partie par certaines pressions et demandes de clarifications provenant à la fois d'éditeurs, désireux d'entrer sur ce marché et de la société Swisslex, soucieuse de préserver ses intérêts vis-à-vis des éditeurs et de la Confédération.

1.3 Swisslex en situation de monopole

Le 10 décembre 1984, le Conseil fédéral décida d'adhérer à l'Association banque suisse de données juridiques (ABSDJ), fondée en janvier 1985 à la demande de la Fédération suisse des avocats (FSA) et de la Société suisse des juristes (SSJ), par la FSA, la SSJ et la Confédération, soutenues par l'Office fédéral de la justice. L'ABSDJ regroupe aujourd'hui tous les cantons (à l'exception de Bâle-Ville et du Jura), l'Institut du fédéralisme à Fribourg, ainsi que de nombreuses organisations et individus. Le Tribunal fédéral délègue un observateur permanent au comité. Les efforts de l'ABSDJ ont abouti au printemps 1986 à la fondation de Swisslex Banque suisse de données juridiques SA, société de droit privé, à laquelle l'ABSDJ participe symboliquement, et la Confédération pas du tout. Le capital social de Swisslex est alors

---

2 http://www.admin.ch/cp/f/1997Feb21.173437.7348@idz.bfi.admin.ch.html

détenu en grande partie par les éditeurs juridiques suisses. La Confédération traite Swisslex en partenaire privé pour la réalisation d'une banque suisse de données juridiques, et défend ses intérêts vis-à-vis de Swisslex par le canal de l'ABSDJ.

Swisslex a obtenu par contrat l'exclusivité de l'exploitation électronique des données juridiques de la Confédération. A l'époque, les coûts de mise à disposition des informations étaient tels, à cause entre autres de la nécessité de saisir les données dans le système, que la viabilité économique de cette base de données ne pouvait être assurée que par des tarifs d'accès élevés et un monopole. En 1987, la première base de données juridiques en ligne était inaugurée. Il s'agissait d'une solution 'Mainframe' installée sur un serveur central avec des connexions des clients par lignes téléphoniques.

Depuis 1995, Swisslex vend un CD-Rom contenant les ATF (arrêts du Tribunal fédéral), au prix de 1'450 Fr. (+ 7,5% de TVA) et 850 Fr. pour deux mises à jour annuelles. Mais Swisslex a des concurrents dans son propre camp, celui des éditeurs spécialisés: certains cantons sous-traitent la publication électronique de leur législation à des éditeurs spécialisés, éditeurs qui publient également des CD-Rom dans le domaine des commentaires.

Par exemple, le Tessin a été le premier canton suisse à éditer, en mai 1996, un CD-Rom avec l'aide de la société Archilex. Ce CD-Rom contient tous les textes de lois de la Confédération, en italien, ainsi que les lois et règlements du Tessin, les règlements des communes tessinoises, la jurisprudence, le droit fiscal, les assurances sociales, etc... Il est vendu par abonnement à plusieurs centaines d'exemplaires (250 Fr. pour trois CD-Rom par an, les mises à jour ayant lieu tous les quatre mois). D'autres cantons, comme Genève, ont suivi cette voie.

En janvier 1997, la banque de données Swisslex est proposée sur Internet, mais toujours selon le principe du paiement d'un abonnement mensuel, proportionnel au nombres de juristes de l'entreprise ou de l'administration, et au volume d'informations consultées (180 Fr. d'abonnement par mois pour un ou deux juristes, par exemple).

La structure du capital de Swisslex a beaucoup changé, afin de faire face aux nouvelles contraintes techniques et financières: au printemps 1998, Westlaw-Europe prend une participation financière. Westlaw-Europe est une société du groupe Thomson Corporation, le leader américain des banques de données juridiques et économiques.

Graphique 1

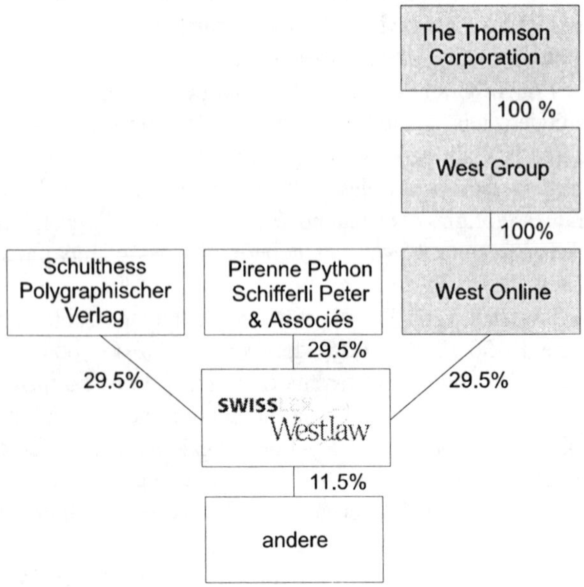

(source pour le graphique: http://www.Swisslex.ch/french/faits.htm)

Sous 'andere' ('autres' en allemand) sont regroupés les actionnaires minoritaires, à savoir différentes maisons d'édition suisses: Edipresse Publications SA, Lausanne; Stämpfli Verlag AG, Berne; Helbing und Lichtenhahn Verlag AG, Bâle; Verein Schweizerische Juristische Datenbank, Fribourg; National Zeitung & Basler Nachrichten AG, Bâle; Sauerländer AG, Aarau.

L'abonnement de base à Swisslex-Westlaw contient la législation et la jurisprudence fédérales (le RS, recueil systématique, est disponible depuis le mois d'octobre 1999 seulement) ainsi que la jurisprudence des grands cantons. Les périodiques à grand tirage sont également inclus. Des abonnements supplémentaires sont nécessaires pour accéder aux périodiques, à la doctrine et aux commentaires se rapportant à différents domaines juridiques (droit civil, droit commercial et bancaire, droit de la concurrence et de la propriété intellectuelle, droit fiscal).

2 Vers un service universel (années 1996/2000)

Les techniques informatiques évoluant, notamment avec Internet, le maintient d'un monopole n'a plus les mêmes justifications économiques qu'il y a dix ans.

2.1 La fin du monopole de fait

En janvier 1997 déjà, le Conseil fédéral, prenant acte du rapport 'étude d'une conception fédérale pour la diffusion et la consultation du droit par voie informatique',[3] a décidé que le RS (Recueil systématique) devait être rendu accessible sur Internet.[4] Environ 200 textes sont diffusés par la Confédération, sur Internet: principalement ceux du droit public ainsi que tous les textes concernant les assurances sociales. Depuis mars 1998, il est aussi possible de consulter l'intégralité du droit interne en format PDF (le programme gratuit Acrobat Reader permet d'accéder au texte intégral). Les données sont exclusivement destinées à un usage privé et ne doivent pas être réutilisées dans un but commercial.

Les arrêts du Tribunal fédéral (ATF) sont toujours proposés par Swisslex-Westlaw sous forme de CD-Rom et en ligne, au choix des utilisateurs, contre paiement. Eurospider met également ces arrêts à disposition sur Internet gratuitement, au nom du Tribunal fédéral, depuis décembre 1996. En mars 1999, cette société a amélioré les fonctions de recherche dans les arrêts du Tribunal fédéral. Le Tribunal fédéral fournit à Eurospider les informations et finance ce service Internet. Le Tribunal fédéral a pris la décision de reprendre techniquement en main, en l'an 2000, la gestion de ce service Internet, plutôt que de continuer à le sous-traiter à Eurospider: il assumera la gestion du serveur et la mise à jour des informations, tout en continuant à payer une licence pour l'utilisation du logiciel développé par Eurospider.

En interne, les juges du Tribunal n'utilisaient aucun de ces services jusqu'en l'an 2000.

Des négociations avec Swisslex-Westlaw pour la conclusion d'un contrat d'utilisation d'un an ont finalement abouti. Ces négociations ont longtemps achoppé sur la question du prix (plusieurs dizaines de milliers de francs demandés au départ. Les termes de l'accord restent confidentiels). La première version de Swisslex (version Mainframe) avait été l'objet de tests à l'époque, mais n'a jamais été considérée comme un outil de travail par le Tribunal fédéral.

Le Tribunal fédéral a recours, depuis 1991, à une base informatique des ATF strictement interne. Même les juges suppléants doivent se déplacer dans les locaux du Tribunal fédéral pour la consulter. La politique déclarée du Tribunal fédéral est de ne pas ouvrir cette base à une consultation extérieure. Cette base interne est plus étendue que les bases publiques (Swisslex-Westlaw et Eurospider, qui ne reprennent que 10 % des arrêts, c'est-à-dire ceux qui sont publiés): elle contient environ 25 % des ATF, et surtout une indexation réalisée grâce au thesaurus juridique monohiérarchique multilingue Jurivoc.[5]

Jurivoc, élaboré par le Tribunal fédéral suisse et le Tribunal fédéral des assurances, en collaboration avec les bibliothèques juridiques suisses, est destiné à

3 'Etude d'une conception fédérale pour la diffusion et la consultation du droit par voie informatique', rapport daté de septembre 1996: http://www.admin.ch/bj/rechtinf/rik0297/ri-konzf.pdf

4 Recueil systématique du droit fédéral (RS): http://www.admin.ch/ch/f/rs/rs.html

5 http://www.bger.ch/jurivoc/f/

l'indexation des trois principales sources du droit: les lois, la jurisprudence et la doctrine juridique. Ce projet est né au début des années 90, d'un désir de fusionner les vocabulaires d'indexation existants pour les différentes bases de données juridiques. L'application Jurivoc, développée en Java, est disponible gratuitement, depuis novembre 1998, sur le site Internet du Tribunal fédéral. Le thesaurus Jurivoc comprend environ 8'000 descripteurs et 10'000 non-descripteurs (synonymes, quasi-synonymes, antonymes dans certains cas) pour chacune des langues[6] (actuellement le français et l'allemand, prochainement l'italien, et ultérieurement l'anglais). Les descripteurs qui sont têtes de hiérarchies se rapprochent le plus possible de la systématique du droit fédéral, systématique connue de tous les juristes suisses.

En interne, l'informatique est devenue indispensable au Tribunal fédéral: en cas de panne, les juristes ne pourraient plus travailler. Le Tribunal fédéral ne dispose pas d'outils d'aide à la décision, mais de textes standard pour répondre à certaines questions. La doctrine et la jurisprudence sont informatisées, la bibliothèque également. Les fiches cartonnées de la bibliothèque ne sont plus mises à jour. Pour autant, tous les juges ne se sont pas convertis à l'informatique. Certains font appel à leur assistant plutôt que d'utiliser eux-mêmes l'un des systèmes informatiques à leur disposition. Les versions papier des documents de référence comme le Recueil systématique du droit fédéral (RS) continuent à être utilisées par une partie des juges, les plus jeunes ayant tendance à adopter plus facilement la version Internet fournie par la Confédération.

Toutes ces bases de données informatisées et ces réseaux n'ont pas entraîné de modification notable des relations du Tribunal fédéral, ni avec les cantons (les échanges se font toujours exclusivement sous forme papier), ni avec la Confédération (au nom de la séparation des pouvoirs, le Tribunal fédéral ne reçoit aucune directive de la Confédération, et n'est pas concerné par l'ordonnance RS 170.512.2 sur la publication électronique de données juridiques, dont nous allons parler). Pas de modification des relations avec les justiciables non plus, bien qu'on note une légère baisse du nombre des recours au Tribunal fédéral. Il est trop tôt pour savoir si cette baisse est une nouvelle tendance qui se confirmera, et si elle a un quelconque lien de cause à effet avec une meilleure information des justiciables.

2.2 L'ordonnance RS 170.512.2: l'annonce d'un service de base gratuit

Les textes juridiques européen introduisent parfois une différence entre un service de base gratuit (ou très peu coûteux), et une service complet payant, commercial.

En Suisse, l'Etat et ses services peuvent légalement se charger directement de la diffusion du service de base: l'ordonnance fédérale, concernant la publication électronique de données juridiques (RS 170.512.2[7] du 8 avril 1998), entrée en vigueur le 1er juillet 1998 est venue clarifier la situation. Elle ne s'applique qu'au domaine des

6 Les langues des décisions du tribunal fédéral se répartissent comme suit pour 1998: allemand: 58,8%, français: 31,8%, italien: 9,5%

7 http://www.admin.ch/ch/f/rs/c170_512_2.html

données juridiques quoiqu'elle définisse une réglementation qui pourrait s'appliquer à toutes les publications de données du secteur public.

Le commentaire[8] se rapportant à l'ordonnance précise que 'le Parlement et les tribunaux fédéraux ne seront pas régis par l'ordonnance. Il serait toutefois opportun, afin que les autorités fédérales mènent une politique uniforme dans le domaine de l'information juridique, que ces deux organes ne s'engagent pas dans une voie diamétralement opposée.'

L'ordonnance RS 170.512.2 donne, article 3, quelques définitions:

> 'a. *données juridiques:* la législation et les traités internationaux (y compris les travaux préparatoires et les procès-verbaux des chambres afférents), la jurisprudence, la doctrine des autorités fédérales et les données émanant de registres ayant une portée juridique;
> b. *publication électronique:* la diffusion de données par des moyens électroniques (p. ex. Internet) ou sur des supports informatiques (p. ex. CD-ROM).'

L'article 4 définit l'étendue de la publication électronique: 'La Confédération se borne à publier des données juridiques, y compris les principaux outils d'accès, tels que les répertoires, les index et la recherche en texte intégral, ainsi que des commentaires de données juridiques destinés au public.'. L'Etat doit donc impérativement, selon l'ordonnance, se limiter à la desserte de base et laisser le marché des ouvrages dérivés au secteur privé. La définition de cette desserte de base pose un réel problème, étant données les évolutions technologiques. Un site Internet avec moteur de recherche intégré était introuvable il y a seulement 5 ans.

Actuellement, le moteur de recherche est considéré comme un minimum indispensable à l'accès de l'information sur un site Internet. Quels seront dans 5 ans les outils disponibles en standard et considérés comme indispensables, donc 'de base'? (agents, traducteurs, etc??).

Le commentaire de l'ordonnance ne clarifie pas beaucoup les choses quand il précise, p. 5:

> 'Dans la plupart des cas, les produits électroniques de l'administration fédérale ne sont pas développés directement pour le public, mais servent en premier lieu à l'accomplissement d'un mandat légal ou à des fins internes (...) Au cours de leur cycle de vie, les produits internes à l'administration sont toutefois constamment développés et tendent à s'enrichir de multiples fonctions. Ainsi, il se peut qu'un produit relève au début, de par sa fonction et sa mise en forme, de la desserte de base, mais qu'au fil du temps il devienne un véritable système d'information qui – si l'administration le propose au public – pourrait supplanter ou, du moins, concurrencer sensiblement des produits ou initiatives privés. Il convient donc de

8 http://www.admin.ch/bj/rechtinf/ris-vo/ris-vo-erl-f.pdf

surveiller les produits électroniques de l'administration pendant toute leur durée de vie en examinant si de nouvelles fonctions sont compatibles avec la répartition des tâches entre la desserte de base et les ouvrages dérivés, et si elles ne menacent pas le marché libre. En cas de risque, il faut envisager de ne mettre qu'une partie des fonctions d'un produit interne à la disposition du public. Il ne faut toutefois pas que cela empêche l'administration d'innover.'

Les choses deviennent un peu plus confuses encore quand le commentaire précise 'que, dans des cas exceptionnels et moyennant certaines conditions, des publications qui ne font pas partie des données juridiques essentielles (art. 3, let. a), mais qui relèvent de la desserte de base (comme p. ex. la JAAC[9] ou d'autres revues produites par l'administration fédérale)' pourraient être 'confiées à des diffuseurs privés en vue de leur publication.

Ce cas peut notamment se présenter lorsque l'administration a ainsi la possibilité de réaliser des économies et lorsque, en même temps, on peut s'attendre à une diffusion plus vaste du produit en question. Contrairement au 1er alinéa, le 2e alinéa utilise le terme d''ouvrages'. Lorsqu'on qualifie un recueil de données d''ouvrage' (notion qui implique en plus une composante créative), on cherche donc à indiquer par là qu'il s'agit d'un produit dérivé, qui dépasse le cadre de la desserte de base pour entrer dans la sphère réservée au secteur privé.'

Toujours dans les commentaires de l'article 5 de l'ordonnance, nous découvrons 'qu'il est inadmissible, dans le domaine de la desserte de base, de prélever des taxes ou d'exiger des taxes plus élevées dans le simple but de protéger des produits privés.' Une confirmation, donc, de la légitimité d'un service minimum, gratuit ou presque. Mais confirmation également des problèmes de survie qui se posent aux entreprises privées sur ce marché.

2.3 Une multiplication de l'offre

Actuellement, toutes les maisons d'éditions peuvent acheter à la Confédération ses informations légales. Par exemple, la collection des lois dans les trois langues officielles (allemand, français et italien) peut être achetée, selon la nouvelle liste des prix de juin 1999[10] pour 3000 CHF (plus 300 CHF pour les mises à jour chaque trimestre). L'information est fournies sous forme Word ou HTML. Le tarif précédent pour les mêmes données était de 100'000 CHF (environ 35'000 CHF pour chacune des langues).

Une floraison d'offres électroniques d'informations juridiques est apparue en Suisse, entraînant un problème d'identification des différentes sources.

---

9 La revue 'Jurisprudence administrative des autorités de la Confédération', finalement mise à disposition sur Internet depuis février 2000 par la Confédération, gratuitement: http://www.vpb.admin.ch/homepage_fr.html

10 'Ordonnance de la Chancellerie fédérale concernant les taxes de transmission de données juridiques' (RS 172.041.12, 24 juin 1999, p. 1699). http://www.admin.ch/ch/f/as/1999/1699.pdf

Selon art. 10 de l'ordonnance concernant la publication électronique de données juridiques, la Chancellerie fédérale prend en charge la coordination dans le domaine des publications électroniques de données juridiques. Concrètement, cela se traduit par la mise en place d'un service de coordination (COPJUR),[11] qui a commencé son travail le 1er octobre 1998.

Sa tâche principale est le recensement des publications électroniques de données juridiques en Suisse: répertoire des sources électroniques (législation, jurisprudence, registres...) des communes, des cantons et de la Confédération, de l'Europe, y compris éditées par le secteur privé. Dans un premier temps, le COPIUR a publié un bulletin d'informations trimestriel adressé gratuitement à plus de 2000 abonnés. Ce service publie sur Internet[12] depuis décembre 1999 un répertoire des publications électroniques contenant des données juridiques.

Les services de base gratuits sont souvent suffisants pour les utilisateurs occasionnels. S'ils sont très utilisés (plus de 100'000 consultations chaques semaine pour les Arrêts du Tribunal Fédéral sur le seul site d'Eurospider), ils ne peuvent en aucun cas répondre à tous les besoins, en particulier des professionnels, fonctionnaires ou non (magistrats, études d'avocats, etc.). Un service plus complet et payant est donc prévu.

2.4 Un service complet payant

Les sociétés comme Swisslex-Westlaw, titulaires de la concession, passée ou actuelle, de service public des bases de données juridiques semblent avoir du mal à garantir un bon service d'une part, et à rentabiliser ce service payant d'autre part.

Il est difficile d'avoir des chiffres précis. Par exemple, dans son dernier communiqué de presse daté du 28 septembre 1999, Swisslex-Westlaw indique que 'la Confédération, la moitié des cantons et nombre d'études font quotidiennement leurs recherches sur Swisslex-Westlaw'. Impossible d'obtenir le nombre même approximatif d'utilisateurs (institutions et/ou juristes) ou de recherches effectuées, alors que d'autres informations sont fournies à la virgule près (capital action et sa répartition entre les actionnaires, marché potentiel, nombre de documents dans la base et nombre de liens entre les documents...).

Ces sociétés semblent avoir des difficultés à équilibrer leurs comptes. Les rentes de situation des années quatre-vingt sont finies: des services en lignes, même partiels, sont proposés gratuitement. La Suisse a confirmé cette notion de gratuité le 24 juin 1999 dans l' 'ordonnance de la Chancellerie fédérale concernant les taxes de transmission de données juridiques'.

De plus, les utilisateurs tout désignés de ces systèmes payants sont souvent aussi les producteurs de l'information (magistrats pour la jurisprudence par exemple). La jurisprudence étant généralement exclue du 'service de base' gratuit (comme en France), les magistrats dans leur grande majorité sont hostiles à ce système. Ils

---

11 Chancellerie fédérale, COPJUR (Service de coordination des publications électroniques de données juridiques), Tel +41 (0)31 323 56 80 bernard.ayer@bk.admin.ch

12 http://informationjuridique.admin.ch/

estiment que le contribuable a déjà payé par ses impôts la production des juges et qu'il appartient à l'Etat, dans un Etat de droit, de faire en sorte que chacun puisse accéder au droit, y compris celui créé par la jurisprudence.

3 Le dilemme transparence des décisions / protection de la vie privée

La publication des seuls textes législatifs n'a pas beaucoup de sens. Elle est utile quand elle est associée à la publication de la jurisprudence et de la doctrine. Se pose alors la question de la protection des données personnelles.

> 'Ce n'est pas parce que des informations nominatives sont prévues comme devant être publiques que des particuliers doivent voir leur vie privée atteinte par une exploitation détournée de celles-ci. C'est pourquoi il est proposé de limiter les indications nominatives accessibles, pour garantir la protection de la vie privée des personnes concernées.'[13]

Le Tribunal fédéral a le projet de publier de toutes les décisions rendues, sur Internet. Une solution a été retenue pour protéger la vie privée: les données seront anonymisées en supprimant toute référence, non seulement aux noms des personnes, mais également aux noms de lieus.

La protection des données est abordée par l'article 7 de la LPD:[14] 'Lors de l'élaboration de la constitution et de la mise à jour de systèmes d'information internes, la Confédération veille à ce que les données devant être protégées et celles qui ne sont pas destinées à être publiées puissent être aisément séparées ou rendues anonymes lors d'une future publication'.

Concrètement, par 'données devant être protégées', il faut comprendre 'données personnelles, nominatives'. Les nouveaux moyens d'accès électronique permettent beaucoup plus facilement qu'auparavant de rechercher et croiser des informations. Par exemple, la FOSC, Feuille officielle suisse du commerce, contient des informations sur les entreprises, avec le nom de personnes et d'organismes qui entretiennent des relations avec ces entreprises. L'accès à l'information se faisait toujours par le nom de l'entreprise. Il serait maintenant techniquement possible de faire apparaître toutes les relations entre une personne et les entreprises figurant dans la FOSC, ce qui serait contraire à la loi fédérale du 19 juin 1992 sur la protection des données (LPD).

Cette loi n'est pas encore très contraignante. Ses dispositions transitoires (Art. 38) permettent aux organes fédéraux de 'continuer à utiliser jusqu'au 31 décembre 2000, les fichiers existants qui contiennent des données personnelles sensibles ou des profils de la personnalité, quand bien même les conditions de traitement posées à l'article 17,

---

13 BERTRAND (Bruno), *Peut-on publier les décisions de justice sur Internet?*, Gazette du Palais

14 Loi fédérale sur la protection des données (LPD) du 19 juin 1992 – Etat au 21 septembre 1999 – http://www.admin.ch/ch/f/rs/2/235.1.pdf

2e alinéa, ne seraient pas réunies.'. Cet article 17, alinéa 2, définit les bases juridiques du traitement des données personnelles par des organes fédéraux: 'Des données sensibles ou des profils de la personnalité ne peuvent être traités que si une loi au sens formel le prévoit expressément, ou si exceptionnellement:

a. l'accomplissement d'une tâche clairement définie dans une loi au sens formel l'exige absolument;
b. le Conseil fédéral l'a autorisé, considérant que les droits des personnes concernées ne sont pas menacés ou
c. la personne concernée y a, en l'espèce, consenti ou a rendu ses données accessibles à tout un chacun.'

4 Conclusion

<table>
<tr><th>Public</th><th>Privé</th></tr>
<tr><td></td><td>1986
Création de Swisslex Banque suisse de données juridiques SA, société de droit privé, dont le capital social est détenu en grande partie par les éditeurs juridiques suisses.</td></tr>
<tr><td></td><td>1987-1997
Swisslex a par contrat l'exclusivité de l'exploitation électronique des données juridiques de la Confédération.</td></tr>
<tr><td>1991
Le Tribunal fédéral créée une base des ATF informatique interne.</td><td></td></tr>
<tr><td>Années 1990
Jurivoc, le Thesaurus juridique multilingue monohiérarchique, élaboré par le Tribunal fédéral suisse et le Tribunal fédéral des assurances, en collaboration avec les bibliothèques juridiques suisses, est né d'un désir de fusionner les vocabulaires d'indexation existants pour les différentes bases de données juridiques.</td><td>1995
Swisslex propose les ATF sur CD-Rom.</td></tr>
<tr><td colspan="2">Mai 1996
Le Tessin est le premier canton suisse à éditer un CD-ROM avec l'aide de la société Archilex. Ce CD-ROM contient tous les textes des lois de la Confédération, en italien, ainsi que les lois et règlements du Tessin, les règlements des communes tessinoises, la jurisprudence, le droit fiscal, les assurances sociales, etc... Il est vendu par abonnement à plusieurs centaines d'exemplaires (250 Fr. pour trois CD-ROM par an, les mises à jour ayant lieu tous les quatre mois).</td></tr>
</table>

Décembre 1996 Eurospider Information Technology AG met au nom du Tribunal fédéral, ses arrêts à disposition sur Internet, gratuitement.	
Février 1997 Chancellerie fédérale et Département fédéral de justice et police proposent au Conseil fédéral 'une claire répartition des tâches entre l'Etat et l'économie privée dans la publication électronique des données juridiques'.	Janvier 1997 La banque de données Swisslex est proposée sur Internet, toujours selon le principe du paiement d'un abonnement mensuel.
Mars 1998 En 1997, le Conseil fédéral, prenant acte du rapport de septembre 1996 'étude d'une conception fédérale pour la diffusion et la consultation du droit par voie informatique' a décidé que le RS devait être rendu accessible sur Internet. Ce qui est fait, gratuitement, en mars 1998.	Printemps 1998 Westlaw-Europe prend une participation financière dans Swisslex. Westlaw-Europe est une société du groupe Thomson Corporation, le leader américain des banques de données juridiques et économiques.
Juillet 1998 L'ordonnance fédérale, concernant la publication électronique de données juridiques (RS 170.512.2 du 8 avril 1998), entrée en vigueur le 1er juillet 1998consacre la création d'un service de base.	
Octobre 1998 La Chancellerie fédérale prend en charge la coordination dans le domaine des publications électroniques de données juridiques: mise en place d'un service de coordination, le COPJUR.	
Juin 1999 'Ordonnance de la Chancellerie fédérale concernant les taxes de transmission de données juridiques' (RS 172.041.12, 24 juin 1999, p. 1699)	
Décembre 1999 Le répertoire des publications électroniques de données juridiques réalisé par le COPIUR est disponible sur Internet	
Février 2000 La revue 'Jurisprudence administrative des autorités de la Confédération', est mise à disposition gratuitement sur Internet par la Confédération	

Pendant une dizaine d'années, le terrain de la publication était occupée en Suisse par une société privée, ayant un monopole. Les années 1996/1998 ont constitué un tournant, avec l'arrivée d'une offre gratuite, faite par les administrations et tribunaux eux-mêmes. Les offres se sont ensuite rapidement multipliées.

Les motifs de différends potentiels entre l'administration pub ique et le secteur privé sont donc nombreux. Des différends risquent fort de se produire à brève échéance, d'autant plus que les administrations suisses, comme les entreprises privées, sont soumises à de fortes pressions financières.

On demande de plus en plus aux administrations publiques suisses de travailler avec des contrats de prestation (en échange d'une enveloppe budgétaire, elles doivent s'engager à fournir certaines prestations, certains services, quitte à trouver des ressources propres... comme par la vente d'informations: le cas s'est produit avec les informations météorologiques).

L'article 12 de l'ordonnance prévoit expressément que le Conseil fédéral puisse mettre sur pied des organes chargés 'de régler les différends concernant la distinction entre la desserte de base assurée par la Confédération et l'offre privée. Les diffuseurs du secteur privé et ceux du secteur public de même que les utilisateurs seront représentés équitablement dans ces organes.'

Reste que les sociétés privées, concessionnaires ou non, auront à trouver leur nouvelle place, à justifier leur 'valeur ajoutée', si elles veulent survivre économiquement: analyse des textes, liens avec la jurisprudence et la doctrine, aide à la recherche, traduction...

Références

Baquiast, Jean-Paul, *Internet et les administrations: La grande mutation,* Berger-Levrault: Paris, 1999, 284 p. (coll. Gestion Publique)

Bertrand, Bruno, *Peut-on publier les décisions de justice sur Internet?*, Gazette du Palais du Tribunal d'instance de Melun n° 18 à 20, du 18 au 20 janvier 1998 pp. 30 à 33 (gazette du droit des technologies avancées)

'Etude d'une conception fédérale pour la diffusion et la consultation du droit par voie informatique', septembre 1996
http://www.admin.ch/bj/rechtinf/rik0297/ri-konzf.pdf

'Jurisprudence administrative des autorités de la Confédération' (revue)
http://www.vpb.admin.ch/homepage_fr.html

Loi fédérale sur la protection des données (LPD) du 19 juin 1992 - Etat au 21 septembre 1999 -
http://www.admin.ch/ch/f/rs/2/235.1.pdf

Ordonnance de la Chancellerie fédérale concernant les taxes de transmission de données juridiques (RS 172.041.12, 24 june 1999, p. 1699)
http://www.admin.ch/ch/f/as/1999/1699.pdf

Recueil systématique du droit fédéral (RS)
http://www.admin.ch/ch/f/rs/rs.html

Répertoire des publications électroniques de données juridiques suisses
http://informationjuridique.admin.ch

About the Authors

Charles Blake is a solicitor. He previously practised law in London and taught at Thames Valley, Brunel and London Universities. For nine years he was head of civil litigation at the Departments of Health and Social Security in London. He was a consultant to the Bar on the proposals which became the Access to Justice Act 1999. He has written widely in the fields of public law, welfare law and legal services. He is currently engaged with co-contributor Gavin Drewry and Sir Louis Blom-Cooper QC in a large-scale research project looking into the workings of the English Court of Appeal, a project which is funded by the Nuffield Foundation.

Edo C. Brommet has since 1998 been a civil servant at the adminstration of justice department for the judiciary at the Ministry of Justice, the Netherlands. In 1999 he became the manager of the 'The Administration of Justice in the 21st Century'. In that function he is in charge of the coordination between the several parts of this operation, such as the legislation, the preparations for implementation and 'The Reinforcement of the Judiciary' project, which is being implemented by the Dutch judiciary, the Netherlands.

Odette Buitendam started her law studies at Leiden University, after her education in juvenile welfare at Rijkshogeschool Groningen. Her thesis was on the role of mediation in divorce proceedings. She has worked as a law clerk in the family and juvenile section of the District Court of The Hague. From December 1997 she worked in the Legal Aid and Legal Professions Department of the Ministry of Justice on the International Conference on Mediation project (25-28 March 1998). Since June 1998 she has been working at the Policy Section of the Administration of Justice Department at the Ministry of Justice.

Christina P.M. Cleiren (1955)Christina P.M. Cleiren (1955) obtained her doctorate (cum laude) at the University of Leiden in 1989. The subject of her Ph.D. thesis was: Principles of proper procedure. An analysis of case law in criminal cases. From October 1991 Cleiren was Professor of Criminal Law and Criminal Procedure at the Faculty of Law, Erasmus University, Rotterdam, and as of January 2000 also at the University of Leiden. In Leiden she is also responsible for co-ordinating the inter-faculty research project 'Judicial Dispute Arbitration' at the E.M. Meijers Institute for Jurisprudential Research. During the period February 1997 - September 1998 Cleiren was Director-General of Legislation, Administration of Justice and Law enforcement, and from September 1998 untill Januari 2000 onwards of Legislation, Administration of Justice and Legal Aid at the Ministry of Justice of the Netherlands. She has practiced as (deputy) Judge in the District Court of Rotterdam (penal section) and (deputy) Judge in the Court of Appeal, Amsterdam; in addition she was a member of the UN Commission of Experts established pursuant to Security Council Resolution 780 (19-92), with the mandate to provide the Secretary-General with conclusions on evidence of grave breaches of violations of international humanitarian law committed in the former Yugoslavia. She is a member of the committee for the selection of the Members of the Judiciary Appointments Committee in the Netherlands. A recent publication relating to the administration of justice is: 'Een pleidooi voor (meer) rechterlijke samenwerking' (A plea for (more) legal cooperation), in: *De mogelijkheden en grenzen van rechterlijke samenwerking*, Prinsengrachtreeks 1997/4, pp. 27-37, Amsterdam.

Francesco Contini is a researcher at the Research Institute on Judicial Systems of the Italian National Research Council. His main research interests cover the topics of organizational change, court technologies and judicial reform. He is currently in the process of publishing a comparative study on quantitative indicators of eight European judicial systems and is engaged in research on the merger of judicial offices. He is also involved in the design and implementation of a web- based training program for the Italian Ministry of Justice.

Maria Dakolias is counsel at the World Bank's Legal Department where she advises and manages legal and judicial reform projects. The views expressed in this article are her own and are not necessarily those of the organization she represents. She is a graduate of Haverford College (B.A.), George Mason University School of Law (J.D.), and the University of Amsterdam (L.L.M.). Her publications include 'Court Performance Around the World: A Comparative Perspective' (*Yale Human Rights & Development Law Journal*, Volume 2, 1999) and 'A Strategy for Judicial Reform: The Experience in Latin America' (*Virginia Journal of International Law*, Volume 36, Number 1, Fall 1995).

Frans C.J. van der Doelen graduated in political science at Nijmegen University and in 1989 he received his Ph.D. at the faculty of public administration at Twente University, the Netherlands, with a dissertation on policy instruments and the Dutch energy savings policy. He worked at the Rekenkamer (the Dutch national audit office), and is currently Head of the Policy and Instrumentation Division of the Administration of Justice Department of the Dutch Ministry of Justice. Among his 50 publications are: 'The Sermon: Information Programs in the Public Policy Process: Choice, Effects and Evaluation', in: M. Bemelmans-Videc, R. Rist en E. Vedung (eds). *Carrots, stick & sermons. Policy instruments & their evaluation*, New Brunswick (Transaction publishers), 1999, pp. 103-129 (with E. Vedung) and 'Expertise van de rechterlijke macht: grenzen aan de Generalistendoctrine inzake rechters', in: J.M. Barendrecht et.al. (eds.), *Rechtspleging, samenleving en bestuur: een gerichte onderzoeksagenda*, Utrecht (Lemma), 2000, pp. 153-161.'

Wim B.H.J. van de Donk (Professor at Tilburg University, Centre for Law, Public Administration and Informatization) co-chairs EGPA's permanent study-group on informatization in Public Administration that has been working and publishing in the domain of informatization in public administration since 1986. He recently edited (together with Prof.Dr. Ignace Snellen) *Public Administration in an Information Age. A Handbook*, which was published by IOS Press.'

Gavin R. Drewry is Professor of Public Administration and Director of the Centre for Political Studies at Royal Holloway, University of London. He is a former Chairman of the Study of Parliament Group, and is co-convenor of SPG study groups on Law and Parliament and on Westminster and Europe. He is also co-convenor of the EGPA Permanent Study Group on the Development of Contractualisation in The Public Sector. His recent publications include (as co-author), *Public Sector Reforms: Issues of Accountability and Public Law* (Pinter, 1996); (as co-editor), *The Law and Parliament* (Butterworths, 1998); and (as co-editor), *Law and The Spirit of Inquiry* (Kluwer, 1999). He is currently directing a major research project, funded by the Nuffield Foundation, on the operation of the civil division of the Court of Appeal for England and Wales.

Thibaut Duvillier est Aspirant du Fonds National de la Recherche Scientifique de Belgique auprès du Centre d'Etudes et de Recherches en Administration Publique (CERAP) de l'Université Libre de Bruxelles (U.L.B.). Sous l'angle de la sociologie des organisations et du droit, il y réalise des recherches sur les modes d'adaptation du système juridique aux mutations sociétales et en particulier, sur les modalités de prise de décision judiciaire. Par ailleurs, M. Duvillier est coordinateur-adjoint de *Pyramides* (Revue du CERAP) et assistant volontaire en gestion des Ressources Humaines et en sociologie de l'administration publique à cette même université.

Carla Eradus is President of the Court of Appeal of Leeuwarden, the Netherlands.

Marco Fabri is a senior researcher at the Research Institute on Judicial Systems of the Italian National Research Council. He has served as a consultant for the Italian Ministry of Justice and the World Bank. His research interests are in the areas of judicial administration, judicial reform, court technology, organizational learning and the management of innovation. He is currently organizing the First European Seminar on Court Technology, sponsored by the European Commission.

Jean-Paul Jean est magistrat, substitut général près la cour d'appel de Paris et directeur de la Mission de recherche droit et justice, [groupement d'intérêt public associant le ministère de la justice, le ministère de la recherche, le centre national de la recherche scientifique, les universités, l'école nationale de la magistrature, les avocats et les notaires]. Il a été auparavant membre de l'inspection générale des services judiciaires, conseiller du ministre des affaires sociales puis conseiller du ministre de la justice. Collaborateur régulier de plusieurs revues ou périodiques, il est l'auteur de deux livres et de nombreux articles relatifs aux questions de justice, aux questions sociales et aux politiques publiques, ainsi que de plusieurs rapports qui ont servi de base à des réformes dans la justice et administration pénitentiaire.

Philip M. Langbroek graduated in political science at Leiden University and received his Ph.D. in 1988 at the Faculty of Public Administration, Twente University, the Netherlands, with a dissertation on separation of powers and decentralisation. Today, he is an Teacher and Researcher at the Department of Constitutional and Administrative Law of Utrecht University, Utrecht, the Netherlands, where he teaches administrative law and public administration. He worked as a counsel for the Dutch Ministry of Justice in several projects invoking change in the Dutch judicial organization from 1996-1998. In 1997 he organized a conference on quality management for the judiciary together with mrs. K. Lahuis of the Dutch Study Centre for the Judiciary and the Administration of Justice (SSR). Nowadays he chairs the permanent EGPA study group on management and delivery of justice together with Albert W. Koers. He is especially interested in quality management and accountability of public sector agencies and the judiciary. He has recently published: 'Normering van kwaliteitszorg in de rechterlijke organisatie, een verkenning', (Regulation of quality management in the judicial organisation), in: *Bestuurswetenschappen 2000*, pp. 96-122)

Barry Loveday is a Principal Lecturer at the University of Portsmouth at the University's Institute of Criminal Justice Studies. He has published widely in the field of criminal justice policy, crime prevention and policing and is currently co-editing a book entitled *After Macpherson. Policing After the Stephen Lawrence Inquiry*. Most recently he has been involved in research generated by the 1998 Crime and Disorder Act which has initiated major changes in the crime prevention and crime reduction field within England and Wales. Prior to joining Portsmouth University he was Principal Lecturer at the University of Central England, Birmingham where he introduced the BA (Hons.) Criminal Justice and Policing degree.

Luigi Marini has been a member of the Italian judiciary since May 1981. From September 1982 to June 1998 he worked as a judge in the criminal court. From June 1988 to November 1996 he worked as a Public Prosecutor, and was a member of the group specializing in investigating economic and tax crime. Since November 1996 he has been working at the Ministry of Justice, dealing with organisational issues (distribution of personnel, appointment of personnel; best practices; internal auditing; management and management evaluation). He was appointed as the Director of the Ministry's 'Office of Statistics' in October 1999. He has published several comments on the Italian Criminal Code, in: *Commentario sul Codice di procedura penale* (Comments on the Procedural Code), published by UTET, and Corruption in Italy, in: *Criminality*, 12th volume in *Annali della Storia Italiana* (Italian History Yearbooks) edited by Einaudi. He is also the co-author of *Economics and Criminality*, published by the Deputy Chamber of Parliament.

Anna Mestitz is the research director of the Italian National Research Council at the Research Institute on Judicial Systems (irsig-cnr) in Bologna. She is a social psychologist mainly engaged in research into judicial administration. She has sat in scientific boards and in some national committees for the reform of various aspects of the

Italian judicial system. Her research activities deal with: recruitment and socialization of the legal professions in Western Europe, technological innovation in Italian courts, organization and management of the Italian juvenile justice system, beliefs and ideology of the Italian legal professions. She is the author of many articles and other publications including *Selezione e formazione professionale dei magistrati e avvocati in Francia* (Padova: Cedam 1990). She is the co-editor, with Giuseppe Di Federico and Giovanfrancesco Lanzara, of *Verbalizzazione degli atti processuali, tecnologie video e gestione dell'innovazione nell'amministrazione della giustizia* (Roma: CNR 1993); the editor of *La tutela del minore tra norme, psicologia ed etica* (Milano: Giuffré 1997) and the co-author of *Avvocati, magistrati e processo penale* (Roma: Carocci 1998). Her principal area of interest is psychology and law. She is a member of the governing council of the Italian Association of Psychology and Law.

Christine Poupa is a researcher at the Idheap (Swiss Graduate School of Public Administration). Idheap is the only university-level institution in Switzerland offering an MPA programme (Master of Public Administration). Christine Poupa specializes in information system management in education (distance learning) and public administration (cyber-administration, cyber-democracy). She is a member of the Swiss interdepartmental co-ordinating group on the information society (CGIS), which was created in 1998 in order to co-ordinate the various initiatives within the Confederation dealing with the information society. Christine Poupa has been Webmaster of www.-gov.ch since 1997. She has published: *Electronic Publication of the Norms: From a Monopoly to Universal Information Service, the Swiss and French experiences, Pre proceedings of the IFIP 8.5 Working Conference on Advances in Electronic Government*, Universidad de Zaragoza, Spain,10-11 February 2000, pp. 133-147; 'Démocratie directe et cyber-démocratie en Suisse', Idheap : Chavannes, mai 1998, 35 p. (Discussion paper de l'Idheap no. 12) http://www.unil.ch/idheap/downloads/discno12-.PDF, and; 'Direct Democracy and Cyberdemocracy in Switzerland', in: *Public Administration in an Information Age: A Handbook*, I.Th.M. Snellen, W.B.H.J. van de Donk, (eds.), IOS Press: Amsterdam, 1998, 579 p. (pp. 137-157).

François Staechelé est magistrat depuis 1975. Il a exercé successivement les fonctions de juge, de juge de l'application des peines à Besançon (il a été le président de l'association nationale des juges de l'application des peines et a enseigné cette matière pendant de nombreuses années à l'École nationale de la magistrature et à la faculté de droit), puis conseiller à la cour d'appel de Colmar et de Metz où , entre autres, il présidait la cour d'assises (il a été le fondateur et le secrétaire général de l'association nationale des praticiens de la cour d'assises). Au moment où, en 1995, il avait pris les fonctions de premier vice-président du tribunal de grande instance de Metz, il s'est intéressé à l'internet et a créé la liste de discussion Themis-France, qui rassemble aujourd'hui près de 500 magistrats français. A présent il exercise les fonctions de président du tribunal de grande instance à Épinal. Il continue activement de contribuer au développement de l'internet judiciaire français, en sa qualité de propriétaire de plusieurs listes de discussion, de formateur de magistrats à l'internet à l'École nationale de la magistrature et au Juripole de Lorraine (http://juripole.univ-nancy2.fr). F. Staechelé a publié un ouvrage consacré à la pratique de l'application des peines, (426 pages, 1995 LITEC).

Marie-France Christophe Tchakaloff is Professor of Public Law, and holds a Jean Monnet Chair financed by the European Communities. She is the Director of Research and Publications at the Institut international d'administration publique (the International Institute of Public Administration), and has been co-director of the Center of European and comparative Law at Paris V from 1998. Furthermore, she is the editor of the *Revue française d'administration publique*. She teaches European law at Paris I, Pantheon Sorbonne University in post graduate courses. She is a member of EGPA, from the Commission for studies of the European Communities and of the French Constitutionalist Association (AFC). Her current field of interest is the relationship between public law and European Law from a national as well as from an international comparative perspective. Last but not least, Mrs. Tchakaloff organises the network EFAP (Espces francophones des administrations publiques) with ENAP of Québec. Mrs. Tchakaloff recently directed: *Le concept d'association dans les accords passés par la Communauté européenne*, éd. Bruylant, novembre 1999

Kim Thachuck works on issues related to corruption and organized crime in the Americas. She has a doctorate in criminology and political science from Simon Fraser University, Canada, and a B.A., and M.A. from the University of British Columbia, Canada.

George O. Tsobanoglou received his Ph.D. from Carleton University, Ottawa, Canada. He has been a researcher and a lecturer at the Institute for Social Research, and the Criminology Institute, Oslo University, Oslo, Norway as well as the Department of Sociology of the London School of Economics, London, UK. He is the Secretary of the Research Committee on Sociotechnics-Sociological Practice of the International Sociological Association and a member of the International Group of Ombudsman Scholars affiliated with Reading University's Centre for Ombudsman Studies. His present research concerns legal and social systems in the European Union and the modalities of management in the public and third sectors. He is presently with the Institute for Social Development, Athens, Greece.

Author Index